Ruth Miles
Bus260E

D1456595

Introduction to
Electronic
data processing

Irwin Series in Information and
Decision Sciences

Consulting editors

Robert B. Fetter
Yale University

Claude McMillan
University of Colorado

Revised edition

Introduction to
Electronic
data processing

ANDREW VAZSONYI

Professor of Computer and Management Science
University of Rochester

1977

RICHARD D. IRWIN, INC.   Homewood, Illinois 60430
Irwin-Dorsey Limited   Georgetown, Ontario L7G 4B3

© RICHARD D. IRWIN, INC., 1973 and 1977

All rights reserved. No part of this publication may be
reproduced, stored in a retrieval system, or transmitted,
in any form or by any means, electronic, mechanical,
photocopying, recording, or otherwise, without the prior
written permission of the publisher.

Revised Edition

3 4 5 6 7 8 9 0   K 5 4 3 2 1 0 9 8

ISBN 0-256-01834-0
Library of Congress Catalog Card No. 75–39359
Printed in the United States of America

*To my wife Laura,
a constant helpmate in
this more mundane adventure*

Preface

This revised edition of *Introduction to Electronic Data Processing* consists of three parts: (1) the *main text,* Chapters 1 to 11, which covers data processing and is independent of any programming language; (2) Appendix One, the *Language Supplement* (Chapters A to D), which presents simplified versions of FORTRAN, COBOL, and BASIC; and (3) Appendix Two, the *Data Processing Applications and Flowcharting Supplement* (Chapter E), which presents a set of data processing case studies. Because the main text does not rely on the supplements the instructor has complete flexibility as to when to introduce programming and how much time to allocate to programming and flowcharting.

The main text stresses the social impact of computer systems, the basic concepts of data processing, the fundamental principles of computer-based information systems, the role of the data processing professional, what data processing is, and what computers do. A broad conceptual framework is developed, relying heavily on illustrations and case studies. Many concepts are presented as flowcharts to build a bridge between data processing and programming.

The programming approach in the supplements is based on *translating* flowcharts into computer programs. The material is presented so that a typical student can write successful computer programs within the first two weeks of the course. Enough complete programs, flowcharts, case studies, and exercises are included to give the student the immediate reward of a series of successful computer runs.

A typical course allocates two thirds of classroom time to the main text and one third to programming, using the supplements. The text is flexible and fits a wide variety of curricula. The instructor may choose to: (1) use the language supplement as a survey of computer programming; (2) stress programming and take full advantage of the variety of simple case studies presented in the Data Processing Applications and Flowcharting Supplement; or (3) use and stress this supplement as a survey of simple data processing case studies.

The detailed Table of Contents gives the outline of the text. Here only the highlights and organization of the Revised Edition are discussed. This Revised Edition represents a major change from the First Edition. It stresses modern concepts of data processing which can prepare the student for the use of computer systems. To keep the size of the book unchanged, material of lesser importance has been condensed or deleted.

The changes in this Revised Edition are based on the comments and advice of a group of consultants and reviewers as well as on a most rigorous classroom testing and verification process. Chapters 1 to 4 are the foundation of the text, and are substantially new. Chapter 1, which is entirely new, makes a case from the societal point of view for data processing and the data processing professional. Chapter 2 is substantially new and develops a simple but precise approach to data processing.

Chapter 3, which has been updated, illustrates the principal concepts of information processing systems and Chapter 4 now includes coverage of minicomputers, interrupt systems, distributed computing, and other recent developments. Chapter 5 stresses principles and methodology of programming including structured programming. Chapter 6 covers data representation in an abbreviated form. Chapter 7 has been updated to describe new types of input/output devices and other developments. Chapter 8 has been simplified, and stresses remote processing, distributed systems, and structured processes.

Chapter 9 starts with procedure-oriented languages, proceeds with a discussion of structured programming, and ends with optional sections on assembler language programming and input/output control systems. Chapter 10 is a new, optional chapter on data base management systems. Chapter 11 starts with a new statement of a general principle of computer systems development, but remains otherwise unchanged.

The supplements now include a man-machine dialog to teach BASIC programming in a time-sharing mode.

An extensive Study Guide with vocabulary drills, self-tests (true-false, matching, and multiple choice), and essay-type questions is available. A comprehensive Instructor's Manual is available with: (1) statement of objectives; (2) suggested approach; (3) objective test questions; (4) answers to tests in the Study Guide; (5) transparency masters of the most important illustrations; and (6) a chapter on PL/I Programming.

ACKNOWLEDGMENTS

The author gratefully acknowledges the valuable help given by a number of educators in the form of guidelines, general advice, comments, and corrections. The following contributors have been particularly helpful: Bob C. Cohoon, University of Alberta, Dan O'Donnell, De Anza College, Robert Fedrick, El Camino College, Robert B. Fetter, Yale University, Carl A. Grame, De Anza College, John A. Guin, Riverside City College, Claude McMillan, University of Colorado, Gerald E. Wagner, California State Polytechnic University, Howard L. Morgan, University of Pennsylvania, David Rosenberg, University of Hartford, Bruce M. Saulnier, Quinnipiac College, William A. Shrode, Florida State University.

Special thanks are due to Herbert F. Spirer, University of Connecticut, whose innumerable comments and suggestions made a profound impact both on the substance and appearance of this Revised Edition.

December 1976   ANDREW VAZSONYI

Contents

Why study data processing? The social implications

During the past quarter century there has developed a new resource of great importance, described by words like computer, data, information, processing, and system[1] combined into expressions like information systems, data processing, and computer and information technology. This resource is bringing about significant changes in society, as it will continue to do in the future. If we are to appreciate the significance of the societal changes brought about by computer systems we cannot think of the computer merely as a calculating machine. It must be considered an entirely new resource, potentially capable of bettering our lot (Figure 1.1a and b).

OPPORTUNITY AND DILEMMA

We usually think in terms of supplying and supporting our needs by material resources, but we have begun to realize that the material resources of the earth are limited. Our material resources are harnessed by energy, and we have learned that the energy resources of the earth are also limited. Thus it appears that our horizons have been foreshortened by the limitations of available resources. If information is compared with energy, however, it can be considered a new resource. *The instrument of this new type of energy—mental energy* is the computer. In the sense that our material and energy resources alike are controlled by information, this third resource may be the most important one (Figure 1.2). Information is also a

[1] Terms printed in color are defined at the end of the chapter.

FIGURE 1.1a
Modern large-
scale computer
system.

Courtesy Control Data Corporation.

virtually unlimited resource, and we have only begun to explore it.

While material and energy resources have contributed to our welfare, our use of them can bring about destructive social consequences and raise serious doubts and inspire fears. Information, the new resource, can be harnessed to benefit us or misapplied to deter us from our goals. *Our challenge is to harness the power of this new invention to the benefit of the human race.* The computer can become an agent of social progress, but it can also create social, political, cultural, and economic problems. However optimistic we may be about the possible accomplishments of the computer, we cannot reap its full benefits unless we recognize both its potentialities and its pitfalls. While to an extent this awareness can be gained only through experience, an educational foundation is essential to a balanced knowledge of the subject.

In the past, most members of our society were involved in producing material goods and services. Today society is rapidly turning from concern only with the production of physical goods to an equal concern with the production of information and knowledge. The purpose of this book is to provide introductory knowledge about computers and data processing. Mastery of this subject will start

FIGURE 1.1b
Modern portable
computer.

Courtesy IBM.

you on the road to becoming a data processing professional or a manager knowledgeable in the use of computers.

In summary, there are four reasons you should study data processing:

1. To fulfill your responsibilities as a citizen in helping assure that the new technology will be beneficial and not harmful to society.
2. To enable you to cope with the expanding use of computers, which is necessary if you are to be an effective, productive member of modern society.
3. To enable you, as a manager, to use the computer as an instrument in decision making.
4. To start you on the road to becoming a data processing professional.

In the first chapter of this book we stress the societal impact of this new resource and the role the data processing professional plays in its development and application. Technical discussion of data processing and computers is reserved for subsequent chapters.

FIGURE 1.2
Comparison of
human resources
with three-
dimensional
space. Space has
three dimensions:
length, width, and
height. Human
resources also
have three
dimensions:
matter, energy,
and the new
dimension—
information.

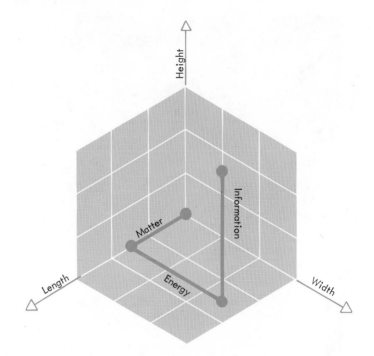

REACTIONS TO THE COMPUTER

The computer has appeared on the industrial scene only recently.
As late as the middle of the 20th century there was no computer
industry as it is known today. Now hundreds of thousands of
people are employed in computer-related work, and over ten
billion dollars worth of computers and services are sold yearly.
The stock exchanges list over 150 corporations either engaged
exclusively with computers and services or closely allied with
the computer industry (Figure 1.3).

Thus not only is the computer encountered in all facets of modern
life, it is also the focus of a substantial level of industrial activity.
It is natural that the ever-accelerating trend toward computerization
should attract much public attention, reaction, and criticism.
Significant changes and innovations by their very nature trigger
such responses. Where computers are concerned, *there is an optimistic and a pessimistic outlook; there is a bright and a dark side;
there is admiration and cynicism.* To develop a balanced and
positive view of computers we must examine these extreme views.
We need not blindly accept them but must evaluate them so we can
take what is valid and sound into account and reject what is unfounded and emotional.

Computerworld Stock Trading Summary

All statistics compiled, computed and formatted by TRADE*QUOTES, INC. Cambridge, Mass. 02139

TRADE*QUOTES

COMPUTER SYSTEMS

BURROUGHS CORP · COMPUTER AUTOMATION · COMMA DATA CORP · DATA GENERAL CORP · DATAPOINT CORP · DIGITAL COMP CONTROL · DIGITAL EQUIPMENT · ELECTRONIC ASSOC. · ELECTRONIC ENGINEER. · FOXBORO · GENERAL AUTOMATION · GRI COMPUTER CORP · HEWLETT-PACKARD CO · HONEYWELL INC · IBM · INTERDATA INC · MEMOREX · MICRODATA CORP · NCR · RAYTHEON CO · SPERRY RAND · SYSTEMS ENG. LABS · ULTIMACC SYSTEMS INC · VARIAN ASSOCIATES · WANG LABS. · XEROX CORP

LEASING COMPANIES

COMDISCO INC · COMMERCE GROUP CORP · COMPUTER INVSTRS GRP · DATRONIC RENTAL · DCL INC · DPF INC · DATA RESOURCES · GRANITE MGT · GREYHOUND COMPUTER · ITEL · LEASCO CORP · LEASPAC CORP · NPG TNC · NPG INT MGT INC · PIONEER TEX CORP · ROCKWOOD COMPUTER · U.S. LEASING

EXCH: N=NEW YORK; A=AMERICAN; P=PHIL-HALT-WASH; L=NATIONAL; M=MIDWEST; O=OVER-THE-COUNTER

O-T-C PRICES ARE BID PRICES AS OF 3 P.M. OR LAST BID

(1) TO NEAREST DOLLAR

SOFTWARE & EDP SERVICES

ADVANCED COMP TECH · APPLIED DATA RES. · AUTOMATIC DATA PROC · BRANDON APPLIED SYST · COMP DATA SYSTEMS · COMPUTER DIMENSIONS · COMP ELECTION SYSTEMS · COMPUTER HORIZONS · COMPUTER NETWORK · COMPUTER SCIENCES · COMPUTER USAGE GROUP · COMPUTER USAGE · COMSHARE · DATATAB · ELECT COMP PROG · ELECTRONIC DATA SYS. · IPS COMPUTER MARKET · KEANE ASSOCIATES · KVDATA CORP · LOGICON · MANAGEMENT DATA · NATIONAL CSS INC · NATIONAL COMPUTER CO · ON LINE SYSTEMS INC · PLANNING RESEARCH · PROGRAMMING & SYS · RAPIDATA INC · SCIENTIFIC COMPUTERS · SIMPLICITY COMPUTER · TYMSHARE INC · UNITED DATA CENTER · US SYSTEMS · WYLY CORP

PERIPHERALS & SUBSYSTEMS

ADDRESSOGRAPH-MULT · ADVANCED MEMORY SYS · AMPEX CORP · ANDERSEN JACOBSON · APPLIED MEDICAL ELEC · BOLT-BERANEK & NEW · BUNKER-RAMO · CALCOMP · CAMBRIDGE MEMORIES · CENTRONICS DATA COMP · CODEX CORP · COGNITRONICS

COMPUTER COMMUN.

COMPUTER CONSOLES · COMPUTER EQUIPMENT · COMPUTER MACHINERY · COMPUTER TRANSCEIVER · COMTEN · COMPAC CORP · DATA ACCESS SYSTEMS · DATA PRODUCTS CORP · DATA TECHNOLOGY · DATUM INC · DECISION DATA COMPUT · DELTA DATA SYSTEMS · DIVA CONTROLS · ELECTRONIC M & M · FABRI-TEK · GENERAL COMPUTER SYS · HAZELTINE CORP · HARRIS CORP · INCOTERM CORP · INFOREX INC · INFORMATION INTL INC · LINDY ELECTRONICS · MANAGEMENT ASSIST · MAGNE-HEAD · MOHAWK DATA SCIENCES · ODEC COMPUTER SYST. · OPTICAL SCANNING · PERTEC CORP · POTTER INSTRUMENT · PRECISION INST. · QUANTOR CORP · RECOGNITION EQUIP · SANDERS ASSOCIATES · SCAN DATA · STORAGE TECHNOLOGY · SYCOR INC · TALLY CORP. · TEC INC · TEKTRONIX INC · TELCO INC · TRIDEO INC · WILTEK INC

SUPPLIES & ACCESSORIES

BALTIMORE BUS FORMS · BARRY WRIGHT · CYBERMATICS INC · DATA DOCUMENTS · DUPLEX PRODUCTS INC · ENNIS BUS. FORMS · GRAHAM MAGNETICS · GRAPHIC CONTROLS · 3M COMPANY · MOORE CORP LTD · NASHUA CORP · STANDARD REGISTER · TAB PRODUCTS CO · UARCO · VANIER GRAPHICS CORP · WABASH MAGNETICS · WALLACE BUS FORMS

FIGURE 1.3 The various stock exchanges list over 150 corporations either engaged exclusively with computers and services or closely allied with the computer industry.

The enthusiastic view

A few years ago it was popular to predict the development of giant computer "brains" which would bring about the millennium. We were told that with the proper computer all problems would be solved. We were promised unlimited leisure and relief from drudgery. Clerks, managers, administrators, technicians, educators—everyone—would be relieved of all tedious work and allowed to concentrate on challenging and pleasant activities. The great increases in productivity in chemical plants employing automation promised similar increased productivity in factories, offices, and various endeavors. All records in banks, insurance companies, hospitals, government offices, and so on would be kept automatically, without error, at low cost, and would be instantly available to all concerned. We were told the computer would do many other things to aid society.

The computer *should* bring better service in all walks of life—instantaneous, accurate service from airlines, and hotels, and at the checkout counters of supermarkets. It *should* relieve educators of clerical tasks so they can concentrate on real educational problems. The scientific and engineering community *should* be provided with inexpensive and accurate computations so that better devices can be designed, more discoveries made in less time. The drudgery limiting creativity *should* be eliminated. Finding and arresting criminals *should* become instantaneous, and our courts *should* be enabled to operate in an equitable, efficient, uncluttered manner.

Yet this is not all. Computers *should* and in fact *do* enable us to do things we could never do before. We *can* travel in space. Medical diagnosis *can* be performed by the computer. Gas *can* be saved by computerized cars.

We could continue at length to describe the benefits promised by enthusiasts. Some of these have been actually realized; others are on the way to becoming reality in the near future; and still others are still far off. But benefits do not come without a price. It is rare indeed to realize an advantage without some accompanying disadvantage.

The pessimistic view

Some people recognize that much of what has been said about the computer is true, but they maintain that the effects it has had on human behavior far outweigh the benefits that have been obtained. The pessimist looks to the future and predicts a dismal one: The computer will disrupt the family, the community, the nation, and will even be detrimental to international relationships and to our global position.

It is said that the computer is causing a second industrial revolution comparable to the Industrial Revolution of the 18th and 19th centuries. In the first Industrial Revolution, the invention of the steam engine, which greatly increased the energy supply, changed concepts of society and people's powers in relation to their physical environment. Those who want to go back to the "good old days" claim that the Industrial Revolution has destroyed our customs, traditions, social organization, and the economic structure of the world (Figure 1.4). For example, it is admitted that locomotives and steamboats are great conveniences for transportation, but

FIGURE 1.4 Charlie Chaplin, in the motion picture *Modern Times* (1936), becomes a "cog" in the industrial machine, goes insane, and turns the factory into a madhouse.

Courtesy The Museum of Modern Art/Film Stills Archive, 11 W. 53d Street, New York City.

increasing the mobility of people leads to the breakdown of family relationships, and the creation of monstrous cities, with the accompanying pollution, crime, and chaos. Ethical and moral issues aside, the Industrial Revolution has adversely affected ecology and demography.

The pessimist sees other disadvantages of computerization. While the Industrial Revolution has shortened the average weekly work load from 72 hours to 40 hours, and will further reduce working hours to perhaps 16 in the next quarter century, the pessimist asks whether we know how to use the leisure we have. If we have lost our natural ability for joy, we will be unable to gain any advantage from having shorter working hours. The invention of power machines may have relieved us of hard work, but technological advances are said to lead to unemployment, increased production to indulgence, and the use of machinery to lower levels of self-reliance and ingenuity. The computer will become indispensable when we forget how to add and subtract. We will have better service to travel but nowhere to go. The computer may aid the educator while simultaneously removing human contact between teacher and pupil, and this leads to mechanistic and impersonal relationships.

In the pessimistic view, providing computers to engineering and scientific communities will make them so computer-reliant that individual creativity will become impossible. Providing computers to the police will aid in the arrest of criminals, but in no way will it cure social conditions leading to crime. Our government, keeping voluminous records on everyone, will run more smoothly, but individual rights and privacy will suffer, and we will find ourselves centrally controlled by dictators. Thus instead of enhancing our lot, the computer will retard social progress. Computerized medical diagnosis must lead to second-rate physicians. The pessimist has an unfavorable view of every possible computer application.

The rational view

Every one of the statements in the sections above has some element of truth as well as falsehood. Like coins, the computer issue has two sides and must not be judged only from one. *We must take a rational, not an emotional, position to chart the best course.* Thus we must recognize that if the computer is controlled properly it can bring great benefits, but if it is directed wrongly its effects may actually be harmful.

It is our opinion that the solution lies in knowledge of both computers and society's needs. To obtain such knowledge and arrive at a balanced view it is necessary to understand wherein the power of the computer lies.

THE POWER OF THE COMPUTER

The computer can calculate with lightning speed; millions, even hundreds of millions, of numbers can be multiplied in a second. The computer can store billions of data items and retrieve them accurately and quickly. These capabilities are remarkable, but they do not explain the power of the computer. Large numbers in themselves are not significant; for example, light covers 186,000 miles a second, and there is an unthinkably large number of grains of sand on every beach. *The key to the power of the computer lies in its ability to deal with information.* It can receive, manipulate, change, and transmit information and thereby influence our actions.

Perhaps the best way to appreciate the importance of information is to describe how it is used. Consider the human body and the nervous system (Figure 1.5). The brain issues commands (that is, information) through the nervous system to various parts of the body. The parts of the body function only with the information transmitted through the nervous system, and without information, they are ineffective. If the nervous system is damaged by disease, poison, or accidents, parts of the body cannot perform and cells become useless. If the brain is damaged severely the entire body can become useless, the personality lost; the human being turns into a vegetable. Severe brain damage leads to death. *It is information that keeps the human body functioning.*

Consider society. Primitive man lived in small groups, the family and the tribe. All communication was through words; there were no written records. The first important development in the communication of information was the written word, which made it possible to organize geographically distant human groups and to record history. The discovery of printing was another milestone in communication. The 19th and 20th centuries witnessed the discovery of the telegraph, telephone, radio, and television. All the various factors of *modern society are held together by communication* (Figure 1.6).

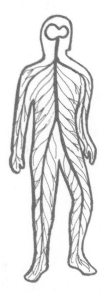

FIGURE 1.5 The human body is controlled by information transmitted by the nervous system.

To appreciate the point imagine all our communication channels cut—no newspaper, mail, telephones, radio, or television. As just two consequences, there would be no way to take care of emergencies, and airplanes could not land, take off, or fly. Gradually our society would cease to progress and would come to a halt. Occasional relatively minor failures in communication systems do occur, and such events have been experienced, at least partially.

The computer provides the technology to deal with information. Because it impacts on the communication systems coordinating society, it is an instrument of the greatest significance. To appreciate how the information capabilities of the computer give it power and enhance its importance, two immediate considerations must be examined.

First, if the computer can deal with information in a superior manner, some human tasks could be performed by robots, and might create machines which could displace people. Thus the computer is involved in the issue of automation and its effects on leisure time and unemployment. This issue is the subject of the next section.

The second consideration involves the impact of the computer on human forms of organization. If it is indeed communication of information that keeps our society functioning, the computer may be able to create a more efficient, more smoothly running society. It can also adversely affect how individuals act in groups, however.

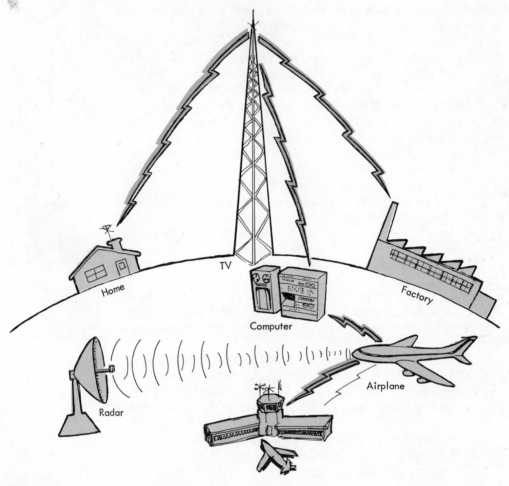

Home

TV

Computer

Factory

Radar

Airplane

FIGURE 1.6
Communication
plays a role in
almost everything
we do. What we
communicate is
information. It is
information that
the computer
processes.

If it is through information that groups mold individual habits, attitudes, and ideas, then the computer is equally able to change society for the worse. If the individual loses his ability to exercise his political influence on the government, for example, the result will be a loss of human dignity and endangered freedoms.

There are many concerns about the impact of the computer. Most of them can be classified into four groups: (1) automation, (2) threats to privacy, (3) loss of individuality and regimentation, and (4) abuse of political power. It is not the purpose of this book to provide a complete discussion of the societal aspects of the computer, however. We will restrict our discussion to brief statements on the issues of automation and threats to privacy.

THE ISSUE OF AUTOMATION

According to the Bible, labor is a curse imposed by God on humans as a punishment for a crime committed in the Garden of Eden. Humans have been striving for years to avoid this curse by the invention of mechanical servants. In Jewish mythology there is the golem, a creature made of clay but endowed with life to serve its creator. According to the legend, the golem runs amuck and its creator destroys it. A 19th-century version of a similar myth is the horror tale written by Mary Wollstonecraft Shelley in which a German student, Frankenstein, learns the secret of infusing life into inanimate matter and creates a monster which ultimately destroys him. The 20th-century version of this myth was introduced on the stage by the Czech dramatist Karel Capek. He coined the word *robot* (from the Czech word for "compulsory service") a concept which today causes apprehension in most people.

From time to time sensational stories in the newspapers or on TV describe an ingenious robot which is able to replace people in all walks of life. A careful examination of 20 years of releases shows that all of them were mere predictions, and none have come true. However, research is being conducted on the development of devices to perform human functions that require some "intelligence." A recent example is a robot called Shakey (Figure 1.7), which prowls a room at Stanford Research Institute, maneuvering a path through a maze of obstacles. As it gropes forward it senses obstacles with its cat-whiskerlike antennas, and it unsteadily zigzags to the goal. Scientists at the institute hope a machine like Shakey *may* some day explore dangerous environments such as those humans might encounter on Mars. Stress the words *hope* and *some day*. No responsible scientist would predict when this will be and what tasks such a robot could perform, in particular what level of "intelligence" such a machine would exhibit.

There is no denying that computers have replaced some human functions and humans. But so have other inventions. In 1801 Joseph-Marie Jacquard, a Frenchman, invented an automatic loom operated by paper punched cards much like those used today in computers. By 1810 there were 11,000 such looms operating in France alone, and the mass manual production of textile fabric has disappeared. After Elias Howe invented the modern sewing machine in 1846 the clothing industry was revolutionized, and hand sewing as a mass industry also disappeared.

It is unnecessary to go through a long list of inventions to describe how they have changed our lives. The fear that automation will lead to unemployment and dehumanization is not new. During the depression of the 1830s, well over a century ago, some people demanded a law to forbid all inventions so new machines would not replace workers. Had Congress passed and enforced such a law, even for a brief period, the sewing machine would not have been invented. Neither would the harvester-reaper (in 1834) and the telegraph (in 1840). Thus the computer is no exception to the rule that inventions have good and bad effects.

FIGURE 1.7
Shakey, a research robot, prowls a room at Stanford Research Institute and maneuvers a path through a maze of obstacles.

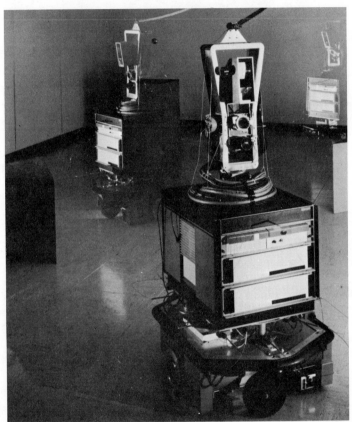

Courtesy Stanford Research Institute, Menlo Park, Calif.

From a societal point of view the rational approach is to appraise the benefits and the disadvantages of innovations and introduce them only when potential benefits outweigh possible disadvantages. Because we cannot foresee the future precisely, we can only appraise the possibilities of what may come. All innovation and progress involve uncertainty and an element of risk. Society can afford to take moderate risks for great benefits, small risks for moderate benefits, and no risks for no benefits.

We must be braced to expect some bad along with the good. We despair about the accidents caused by the automobile but are unwilling to eliminate this mode of transportation, since the benefits far outweigh the harm. We do not ground *all* airplanes because of an occasional catastrophe. However, we must face up to the ethical issue of protecting humans from avoidable adverse consequences of innovations and must shield and compensate the victims. Social organization allows the removal of the incompetent employee or the obsolete one, but it provides aid to the unemployed. Most nations insist on liability insurance for automobile drivers, supply medical aid for the disadvantaged, and provide retirement plans for the aged.

When a computer is introduced to automate a job, the issue of good and bad effects must be raised and evaluated. Are more or fewer jobs being created? Are the jobs more challenging, or less so? Will there be more or less boredom? Better or worse working conditions? Will more or fewer skills be required? Will productivity rise or decrease? Will automation mean a higher standard of living? A shorter work week? Earlier retirement? More leisure? Longer vacations?

A great deal of inquiry has been directed to finding the truth in these matters. *In spite of the predictions of the prophets of doom it has been found that the benefits of the computer far outweigh the disadvantages.* Undoubtedly some people have been replaced by computers, but most have found substitute jobs. Substantial unemployment has been created not by computers but by economic dislocations, recessions, and depressions. However, it is possible that problems in this area may arise in the future. Society must watch closely the potential political problems of automation and establish broad safeguards to protect human welfare.

PROTECTING PERSONAL PRIVACY

With expanding requirements for information by business, government, and other organizations, there is a growing recognition that steps must be taken to guarantee the individual's right to privacy. There are records on over 10 million people who have sought insurance in more than 700 major life and health insurance companies. Credit agencies, local, state, and federal law enforcement agencies, the Social Security Administration, and tax bureaus all keep extensive records.

While such computerized bureaus all maintain voluminous records, the effect of the computer on the magnitude of these records is not entirely clear. A three-year effort by a team of scholars for the prestigious National Academy of Sciences demonstrated that much of the alarm about computer invasion of privacy is unfounded, and *in some instances the introduction of the computer actually caused a decrease in the amount of information held.*[2] However, we should be concerned about these adverse possibilities. The Federal Privacy Act of 1974, which went into effect in September 1975, is designed to prevent potential abuse of personal privacy. The establishment of sound public policy on this issue should be based on the following principles:

1. Individuals should have access to information about themselves.
2. Individuals must have the freedom to find out how information about themselves is being used.
3. Each individual should have a way to correct or amend inaccurate information.
4. Each individual should be able to prevent information from being improperly used for other than authorized purposes without his or her consent, unless required by law.
5. Recordkeeping agencies must take precautions to see that sensitive information is reliable and is not misused.

THE USERS OF COMPUTER SYSTEMS

We have seen that our society is profoundly influenced by the computer; there are literally millions of people in all walks of life — banks, offices, department stores, schools, government offices — who are users of computers. The word user is a general term referring to anyone who requires the services of a computing system, though in this book we will concentrate on those who cannot fully benefit from the computer unless they have a good knowledge of what computer systems are about.

Specifically, in this book we are concerned with two types of users. The first is managers who use computers for the purpose of doing a better job. They need to know *how* to apply computers to their activities. They also need to know about computer systems so they can decide whether to acquire and use them to achieve particular benefits. The second type of user in whom we are interested is the data processing professional or information systems specialist who uses the computer to provide information to others. We could call managers and data processing professionals *sophisticated* users, in contrast to users who need to know very little about computer systems. *Our main interest in this book is the sophisticated computer user — that is, the manager, the information system specialist, and the data processing professional.*

[2] Alan F. Westin and Michael A. Baker, *Databanks in a Free Society* (New York: Quadrangle Books, 1973).

THE MANAGER AND THE COMPUTER

Managers, in both the private and public sectors of society and in both profit and nonprofit organizations, must have knowledge about computers and data processing. They are the ones who make the decisions whether or not a computer system is to be acquired and how it is to be used, so they are responsible to a great extent for the use or misuse of the resource. They also must know about the computer because it influences their management style.

When managers are faced with the decision of installing information systems, it is not enough for them to consider advantages and disadvantages in general. They must also think in terms of eco-

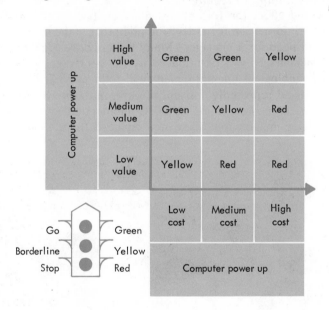

FIGURE 1.8 Cost/ benefit analysis compared to a traffic-light control system.

nomics, values, costs, and benefits. As computer capabilities increase, costs and values to the firm also increase. The decision to install a computer cannot be based on either value or cost, however, but on the difference between the two—the net benefit.

The cost/benefit analysis can be compared to a traffic-light system (Figure 1.8). For example, medium cost and high value mean positive net benefit, or a green *go* signal. High cost and medium value mean a net loss, or a red *stop* signal. When costs and values are comparable, the manager has a borderline case, or a *yellow,* or caution signal. Thus what the manager needs to know is not so much how the computer system works as its performance capabilities and associated benefits, values, and costs.

But such a cost/benefit analysis is not enough. The manager must also understand the psychological and societal aspects of organizations to be able to appraise the operational soundness of a computer installation. There is a widespread tendency to resist change. Unless appropriate motivation is provided, an otherwise technologically and economically sound system may fail.

There is another reason why managers need to know about computers; the modern manager is considered a decision maker, and must have information on which to base decisions. At the crossroads the manager must set foot on one or another of the routes that lead to the future, and it is information that points to the rational choice. *The computer is playing an increasing role in providing needed information for managers.*

This could affect the role of the manager. If the computer can provide the information for a decision and process the information, is there any need for a manager? Many writers have predicted that the middle manager will be replaced by the computer, and a new type of technological unemployment will follow. While this issue has been raised repeatedly, *careful research has shown that none of the predictions have come true.* Computerized systems have aided decision makers but have not replaced them (Figure 1.9).

FIGURE 1.9
Computerized
systems have
aided decision
makers but have
not replaced them.

Courtesy Gordon Baer, Cincinnati and Business Week.

So far computers have not significantly influenced the organizational structure of corporations, and no discernible trend toward centralization or decentralization has been found as a result of computer installation.

RESOLUTION OF THE DILEMMA: THE KNOWLEDGE WORKER

We have stressed the potential of the new resource known as the computer and the dilemma involved in assuring the benefits of such technology while avoiding its pitfalls. The resolution of this dilemma lies in a rational and thoughtful approach to the problem through knowledge—knowledge of both technology and social issues. And this is the crux of the matter: We believe that *the computer revolution in our society lies not in the computer itself or its technology but in the manner in which society is organized and the functions that people perform.*

The social revolution we are undergoing is closely tied to the change from predominantly manual work to work in areas of knowledge production. The "knowledge industry" is a term coined by the Princeton economist Fritz Machlup in 1962 to contrast the production and distribution of ideas and information with the production and distribution of goods and services. Up to World War II, U.S. industry was primarily concerned with goods and services. As the knowledge industry started to grow in the postwar era, there was a dramatic increase in the number of people occupied with such areas as education, communication, publication, and computers. Depending on how information is defined, it has been variously estimated that between one third and one half of the work force in the United States is concerned with knowledge and information. And the number is steadily increasing.

Now we can identify wherein the real power of the computer lies. *Our society is changing into a knowledge society, and the computer is the prime instrument of this change.* As knowledge workers modern managers must have a knowledge of the computer if they are to fulfill their obligations effectively. And data processing professionals must have a positive societal conscience so they can serve as guardians of the computer and assure that the full benefits of the new resource for society will be realized.

THE WORLD OF THE DATA PROCESSING PROFESSIONAL

The computer, as any other machine, must be designed, built, operated, and maintained. Although the computer is primarily an electronic device, electronic engineers, circuit designers, and electronic technicians are not the only ones to participate in its design and construction. Because a computer system contains

FIGURE 1.10
The classified
advertisement
section of a news-
paper provides an
up-to-date listing
of opportunities for
data processing
professionals.

many mechanical devices, mechanical engineers and technicians also must participate.

Manufacturers of computers, as of any complex, specialized equipment, require highly trained and skilled production and assembly workers. Computer factories are desirable places to work because no smoke or noise is produced. Some electronic com-

---

POSITIONS AVAILABLE   POSITIONS AVAILABLE

IBM SYSTEMS PROFESSIONALS

We are seeking the one right Systems Professional to take charge of a challenging program to develop and test IBM-compatible processing hardware systems. If you are this person, or know of such a person, please contact us by telephone or know or resume for a confidential discussion of your qualifications. Qualifications should include facility in working with internals of DOS/VS, OS/VSI, OS/VS2, or VM/370, DASD programming; and System Utilities. If you are the right person, you can expect attractive compensation, and the opportunity to be responsible for state-of-the-art hardware systems.

Please respond to: ....

PROGRAMMERS
The individual we seek must have a minimum of 2 yrs. programming experience in a DOS or OS environment, using ANS Cobol. Candidate should possess a good working knowledge in financial and manufacturing applications within a manufacturing environment. An Associates Degree or equivalent is desirable. For immediate consideration, please submit a detailed resume including salary history in strict confidence to: Box 137MX this newspaper.

PROGRAMMER: Experience and a desire to grow are needed by local firm. to develop programs in BAL or IBM 370/135-145 OS. JCL a plus. Salary $15,000. Burns Personnel Agency, 701 Security Tower, 1 East Ave., 232-7470.

PROGRAM DIRECTOR: In Rehabilitation setting. M.A. or B.A. with 2-5 yrs. administrative and grant experience. Send resume to T.A. Sprague, Executive Director, Genesee County Association for Retarded children. 3837 West Main St. Batavia, N.Y. 14020.

Programmer $17,000
Assembler, mini-computers.
KRUPK...

CAREER OPPORTUNITIES
OUTSTANDING SYSTEMS AND PROGRAMMING PROFESSIONALS

SYSTEMS ANALYST
Work with user departments in the development of real-time general ledger and library systems. Bachelors degree required plus minimum of 2 years systems experience. Total 5 years program systems involvement. Educational and accounting background is a plus.

SYSTEMS PROGRAMMER/ANALYST
Work full time on hardware/software applications including systems generations, maintenance and optimization of operating systems. Bachelors degree required or equivalent work experience. Minimum of 2 years technical software items supportive activities. Total of 6 years experience data processing.

PROGRAMMER
Work on real-time and batch programming on receivable, general ledger, registration and library systems. Bachelors ... equivalent work experience plus minimum ... programming.
... be familiar with IBM 370 DOS/VS ... ge benefits and vacation. Tuition

Reply In Writing Stating Salary
Ms. Yvonne Lowen

CHIEF EXECUTIVE OFFICER
$75,000/YEAR PLUS INCENTIVES

Internationally based Leasing and ... specializing in the Computer Field se... for domestic operation. Financially ori... ly connected Executive with Leasing ... ...and understanding of relat...

INFORMATION SYSTEMS SPECIALISTS

Manufacturing Applications
Salaries: To $25,000

Due to internal promotions, two key available within our corporate Mana consultants to multiple-plant corpora headquartered in Northeast New Jer in the greater Philadelphia area) pr ties will involve the planning, design computer systems to control product flow.

Professional qualifications call for ind working independently with at least 5 experience in planning, designing and cant computer base manufacturing int including multiple aspects of line com terial control employing on line com cellent communications skills, strong edge of computers and solid financial might also required. B.S. in I.E. required. Master's De gree preferred. Ideal candidates will also have actual plant operating exposure and project management ex perience.

These high visibility positions on our Corporate Staff offer top professional challenge, lucrative compensation packages and exceptional career growth opportunities ... growing $1.3 billion corporation. Reply to ...

COLLEGE

Senior Software Development Analysts
San Francisco

Three to five years' experience in development of telecommunications software in an OS/MVT/HASP environment. Specific areas include: CICS/VS/VTAM...

Marketing Opportuni...
DATA PROCESSING

Computer Machinery Corporation, one of the natio... firms in data entry and remote batch processing syst... highly qualified individuals for newly created sales positi... rapid expansion, the following opportunities are immedi... able:

● REMOTE JOB ENTRY/DATA ENTRY SALESMEN
Openings available in New York City, Philadelphia, Detroit, Houston, St. Louis, Dallas, San Francisco, Los Portland, Springfield, Illinois; and Columbus, Ohio.

● ACCOUNT/CUSTOMER REPRESENTATIVE
Openings available ... ork City, Ch...

COMPUTER PROGRAMMING

LEARN IBM COMPUTERS LEARN
360 PROGRAMMING $649
CONSOLE OPERATION $449
KEY PUNCH $199
APPVD. FOR VETS & STATE LOANS
AUTHORIZED TO ACCEPT
NON-IMMIGRANT ALIEN STUDENTS
COMPARE!
CPU 853 B'WAY, N.Y.C.
982-4000

PROGRAMMER: Cobol, to coordinate activities of small programming staff, including applications programming and systems analysis, supervisory experience preferred, minimum 5 yrs. in top including detailed exposure to operating systems and extensive Cobol experience. Write: Personnel Dept., University of Rochester, 260 Crittenden Blvd., 14642. An Equal Opportunity Employer, M/F.

PROGRAMMER: 18K, Fee paid. Experienced with BAL-COBOL, CICS and Systems debugging. Will be working with conversion from DOS/VS to OS/VS. Resume required. Contact Jim Wright, EXECUTIVE PLACEMENT CORP., Agency. 949-49 Sibley Tower, 454-1424.

POST OFFICE BOX 923
LOS ANGELES, CALIFORNI...

ELECTRONIC ENGINEERS
DATA COMMUNICATI... EQUIPMENT DESIG...

We are a dynamic, rapidly growing turer of data communications equipm... world wide. We seek talented, innov... dividuals experienced in logic and c... sign, capable of following projects fr... tion through production. BSEE requ... preferred. Minimum of 3 yrs experie... sional travel. Excellent salary an... program. Located in Suffolk Cou... Island.

Send resume with salary histor...
Y 7045 TIMES

CUSTOMER SERVICE MANAGER COMPUTERIZED TYPESETTING

We are a subsidiary of one of the largest printing conglomerates in Europe. WE are seeking an individual with a good background in text-oriented data processing and graphics in the computerized typesetting industry. Your key functions will be to act as a liason between customers and production, working with, and reporting to our Vice President of Marketing. Should be personable and enjoy with people.

loccation - Huntington, Long Island, New York.

For further information, please call Nick Battaglino, V.P. marketing, (212) 751-0815, or send resume to:

Esselte Digitype   866 Third Avenue New York, NY 10022

ponents are made in an air-conditioned environment that is cleaner than hospital operating rooms.

Repair and maintenance are much more complex for computers than for most other machinery. People performing these tasks are called field or maintenance engineers and have interesting, well-paid jobs.

All these positions are in firms associated with the production of computer systems. The computer professional is the knowledge worker who is employed to use the computer.

The role of the data processing professional is changing so fast that by the time this book is in print it will undoubtedly present new challenges. Better jobs and more pay are likely to be available. Perhaps the best way to find out what the computer professional does is to pick up your daily newspaper, look in the classified advertisement section, and review the jobs available (Figure 1.10). You will find that there are many openings. If you compare today's help-wanted section with an old paper, you would find that the number of positions has greatly increased. All signs indicate that the profession is still expanding, and more jobs are promised in the future.

In surveying the positions open to data processing professionals you will occasionally find words with which you are not familiar. Do not be discouraged; as you proceed with your studies, the data processing words will become clear.

To aid you in appraising the opportunities, Figure 1.11 presents information about positions in data processing in 1975. Positions can be classified into three main groups: computer operations, application and system programming, and systems analysis. In each of these groups there are also supervisory and managerial positions. The most important position is the director-manager of data processing or the vice president of data processing.

Computer operators

Computer operators are the people who see and touch the machine; they deal with the physical, tangible, and permanent components of the computer or data processing system, or the computer hardware. Chuck Pearson was a driver in a car wash when his high school counselor suggested that he get into "computer work." At first it frightened him even to think about computers, but with encouragement from his counselor he enrolled in a computer course. As he lost his fear and realized that running a computer can be fun, he learned much about operating a computer and a few things about programming. After he took his first job he learned more through on-the-job training.

Representative Title	Salary (in thousands)	Number in the U.S.	Typical functions	Typical training and experience
Vice president or director of information systems	$20–60	12,000	Manage 10–500 persons and $200,000 to several million dollar budget, allocating resources to projects, motivating, and controlling progress	College degree, possible graduate degree, technical and analytical skills, knowledge of the business problems and management ability, 10–20 years experience, mostly in information processing
Manager of systems analysis	$16–30	30,000	Manage information systems development	Usually college degree, five or more years of computer experience, and working knowledge of the organization's problems
Systems analyst	$12–25	150,000	Analyze and design information systems to solve user needs	Former programmer or business analyst, with college likely
Programmer	$10–25	250,000	Design and develop programs	One to ten years' programming experience after college or programming school
Coder	$ 8–12	100,000	Low-level programming conversion	Programming language school without college degree and under two years' experience
Operations manager	$12–25	20,000	Manage staff operating computer	Operator school and three years' experience
Computer console operator	$ 8–16	100,000	Load and run computer	Operator school and some experience

FIGURE 1.11
Information about positions in data processing (1975).

Pearson's new know-how of computers prepared him for his current job, on which he is responsible for input/output operations, such as mounting tape and disk drives and getting paper ready for the printer. Off the job he listens to music on the radio, and on the job he likes to think of himself as an input/output jockey. He enjoys being on his feet and taking part in the action. He really admires Keith, the console operator, the interface between people and computer.

Keith Crown is a high school graduate with five years of experience in computer operation. To an outside observer Crown's job may look boring; all he does is push buttons and type messages to the computer. But Crown has a different feeling about it. Isn't he the commander who directs the computer? Isn't he the one who, in the final analysis, decides what the computer should do?

Almost every day Crown manages, by ingenious scheduling, to squeeze another computer job into the work day. He has been told by the director of data processing that he is saving $10,000 a month for the company! Crown likes his job and wants to stay with it. When new equipment comes in (and this happens often) he must learn all about it and figure out how to put it to the best use. He will never run out of problems, and he does not want to become a computer programmer. He wants action, not a desk job that requires a great deal of patience. He also loves the quiet elegance, the air-conditioned environment of the computer room where he does his work.

Rita Haber, a computer operator in operations, regards her job differently than either Pearson and Crown do theirs. She knows a great deal about computer systems and programming and often works with programmers and helps them with their problems. She likes this accurate, abstract, thinking type of work. She learned some computer programming in a business school and is taking part in an in-house training course to become a computer programmer.

Thomas Baker is the manager of operations shown in the organization chart in Figure 1.12. He is a high school graduate who worked his way up from computer operator to manager. He likes to supervise people, run projects, organize, and plan operations. He enjoys supervising the computer and the keypunch operators and the people preparing data. He regards the computer as a machine in a factory, which produces data rather than manufactured products, and considers himself a part of the knowledge industry. Some day he hopes to get promoted out of data processing to the factory to manage other operations like assembly-line or machine-shop production.

Application programmers

Application programmers are one example of the people in data processing who write programs or perform programming, to solve the problems of the ultimate users, who are outside the data processing function.

Yolanda Hutchins is a programmer trainee, a coder who per-

FIGURE 1.12 Organization chart of the data processing functions.

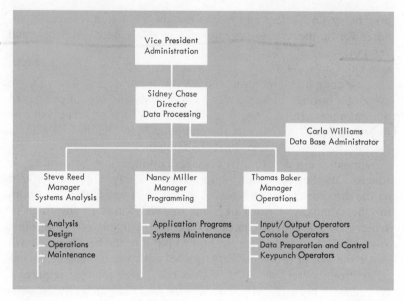

forms coding under Hilda Gardner, a senior programmer. Hutchins studied programming in junior college and is learning practical knowledge from Hilda Gardner (see below). Hutchins's job is to write program segments to support Gardner's work. She is good with figures and attends to details, but she does not like mathematics and has little knowledge of it. She always liked accounting, however, and finds that her knowledge helps her understand data processing methods.

Hilda Gardner is a college graduate who has had some education in mathematics and business. She has a logical mind and good reasoning ability. An excellent student of programming in college, she has learned a great deal on the job since. In addition to writing application programs, she maintains the programs provided by the manufacturer, and each time the manufacturer changes the programs she is the one who makes them operational. She finds these assignments interesting because the programs provided by the manufacturer are much more complex than the application programs. Some day she may work her way up to systems programmer (see below).

Arthur Knodel is a college graduate who majored in computer sciences and also studied business and mathematics. He is not only an excellent programmer but has a good command of English, both oral and written. He likes to solve problems and works closely with systems analysts (see below). Some day he hopes to be transferred to that group.

Nancy Miller (see Figure 1.12) is the manager of programming.

She was a top programmer before being promoted to her managerial job. She enjoys her work because she likes to deal with people, though sometimes she regrets not using more of her technical training, and she does not have time to keep up with new developments. She works closely with systems analysts and the users of the application programs. She is under constant pressure from management to produce accurate results, on time, and within a budget. She finds this stimulating.

Systems analysts

Systems analysts work with the users for each application, determine their requirements, and prepare specifications so the programmers can write the programs. They define and recommend new systems; estimate costs and benefits; design, implement, and modify systems; and hold overall responsibility for system performance.

Estelle Novak is a college graduate who majored in accounting, management, and computers. She became interested early in systems, computers, and programming. Initially, she was a programmer and later was transferred to systems analysis. She has a knack for dealing with computer users and understanding their problems. She likes to attack generalities and translate them into specifics.

Novak considers herself the link or interface between the user and the programmer, and her knowledge of both business and the computer well qualify her for this role. She feels that the highly abstract nature of her work fully challenges her logical and creative abilities. One of her most important skills is the ability to conceptualize complex problems and situations.

Robert Blake holds a similar systems position, though he has a very different background. He is a college graduate who majored in accounting and worked in accounting systems. Because he dealt with computer professionals, he got interested in systems analysis and computer programming. He went to night school to learn data processing and programming and later took a position as a programmer. Soon after he was transferred to systems analysis, where his background in business and computers could be used best.

Steve Reed is manager of systems analysis (see Figure 1.12) and is responsible for the analysis, design, operations, and maintenance of systems. He is a college graduate who majored in computers and information systems. He started as a programmer and worked his way up to senior programmer, to senior systems analyst, and finally to the managerial position. He is equally competent in strictly technical problems and the business problems of the users. He is responsible for all the functions to be performed by systems analysts and the achievement of the goals assigned to the professionals working for him.

✳ Systems programmers

Systems programmers are the "super" programmers of the profession. The programs they write may contain tens or hundreds of thousands of program steps. Some are college graduates who majored in computer science; others worked up from the ranks of application programmers. Systems programmers do the most abstract programming, and they are said to be the aristocrats of the profession and often receive the highest pay. They deal with the most complex type of software, the term used to describe all items pertaining to the operation of a data processing system except hardware. Thus systems programmers usually work for computer manufacturers and "software houses."

✳ Data base administrators

Carla Williams (see Figure 1.12) is on the staff of the director of data processing and is responsible for keeping all computerized data on the operations of the corporation. Her position, a relatively new one, has resulted from the growing importance of data in data processing operations.

Williams likes to compare herself to the chief librarian of a university, who is responsible for the purchase, maintenance, and replacement of all books, magazines, newspapers, and documents. The librarian maintains up-to-date records and makes it possible for students and faculty to obtain material required for studies and research. In a similar fashion Williams administers the data base or data bank for the corporation. No one can add, change, or remove data without checking with her. She knows where the data is and keeps descriptions, definitions, dictionaries and indexes for data. She is responsible for the integrity of the data, that is, for the maintenance of sound principles of data keeping. She assures that various rules pertaining to data are properly established and observed and maintains the necessary records.

Williams's functions are not only technical but organizational. She deals with programmers, systems analysts, and the user and must make the proper compromises for the benefit of all. Her position and in fact her field of work are relatively new, and she has no people working under her. The trend in data processing is toward increased emphasis on data base administration, however, and it should not be long before she will have one or more assistants to support her important activity.

Directors of data processing

Sidney Chase (see Figure 1.12) is a college graduate who majored in management. He considers himself a manager and likes to supervise people and run things. He is good at planning, implementing, installing, and controlling the complex projects that make up the data processing operations. Chase was promoted from the ranks of systems analysis because of his familiarity with such management functions as marketing, finance, and manufacturing. He is effective in dealing with management and users. Chase hopes that some day data processing will be so important that he will make a vice president of data processing.

Skills required   What skills are required to reach the top in the data processing profession as a director of data processing? Must you be scientifically oriented, knowledgeable in mathematics and science? Not necessarily. Surveys have determined the skills required.

In one survey, executives were asked to name the most critical qualities a director of data processing could have to uniquely fit that position. Figure 1.13 shows the answers received. Only 8 per-

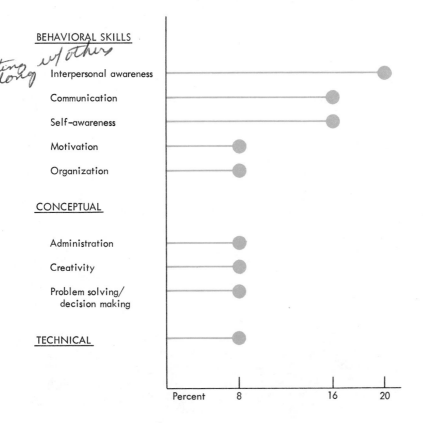

FIGURE 1.13
Skills required in a director of data processing. The horizontal dimension shows the percent of executives reporting the indicated skill as the most critical one.

BEHAVIORAL SKILLS

Interpersonal awareness

Communication

Self-awareness

Motivation

Organization

CONCEPTUAL

Administration

Creativity

Problem solving/
decision making

TECHNICAL

Percent   8   16   20

cent of the respondents considered technical knowledge as the most critical factor. Interpersonal awareness was listed as the most desirable characteristic for a successful data processing director by 20 percent, and skills associated with communication and self-awareness were listed by 16 percent. The rest of the respondents equally cited (8 percent) the behavioral skills of motivation and organization and the conceptual skills of administration, creativity, and problem solving/decision making.

To summarize, there are great professional opportunities in data processing administration for systems analysts with the following profile:

1. Understands the management process.
    a. Is knowledgeable in functional areas of business.
    b. Is systems oriented.
    c. Differentiates between the practical and theoretical.
2. Considers computers a resource.
    a. Understands the basis of computer applications.
    b. Knows computer hardware and software.
3. Is aware of problems connected with creating changes.
    a. Recognizes the role of the emotions.
    b. Can deal with behavioral situations.
    c. Balances benefits with costs and risks.
    d. Is sensitive to change and changed relationships.

Of course, technical knowledge is a prerequisite for advancement in data processing, but behavioral and conceptual skills are also of great importance.

THE JOYS OF DATA PROCESSING

People become data processing professionals for many reasons. The primary reason may be to make a living, and to do it with an interesting, pleasant, well-paying job. But there is more to it. In particular, there is more to programming. Frederick P. Brooks, Jr., who might be called a "super" systems programmer, beautifully describes the joys of the craft in *The Mythical Man-Month: Essays on Software Engineering.*

THE JOYS OF THE CRAFT

Why is programming fun? What delights may its practitioner expect as his reward? First is the sheer joy of making things. As the child delights in his mud pie, so the adult enjoys building things, especially things of his own design. I think this delight must be an image of God's delight in making things, a delight shown in the distinctness and newness of each leaf and each snowflake.

Second is the pleasure of making things that are useful to other people. Deep within, we want others to use our work and to find it helpful. In this respect the programming system is not essentially different from the child's first clay pencil holder "for Daddy's office."

Third is the fascination of fashioning complex puzzle-like objects of interlocking moving parts and watching them work in subtle cycles, playing out the consequences of principles built in from the beginning. The programmed computer has all the fascination of the pinball machine or the jukebox mechanism, carried to the ultimate.

Fourth is the joy of always learning, which springs from the non-repeating nature of the task. In one way or another the problem is ever new, and its solver learns something: sometimes practical, sometimes theoretical, and sometimes both.

Finally, there is the delight of working in such a tractable medium. The programmer, like the poet, works only slightly removed from pure thought-stuff. He builds his castles in the air, from air, creating by exertion of the imagination. Few media of creation are so flexible, so easy to polish and rework, so readily capable of realizing grand conceptual structures.

Yet the program construct, unlike the poet's words, is real in the sense that it moves and works, producing visible outputs separate from the construct itself. It prints results, draws pictures, produces sounds, moves arms. The magic of myth and legend has come true in our time. One types the correct incantation on a keyboard, and a display screen comes to life, showing things that never were nor could be.

Programming then is fun because it gratifies creative longings built deep within us and delights sensibilities we have in common with all men.[3]

THE CHALLENGE: TOWARD A POSITIVE FUTURE

The computer may be the greatest invention of modern times. More than any other it has the potential to change our way of life. We can assume that all organizations—private industry, government, scientific, educational—will come to rely on computers, and they will penetrate the home, affecting both individuals and the family group.

With the computer here to stay, the issue is not how to limit its use but how to assure that this use will be in the service of humanity. There are potential risks and dangers, as in all innovations, and caution is in order. But progress is made not by the timid but by the bold. We believe that the computer offers great benefits at small risk; the challenge is to use it to the best advantage to enrich our lives. The computer cannot do this for us. We alone are responsible. (See Figure 1.14.)

---

[3] Frederick P. Brooks, Jr., *The Mythical Man-Month: Essays on Software Engineering* (Reading, Mass.: Addison-Wesley, 1975), pp. 7–8.

FIGURE 1.14
The name of
the game.

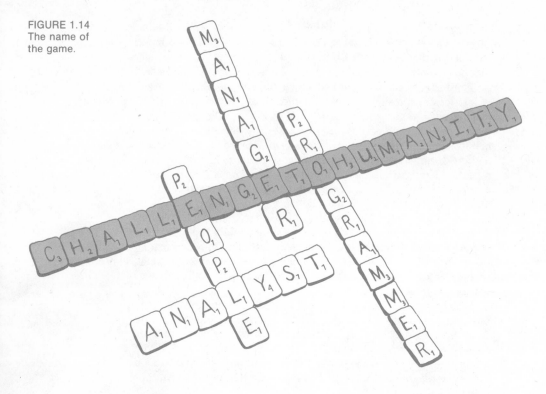

SUMMARY

1. Information is a resource, in a sense the most valuable of all resources, since it can control all other physical resources, as represented by energy and matter.
2. The computer, a revolutionary invention, is a source of mental energy which changes the social, political, cultural, and economic fabric of our society.
3. The computer can be controlled for the benefit of the individual, to protect his rights and enhance his responsibilities, or it can be misapplied and become an agent of social retrogression.
4. Management controls organizations and makes decisions through information systems. Thus the computer is a critical instrument for the modern manager.
5. Prerequisites in the beneficial use of information systems are:
    a. Citizens knowledgeable as to the potential of the computer and its limitations.
    b. Managers sophisticated in the economical use of computers.
    c. Data processing professionals with social, political, cultural, and economic awareness.

6. The successful data processing professional must have technical knowledge and the skills necessary to conceptualize problem solving and to deal with behavioral situations.
7. The data processing professional is challenged to become a societal agent who can assure the full benefits of computer use for humanity.

KEY CONCEPTS AND WORDS[4]

coder: a person involved mainly in writing but not designing computer programs.

coding: work performed by a coder.

computer: a data processor which can perform substantial computations, including numerous arithmetic or logical operations, without intervention by a human operator during the run.

console: part of a computer used for communication between the operator and the computer.

data: any representation such as characters or other symbols to which meaning is or might be assigned.

data base: a collection of data fundamental to an enterprise.

hardware: physical equipment as opposed to the computer program or method of use; for example, mechanical, magnetic, electrical, or electronic devices. Contrast with *software*.

information: the meanings assigned to data by the known conventions used in its representation.

input: (1) the data that is delivered to a data processing device from the external world, (2) the process of delivering this data to the equipment that performs this process, (3) a keyboard-actuated device that punches holes in a card to represent data. Contrast with *output*.

interface: a device or person forming a shared boundary or link between two entities.

keypunch: a keyboard-actuated device which punches holes in a card to represent data.

output: (1) the data that is delivered by a data processing device to the external world, (2) the process of delivering this data.

processing: a broad term used in expressions like data processing, automatic data processing, business data processing, electronic data processing, industrial data processing, information processing.

program: usually refers to a computer program, a series of instructions or statements in a form acceptable to a computer which has been prepared to achieve a certain result.

---

[4] The language of data processing is constantly changing, and it is impossible to provide universally accepted definitions. There are a number of dictionaries, but often the terminology is conflicting. We have tried to strike a reasonable compromise, which sometimes leads to minor discrepancies. Occasionally we introduce synonyms to help students to use other books.

programmer: a person mainly involved in designing, writing, and testing computer programs. An application programmer is mainly concerned with writing application programs. A systems programmer is concerned with designing, writing, and testing programs designed to help a computer system operate more efficiently and make it easier to program.

programming: The design, writing, and testing of computer programs.

software: a set of programs, procedures, and possibly associated documentation concerned with the operation of a data processing system. Contrast with *hardware*.

system: (1) an assembly of methods, procedures, or techniques united by a regulated interaction to form an organized whole, (2) an organized collection of men, machines, and methods required to accomplish a set of specific functions.

systems analyst: a person who defines problems and designs information systems and procedures to meet users' needs.

user: a broad term referring to anyone who requires the services of a computing system.

DISCUSSION QUESTIONS

1. Define and explain in your own words: *computer, information, processing, system.* Give examples. Compare your definitions with those in your dictionary and explain differences, if any.[5]

2. Start a collection of newspaper, magazine, and television items on computers and data processing. Analyze these items critically and separate fact from opinion. If the issue is controversial, develop your own position. You will be asked to report on your collection at the completion of each chapter.

3. Start a collection of cartoons, jokes, and anecdotes about computers and data processing. Analyze each item and explain the attitudes expressed in them. You will be asked to report on your collection at the completion of each chapter.

4. Search the classified section (Yellow Pages) of your telephone directory and find the sources of computer products and services. Classify them into categories: hardware, data processing services, software, consulting, input processing, and so on.

5. What is a *resource?* Give a definition in your own words, and provide examples. Cover both material resources and others. Are there any free resources?

6. What do we mean when we say that our resources are limited? Are there any unlimited resources? Were there any unlimited resources in the United States 200 years ago?

7. Explain how resources are being consumed. Is information ever con-

---

[5] In all word problems you need make comparisons only if the word or phrase is in your dictionary.

sumed? What do we mean when we say information is an unlimited resource?

8. Describe how our lives have been changed by the invention of: (*a*) the telephone, (*b*) motion pictures, (*c*) television. Discuss three other inventions the same way.

9. Discuss four reasons for studying computers and data processing.

10. Why do some people have an enthusiastic view of computers and data processing? Are some of these views based on self-interest?

11. Discuss the previous question in terms of the pessimistic view.

12. Discuss the rational view of computers and data processing. Would self-interest influence the rational view?

13. Give three examples of failure in the functions of the human body which can be associated with lack of information.

14. Give five examples of disasters in our society which can be related to failure of an information system. (Hints: the bombing of Pearl Harbor, the sinking of the Titanic, failure to reach police or fire stations.)

15. Why are some people against automation? Give examples of the detrimental effect of automation.

16. Give three examples of how computers violate our personal privacy.

17. Give three examples of potential managerial failure that can be related to lack of information.

18. How is it possible that a more powerful computer which provides more information to an organization results in an overall detrimental effort? Why is economics important in connection with the use of computers?

19. Give a definition and five examples of *users* of computers and data processing.

20. Define: *knowledge industry* and *knowledge worker*. Why is our society increasingly turning to knowledge workers?

21. Is the data processing professional a user? Are all users data processing professionals?

22. Search your local newspaper for data processing positions. Classify them by whether the employers are in: (*a*) the computer business, (*b*) other private enterprise, (*c*) government, (*d*) education. Also classify the positions by salaries, either as given or as you assume them to be.

23. If you have visited a computer installation, describe what you saw. If you have not yet visited a computer installation, do so. You will be asked to report on your visit by the completion of Chapter 2.

24. Define and explain in your own words: *hardware, input/output, console, interface, keypunch*. Give examples. Compare your definitions with those in your dictionary and explain differences, if any.

25. Describe the principal jobs in data processing and compare training and education required, relationship to management, and salaries earned.

26. Define and explain in your own words: *coding, software, data base, program*. Give examples. Compare your definitions with those in your dictionary and explain differences, if any.

27. Discuss the various skills required in data processing and their relative importance.

28. At the end of the course you will be asked to present a 550-word (50 words per chapter) Personal Summary of this course. Prepare a 50-word summary of Chapter 1. (You will be asked for an interim report at the end of Chapter 6.)

What is data processing?
The conceptual framework

The case for data processing and the data processing professional was developed in Chapter 1, which showed that information is a resource of great potential value. As we examine in detail the nature of data processing we find that information is a commodity as well as a resource.

Commodities such as corn, steel, and lumber are raw materials which can be bought and sold; data is also bought and sold. The upper part of Figure 2.1 shows the flow of physical goods in a manufacturing situation. Raw materials are supplied for manufacturing processes; from them products are created to be sold to consumers. Similarly, the raw material data is the input to data processing; from this process information is created as an output and is communicated (sold) to the user.

Like the study of manufacturing processes, data processing (the production of information) is a complex subject. To study all the possible kinds of data processing would be difficult because there is an immense variety of data processing systems. Therefore our approach in this text is to develop the concepts, the basic ideas which underly all data processing systems. With mastery of these concepts and ideas you will be able to create the combinations that describe complex, real-world data processing operations.

For example, the operations of a machine shop manufacturing many different parts can be compared with a data processing department. In a machine shop there are a few basic processes: drill-

FIGURE 2.1
Comparison of the
manufacture of
goods with the
production of
information.

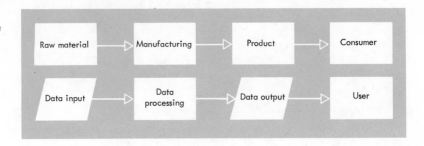

ing, lathing, milling, and so forth. Similarly, data processing can
be reduced to a few basic processes. You need only develop a firm
idea of what these basic processes are. The complexity of data
processing does not stem from complex processes but from the
manner in which these processes are linked together — that is, from
the structure of data processing (Figure 2.2). The architectural
marvel of a cathedral does not lie in the bricks, mortar, and other
raw materials used but in the manner the components are put together by the artist, the architect.

In this chapter we discuss some of the basic processes from
which all data processing operations can be formed. We also present

FIGURE 2.2 The
complexity of data
processing stems
from the way the
operations are
linked together,
or the structure
of the system.

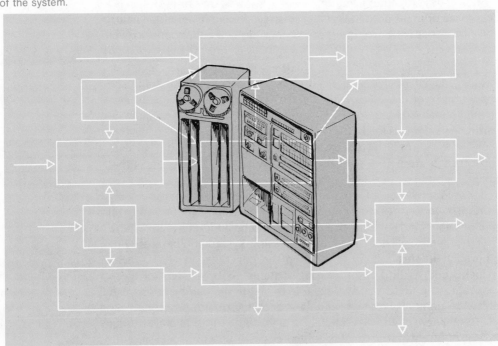

the fundamental technique of the flowchart,[1] which shows the structure or architecture of data processing, that is, the relationships among the component processes. The conceptual framework we develop applies equally to manual or automatic data processing and is independent of the computer. The study of the computer itself is postponed to later chapters.

If you wish to learn what a data processing professional does you must also know about programming—that is, the technique of instructing the computer to perform specified tasks. You can start learning programming with little knowledge of the computer itself. After you have worked through the two flowcharts in this chapter you will be ready to start programming, with the help of the appropriate chapters in the supplements in Appendixes one and two.

A SIMPLE CALCULATION: THE ACCOUNT-BALANCING PROBLEM

In this chapter we work with a few extremely simple basic processes of data processing. Do not be misled by the simplicity of the problems shown; most data processing problems are more complex. Following the same type of analysis we use here, however, a complex task can be broken into simple problems, which in turn can be broken into even simpler problems. If you learn to solve the simple problems you are on your way to understanding those that are more complex.

First we discuss the process of computing, one of the important data processing operations. With the aid of computational processes we can easily illustrate the concept of how complexity can be reduced to simplicity. Even the most complicated sequence of mathematical computations consists of the four elementary arithmetic operations: addition, subtraction, multiplication, and division. The complexity of some mathematical computations comes from the sequence, that is, the structure of the computations. Since complexity does not depend on the size of the numbers, small numbers are used in the examples to simplify.

The first problem is the computation of the new balance shown on a bank statement when simultaneously a deposit is made and a check is cashed. Figure 2.3 shows a simple work sheet for carrying out these calculations manually. Bank records, deposit slips, and the checks which provide the data to fill in the first three columns in Figure 2.3 are source documents. The problem is to specify how to fill in the fourth column. This is a considerable simplifica-

---

[1] Terms printed in color are defined at the end of the chapter.

FIGURE 2.3 Work sheet for carrying out the account-balancing calculation.

CUSTOMER	OLD	DEP	CHECK	BAL
Mildred Crowe	500	800	400	
Howard A. Davis	200	50	120	
Donald D. Dobson	1327	243	1005	
John W. Dunham	12192	5172	523	
Paul P. Ellis	213	417	115	

tion of the real-world process; all a clerk would have to do is add the deposit to the old balance and subtract the check. Such an instruction would be perfectly adequate as a verbal statement to a clerk, but it is not suitable for a computer. If we had a hundred columns on the work sheet and the calculations to be performed were more intricate, a verbal statement would be quite difficult even for a clerk to follow.

The problem is not in each step of the calculation but in how the calculations fit together. We must have a formal way to write commands and instructions to this most simple-minded clerk, the computer. For this very simple calculation of balancing an account we simply write the assignment statement:

$$BAL \leftarrow OLD + DEP - CHECK$$

This statement is understandable to a computer and can replace the verbal statement.

This simple problem has only four variables, the names of which are OLD, DEP, CHECK, BAL. There are three *input* variables on the right side and one *output* variable on the left side. In a complex calculation there might be a large number of input variables on the right side, but there must be only a single output variable on the left side — the one to be computed, the output variable.

In spite of the simplicity of the illustration, the concepts involved are of the greatest importance. There are only four variables, and each of these can assume various numerical values. For example, the variable OLD in Figure 2.3 assumes in sequence the values 5.00, 2.00, 13.27, and so on. The assignment statement is valid for any value of the variables, and there is no reason at all why OLD could not assume the value of 1,235,731.15. This would make the calculation more time-consuming but would add nothing conceptually. The example used only the arithmetic operators: addition (+) and subtraction (−). There are two more arithmetic operators: multiplication (×) and division (/). Each of these operates on two variables called operands.

Here are three assignment statements for illustrative purposes:

BONUS ← .02 × OVER

COMMISSION ← 6.00 + 0.02 × (AMOUNT − 150.00)

C ← P1 × W1 + P2 × W2 + P3 × W3 + P4 × W4 + P5 × W5 + RATE × W

Each of these assignment statements will be used in our later work.

You may wonder why we use the left arrow (←) and not the mathematical equal sign (=). In fact, most programming languages use the equal sign. In developing our conceptual framework, however, we use the left-side arrow to stress the point that we are dealing with commands either to a clerk or to a computer to perform arithmetic operations. We must make certain that we do not get confused between the mathematical equal sign expressing equality on both sides of the equal sign, as opposed to a command to perform operations.

When you write $5 = 2 + 3$ you are saying something which is known to be true. If you write $2 + 3 = 4 + 2$ you are saying something false. It would make no sense to ask whether

BONUS ← .02 × OVER

is true or false because this is an instruction to multiply .02 by the value of OVER and assign the result to BONUS.

Note that in the three illustrative assignment statements above, the first and second statements have not only variables but the constants .02, 6.00, 0.02 and 150.00. Variables assume different values as the operations are performed; constants do not change.

Input/output (I/O)

Assignment statements deal only with calculations; to carry out calculations also requires input and output. To illustrate, assume

FIGURE 2.4 The
input deck for the
account-balancing
problem.

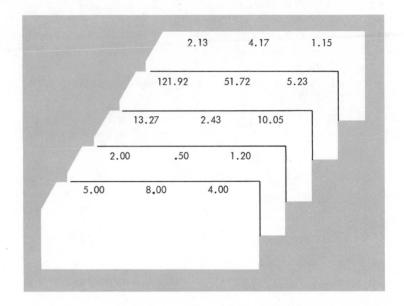

that the input is provided by a deck of cards (Figure 2.4). Each card
is a record containing the three data items of the old balance, deposit, and check. Cards are used only for convenience; the input
could be provided by handwritten records, slips of paper, or by any
other source document. To simplify, the names of the customers
are omitted in the cards in Figure 2.4.

Figure 2.5 shows a typewritten output of the account-balancing
calculation. The problem is to prepare from the input of old balance,
deposit, and check an output consisting of old balance, deposit,
check, and new balance. From the general conceptual point of view
we are dealing here with a step-by-step procedure or process which
transforms the input into output. We are also implying that this
process will be repeated time and again until the cards run out. Thus
it is implied that there is a loop in the process of producing the output from the input.

The account-balancing problem is simple, and a verbal description of the process would be adequate. But we want to present

FIGURE 2.5 The
output of the
account-balancing
calculation.

5.00	8.00	4.00	9.00
2.00	.50	1.20	1.30
13.27	2.43	10.05	5.65
121.92	51.72	5.23	168.41
2.13	4.17	1.15	5.15

broad concepts which can deal with any data processing operation, and so a formal technique to describe the operations and their sequence is necessary.

The concept of the flowchart

This most important data processing technique is illustrated in Figure 2.6, which shows the flowchart description of the simple account-balancing problem. On the left side the operations are

FIGURE 2.6 Flow-charts for the account-balancing problem. The chart at the left uses plain English, and the one at the right uses the abbreviated, symbolic notation to be used throughout the book.

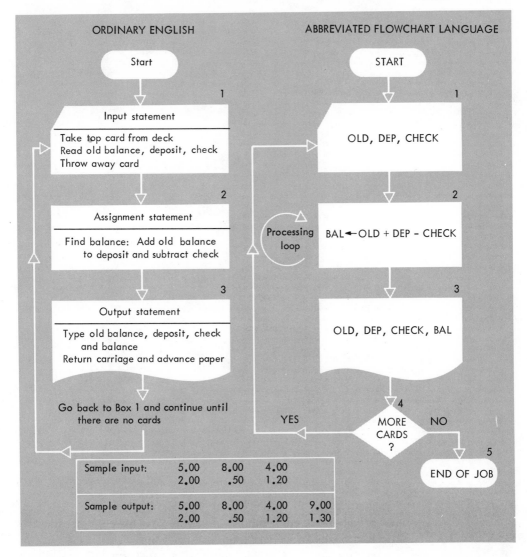

FIGURE 2.7 Flow-
chart representa-
tion of a straight-
line program
consisting of
inputs, calcula-
tions, and outputs.

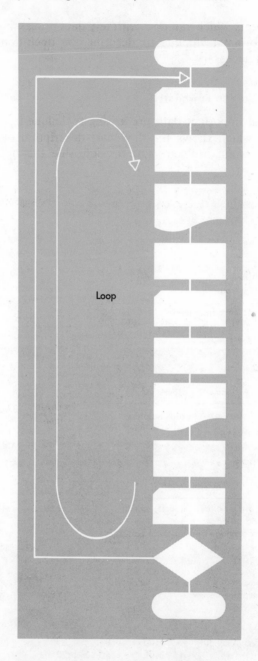

Loop

described in the flowchart boxes in plain English. The right side uses an abbreviated symbolic notation. We have numbered the flowchart boxes so we can reference each box.

Consider Box 1. The left side explains that this is a card input statement. The right side only lists the data names for three variables. The shape or form of the box indicates it is a card input box; when the upper left corner is cut, this implies cards. Box 2, a simple rectangle, gives the assignment statement. Box 3, with a wavy bottom border, indicates printed output. The diamond-shaped Box 4 indicates the process of making a decision whether to return to Box 1 to input another card or to stop the processing by the oval-shaped terminal Box 5, because all the cards have already been inputted.

The lines and the arrows indicate the sequence. This is the structure of the processing. It is customary in data processing to designate the flow of processing as in the normal direction when the arrows point downward, or left to right, and in the reverse direction when the arrows point upward (as from Box 4 to Box 1), or right to left. To clarify, we have indicated all the flow lines with arrows, though arrows indicating normal flow can be omitted.

We have discussed the three flowchart forms serving the input, the assignment statement, and the output. The decision box is used to indicate that a decision whether a calculation should be terminated is in order. The ovals start and terminate the process. Figure 2.7 shows how these flowchart forms can be used to build a sequence of inputs, calculations, and outputs of any length. Such programs are often referred to as straight-line programs because the structure is a simple straight line from the top to the bottom of the diagram. More complex structures can be simplified by dividing them into three steps: (1) input, which may involve reading many cards, (2) calculations, which may involve many assignment statements, and (3) output, which may involve many lines of printing. The fundamental structure of such computations (Figure 2.8) can be described as the "IN–PROCESS–OUT" loop of data processing. Note that Figure 2.8 indicates input and output with parallelo-

grams ▱ —the generalized flowchart form used in data processing.

In spite of the apparent simplicity of the concept of the IN–PROCESS–OUT loop of data processing, it is a concept that will serve you well as you build your knowledge of data processing.

LOGICAL COMPUTATIONS: THE COMMISSION PROBLEM

The straight-line program illustrated in Figure 2.7 is simple because each time the process is carried out the sequence of operations is unchanged. In most data processing operations there is a need to provide choices and variations in the sequence of calculations.

The situation can be compared with railroad tracks (Figure 2.9). Without branching points or switches there would have to be innumerable tracks connecting various places. By routing trains through switches in various ways, a network of tracks can be built. The basic idea is the switch. The corresponding data processing concept can be illustrated with an example requiring only a single switch.

Consider the problem of Ben Reeves, a salesman who gets a $6 "base" commission on each sale he makes. If the amount of sale

FIGURE 2.8 The simplified IN–PROCESS–OUT structure of a data processing loop.

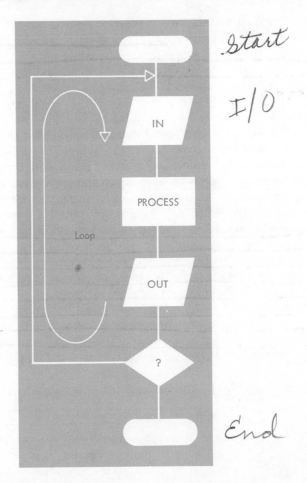

is over $150 he gets in addition a 2 percent bonus on the amount above the $150. For example, if the amount of sale is $200 he gets his base commission of $6 plus 2 percent of $50, the amount over $150; that is, another $1. Thus his commission on a sale of $200 is $6 + $1 = $7.

The flowchart for solving this commission problem and sample input and output data is shown in Figure 2.10. Examine first Boxes 10 and 30, which contain the assignment statements. Box 30 ap-

plies when Reeves's sales are less than or equal to $150. Then the
commission will be $6. Box 10 contains three assignment statements
(we are allowing a single assignment box to contain any number of
assignment statements). These statements are used to compute
the commission when sales are over $150. The first assignment
statement computes OVER; the second BONUS; the third COM-
MISSION.

FIGURE 2.9 By
routing trains
through switches
in various ways, a
network of railroad
tracks can be
built.

The difficulty is to determine, with the aid of the flowchart, when
to use Box 10 and when to use Box 30. The diamond-shaped decision box introduced in Figure 2.6 must be used here. Box 5 is a
branch instruction specifying the appropriate sequence of the data
processing operation, depending on the value of AMOUNT. It
describes a logical operation which provides a transfer of control
of the operations to Box 30 when the amount is less than or equal
to $150 and to Box 10 when the amount is over $150.

The importance of branching cannot be overemphasized. A
simple example does not do justice to the power of this operation.
As with railroads, once branching is used it is possible to construct
extremely intricate computational structures. Figure 2.11 shows a
flowchart with many branch points and conditional jumps. The
branch points are connected by sequences of instructions called
branches.

FIGURE 2.10
Flowchart for the
commission
problem.

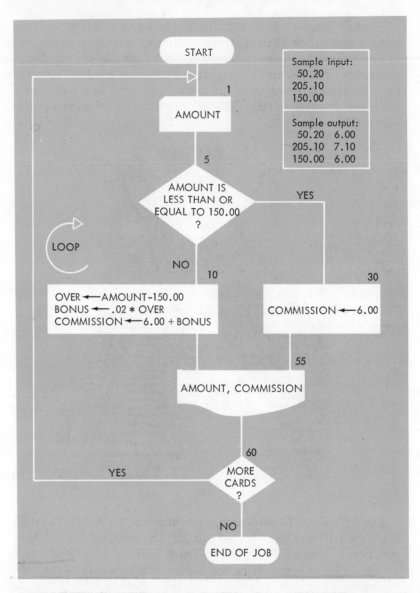

Do not confuse the logic of the flowchart, which shows in what
sequence the operations are to be performed, with the physical
layout of the flowchart on the sheet of paper. The decision boxes
and arrows, not the way in which the boxes are placed, control the
flow of processing. To demonstrate, in Figure 2.12 the flowchart for
the commission problem is drawn in various ways, but the logic
of these flowcharts is precisely the same.

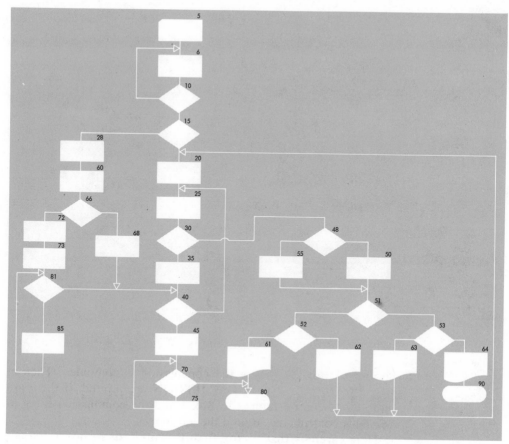

FIGURE 2.11
Using branching
instructions, it is
possible to build
extremely intricate
computational
structures.

Alternate flowcharts

While in Figure 2.12 the logic of the various flowcharts is the same, this does not mean that a problem can be solved in only one way. There are usually many ways to solve a data processing problem, and many of the solutions may be equally satisfactory.

Figure 2.13 shows a somewhat different approach which can be used to solve the commission problem. Box 1 sets COMMISSION to $6. Box 3 provides the input for AMOUNT. Box 5 examines the value of AMOUNT. If it is less than $150 control is transferred to Box 50, the output is printed, and, if there are more cards, a return is made to Box 3 to get a new input for AMOUNT. As long as the amount is less than $150 control will go around the right loop, and the commission will be $6.

On the other hand, if the amount is over $150, Box 5 transfers

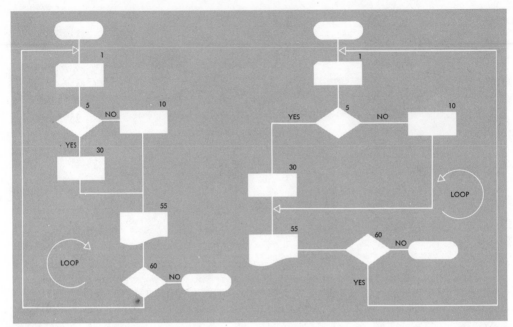

FIGURE 2.12
Varied flowcharts
for the commission
problem demon-
strate that data
processing
structure depends
on the logic and
not on the physical
layout of the
flowchart.

control to Box 20, where the commission is computed. Then in
Box 40 AMOUNT and COMMISSION are printed. If there are
more cards control returns to Box 1 and the commission is set to
$6. Thus control goes around the left loop.

Note carefully that control from Box 40 leads to Box 1 and not
to Box 3. By working an example manually you can easily verify
that if the line from Box 40 leads to Box 3 you could get the wrong
answer.

MORE ABOUT FLOWCHARTS

How to construct a flowchart

Constructing a flowchart is more of an art than a science. Still
we can give you some good advice on how to make a flowchart
and spell out some of the rules you must follow to obtain a valid one.

As Figure 2.14 shows, the first step in making a flowchart is to
lay out the output (Box 5). What is the desired output? What numbers are to be printed on what line and in what order? Then lay out
the input (Box 10). Work with sample data; imagine some sample
data input and consider the output you want. When you fully understand the problem and know the output and input, then plan the
flowchart.

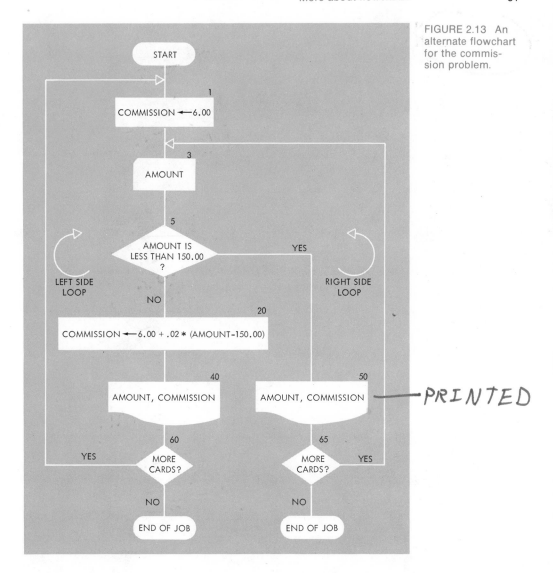

FIGURE 2.13 An alternate flowchart for the commission problem.

3. You cannot write the assignment statements (Box 15) before you have the <u>names of the variables. Select the simplest names possible</u>. Overlong names require too much writing, and too short names will not do either. For example, in the account-balancing problem we could have used O instead of OLD, C instead of CHECK, D instead of DEP, and B instead of BAL. Our assignment statement then would be:

$$B \leftarrow O + D - C$$

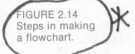

FIGURE 2.14
Steps in making
a flowchart.

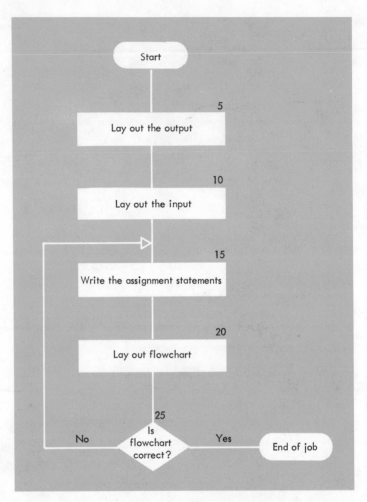

This is a valid notation, but how would you remember which variable is which? It is better to use names you can recognize easily. Two rules you must remember:

1. Start the name of a variable with a letter of the alphabet. (You cannot use 5PAYROLL, but you can use PAYROLL5.)
2. Use only letters of the alphabet and digits with no blanks or other symbols between. (You cannot use OLD BALANCE or OLD-BALANCE, but you can use OLDBALANCE. You cannot use PART #5 or A + B.)

Now lay out the flowchart (Box 20). Start writing assignment statements where you can. Do not number the flowchart boxes in consecutive numbers (1, 2, etc.), because if you forget a box and need to insert it the numbers will be scrambled. It is better to use nonconsecutive numbers like 5, 12, 23, or 10, 20, 30. You will then be able to make an insertion using whole numbers.

When the flowchart is completed you must establish whether the flowchart is correct (Box 25). To do so you should carry out by hand the operations indicated by the flowchart for the same data. Choose small numbers for data so you do not waste time with lengthy calculations. Become a simple-minded computer: forget your knowledge of the meaning of the problem. Just follow the instructions on the flowchart and do nothing more. Very likely you will find errors, and then you can debug the flowchart.

More about assignment statements

In making a flowchart it is important that you clearly understand the meaning of the assignment statement. For example, consider:

LENGTH + WIDTH ← GIVEN + GARBAGE

The symbols

LENGTH + WIDTH

could not stand for the name of a variable because one of the symbols is a plus sign (+). Thus this is a nonsense assignment statement. In the statement

2.57 ← PRICE

the number 2.57 cannot be the name of a variable.

Suppose you write:

A = 5

This is not an assignment statement because we use the left arrow symbol, not the equal sign. You can write:

DOG ← CAT + RAT

NUMBER ← NUMBER − FIGURE

These are perfectly legitimate assignment statements. Observe that in the second of these assignment statements NUMBER appears on both sides of the left arrow.

Consider the assignment statement:

$$\boxed{\text{AMOUNT} \leftarrow \text{ONHAND} + \text{ADDITIONAL}}$$

Suppose the output statement refers to AMNT. The flowchart will be useless because there are two different variables, AMOUNT and AMNT, and the second variable will not be computed.

The dynamics of flowcharts

There is one further point about flowcharts we must stress. A flowchart as it appears on paper is a static picture of a dynamic, ongoing sequence of processes. We have interpreted the flowchart in Figure 2.13 by stating that the process flows around the right or left loop, but it would take a motion picture or flashing neon sign to show how the flow of data occurs. It is important to understand that the flowchart conceptually represents a sequence of events. The importance of the flowchart lies in the fact that it can be applied thousands of times, over and over again, depending on the particular values of the variables. It describes how the process occurs and how the computations and other data processing functions are performed. You should bear in mind that the computational power of the computer is related to the fact that the same flowchart (or program) is used many times with different sets of data fed into the system.

CONCEPTS OF DATA PROCESSING SYSTEMS

The structure of data

We have compared data processing to manufacturing, but so far we have stressed processing and said little about data. In manufacturing we need to consider both the techniques of processing and the materials to be processed. Like these materials, data is an important resource. In any large organization millions of dollars are invested in data, and data professionals are concerned with managing this resource.

There are very many different materials in the world, all composed of about 102 fundamental chemical elements like oxygen and silicon. Similarly, data is composed of various characters. We have the digits from 0 to 9 and the alphabetic letters from A to Z. We have special characters like the period, comma, hyphen, and question mark. The blank, that is the space between characters, is considered a character in data processing. From these elementary building blocks we can construct all other data by structuring the elementary characters in the appropriate manner.

These concepts can be introduced in a practical way by considering part of the first page of Form 1040, U.S. Individual Income Tax Return (Figure 2.15). Note that filling out the form involves not only numbers but also other alphabetic and special characters. In data processing a small group of characters is called a field or data item. An example in Figure 2.15 is Field 9, where wages and other

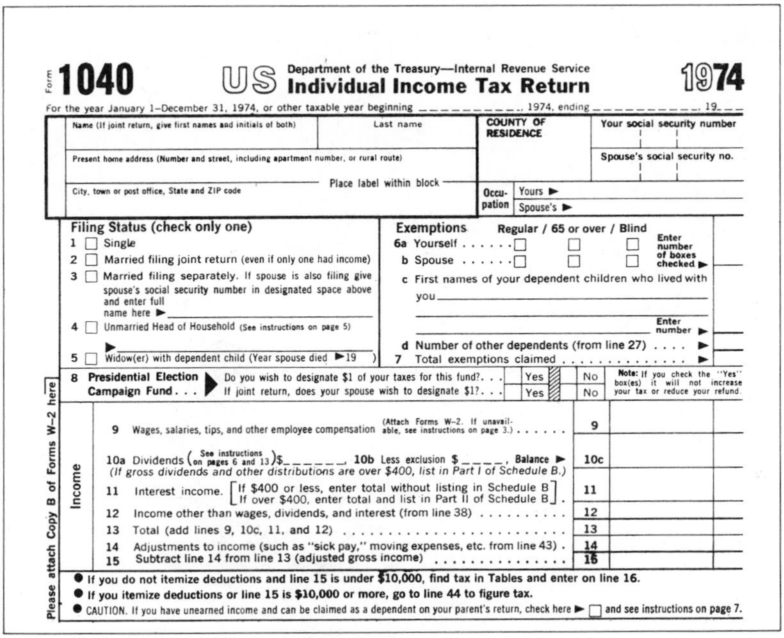

Form 1040 US Department of the Treasury—Internal Revenue Service Individual Income Tax Return 1974

For the year January 1–December 31, 1974, or other taxable year beginning ______, 1974, ending ______, 19__

Name (If joint return, give first names and initials of both) | Last name | COUNTY OF RESIDENCE | Your social security number

Present home address (Number and street, including apartment number, or rural route) | Spouse's social security no.

City, town or post office, State and ZIP code | Place label within block | Occupation: Yours ▶ Spouse's ▶

Filing Status (check only one)
1 ☐ Single
2 ☐ Married filing joint return (even if only one had income)
3 ☐ Married filing separately. If spouse is also filing give spouse's social security number in designated space above and enter full name here ▶
4 ☐ Unmarried Head of Household (See instructions on page 5)
5 ☐ Widow(er) with dependent child (Year spouse died ▶19)

Exemptions — Regular / 65 or over / Blind
6a Yourself ☐ ☐ ☐
b Spouse ☐ ☐ ☐ — Enter number of boxes checked ▶
c First names of your dependent children who lived with you — Enter number ▶
d Number of other dependents (from line 27) ▶
7 Total exemptions claimed ▶

8 Presidential Election Campaign Fund ▶ Do you wish to designate $1 of your taxes for this fund? Yes No — If joint return, does your spouse wish to designate $1? Yes No — Note: If you check the "Yes" box(es) it will not increase your tax or reduce your refund.

Income
9 Wages, salaries, tips, and other employee compensation (Attach Forms W-2. If unavailable, see instructions on page 3.) — 9
10a Dividends (See instructions on pages 6 and 13) $____, 10b Less exclusion $____, Balance ▶ — 10c
(If gross dividends and other distributions are over $400, list in Part I of Schedule B.)
11 Interest income. [If $400 or less, enter total without listing in Schedule B; If over $400, enter total and list in Part II of Schedule B] — 11
12 Income other than wages, dividends, and interest (from line 38) — 12
13 Total (add lines 9, 10c, 11, and 12) — 13
14 Adjustments to income (such as "sick pay," moving expenses, etc. from line 43) — 14
15 Subtract line 14 from line 13 (adjusted gross income) — 15

● If you do not itemize deductions and line 15 is under $10,000, find tax in Tables and enter on line 16.
● If you itemize deductions or line 15 is $10,000 or more, go to line 44 to figure tax.
● CAUTION. If you have unearned income and can be claimed as a dependent on your parent's return, check here ▶ ☐ and see instructions on page 7.

Please attach Copy B of Forms W-2 here

FIGURE 2.15 Concepts of data processing can be explained using part of Form 1040, U.S. Individual Income Tax Return.

compensation are filled in. The use of numeric data was illustrated in the discussion of flowcharts previously. Illustrations of nonnumeric fields are "last name," and "single."

As Figure 2.16 shows, data structures can be arranged in a hierarchy. Characters are the first level and fields are the second. At the next level of complexity fields are combined to form groups of fields. For example, in Form 1040, item 6, "exemptions" is a group composed of four fields—a, b, c, and d. From simple groups entire records can be composed. If you have ever filed a U.S. income tax return, the Treasury Department has a record on you. This record has many groups, groups within groups, fields, and fields within fields, all containing data items made up of elementary symbols.

FIGURE 2.16 The hierarchy of data structures.

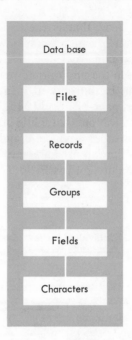

FIGURE 2.17 The Social Security Administration's data base contains about five trillion characters. Keeping the records in the form of books would require a bookcase 300 feet long and 50 stories high.

At the next higher level in the hierarchy of data structures records are combined into files; and at the top level files are organized into the data base, the largest unit of data maintained by any organization. One of the largest computerized data bases in the world, containing about five trillion characters, is kept by the Social Security Administration (Figure 2.17).

Differences between data and information

We have made some distinction between data and information; now we will more rigorously define the conceptual differences between the two. Data is a mere collection of characters which may or may not have meaning and may or may not be used. Data becomes meaningful information through a context which enables the receiver of the information, the user, to act upon receipt of it.

Consider three data items: 40, 65, and 78. These three numbers in themselves have no meaning, but Figure 2.18 provides alternate meanings for them. The first meaning is that Stratton is 40 inches tall, 65 years old, and has $78 thousand. The three data items also could mean that Fagan is 65 inches tall, 78 years old, and has $40 thousand. Or another variation: Ferguson is 78 inches tall, 40 years old, and has $65 thousand.

Figure 2.19 illustrates the concepts of information, context, and data more specifically. The left side provides a narrative description about information pertaining to Mildred Crowe. The middle column shows only the context, and the right side shows the data which is to be inserted in the context to provide information.

FIGURE 2.18 Data compared to information. The three data items 40, 65, and 78 give no information unless context is provided.

Stratton is 40 inches tall, is 65 years old, and has $78 thousand
Fagan is 65 inches tall, is 78 years old, and has $40 thousand
Ferguson is 78 inches tall, is 40 years old, and has $65 thousand

Information	*Context*	*Data*
The *name* of the customer is **MILDRED CROWE,** her *account number* is 125, her *balance* was $5.00 before the *deposit* $8.00 was made and the *check* of $4.00 was drawn. After these transactions her *new balance* was $9.00	The *name* of the customer is ...., her *account number* is _____, her *balance* was $ _____ before the deposit $ _____ was made and the *check* of $ _____ was drawn. After these transactions her *new balance* was $ _____	**MILDRED CROWE** 125 5.00 8.00 4.00 9.00

FIGURE 2.19
Context turns
data into
information.

In the income tax return in Figure 2.15, the form provided by the Treasury Department provides the context. We fill in the data to create information to compute the federal tax we owe.

Note that the context provided in Figure 2.19 is the same for all records, but each individual record contains different data items. When we introduced the concept of variables we observed that for each calculation the variables assume values. When dealing with calculations the variables are numeric. The variables can also be nonnumeric, as in Figure 2.19, where the name of the customer is composed of characters. Note again that data processing deals not only with numbers but with characters.

The importance of providing a precise context for data cannot be overemphasized. When the meaning of data is not rigorously defined, the reports produced can be useless or misleading in spite of the most elaborate data processing system.

Other basic data processing operations

When records are received they are not always in order. For example, the records on the left side of Figure 2.20 are not in alphabetic order by family name of customer. The right side shows the result of a sort, which puts the records into alphabetic order. Records can also be sorted in numeric order, as by account number or payroll number.

Figure 2.21 illustrates a manual operation dealing with records in a file. The basic operations are to search for particular records, with the objective being to retrieve them, and to store the records. The same operations can be performed by the computer.

It may be necessary, for example, to retrieve a record from a personnel file because the employee has moved and his address must be changed and the employee file updated. Retrieving a record, working on it, and storing it again is called processing a transaction.

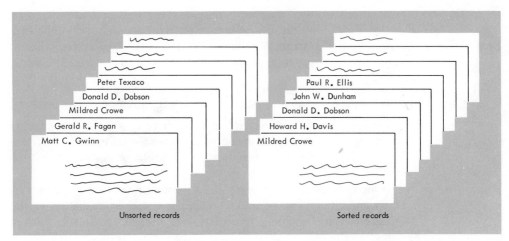

Unsorted records   Sorted records

FIGURE 2.20 The right side shows the result of a sort operation which puts records into alphabetic order.

For example, we may take a **master file** for personnel records, **retrieve** an individual's record, **copy** from a source document his most recent earnings, and then **store** the updated record in the file. If we have to create a new file for a class of employees, we may retrieve the records of male employees, retrieve only some of the field from the records, rearrange the fields in different sequence, copy the data, or **move** the data to another record.

When data is entered into a data processing system it must often be **edited** to conform to input requirements. For example, $1,195.95 may be entered as 119595. Similarly, output must be edited to meet user requirements. For example −000119595, the result of a computer computation, might be printed in the output as a debit: $1,195.95DB. (The abbreviation DR is also used.)

Remember that there are only a few basic data processing

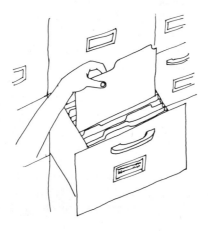

FIGURE 2.21 Illustration of manual information storage and retrieval.

operations. As we more fully develop the details of data processing we will combine these elementary data processing operations into more complex structures. Knowledge of these structures will enable you to apply data processing operations to real-life processes.

Economic benefits of data processing and information systems

Management's interest in computers is based on the benefits that can be realized from processing data into information. Certain computer system characteristics are particularly important from the point of view of economic value.

One of these is timeliness. In an airline reservation system the customer must know quickly whether a seat is available on the desired flight; obsolete information is useless. A closely related concept is access time, the time it takes to get a response to a query. The user may want an answer in minutes, hours, or days. In the latter cases an essentially instantaneous response is not so necessary as it is when the user wants information on seat availability on the next flight.

Another important characteristic of an information system is its storage capacity, the quantity of data that can be stored. An extreme example is the enormous data base requirement for the Social Security Administration.

The accuracy of information and the number of errors committed are also important. While it may be impractical or uneconomical to achieve complete accuracy, too many errors lead to a lack of credibility for the computer's output. Such results are of little value.

Reliability of the equipment and time required for maintenance are also important. Downtime refers to the period when the computer is not available to the user. Excessive or untimely downtime impairs the usefulness of the system.

Relevancy and completeness are other aspects of information systems that can affect economic benefits. It is useless to maintain data that users do not need, but it is impractical to keep all data in storage. The throughput of the system, that is the volume of work it performs, is a characteristic that distinguishes large, medium-size, and small systems.

Balancing costs and benefits

Computers are used in practically all sectors of our society: business, government, leisure, education, and so on. However, only those applications in which benefits are higher than the costs incurred will survive. Each of the various characteristics of information systems discussed ties in directly with costs and benefits. For example, a high-response system may lead to more timely data, faster order entry, and faster production, manufacture, and delivery of goods, but it will also be more costly. In balancing costs and benefits, there are three main trends to be considered:

1. A data processing system can provide the same service presently available to the user at a lower cost. This will lead to higher profits and greater value to the firm.
2. Other data processing systems may not reduce costs of data processing but can provide higher operational effectiveness; for example, manufacturing costs may be reduced. Here higher profits are obtained by increasing operational efficiency.
3. Better information systems can lead to higher sales and more revenue without an increase in the cost of the data processing system or other costs of the firm.

In real-life situations these three techniques can be combined in an infinite variety of ways to lead to higher profitability.

SUMMARY

1. Information is created from data. Data is processed into information which is then used or stored for later use.
2. Data processing concepts hold for manual or computerized operations.
3. All data processing can be broken into simple, elementary operations.
4. The complexity of data processing lies not in complex operations, but in the manner in which the operations are sequenced or structured.
5. The basic, simplified structure of data processing is the loop: IN–PROCESS–OUT. The PROCESS part of data processing consists of operations like calculating, logical operations, sorting, storing, retrieving, and editing.
6. All calculations can be broken into the four arithmetic operations of addition, subtraction, multiplication, and division.
7. Logical operations (branching, transfer of control) make possible the great variety of data processing structures.
8. The flowchart is the important graphic tool used to describe the structure of data processing.
9. Data is structured from the building blocks of elementary characters combined into fields, groups, records, files, and, finally, the data base.

10. Important characteristics of data processing systems are: speed, storage capacity, response time, accuracy, reliability, relevance, throughput.

11. The economics of computer systems depends on costs and benefits. Each characteristic of data processing systems contributes to both costs and benefits.

12. Business management is interested in profit and value, which can come from three different factors: (1) cost reduction, (2) increase in operational efficiency, (3) increase in revenue.

KEY CONCEPTS AND WORDS

access time: (1) the time interval between the instant data is called for and the instant delivery begins, (2) the time interval between the instant at which data is requested to be stored and the instant at which storage is started.

accuracy: the degree of freedom from error.

assignment statement: the variable on the left side of the arrow is given the value obtained by carrying out the computations indicated on the right side.

blank character: a nonprinting character used to separate words or symbols.

branch: a set of instructions that are executed between two successive decision instructions.

branch instruction: an instruction to select a branch in a flowchart or program.

branch point: a box in a flowchart where a branch is selected.

character: a letter, digit, or other specific symbol used as part of data representation.

command: see *instruction*.

conditional jump: a jump that occurs if specified criteria are met.

constant: a fixed or invariable value or data item.

context: the parts of a text that surround a word or passage and can throw light upon its meaning.

control: a broad concept referring to means or devices to direct and regulate a process or sequence of events.

copy (move) data: to reproduce data in a new location, replacing whatever was previously stored there, usually leaving the data unchanged in the original location.

data item: smallest unit of named data. Also called field, data element, elementary item.

data name: the word used to refer to data.

decision: (1) determination of future action, (2) abbreviation of a decision instruction which determines the selection of a branch of a program, also called a *conditional jump* instruction.

decision box: flowchart form containing a decision instruction.

debug: to detect, locate, and remove mistakes (bugs) from a flowchart or computer program.

diamond-shaped box: see *decision box.*

downtime: the time interval during which a device is not operating correctly due to machine malfunction.

edit: to modify the form or format of data; for example, to insert or delete characters such as page numbers or decimal points. Edit is also a computer instruction to perform the function defined above.

field: a specified area in a record used for a particular category of data, usually consisting of a small group of characters.

file: a collection of related records treated as a unit.

flowchart: a graphical representation for the definition, analysis, or solution of a problem in which symbols are used to represent operations, data, flow, equipment, etc.

flowchart form, symbol, shape: a symbol used to represent operations, data flow, or equipment on a flowchart.

group of fields: a set of one or more fields or groups which can be referenced by name.

instruction: a statement which specifies an operation and the values or locations of its operands.

logical operation: see *branch instruction.*

loop: a sequence of instructions which is executed repeatedly until a terminal condition prevails.

master file: a file that is either relatively permanent or is treated as an authority in a particular job.

move data: see *copy.*

normal direction flow: a flow in a direction from left to right or top to bottom on a flowchart.

operand: that which is operated upon by an operator.

operation: a process that obtains a result from any permissible combination of operands or the sequence of actions resulting from the execution of one computer instruction.

operation, arithmetic: addition, subtraction, multiplication, division.

operator: that which indicates the action to be performed to obtain the result of an operation.

procedure: a broad term indicating the course of action taken for the solution of a problem.

process: a broad term indicating a systematic sequence of operations to produce a specified result.

record: (1) a collection of related items of data treated as a unit, for example, a group of fields or a group of groups, (2) a broad term referring to the output of a process.

reliability: the probability that a device will function without failure over a specified time period or amount of usage.

retrieve: refers to the methods and procedures for recovering specific information from stored data.

reverse direction flow: in flowcharting a flow in a direction other than from left to right or from top to bottom.

sort: a process to segregate items into groups according to some definite rule.

space character: see *blank character.*

special character: a character that is not a letter, a digit, or a blank.

storage capacity: the amount of data that can be contained in a system or a device.

store: (1) to enter data into a storage device, (2) to retain data in a storage device, (3) a storage device.

throughput: the total volume of work performed by a system over a given period of time.

update: to modify a record or file with current data according to a specified procedure.

variable: a quantity that can assume any of a given set of values.

DISCUSSION QUESTIONS AND EXERCISES

1. Report on your collection of newspaper, magazine, and television items and cartoons, jokes, and anecdotes.

2. Report on your visit to a computer installation (see Exercise 23 in Chapter 1).

3. Are national parks commodities, resources, both, or neither? Define and compare *resource* and *commodity.* Explain the differences and similarities.

4. Describe: (*a*) a manufacturing process, (*b*) a food distribution process, (*c*) a supermarket operation. Go to your library or to any other source if you lack information. Explain the similarities and dissimilarities between each of these processes and data processing.

5. Define *structure* and *architecture* and provide examples from everyday life.

6. Explain the difference between the symbols: left arrow (←), mathematical equal sign (=). Give examples of each.

7. Define and explain in your own words: *command, instruction, assignment statement, variable, operator, operand, constant.* Give examples. Compare your definitions with those in your dictionary and explain differences, if any.[2]

8. Change the flowchart for the account-balancing problem (Figure 2.6) by assuming that each customer makes one deposit and cashes two checks, CHECK1 and CHECK2. The assignment statement is:

---

[2] In all word problems you need make comparisons only if the word or phrase is in your dictionary.

$$BAL \leftarrow OLD + DEP - CHECK1 - CHECK2$$

Use for input:

OLD	DEP	CHECK1	CHECK2
5.00	8.00	3.00	1.00
2.00	0.50	0.80	0.40
2.00	0.50	1.20	0.00
5.00	8.00	0.00	4.00
13.27	2.43	10.50	4.50

Determine the output.

9. This exercise is similar to the previous one except it assumes that each customer makes two deposits and cashes two checks. Therefore the assignment statement is:

$$BAL \leftarrow OLD + DEP1 + DEP2 - CHECK1 - CHECK2$$

Use for input:

OLD	DEP1	DEP2	CHECK1	CHECK2
5.00	8.00	2.00	2.00	1.00
2.00	0.50	0.00	0.80	0.40
2.00	0.00	5.50	1.20	0.00
5.00	8.00	3.20	0.00	4.00
2.50	12.00	0.00	2.50	0.00
13.27	2.43	1.27	10.50	4.50

Determine the output.

10. Define and explain in your own words: *record, procedure, process, loop, flowchart, data name, diamond-shaped box, decision, normal direction of flow, reverse direction, flowchart form.* Give examples. Compare your definitions with those in your dictionary and explain differences, if any.

11. Discuss the importance of branching and logical operations.

12. Change the flowchart for the commission problem (Figure 2.10) by replacing the statement in Box 5 with the following:

AMOUNT IS LESS THAN 150.00

Calculate the output when AMOUNT is $150. Is the new calculation the same as the old one? Do you get the same answer? Can you deduce some general conclusions from this example?

13. Change the flowchart for the commission problem by assuming that the "base" commission is $9.

14. Change the flowchart for the commission problem by assuming that the bonus is 1.5 percent of the amount over $150. For a flowchart use the first diagram in Figure 2.12.

15. Change the commission problem by changing the base commission

to $10 and the bonus to 2.5 percent. For a flowchart use the second diagram in Figure 2.12.

16. Change the commission problem by lowering the $150 (that is, the threshold where the bonus starts) to $100. Use the flowchart in Figure 2.13.

17. Describe the various shapes of flowchart boxes and their meaning. Provide examples.

18. Define and explain in your own words: *branch instruction, logical operation, control, branch point, conditional jump, branch.* Give examples. Compare your definitions with those in your dictionary and explain differences, if any.

19. Describe the rules for valid names of variables. Which of the following are valid names?

    a. A ✔   *e.* XY23 ✔

    alpha num *b.* B5 ✔   *f.* BAL#5 I✔

    c. M-2 I✔   *g.* A-B I✔

    d. 2F I✔

20. Describe the rules for valid assignment statements. Which of the following are valid?

    ✔ *a.* B5 ← C + F

    ✔ *b.* A3 ← B3 + A3

    I✔ *c.* X−Y ← X+Y

    ✔ *d.* TABLE ← CHAIR + LAMP − PENCIL

    I✔ *e.* HAT ← 2DOGS + CLOCK

    I✔ *f.* COUPLE = MAN + WIFE

    g. 352.1 ← A − Z

    ✔ *h.* AB ← A + B

    I✔ *i.* CHECK + 2.1 = BALANCE

21. Describe in your own words the meaning of the word *structure* as applied to data.

22. Define and explain in your own words: *character, special character, blank space.* Give examples. Compare your definitions with those in your dictionary and explain differences, if any.

23. Describe the structure of data in terms of the hierarchy described in the text (Figure 2.16).

24. Define and explain in your own words: *field, data item, group of fields, record, file, data base.* Give examples. Compare your definitions with those in your dictionary and explain the differences, if any.

25. Discuss the distinction between *data* and *information.* Give examples.

26. Define and explain *context* in your own words. Compare your definition with the one in the dictionary and explain the difference, if any.

27. Describe the various data processing operations covered in the text. Provide examples.

28. Define and explain in your own words: *sort, retrieve, store, update, transaction, master file, copy, move, edit.* Give examples. Compare

your definitions with those in your dictionary and explain differences, if any.

29. Describe the most important characteristics of information systems and their economic significance. Provide examples.

30. Why are economic considerations important for information systems?

31. Define and explain in your own words: *timeliness, access time, storage capacity, accuracy, reliability, downtime, relevance, completeness, throughput.* Give examples. Compare your definitions with those in your dictionary and explain differences, if any.

32. Describe three ways profits can be increased.

33. Review and update your Personal Summary of this course (see Exercise 28, Chapter 1).

3

Computer-based information systems in action

Chapter 1 presents the case for data processing and the data processing profession and Chapter 2 outlines a conceptual framework for data processing and identifies the basic processes, building blocks of information systems. A complex data processing system consists of these basic processes, but the performance and value of the system depends on the totality of its parts. *The whole is greater than the sum of the parts.* In this chapter, we study complete information systems to appreciate their significance. Which systems should we study?

There are thousands of different systems in action, and essentially all organizations, whether private or public, profit or nonprofit oriented, use information systems. Figure 3.1 shows some of the most important business areas for computers. We cannot possibly discuss all information systems, so we need to develop concepts and a point of view to organize our knowledge. We will adopt two guidelines.

First, information systems are made up of both people and computers; and we must always consider how people and machines interact; that is, we must stress the problem of man-machine interface.[1] Second, information systems are used to obtain benefits, so these benefits must always be made explicit and specific.

---

[1] Terms printed in color are defined at the end of the chapter.

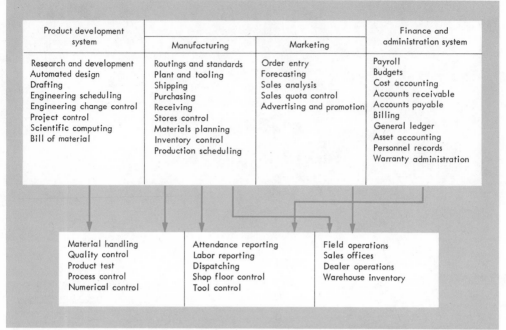

Product development system	Manufacturing	Marketing	Finance and administration system
Research and development Automated design Drafting Engineering scheduling Engineering change control Project control Scientific computing Bill of material	Routings and standards Plant and tooling Shipping Purchasing Receiving Stores control Materials planning Inventory control Production scheduling	Order entry Forecasting Sales analysis Sales quota control Advertising and promotion	Payroll Budgets Cost accounting Accounts receivable Accounts payable Billing General ledger Asset accounting Personnel records Warranty administration
Material handling Quality control Product test Process control Numerical control	Attendance reporting Labor reporting Dispatching Shop floor control Tool control	Field operations Sales offices Dealer operations Warehouse inventory	

FIGURE 3.1
Typical areas of business data processing.

From Joseph Orlicky, *The Successful Computer System* © 1969. Reprinted by permission of McGraw-Hill Book Company, New York.

THE PYRAMID OF INFORMATION SYSTEMS

It is customary to classify information systems into three levels (Figure 3.2). At the base is transaction processing, the bread-and-butter application or most common use of computers. Bank statements are prepared and mailed; bills are paid; sales orders are filled; manufacturing parts are ordered—all with the aid of information systems. Before the advent of the computer, transaction processing was performed either manually or by machines using punched cards. Computer-based systems may not have changed the functions involved, but they do provide such advantages as higher speed and greater accuracy. The reason most often advanced for using computerized transaction-processing systems is cost reduction.

After transaction-processing systems became successful, managers in private and public organizations realized that data processing can be used for various management functions, such as planning, control, and decision making. Thus the concept of management information systems (MIS) evolved. This term is generally understood to mean an integrated man/machine system to support operations, management, and decision-making functions in an organization. Management information systems are usually split into two levels (see Figure 3.2).

Middle-level management information systems deal with operational planning and control, that is with relatively short-range managerial decisions. These systems support the preparation of plans for specific tasks and aid management in assuring that plans for these tasks are actually carried out effectively and efficiently. Typical issues these systems deal with are: what to produce in a

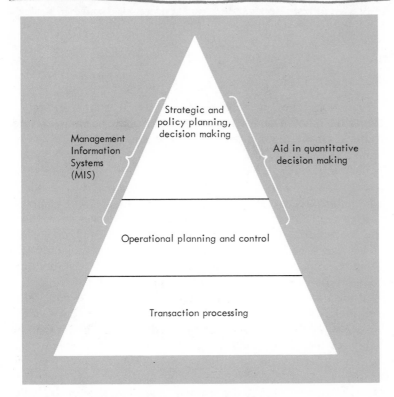

FIGURE 3.2 The three levels of the information systems pyramid.

manufacturing plant; what schedules to prepare; how many parts or goods to keep in inventory; how many items should be on the shelves of a supermarket, in the warehouse, or at the producing facility. The benefits of these systems are higher operational efficiency, reduction in the cost of goods produced, more sales, and more profits.

On the top level of the pyramid is the management information systems for strategic and policy planning and decision making. These are new, emerging fields for computers. The issues involved, such as establishing a new plant, new product development, and marketing strategy, require long-range decisions.

The computer is also used to support management in quantitative decision making. Development of these systems relies on such managerial decision-making approaches as operations research and management science. The computer performs extensive computations required in such quantitative techniques as probability theory, linear programming, and simulation.

This chapter presents case studies for these various types of information systems. The first system illustrated is the most commonly used information system, transaction processing.

TRANSACTION PROCESSING SYSTEMS

Accounting and recordkeeping

When Bob Jones, a mechanic for A. D. Warren Corporation, looks at the amount on his paycheck one Friday, he smiles: a large paycheck. Or did the computer make a mistake?

Jones looks closely at the stub of the paycheck (Figure 3.3)—first at *totals this check, gross,* then *net this check,* then *deductions:* Code 1, *savings plan?* OK. Code 2, *union dues?* OK. Code 3, *credit union?* OK. Code 4, *bonds?* OK. But *F.I.C.A.?* The computer deducted only 25 cents. How come? Last week it was much more. Jones looks at the heading *year to date* on the pay stub and recalls that last week he had almost completed his yearly social security payments, so only 25 cents remains to be paid this year. Good. For the rest of the year there will be no more social security deductions.

But this does not fully explain why the paycheck is so large. Now Jones looks at the *hours* heading and realizes that under Code 4, *overtime—2X,* there are four hours listed. Yes, he recalls working Sunday for the maintenance job on the drill press, in Department 015. This explains the large paycheck. The computer made no mistake.

Jones may not see why a computer is used for a simple task like figuring a paycheck. When Mr. Warren was in charge of the Warren Corporation 30 years ago, the office had no problem handling the paychecks for 50 employees with paper and pencil. But as the corporation grew to 500 employees, the process became much more involved. First calculating and office machines were introduced, then machines using punched cards. Finally, an electronic computer was installed. Why was the transition made from manual to automatic? (Figure 3.4).

Consider for example the four hours of double-time work by Jones. Department 015 will be charged for this work. The 500 employees of Warren Corporation work on thousands of projects in many departments. The computer keeps track of the labor costs

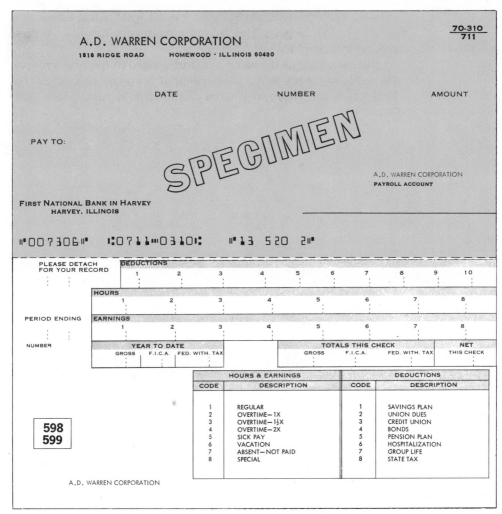

FIGURE 3.3 A blank paycheck.

for each of the departments and projects. It prepares not only payroll records but also cost accounting reports by departments and projects.

In fact, all the deductions in Jones's paycheck find their way into various other reports. His deduction for the savings plan is included in the savings plan account, where the earned interest and new balance are computed. His bond deductions are credited to his bond account, and so on. All these *internal* accounting requirements of the firm are met by the computer, and hundreds of reports are prepared. The computer must also prepare reports to meet *external* requirements, such as the federal withholding tax and the social security report. The federal government handles all these reports by computer.

Still this is not all the computer work related to Jones's paycheck. He sends his check to his bank, where it is computer handled. His bank sends the check to Warren Corporation's bank, where again

FIGURE 3.4
From manual to
electronic
processing.

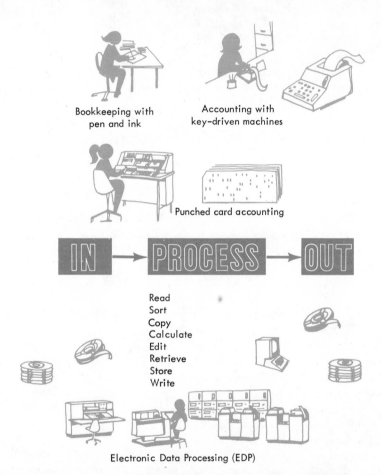

Bookkeeping with pen and ink

Accounting with key-driven machines

Punched card accounting

IN → PROCESS → OUT

Read
Sort
Copy
Calculate
Edit
Retrieve
Store
Write

Electronic Data Processing (EDP)

it is handled by computer. Each year 20 billion checks, or about 3,000 checks each second, are computer handled in the United States. Finally, Jones's check finds its way back to the Warren Corporation computer.

Computers were introduced to the Warren Corporation, as to many other organizations, in a gradual, evolutionary process. When problems arose, computer-based solutions were found. As the company grew and external pressures developed, the manual system became inadequate. There were too many mistakes, reports were late, clerical turnover was high, the volume of information increased greatly, and costs were up. For many years punched card equipment and other mechanical, electric, and electronic accounting machines helped solve the problem. When finally the electronic computer was introduced, the firm's large volume of data could be organized into a computerized data base. Complex and repetitious clerical tasks could be handled by the computer swiftly, accurately, and at low cost.

Thus computers save money for Warren and increase profits. More and better information is provided for management. If the computer at Warren should stop permanently, all work would also stop.

A different kind of transaction processing system is represented by an airline reservation system.

Airline reservation systems

Ed Turner looks nervously at his watch. He is a passenger in a taxi in Manhattan, headed for Kennedy Airport. The Friday afternoon traffic is terrible. Will he catch the 4:00 P.M. flight to Chicago and the connection to Davenport?

No! By the time he arrives at the airline desk the plane has left. So the agent at the ticket counter (Figure 3.5) pushes a few keys on a typewriter-like device, a computer terminal (console), and finds that there is a 6:00 P.M. flight to Chicago on which a seat is available. The connecting flight to Davenport at 8:30 is full, but there is a seat to Davenport on the 9:30 flight which Turner could take. Should he have dinner in New York and take an alternate 7:00 o'clock flight to Chicago? There are only three standbys on the 8:30 flight to Davenport, so Ed Turner decides to chance the 6:00 o'clock flight to Chicago in the hope there will be cancellations on that flight.

The agent again pushes a few keys and the computer, a thousand miles away, updates the records and the availability of seats. One second later someone in Hartford, Connecticut, calls reservations and tries to get a seat on the 6:00 P.M. flight from New York to Chicago, but the computer says no, all seats are sold. Turner has just bought the last seat.

Reservations are not all the computer does for the airline. The system also provides for:

1. Flight confirmation.
2. Ordering menus and food catering.

FIGURE 3.5
Online, real-time
airline information
system.

Flight progress
checks

Reservations
at ticket
counter

Worker in engine
repair hangar types
request into
computer when
ordering parts

Reservation center
can give customers
instant confirmation
of space

Computer terminals
in operations room
show whereabouts
of airplanes

3. Scheduling jet overhaul and maintenance.
4. Fueling.
5. Weather analysis.
6. Arranging connecting transportation.
7. Customs regulations.
8. Hotel availability.
9. Payroll calculations.
10. Revenue accounting.
11. Message switching.
12. Freight control.
13. Recording passenger names.
14. Assignment of crews.
15. Flight surveillance.
16. Parts inventory and control.
17. Flight scheduling and plan preparation.
18. Baggage tracing.

The benefits are lower cost of travel, better service to travelers, more people traveling, and more profit to the airline. Social implications include more jobs with the airlines and more opportunities for travel in a more convenient manner, at lower cost. More mobility also removes barriers between people.

Observe that some of these data processing functions are no longer transaction processing oriented. The system performs some of the functions of operational planning and control, the second level of the pyramid of information systems (Figure 3.2).

Airline reservation systems compared to accounting and recordkeeping

Bob Jones gets his paycheck on Fridays; social security records are sent in quarterly. These accounting and recordkeeping tasks are performed periodically, and such data processing jobs can be scheduled. Input data, such as time cards, are collected and processed only when all the data is ready. Records on files are processed in sequence, that is serially. All work is done locally on site by batch processing.

But Ed Turner wants his seat on the airplane within seconds of approaching the ticket counter. The airline cannot schedule requests for tickets and input/output for the computer; the remote computer must accept the data when it is presented and provide answers on demand. The customer needs a quick-response, online, real-time, remote, teleprocessing system (Figure 3.6.).

Note that the response requirements are completely different in the two systems. In batch processing it is possible to schedule the output; in real-time processing the output must be furnished when needed for action.

The medium, that is the material to carry the information, is also completely different in the two systems. In recordkeeping and accounting the source documents and the output reports are all on paper. Documents and cards can be handled and carried by people. In the airline reservation system the data is entered through terminals and carried through wires (or other electronic means of communication), and the output is produced again on terminals.

There is very little, if any, need for computation in the airline reservation system. The system is primarily an information storage and retrieval system. Information is stored in a data base and retrieved when required.

The airline reservation system is made possible by hooking the computers and the input/output devices of the system into a communication network like the telephone network. This is an online system (Figure 3.7) on which data is directly entered into the system. Contrast this with the traditional transaction-processing application.

FIGURE 3.6 Real
time means getting
the answer in time
for action.

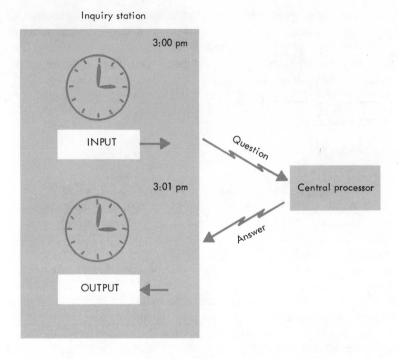

FIGURE 3.7
Online versus
offline system.

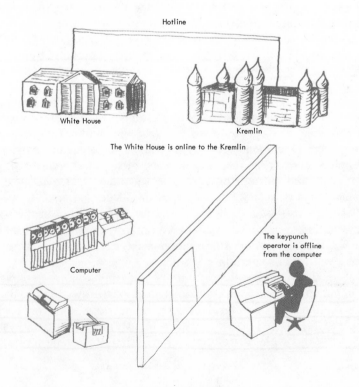

in which docur.ients are prepared and carried prior to entering into the computer in an offline manner.

In the airline reservation system, the man/machine interface between the airline reservation clerks and the computer is relatively simple. In other systems this interface is much more involved.

Online, real-time administrative systems

Robert Holland has had a successful afternoon; he has sold one dozen electric typewriters to the local high school to be used for class work. Washington High wants reconditioned IBM model D standard typewriters with 24-inch carriages. So far so good. But the typewriters must be equipped with certain specific features and delivered within a month. What worries Holland is whether these particular typewriters can be obtained so soon. He knows they are not available in local inventory, but perhaps they can be obtained from another warehouse.

You might think that when Holland gets back to his office he will start to fill out order entry forms and make phone calls to try to find the typewriters. Not so! He works for IBM, the computer corporation which developed the Advanced Administrative System to handle the entering of orders and other associated data processing tasks.

Holland sits down in front of the video display inquiry terminal, completes a phone connection with the remote computer, perhaps thousands of miles away, and types in the confidential code that authorizes him to work with the computer. The computer responds by a display on the cathode-ray tube (CRT) screen. Figure 3.8a

FIGURE 3.8a
Gross transaction display.

GROSS TRANSACTION DISPLAY

1. CUSTOMER RECORD CONTROL
2. ORDER ENTRY CONTROL
3. UNINSTALLED EQUIPMENT CONTROL
4. INSTALLED EQUIPMENT CONTROL
5. MAINTENANCE (SERVICE)
6. BILLING—TAXES INFORMATION
7. SALES ADMINISTRATION
8. INQUIRY

OPERATOR: MAKE A SELECTION

FIGURE 3.8b
Order entry
transaction display.

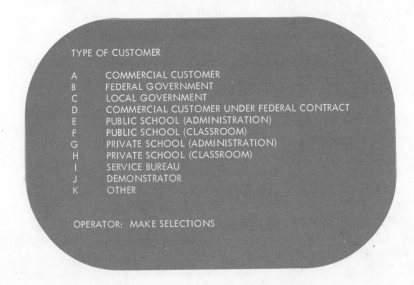

```
ORDER ENTRY TRANSACTION DISPLAY

 1. ORDER
 2. ALTERATION
 3. CANCELLATION
 4. RESCHEDULE CUSTOMER
 5. RESCHEDULE IBM
 6. SPECIAL ENGINEERING REQUEST
 7. SPECIAL ENGINEERING REQUEST APPROVAL/DENIAL
 8. RECEIPT OF SPECIFICATIONS SUPPLEMENT
 9. ADMINISTRATION ACTION REQUEST MESSAGE
10. MISCELLANEOUS EQUIPMENT SPECIFICATION ORDER
11. MISCELLANEOUS EQUIPMENT SPECIFICATION CANCELLATION


OPERATOR:  MAKE A SELECTION
```

shows that the computer is capable of performing eight kinds of functions or "gross transactions." Holland is interested in "order entry control," so he types the code 2. The computer responds with the display shown in **Figure 3.8b.** Now Holland has 11 possibilities. Since he is interested in entering an order (not an alteration, cancellation, etc.), he types the code 1.

Now the computer responds with a list of the type of customers **(Figure 3.8c)** IBM deals with. Holland sold the typewriters to a

FIGURE 3.8c
Type of customer
display.

```
TYPE OF CUSTOMER

    A      COMMERCIAL CUSTOMER
    B      FEDERAL GOVERNMENT
    C      LOCAL GOVERNMENT
    D      COMMERCIAL CUSTOMER UNDER FEDERAL CONTRACT
    E      PUBLIC SCHOOL (ADMINISTRATION)
    F      PUBLIC SCHOOL (CLASSROOM)
    G      PRIVATE SCHOOL (ADMINISTRATION)
    H      PRIVATE SCHOOL (CLASSROOM)
    I      SERVICE BUREAU
    J      DEMONSTRATOR
    K      OTHER


OPERATOR:  MAKE SELECTIONS
```

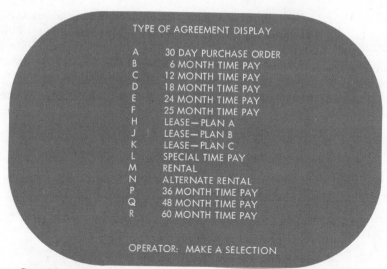

FIGURE 3.8d
Type of agreement
display.

Figure 3.8a to 3.8d reprinted with permission of Macmillan Publishing Co., Inc., from *Computerized Management Information Systems*, by Joseph F. Kelly. Copyright © 1970 by Macmillan Publishing Co., Inc.

public school for classroom use, so he types the code F. The computer responds with the display shown in Figure 3.8d. Holland knows that the high school has a special time-pay arrangement, so he types the code L.

You can imagine now, before we list all the detailed steps, how Holland goes down the inquiry tree (Figure 3.9) and holds a conversation with the computer. At the end of the dialog, Holland finds that for the typewriters he sold (which are (1) reconditioned, (2) not supplied by local inventory, (3) IBM model D standard with decimal tabulation, (4) with 24" carriage), the delivery date is three months, which is, of course, unacceptable to Holland. Does he tell Washington High that he cannot deliver? Hardly.

He keeps typing casually to the computer and retrieves data in a conversational way about the sale and manufacture of typewriters. As he browses through the records he notices that a number of suitable typewriters are being reconditioned, but unfortunately all of them have been already promised to customers. But what about the 20 typewriters assigned to the Duke Corporation? Holland questions the computer and finds that the IBM representative to Duke is Bud Winthrop, a good friend. Holland calls Winthrop, who calls the purchasing agent at Duke and finds that the Duke people don't really need the typewriters right away. The upshot is that Washington High gets the 12 typewriters in one month; Duke gets 8 in one month and the other 12 in three months. Both sales are made. Everyone is satisfied.

The Advanced Administrative System of IBM serves hundreds

of locations where branch offices, regional offices, headquarters, plants, and warehouses of IBM are located. There are over 1,000 terminals, and nearly 10,000 users. The system stores millions of records, with hundreds of millions of data items. All data processing is performed without paper, through electronic means.

The system not only accepts orders but checks the validity of the

FIGURE 3.9 The inquiry tree enables the user to hold a conversation with the computer.

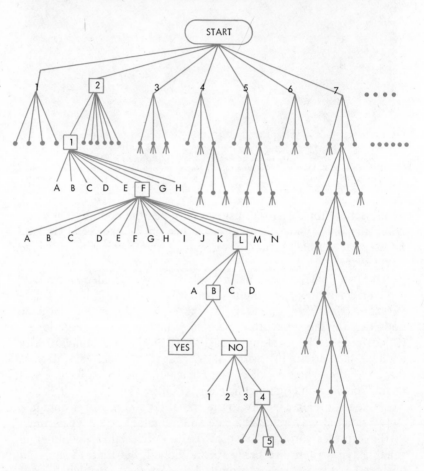

orders, assigns delivery dates, enters the data into the inventory control records, and provides summarized data both for sales and manufacturing control. If the order is for a complex computer system, the Advanced Administrative System determines the various components required for the system and makes certain that the customer will indeed receive a system which can be put together and operated.

In addition to recording orders and determining delivery schedules, the system also performs tasks like territory assignment, payroll, commission accounting, configuration validation, accounts receivable cash applications, the customer master record, an installed machine inventory, and billing. Note that some of these functions involve operational planning and control, which belong to the second level of the pyramid of information systems (see Figure 3.2).

There were many delays and errors in the earlier manual system that took care of these matters. These were, of course, eliminated by the computerized system. More significantly, the system has allowed the corporation a vigorous growth period. Without the system this growth would have been limited by the burden of manual paper work.

There has also been another advantage on the social scale. Holland, being a salesman, likes to work with customers and hates paper shuffling. He finds that working with the terminal is more productive and satisfying than filling out all the forms associated with selling.

OPERATIONAL PLANNING AND CONTROL

Electronic retailing

When Doris Lippitt purchases a coffeepot in a department store, a long chain of computer-supported events is started. First she takes the coffeepot from the shelf (1), (Figure 3.10). Then she takes it to the checkout counter (2), where the salesclerk either keys the numbers into the electronic cash register point-of-sale terminal (POS) or uses the electronic scanner (3), a device which can automatically read the product code on any merchandise (4).

If Lippitt wants to pay with a credit card the scanner picks up the magnetic code and in less than one second clears the card through the branch store's computer. At the same time sales information is provided to the inventory management system of the corporation.

The local computer (5) stores all pertinent accounting data (6) about the coffeepot until nightfall (7). Then the data is transferred to the corporate computer (8) for processing. There Lippitt's credit account is charged, sales and tax figures are entered in the accounting department's records, and the salesclerk's commission record is updated for the payroll department (9).

Sales data is also entered into the corporate inventory management system (10) and presented to corporate sales management (11). If the day's coffeepot sales lower the department's inventory below a predetermined point, the computer automatically prints a purchase

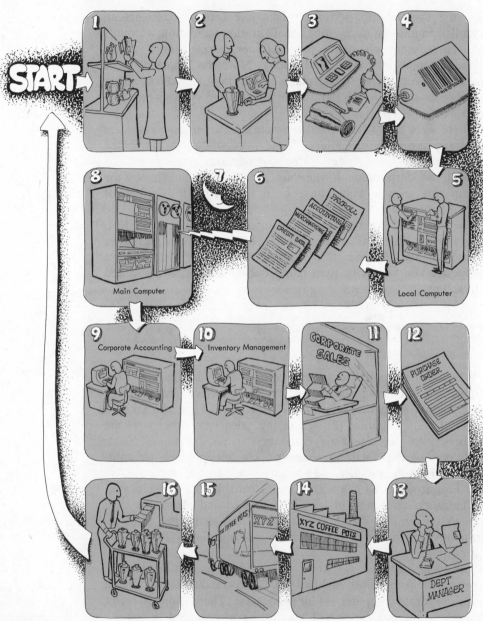

FIGURE 3.10
Sixteen steps in
the purchase of a
coffeepot.

order (12) which is sent to the department manager (13) the next morning. If the manager decides to buy coffeepots the reorder goes to the supplier (14), who then ships the coffeepots (15) to the department store. Here, as the last step in the cycle (16), the coffeepot is received, and an automatic ticket maker produces a ticket to be attached to the coffeepot to indicate color, price, stock number, and department number.

This type of information system is used not only in department stores but also in supermarkets and many other retail merchandising systems. The information system performs not only transaction processing but also operational control and planning. Not only are costs lowered, but many other benefits are derived. Inventory levels are also lowered, so less money must be tied up in inventories. Better forecasts are made for customer needs, and higher sales result. The productivity of sales and check-out clerks increases, and training costs decrease because operations are simpler. Costs are reduced because there is no need for other clerks to process sales tickets. Instant credit verification prevents fraudulent use of credit cards.

The social implications of such systems are that less time is wasted at check-out counters, stores can become more responsive to customer needs, greater product satisfaction is possible, and lowering the cost of goods leads to higher living standards.

MANAGEMENT INFORMATION SYSTEMS FOR STRATEGIC AND POLICY PLANNING

A corporation "war room"

Ben Taylor, vice president of operations of one of the major airlines, is attending the daily morning briefing sessions in what has come to be known as the "war room" (Figure 3.11). Division heads and other executives review the airline's activities of the previous day and plan for the next day. Managers not physically present are connected by telephone lines to loudspeakers.

Day and night, throughout the extended operations of the airline, data is fed into the remote terminals of the central computer. The computer processes all this data and creates information and management reports. These computer-created reports are the chief means by which airline management keeps close tabs on operating details. Pertinent information is retrieved and displayed, and the performance of the entire airline is watched and evaluated. If bottlenecks develop, management decisions are made, quick executive action is taken, and managers in the far-flung operations of the airline are informed of problems and corrective actions to be taken.

FIGURE 3.11
Management
information
systems in action.

The computer system may be the same as the one the company uses to solve the passenger reservation problem. But the computer does a great deal of additional processing to provide information for management decision making.

Note the difference between transaction processing and the management information systems discussed here. The former produces *data* and prepares accurate reports fast and at low cost. The latter provides *information* to executives to help them run their businesses better and enable them to make better decisions.

The following are some of the distinguishing technical characteristics of this and other management information systems:

1. All data (records and files) is organized into a data base, the foundation of the system.
2. Remote, direct, and quick two-way communication is provided between user and data base.
3. Flexibility is provided to respond to planned and unplanned, ad hoc inquiries.
4. Information can be provided in a form specified by management.
5. Management is provided with the ability to "browse" through data and to retrieve information in more and more depth as required.
6. File security is provided to prevent unauthorized users from storing and retrieving data.

MIS benefits include, among others, better management and better products at lower cost. Social implications include the attainment of higher living standards and improvement in the general welfare of people.

Management information systems can be used not just in business but wherever managerial problems arise. One example is in education.

University information systems

Paul Lubin, associate dean for admission and registration at Alpha College, in reviewing registration for the next term, finds that Section 1 of Management 215 has too many students registered, but there is still room in Sections 2 and 3. Rearranging students between sections is not an easy matter, because they may have conflicting course schedules. But the direct, two-way information storage and retrieval system provided by the management information systems of Alpha College permits Lubin to examine rapidly a number of alternate possibilities. Within a few minutes a satisfactory class arrangement is found.

Registration takes advantage of only a small part of the informa-

FIGURE 3.12
Total information system for a college or university.

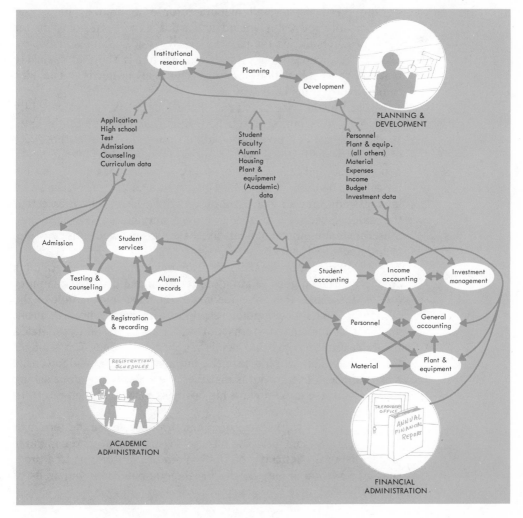

tion systems of Alpha College. As shown in Figure 3.12, information for all three functions of the college, academic administration, financial administration, and planning and development, is handled by computers. Thus not only can operational planning and control problems be supported by the management information systems, but higher level decisions can be based on it as well.

Benefits obtained include relief for the school administration of routine clerical jobs, lower costs, more efficient scheduling, and better educational services.

SYSTEMS TO SUPPORT QUANTITATIVE DECISION MAKING

Decision making with time sharing

Don Pierce is a small manufacturer of hydraulic pumps and high-pressure valves. Demand and sales have been going up for these products during the past six months, and so have inventories. Pierce needs more money for inventory but is short of cash. He makes a short calculation of how much money he needs and decides to borrow from his bank.

Susan Mason, vice president of the local bank, listens carefully to Pierce's story but is not satisfied with his justification for the loan. Is the forecast for inventory buildup correct? What is the effect of the observed slowdown in accounts receivable? What about depreciation and taxes? Pierce protests that he does not have time for all that figuring. Neither can he afford a computer; he is a small businessman, not a large corporation. But Mason tells Pierce that the bank subscribes to a time-sharing service (Figure 3.13), and therefore a computerized analysis of Pierce's problem can be made, at little cost and quickly.

After Pierce provides detailed financial information about his company, Mason goes to a remote terminal and dials the computer on the telephone line. She feeds the financial information to the computer, and the computer responds with comprehensive profit and loss statements. It turns out that Pierce has underestimated his cash requirements and needs much more money for a longer time period. This will increase the interest to be paid and lower his profit forecast. The upshot is that Pierce decides to postpone asking for the loan. He must rework his business plans and then return to the bank with a new request.

When Mason works the computer through the remote terminal, in an interactive manner, she has, so to speak, a private computer at her disposal. Actually, the bank is simply subscribing to a time-sharing service and may be sharing the computer with hundreds of other subscribers. For fractions of a second the bank has the computer to itself, and the computer rotates its service sequentially to all the subscribers.

The subscriber to such a service may be an engineer doing stress analysis for a bridge on a CRT device, a doctor making a diagnosis

FIGURE 3.13 A time-sharing system provides interactive computing power to many users.

in a hospital, a librarian searching for a book, a manager working on a marketing problem. The subscribers to the system are at different locations, but they can directly communicate to the computer and tell the computer what to do, program it, pose questions, and get immediate answers.

None of the users has enough problems to keep a computer system busy full time, nor could any of them afford one. But each user can share the cost and thereby take advantage of a large computer system located at a remote location. One of the social implications of such an arrangement is that it makes it easier for the small businessman to compete with large corporations. A small user can be as effective as a big one in this respect.

Computer simulation

Hugh Blake, vice president of marketing of a large food processing company, is discussing problems with his staff. Sales have been going up, and the marketing effort must be increased and streamlined. Here are some of Blake's questions: How many new warehouses are needed? Where should the warehouses be located? When should the warehouses be built? Which customers should each warehouse service? What volume should each warehouse handle? What new processing plants should be established? And so forth.

John Huang is a highway engineer in charge of construction for a new freeway intersection at Canal Street and Broadway. Huang's staff has expert knowledge about the strength of steel and concrete and can design a permanent structure at low cost. But what about the traffic patterns? How many cars will there be during rush hours in each direction? How many lanes should be built? How sharp should the turns be? How much distance should be allowed for cars to blend into the traffic stream?

Before digital computers were available, answers to such questions were often obtained by judgment or mere guesswork. Perhaps with paper and pencil, a few possibilities could be examined. But there are an unthinkably large number of combinations, and an important one could easily be missed. There are also many unpredictable chance events that cannot even be foreseen.

The modern computer offers solutions to such problems by the technique of simulation. There is nothing new about building scale models of bridges, buildings, or cities. Models of ships are built and tested in water; model planes are tested in wind tunnels. The military use war games to practice wars. In all these examples the real world is simulated by a make-believe world. A computer, however, simulates the real world not by building a physical replica but by using numbers and computations. Each step in a computer simulation could be done with paper-and-pencil computations, but the total simulation involves millions of calculations and can be carried out swiftly and inexpensively only on a computer.

Once the computer is programmed to simulate a system, the user can ask various questions, and the computer will give significant answers. For example, Blake, the marketing manager, will find out what kind of revenue, expense, financial investment, profit, and so on the corporation would obtain if various steps with regard to warehousing and food processing plants were taken. Huang, the highway engineer, might find out that a mile-long third lane for entering the main traffic stream would be very beneficial during rush hours, and the large circular approach proposed is really a waste of money.

Simulation has been used in many areas of management, both in the private and public sectors: manufacturing, assembly-line scheduling, transportation planning, routing of railroad cars, chemical processing, city planning, highway planning, hospital building, and so on. A digital computer can even simulate another digital computer, so answers can be found on how to design a computer or how to use a computer before it is built or acquired.

THE NATIONAL CRIME INFORMATION CENTER (NCIC)

The police officer from the San Bernardino, California, sheriff's office could not believe his eyes. There were two wheelchairs coming down the hill toward his car. He managed to dodge the wheelchairs and stopped to question the two "crippled" people. To his surprise, he found that only one of them was crippled. The other had simply borrowed a wheelchair to go along with his friend for a ride to the store. During questioning, the officer got suspicious and, via his radio terminal (Figure 3.14) ran a routine check. In seconds the message came back that the man who did not need the wheelchair was wanted for armed robbery of a bank in Cleveland.

Some time ago the New Mexico State Police found a car parked along Route 66. The officer was told by the driver, the owner of the car, that the two passengers were hitchhikers. A routine check from the patrol car by the officer revealed that the two were wanted for murdering four women during the robbery of a savings and loan institution in Ohio.

Not long ago a student in Los Angeles was stopped by a policeman for making an illegal left turn. The officer decided to run a check to see if there were any outstanding traffic warrants. In a matter of seconds, less time than it takes to write a citation, the response to his query came in: 48 outstanding warrants, covering a three-year period, with fines totaling $550!

In each of these incidents the officer obtained a quick answer by contacting the computerized communication center of police head-

FIGURE 3.14
Police officer
making a routine
check via radio
terminal.

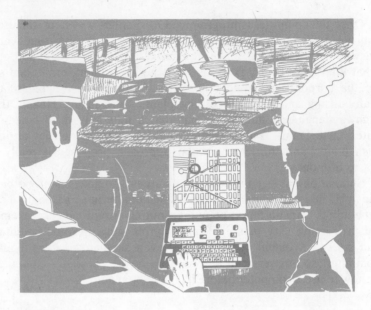

quarters. Some police or sheriff headquarters have their own local computerized system, while others tie in directly to the National Crime Information Center.

The computer helps the officer in apprehending wanted persons in several ways:

1. It tells if there is a warrant out for a suspect, what crime the suspect is accused of, and when and where the crime was committed.
2. It advises whether the suspect is armed and considered to be dangerous.
3. It advises whether a car has been stolen and, if so, where and when.

Some police headquarters are equipped with TV screens, so they know the location of every patrol car. When the officer touches a spot on the map in the car, the same spot lights up at headquarters. Thus the police dispatcher can send the nearest available patrol car to the designated spot.

One benefit is that the apprehension of criminals is facilitated. Social implications include enhanced crime prevention possibilities.

SCIENTIFIC AND ENGINEERING COMPUTING

Newton's laws govern the motion of heavenly bodies, but to compute and predict the precise location of planets, it is necessary to apply Newton's laws through differential and integral calculus. Complicated mathematical formulas must be evaluated many times, perhaps millions or even billions of times. People are neither swift nor accurate. In no other application of computers is their phenomenal computational capability more important than in scientific computations.

There is no limit to the applications of computers in scientific and engineering computations. When a jet aircraft is designed, computations of structural strength, aerodynamic performance of wings, thermodynamics of the engine are made. When a space vehicle is designed, the size and shape of the vehicle, type and amount of fuel, performance of the guidance and control systems must all be computed by digital computer. The path to be followed by the astronauts, the specifications of the various maneuvers, such as take-off, coasting, midcourse correction, and landing, are all computer determined. The design of nuclear weapons and fusion reactors is based on computer calculations.

The computer relieves scientists and engineers from much tedious, repetitive details and enables them to concentrate on creative aspects of their work. It enlarges their scope, and thus the beneficial influence of science on our society and in our environment is enhanced.

AUTOMATION

Some automatic machinery does not use computers. The automatic weaving machine, for example, produces materials such as cloth and carpets with little human assistance. Automatic machines manufacture parts in factories; books, magazines, and newspapers in printing shops; ingots, bars, and plates in steel mills. An airplane, a train, an antiaircraft gun, a chemical plant or a refinery can be controlled without any people, or few of them.

In automatic process control, there are instruments to sense or measure the variables of the process: quantity, pressure, temperature, flow rate, and so on. The output of the instruments is changed by mechanical, electrical, or electronic means: actuators regulate switches, cams, valves, and other devices. The flexibility of such automatic machinery is limited. Much help from man is needed, and if performance specifications are changed, often a new machine must be built.

The digital computer allows much more flexible, versatile, and complex automation and process control. Instruments sense the variables of the process, but the variables are fed as data to the computer. The computer performs operations and provides signals to the actuators.

Machine tools, automatic machinery, and assembly lines can be controlled by computer. Parts and assemblies can be stored in a warehouse and computer controlled. A telephone request to a computer can automatically load the desired item on a truck and dispatch it. Grocery orders can be automated, so that when an order is called in, the entire transaction is performed by computer.

Rolling stock of railroads is kept track of by computer. Empty cars are routed where they are needed, and trains are assembled efficiently. Computers control the start, stop, speed, and switching of railroad and commuter transit systems.

A computer can control an entire parking lot. Signs indicate if parking space is available, and cars are monitored by sensor devices from entry to exit.

Space vehicles are controlled by digital computers. The autopilot normally used in airplanes is not capable of handling the complex maneuvers required to fly a space vehicle.

Federal safety standards require highway vehicles with air brakes to be able to stop in specified distances and lane widths. Computerized braking and antiskid control systems meet these standards.

The automatic factory

Figure 3.15 shows how six computers can automate a nut and bolt factory. Computer 1 checks the supply of raw materials and moves steel rods to the production line. Computer 2, the central factory computer, determines the production schedule, monitors all computers, and directs computer 3 to run machine tools that cut, shape, and thread bolts. Computer 4 cleans and plates nuts and bolts, and computer 5 joins and tests them. Computer 6 directs shipments from the warehouse. All computers feed data to the cen-

FIGURE 3.15 Six computers can automatically run a factory.

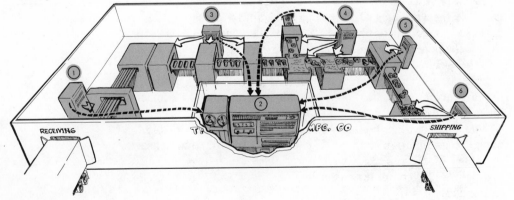

tral factory computer, No. 2, which transmits production and cost data to the computer at corporate headquarters (not shown).

FURTHER APPLICATIONS OF COMPUTERS

Hospital services

In the intensive care unit of a hospital a number of instruments can be attached to each patient to measure data about internal and skin temperature, electrocardiogram wave forms, heart rate, respiration and many other variables and transmit it directly to a computer. The computer analyzes the data and displays information on cathode-ray tubes (CRT) to the nurses. Nurses are specially trained to monitor the screens, watch for unusual occurrences, and either take action or call physicians.

Medical diagnosis and research

Computers are playing an increasing role in diagnosing medical problems and recommending treatment. Computers also lower the cost of testing and analyzing everything from vision and blood chemistry to lung capacity and heart rhythm. Cures for diabetes are on the way through the development of a computerized implant of an artificial pancreas. Computer-based models of the human cell aid in cancer research.

Ground and air traffic control

Computers control traffic lights at intersections to avoid traffic jams and permit more cars to move through them safely. Traffic signs control entry to freeways to regulate the flow of traffic. At airports, radar screens display computerized information about planes so advice to pilots on how and where to land can be given.

Telephone service

Faster, more reliable, and less costly dialing service is provided by computer-controlled telephone exchanges. You dial a number, and the operator tells you that the number has been changed. You tell her what number you dialed. The operator enters the old number by pushing buttons to a computer. The computer responds by voice, taking over for the operator, and tells you the new number to dial.

It is possible to call a computer and enter data or a question by redialing or button pushing. The computer answers by voice, or it can put data directly on the screen of a picture phone.

Computer-assisted instruction (CAI)

Computer-assisted instruction (CAI) can help a student learn by working on a computer terminal equipped with a CRT screen. The computer asks questions, and the student responds by keying in answers. The computer accepts or corrects answers and guides the student through a learning process.

A computer panel at Massachusetts General Hospital displays nine small windows, each containing three-letter words. Johnny, a mentally retarded boy, could not read them until prompted by the computer. Then, in a month's time, he learned words, an achievement that had eluded the efforts of human teachers.

Map making

The computer automates the laborious process of making maps. Aerial photographs are fed as data into the computer, and high-quality maps are automatically produced.

Pollution control

Environmental factors such as wind direction, air temperature, and water currents are monitored and transmitted to the computer for analysis. Based on the existing distribution of pollution, the computer specifies where pollutants may or may not be discharged to minimize harmful concentrations.

Product-injury checks

If a homemaker cuts a finger on an electric mixer, the hospital, after treating the patient, notifies the National Electronic Surveillance System. Within 24 hours the Food and Drug Administration may contact the manufacturer and request that the on-off switch on the mixer be relocated to prevent injury to others by an accidental start.

A computerized stock exchange

When you call your broker on the telephone to inquire about stock or to buy or sell, the broker can receive information through the simple CRT–equipped terminal placed on the desk. Retail salesmen and traders receive essentially instantaneous price quotes, other information on stocks, and industrial indexes. Authorized personnel not only retrieve data but also enter and remove it.

The New York Stock Exchange utilizes a computerized block automation system. Thus the trading of stocks is no longer restricted to a building at Broad and Wall Streets in New York City but is conducted throughout the nation by a computer network.

Computerized typesetting and composing

Johann Gutenberg spent about five years casting and composing the Bible and three years printing some 200 copies of it. Today, through the use of computerized typesetting and composing machines, the Bible can be set in type and composed into pages electronically in about one hour. A book of average length takes about 6 minutes to compose, because the system operates at a rate of approximately 6,000 characters per second.

Fire safety systems

The key to modern fire protection systems is a computerized emergency and communication center. The person in charge sits at a console which automatically reports fire and smoke, pinpoints alarm locations, monitors sprinkler flow, initiates emergency routines, calls the fire department, brings elevators to the ground floor, and so on.

Safeguards against criminals

Computerized building control systems provide not only fire safety, the monitoring of air-conditioning systems, and so on but also security. Employees or residents are issued access cards with which they can open doors. The system can tell instantly who is in and who is out. Rooms and carpets are monitored, and if there is an intruder an alarm is sounded, the police are notified, and other actions are taken to safeguard the building.

SUMMARY

1. Transaction-processing systems are the most common data processing systems and are usually justified by cost savings.
2. Management information systems (MIS)/support the operations, management and decision-making functions of the organization on two levels:
   a. Operational planning and control.
   b. Strategic and policy planning and decision making.
3. The computer is used to support management in quantitative decision making through disciplines and techniques like simu-

lation, probability theory, statistics, and linear programming.

4. Batch processing has the advantage of high computer through-put but a relatively inflexible man/machine interface.

5. Online, remote teleprocessing systems offer the advantages of quick response and a flexible man/machine interface.

6. Time sharing has the advantage of providing individualized computer power in an interactive mode at low cost.

7. In addition computers are used in practically all fields of human activity, such as research, engineering and scientific calcula-tions, automation, and process control.

KEY CONCEPTS AND WORDS

batch processing: (1) the technique of executing a set of computer programs such that each is completed before the next program is started, (2) the sequential input of computer programs or data, (3) the execution of computer programs serially.

computer-assisted instruction (CAI): a computer system used to assist instructors in teaching students.

inquiry terminal: data terminal used for inquiry into a data processing sys-tem.

interactive process: an application in which each query elicits a response. An interactive system may also be conversational, implying a dialog between the user and the system.

management information system (MIS): an information system designed to aid in the performance of management functions.

man-machine interface: a hardware or software component to provide efficient interaction between the user and the data processing system.

medium: the material on which data is recorded, for example paper tape, cards, magnetic tape.

online: (1) referring to equipment or devices under control of the central processing unit, (2) referring to a user's ability to interact with a com-puter. Also called inline.

point-of-sale terminal (POS): a terminal used at the point where a sale occurs.

process control: referring to systems whose purpose is to provide automa-tion of continuous operations. Loosely speaking, referring to systems providing automation for any operation.

punched card: a medium by which data is fed into the computer in the form of holes punched in a card.

real time: when response to input is fast enough to affect action.

remote processing: the processing of data that is received from or sent to remote locations by communication lines.

simulation: to represent some or all the behavior of one system with a different, computer-based system.

teleprocessing: see *remote processing.*

time sharing: a method of using a computing system which allows a number of users to execute programs concurrently, and then to interact with the programs during execution.

transaction processing: loosely speaking, performing data processing operations clerical in nature. Contrast with *management information system.*

DISCUSSION QUESTIONS

1. Report on your collection of newspaper, magazine, and television items and cartoons, jokes, and anecdotes.

2. What is meant by "The whole is greater than the sum of the parts" in relation to a complex data processing system?

3. Explain why studying the man/machine interface is important.

4. Discuss each area of business data processing listed in Figure 3.1.

5. Give three examples of information systems corresponding to the levels of the information systems pyramid shown in Figure 3.2.

6. Define and explain in your own words: *transaction processing, punched card, internal* and *external requirements.* Give examples. Compare your definitions with those in your dictionary and explain differences, if any.[2]

7. Define and explain in your own words: *serial, batch processing, on-line, real time, remote system, teleprocessing system, medium, offline, inquiry terminal, point-of-sale (POS) terminal.* Give examples. Compare your definitions with those in your dictionary and explain differences, if any.

8. Review each information system in the chapter and discuss: (*a*) input/output processing, (*b*) what people do, (*c*) whether the processing is on site, batch, online, offline, real time, time shared, etc., (*d*) benefits obtained. Choose one system for detailed study. Go to your library or any other source and search for more information.

9. Review and classify all case studies into three groups: (*a*) primarily information storage and retrieval oriented, (*b*) primarily data processing and computational oriented, (*c*) oriented both ways.

10. Review each case study and specify its position in the pyramid shown in Figure 3.2.

11. Define and describe in your own words a management information system (MIS). How does it differ from other information systems?

12. Provide three examples in which the computer supports quantitative decision making. State the alternatives available to executives, the decisions they make, what information the computer provides. Compare the computer-based decision-making system with a manual system, and state the benefits when a computer is used.

---

[2] In all word problems you need make comparisons only if the word or phrase is in your dictionary.

13. Define and explain in your own words: *time sharing, interactive process, simulation, model.* Give examples. Compare your definitions with those in your dictionary and explain differences, if any.

14. State in your own words what simulation is. Give three examples and state its benefits.

15. Compare scientific computing with business data processing. What are the similarities? Differences?

16. Give three examples of automation. State advantages and disadvantages.

17. Define and explain in your own words: *process control, actuator, sensing a variable, autopilot.* Give examples. Compare your definitions with those in your dictionary and explain differences, if any.

18. Review Figure 3.10 and describe each step in more detail.

19. Review Figure 3.12 and describe each step in more detail.

20. Review Figure 3.15 and describe each step in more detail.

21. Describe what you know about information systems for: (*a*) hospital services, (*b*) medical diagnosis and research, (*c*) ground and air traffic control, (*d*) telephone service, (*e*) computer-assisted instruction (CAI), (*f*) helping the retarded, (*g*) map making, (*h*) pollution control, (*i*) product-injury checks, (*j*) stock exchange, (*k*) printing, (*l*) fire safety, (*m*) safeguarding of buildings. In each case state: (*a*) input/output processing, (*b*) what people do, (*c*) whether the processing is on site, batch, online, offline, real time, time shared, etc., (*d*) benefits obtained.

22. Choose one of the information systems in Exercise 21 for detailed study. Go to your library or any other source and search for information. Answer the questions posed in Exercise 21 in more detail.

23. Choose an information system not mentioned in this text and perform the study outlined in Exercises 21 and 22.

24. Review and update your Personal Summary of this course (see Exercise 28, Chapter 1).

4

Overview of computer hardware and software

We have discussed why and how computers are used in data processing and information systems. Now we take a preliminary look at the computer itself and explain how the computer's hardware and software operate.

There is such an enormous range of hardware and software detail that only a specialist can possibly know all the ramifications of computer systems. Fortunately, on the introductory level you need understand only the concepts and logic of computers; technological details are not necessary. Therefore, in this chapter we will present a functional view of computers and will provide (so to speak) a guided tour of computer hardware and software. In later chapters we will go into greater depth on each. To help take the mystery out of the computer, computer concepts are related to everyday experience and knowledge, and a historical perspective is taken to show how the computer has evolved.

EARLY HISTORY OF COMPUTING

For thousands of years people used fingers, sticks, and stones to help them count and figure. The abacus, a manual calculating device which uses beads strung on rows of rods or counters sliding in grooves and which was invented about 2,000 years ago, is still used in some countries.

As science and business advanced in the Western world, the

requirement for better computational devices (**Figure 4.1**) became more pressing. Blaise Pascal, a French scientist and philosopher, invented and built the first adding machine in 1642. Gottfried von Leibniz, a German scientist and philosopher, invented (in 1699) the first machine to multiply. These early attempts to build a computing machine were impractical, as technology was inadequate

FIGURE 4.1
Pascal's adding
machine, modern
calculator, cash
register, Jac-
quard's loom,
electronic ac-
counting machine
(EAM), Babbage's
computer (the ana-
lytic engine),
Hollerith's sorter.

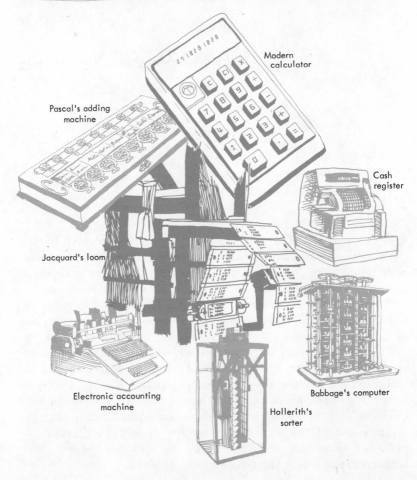

to build accurate and intricate devices. Today's calculator,[1] cash register, and electrical and electronic accounting machines (EAM) are descendants of these early machines.

Charles Babbage, professor of mathematics at Cambridge University, invented the first general-purpose digital computer in 1822.

---

[1] Terms printed in color are defined at the end of the chapter.

Babbage used punched cards to run his analytic engine, as Joseph Jacquard did to run an automatic weaving loom, but Babbage "weaved numbers," not carpets. He built some of the components of his machine and used gears to *compute* in his "mill" and to *store* numbers in his "store." Babbage was 100 years ahead of his time, but his computer was never completed and was soon forgotten.

The first successful mechanization of a data processing operation was by Herman Hollerith. It took two and a half years of manual work to summarize the 1890 census, so Hollerith devised a punched card machine to do the sorting for future censuses.

After World War I accounting machines began to be used to do clerical operations such as billing and payroll preparation. All these machines, including desk calculators, used sets of gears as the medium for doing calculations with numbers. Later, means were found to provide input by punched cards, and the modern punched card data processing system was introduced.

Music machines compared with computing machines

For both music machines and computing machines, an automatic process can be compared with a manual process and a special-purpose machine compared with a general-purpose machine. As Figure 4.2 shows, the cymbal is a special-purpose manual musical instrument, and Pascal's adding machine was a special-purpose

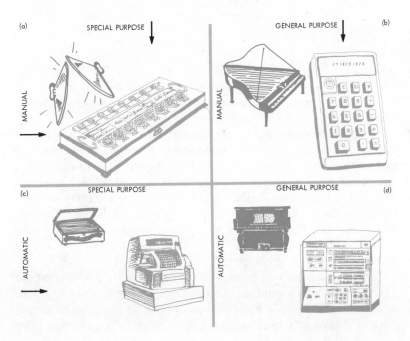

FIGURE 4.2
Comparison between music machines and computing machines.

calculating machine operated by hand. The piano and the calculator are both manual and **general purpose.** The music box is automatic but special purpose; it plays only one tune, like the cash register and the accounting machine. The player piano is automatic and general purpose; it can be made to play many tunes by changing a punched roll of paper. Similarly, the general-purpose computer is programmed to solve all sorts of problems automatically.

COMPUTING INSTRUMENTS

The calculating machines discussed above stored numbers in mechanical gears or mechanical **registers.** You can see how a me-

FIGURE 4.3 The odometer is a special register.

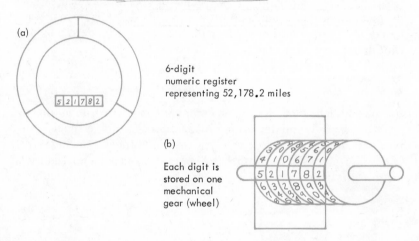

(a)

6-digit
numeric register
representing 52,178.2 miles

(b)

Each digit is
stored on one
mechanical
gear (wheel)

chanical register works by looking at the odometer in a car (**Figure 4.3**). The odometer is a special register that can count by tenths of miles.

In 1937 Howard Aiken of Harvard University conceived the idea of wiring together the components of punched card machines and controlling them by punched paper tapes. This system can be compared with a player piano, which is controlled by rolls of punched paper tapes. Aiken used mechanical registers to store numbers, like all his predecessors (Pascal, Leibniz, Babbage, Hollerith), but he controlled his computer by electric signals released by the registers. Thus the Mark I was not an electronic but an electromechanical computer.

Since there is no way to turn gears fast, the next step in computer development was to replace the mechanical wheels of the computer with electronic wheels. **Figure 4.4** shows one way this can be accomplished: Make a "wheel" with ten light bulbs or ten electron tubes or ten transistors. Instead of turning the wheel to a number (5 in the illustration), turn one bulb on (the fifth in the diagram) and turn all the other bulbs off. Switching on and off electron tubes (or transistors) can replace the mechanical turning of wheels, but electronic signals can be turned on and off millions of times faster than mechanical wheels can be turned. (Note that in this design it would take 100 light bulbs or electron tubes or transistors to store a 10-digit number, a very inefficient design indeed.)

During World War II the first electronic computer, the ENIAC (*E*lectronic *N*umerical *I*ntegrator *A*nd *C*alculator) was created under the direction of Dr. John W. Mauchly and J. Presper Eckert, Jr. In 1945 the EDVAC (*E*lectronic *D*iscrete *V*ariable *A*utomatic *C*omputer) was built, embodying the ideas of a Hungarian-born mathematician, John von Neumann. Finally, in 1951, the first commercially available computer, the UNIVAC (*UNIV*ersal *A*utomatic *C*omputer) was installed in the U.S. Bureau of the Census. Thus 1951 can be considered as the starting date for computer-based information systems. However, most of the computers used prior to 1954 can be characterized by a simple, basic structure; and so we discuss these *classical* computers first.

FIGURE 4.4
Electric or electronic "wheel."

THE CLASSICAL COMPUTER

Binary representation of data

According to Webster, binary means consisting of two things. More specifically, binary has the characteristics of a choice or condition in which there are only two possibilities. Some binary possibilities are heads or tails, up or down, on or off, yes or no.[2]

Binary representation of data means to represent data with binary digits, that is with 0s and 1s. For example, the data item:

0111 0011 1110 0011

---

[2] It will be helpful at this juncture if you have some elementary knowledge of programming. This can be obtained from the first few pages of the Language Supplement (Appendix one).

consists of 16 binary digits. In computer work a *BI*nary digi*T* is called a bit, and a series of bits is called a bit string. Eight bits are usually called a byte.

All data can be represented by bit strings (Figure 4.5).

As an example, think of the Morse Code used in telegraphy. There are only dashes and dots; there is only a binary choice. If dashes are replaced by 0s and dots by 1s, every message can be represented as a bit string.

As a second example, consider the Braille code for the blind. The Braille "cell" is three dots high and two dots wide. By pressing on paper raised dots which can be read by touch, messages and even music can be represented. There is only a binary choice — to raise the dot or not.

FIGURE 4.5 Bit string representation of data.

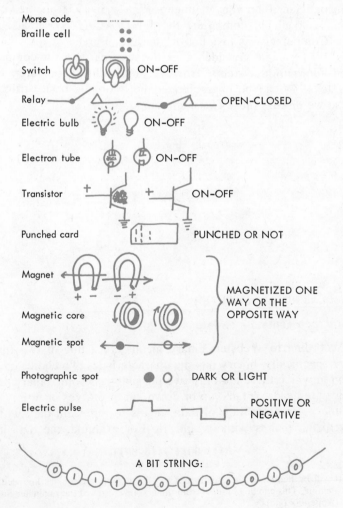

A computer program consists of a series of instructions conposed of characters. *All* computer instructions and programs can be represented by bit strings.

The indivisible bit is the ultimate unit of information.

Every message can be stored in devices like switches, relays, electric bulbs, electron tubes, or transistors. In each of these devices there is only a binary choice. If you represent one of the choices by 1 and the other by 0 you realize that all data and every message can be represented by bit strings.

Data in punched cards is represented by a series of punched holes. The binary choice here is yes, there is a hole, or no, there is no hole. Replace the yeses with 1s, the nos with 0s, and you get bit strings.

Data can be represented magnetically in a magnetizable material like a horseshoe, magnetic core, or a tiny magnetizable spot. When the spot is magnetized in one direction, it represents a 1; when it is magnetized in the opposite direction, it represents a 0.

Organization of classical computers

The diagram in Figure 4.6 summarizes how the components of a classical computer work together.

The peripheral units are the input and output units. The input unit provides data and programs to the computer. The output unit provides answers to the users.

The central processing unit or main frame consists of three components:

1. The arithmetic/logic unit.
2. The storage or memory unit (for data and programs).
3. The control unit.

The arrows in the diagram show the data flow:

1. From input to central processing unit.
2. To and from the arithmetic/logic unit and the storage unit.
3. From the central processing unit to the output unit.

The control unit issues commands to all other units of the computer. It is like a traffic light, but it controls the flow of data rather than vehicles.

Functions of the control unit

To illustrate what the control unit does, consider how it carries out in a simplified manner the calculations involved in the account-

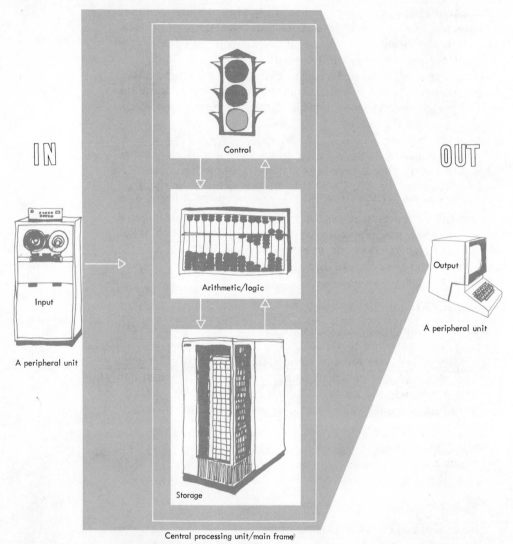

FIGURE 4.6
Organization of
classical computer.

balancing problem discussed in Chapter 1. In this problem the control unit performs the following eight steps:

1. Designate four storage elements by: OLD, DEP, CHECK, BAL.
2. Command the input unit to read the three input data items from the card.
3. Transfer, with the aid of electronic signals, the three data items to the storage elements OLD, DEP, CHECK.

4. Transfer OLD, DEP, CHECK to the registers of the arithmetic/logic unit.
5. Command the arithmetic/logic unit to perform the assignment statement:

$$BAL \leftarrow OLD + DEP - CHECK$$

6. Transfer the value of BAL from the register of the arithmetic/logic unit to BAL in storage.
7. Transfer the values of OLD, DEP, CHECK, BAL in storage to the output unit.
8. Command the output unit to print the results.

This is a simplified version of the functions of the control unit, which we will discuss later in more detail.

COMPUTER SYSTEMS

Generations of computers

It is customary to discuss the history of computers in terms of generations (Figure 4.7). The first generation of computers was used in the time period 1954 to 1959. Computers made prior to 1954 were primarily experimental; they sometimes are referred to as the zero generation computers, or, classical computers as we do in this text. The period 1959 to 1964 is considered to be the time of the second generation of computers, and 1965 is considered the birth date of the third generation of computers.

The first- and second-generation computers were designed either for scientific or business use. Only the third-generation computers can handle both types of applications.

Whether today's computer is still a third-generation computer

FIGURE 4.7
Characteristics of computer generations.

	First generation 1954–59	Second generation 1959–64	Third and fourth generations 1964– ?
Registers and electronics	Vacuum tube	Transistor	Transistor, monolithic, integrated, semiconductor circuits
Internal (primary) storage	Magnetic drum	Magnetic core	Magnetic core, solid state
External (auxiliary, secondary) storage	Magnetic tape	Magnetic disks	Magnetic disks
Communication systems	Single site location	Limited dispersion	Remote processing, time sharing

or not is a matter of opinion. Some prefer to speak of three and one-half or four generations of computers, while others maintain that the fourth generation has not yet been born. The fact is that since 1965 computers have been steadily improved, and they will continue to be perfected. To avoid confusion in this text we will refer to computers after 1965 as third-generation or third- and fourth-generation computers, and when necessary we will specifically identify features of the computer system we are discussing.

Performance of computer systems

The first generation of computers used vacuum tubes, and consequently were bulky, unreliable, and expensive per computation performed. About 1959 transistors and integrated circuits were introduced. This led to a dramatic decrease in size (Figure 4.8) and an increase in speed (Figure 4.9) and storage capacity (Figure 4.10). (Because performance figures differ greatly in computers, all performance figures in this book, unless stated otherwise, are approximate but representative.)

FIGURE 4.8 The shrinking computer.

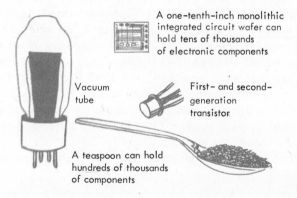

The time required to carry out computations is very short, and so for computer work special units of time have been introduced. A millisecond is one thousandth of a second (1/1,000); a microsecond is one millionth of a second (1/1,000,000); and a nanosecond is one billionth of a second (1/1,000,000,000). Thus a computer can perform multiplication in 50 nanoseconds, meaning 20 multiplications per microsecond, or 20 million multiplications per second. While a jet plane travels one inch a computer can perform 2,000 multiplications.

It is difficult for the human mind to grasp the meaning of these times and speeds. Here are some helpful ideas:

A car may cover 1 inch in a millisecond.
A jet plane may cover .01 inch in a microsecond.
A spacecraft may cover 2 inches in a microsecond.
Light and electronic signals cover 1 foot in a nanosecond.
A 200-page book may have one million characters.
There are as many nanoseconds in a second as there are seconds in
    30 years.

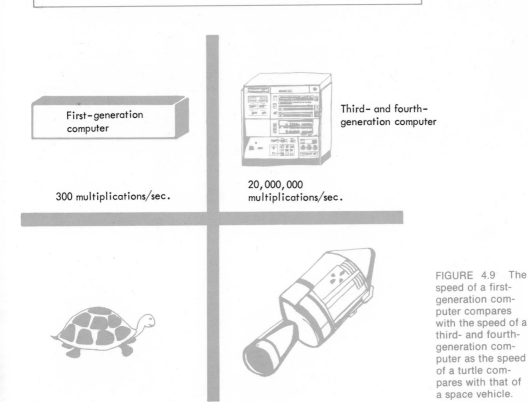

First-generation
computer

300 multiplications/sec.

Third- and fourth-
generation computer

20,000,000
multiplications/sec.

FIGURE 4.9 The speed of a first-generation computer compares with the speed of a third- and fourth-generation computer as the speed of a turtle compares with that of a space vehicle.

Most first-generation computers used magnetic drums for storage. A magnetic drum may be compared with the cylinder of the early Edison phonograph (Figure 4.11). The Edison phonograph stored sound on a cylinder covered with a sheet of soft tinfoil. A magnetic drum stores data in circular tracks on a cylinder coated with magnetizable material such as iron oxide. Tiny spots on the material are magnetized in one direction or the opposite direction, and thereby bit strings are represented. By rotating the drum continuously at high speed, data can be recorded and read.

FIGURE 4.10 The internal storage capacity for a first-generation computer compares with that of a third- and fourth-generation computer as the height of a man to that of the Eiffel Tower.

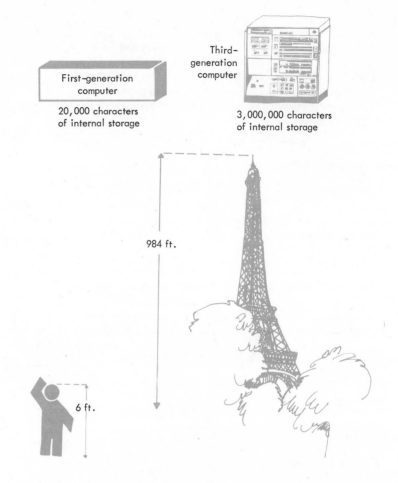

First-generation computer

20,000 characters of internal storage

Third-generation computer

3,000,000 characters of internal storage

984 ft.

6 ft.

Modern drums can hold up to five million characters, the equivalent of a 1,000-page book. The data transfer rate of a magnetic drum can be 1.5 million characters per second; for example, the central processing unit could read or write 1.5 million characters per second on a drum. *It would take one second to read, character by character, a 300-page book.*

But the access time, the time required to find an individual data item, is slow on magnetic drums; it may be between 10 to 100 milliseconds. In the second-generation computers, magnetic drums were largely replaced by magnetic cores. The access time was reduced to about one microsecond. In modern semiconductor memories the access time can be reduced by a factor of 10.

Transfer rate:
   1.5 million characters/sec.
Storage capacity:
   10 million characters
Access time:
   10—100 milliseconds

The early Edison phonograph stored
sound on a cylinder covered with a
sheet of soft tinfoil.

A magnetic drum stores data on a
cylinder coated with a magnetizable
material (like iron oxide).

FIGURE 4.11
Magnetic drum
compared with
Edison phono-
graph.

Peripheral units

The internal storage capacity of magnetic core memories today is
measured by hundreds of thousands of characters, but in data
processing there is the need to store entire files, or tens and hundreds of millions of characters. In the first generation of computers the internal (primary) storage was supplemented by magnetic
tape to serve as external (auxiliary or secondary), mass or bulk
storage. Once a deck of cards is transferred to magnetic tape, all
input/output processing is performed by magnetic tape.

Magnetic tape is like the tape used in a tape player (Figure 4.12).
A magnetic tape can store both sound and bits of data on a plastic
ribbon coated on one side with magnetizable material. A spot magnetized in one direction yields a 1; when it is magnetized in the opposite direction it yields a 0. A reel of magnetic tape can contain
30 million characters, the equivalent of 400 thousand punched cards
fastened together to form a ribbon 50 miles long. The transfer rate
can be 300 thousand characters per second, the equivalent of 4,000
punched cards per second. This means, for example, that the central processing unit could read a 600-page book from a magnetic
tape in 10 seconds.

Figure 4.13 shows the organization of a computer equipped with
an external, auxiliary storage unit. Under commands from the control unit, data is transferred to and fro between the external and internal storage units. Once data is in internal storage, the computer
operates like the classical computer (see Figure 4.6).

There is, however, one serious difficulty with magnetic tapes.
Magnetic tape units do have high data transfer rates, but records
must be processed sequentially (Figure 4.14). Thus individual rec-

FIGURE 4.12
Magnetic tape
compared with
reel-to-reel tape.

Transfer rate:
   300,000 characters/sec.
Storage capacity:
   30 million characters
Sequential access only

A magnetic tape stores sound or data on a plastic ribbon coated on one side with
a magnetizable material.

FIGURE 4.13
Computer organi-
zation with
external storage.

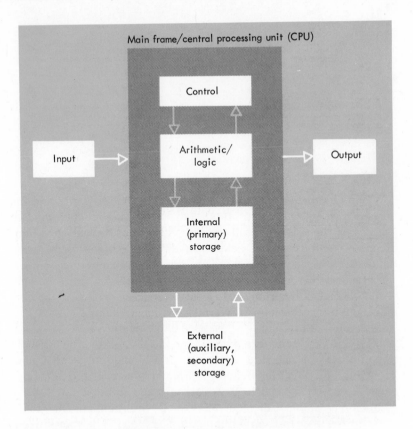

FIGURE 4.13
Computer organi-
zation with
external storage.

ords can be found only by scanning the tape sequentially from the beginning of the tape to the desired record. To provide quick answers requires direct (random) access to storage (Figure 4.15). Therefore, second- and third-generation computers are provided with magnetic disk storage units.

FIGURE 4.14 You climb a ladder step by step sequentially, and a computer processes a deck of cards one after the other. A magnetic tape must be "rolled up"; records can be processed only one after the other.

FIGURE 4.15
Direct-access
storage. Keys are
stored in sequence
but requests for
keys are random.
The clerk has
direct access to
keys.

Magnetic disks can be compared with phonograph records (Figure 4.16). On a phonograph record sound is stored in mechanical grooves. On a magnetic disk, data is stored in circular tracks on a disk coated on one or both sides with magnetizable material. Bits are stored in tiny magnetic spots. By rotating the disks at a high speed and moving arms in and out with read/write magnetic devices, data can be stored and read. Magnetic disks can have data transfer rates up to three million characters per second and a storage capacity up to hundreds of millions of characters. But the real advantage of disks is that any desired record can be found quickly, a requirement for many applications. Disks provide direct or random access to records.

Computer costs ~ gone done

The cost per unit of data processing tasks such as multiplication was 100 times higher in first-generation computers than in third-generation computers, and costs are still decreasing. A million-dollar computer of 1970 may have cost $500,000 in 1975 and perhaps will cost only $100,000 in 1980. Small computers, or minicomputers, may sell between $1,000 and $20,000, and very small microcomputers may sell for under $100. There are even desk- and pocket-size programmable calculators that sell for under $1,000. The total amount of money spent on computers increases with the increasing need for data processing.

FIGURE 4.16
Magnetic disk/
pack compared
with phonograph
record.

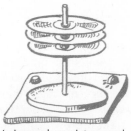

A phonograph record stores sound in mechanical grooves.

A magnetic disk stores data on a disk coated with a magnetizable material.

Transfer rate:
3 million characters/sec.
Storage capacity:
hundreds of millions of characters
Access time:
2–200 milliseconds

DATA COMMUNICATION

A first-generation computer was located at a single site. Input data was carried to the computer in written, typed, or punched card form. Output reports were manually carried to users.

It was soon recognized that data could be transmitted remotely through wires, and gradually remote teleprocessing systems which utilize communication networks emerged. The seven most commonly used types of data communication, shown in Figure 4.17, permit various remote data handling operations.

FIGURE 4.17
Types of data
communication.

1. Remote data entry and storage.
2. Remote job entry.
3. Information retrieval.
4. Interactive system.
5. Remote printing.
6. Data acquisition and control between remote data bases.
7. Data exchange (data base to data base).

Data can be entered remotely to the central processing unit. An entire deck of punched cards (with programs and data) can also be entered remotely, resulting in remote job entry. Data and information can also be retrieved remotely. In an interactive data communication system the user can both enter data and receive answers directly. Remote printing implies operating the printer at a remote location from the computer.

Data acquisition and control permits operating data bases from remote locations, and data exchange is the transfer of large amounts of data from one data base to another located at a distance.

The three principal methods for transferring data are telegraph lines, "voice grade" (telephone) lines, and broad-band channels. Chapter 7 gives a more detailed discussion of communication systems.

ORGANIZATION OF MODERN COMPUTER SYSTEMS

The classical computer (see Figure 4.6) operates in a sequential manner. Input data is read and processed, and output is produced. While one component of the system operates, the others idle. However, the arithmetic/logic unit, being electronic, operates much faster than the electromechanical input/output units. Therefore the resources of the classical computer system are underutilized;

it would be like having a 100-lane highway with single-lane access roads (Figure 4.18).

To grasp the relative speeds of the central processing unit and peripherals, consider the simple situation when the output units are electric typewriters. The central processing unit (CPU) operates 50,000 times faster, meaning that a single CPU could keep 50,000 typewriters continuously busy. Therefore you can get high through-put at low cost by connecting many peripheral units to a CPU and operating them in a simultaneous manner. Such a computer system poses a different control problem from that of the classical computer.

In a classical computer the central processing unit waits until the input and output units complete their assignments. In a mod-

FIGURE 4.18. Having a single input and single output unit attached to an arithmetic/logic unit would be like having a 100-lane highway with single-lane access roads.

ern computer system the CPU commands a peripheral unit to perform a data processing function, and while this processing is being performed the CPU turns its attention to other functions. Thus, while an input unit reads a deck or a tape and transfers the data to storage, the CPU may be commanding other peripheral units to perform other tasks, or the CPU itself may perform some data processing.

When a peripheral unit completes its assignment, it must report back to the central processing unit that its work is done, and it is idle and ready for a new assignment. In this case an interruption said to occur, and the computer system is said to be interrupt driven. From everyday experience we can compare the system with the telephone switchboard operator who operates by responding to incoming calls (Figure 4.19). In fact, a modern computer system must contain means to take care of terminals, to answer and switch messages, and so on.

FIGURE 4.19
Modern computer
compares with
telephone switch-
board operator.
Both are
interrupt driven.

The control system of a modern computer system does even more, and later we will discuss in more detail how such control systems operate. An example from everyday life will illustrate it sufficiently now.

An example of an interrupt system

Anne Roney is performing the various tasks involved in preparing dinner. She is interrupted in her work by the ring of the telephone and moves toward the phone to answer the call. Then the doorbell rings, and she decides the phone call can wait. She moves toward the door, but the baby begins to cry upstairs. Both the phone call and the doorbell can wait; she assigns the priorities: (1) baby, (2) door, (3) telephone. She looks at the baby but finds that only dry diapers are needed, a job that can wait. So she changes her priorities: (1) door, (2) phone, (3) baby. She opens the door, lets in the Avon lady, seats her in the living room. The phone is still ringing so she answers the call. As she is conversing on the phone the washer buzzes that the cycle is completed. She interrupts the phone call but is interrupted in transferring the laundry to the drier because the rice is burning on the stove. She interrupts her work at the washer and attends to the rice. And so on.

The human mind typically operates in an interrupt mode. While you drive, you listen to the radio and make plans for the day, but you are interrupted by a red traffic light. In class you listen to the instructor but also think your own thoughts, and you are interrupted by your neighbor asking for an eraser. Without rapid changes in attention human life would be impossible; we could not, for example, respond to emergencies. Neither could a modern computer operate efficiently without the ability to respond to interrupts.

Central and distributed computer systems

Figure 4.20 is a simplified illustration of the organization of a modern computer system. The central processing unit is connected directly not to the peripheral units but to the interface of the data channels. These are special-purpose computers to deal with the peripherals. The CPU issues commands to the data channels, which in turn control the peripherals. When the peripherals complete their assignments they report back through the data channels to the CPU

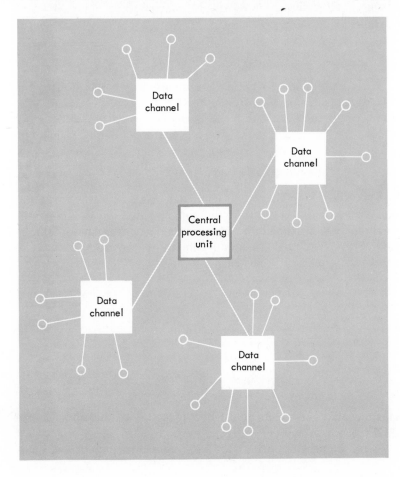

FIGURE 4.20
Simplified
diagram of
organization of
modern computer
system.

and interrupt its function. It must be stressed that the peripheral units can operate simultaneously with each other and with the CPU. A computer system with many peripheral units requires complex organization and can provide high resource utilization and throughput.

A computer system with a single CPU and many peripheral units is often designated as a central computer system because data processing functions are performed at a central point. A more sophisticated computer system emerges when two or more CPUs are connected to work in a coordinated manner. These distributed computer systems operate in a simultaneous manner, both as to the CPUs and the peripherals. Such systems are also designated as a computer network or distributed network. Some of the terminals of the system may be equipped with a limited data processing capability; such devices are called intelligent terminals.

Distributed computer systems offer the potential of optimum resource allocation. They will be discussed in more detail in Chapter 8.

PROGRAMMING AND SOFTWARE

A computer can perform a data processing job only if a program is written specifying each step to be performed. A program consists of many instructions, and each instruction must be stored in the computer as a bit string. Imagine a program consisting of hundreds or thousands of 32-bit machine language instructions like:

0001 0000 0000 0000 0000 0000 1011 1000

This is precisely the way a computer instruction was written for early computers. Soon it became apparent that the task of writing instructions consisting of bit strings was not convenient for humans, and efforts were made to simplify the job of the programmer. Thus the concept emerged that the programmer should write statements like:

ADD	DEP

or

SUB	CHECK

meaning that the value of DEP is to be added and the value of CHECK subtracted.

After the programmer writes a program consisting of statements of this kind, the program is to be used as input to the computer. The computer will translate the program into a program consisting of bit strings. This concept of giving the job of translation to the computer is called automatic programming, though it is to be stressed that the program is written by the programmer, and the computer only translates the program.

Note that program preparation is separated into two different tasks. Systems programmers, often working for manufacturers, write the translator program. The application programmer writes a source program which is translated by the computer into an object (target) program. This concept is the birth of the concept of software. The difference between the source and object programs can be illustrated by a comparison between a computer system and the human circulatory system.

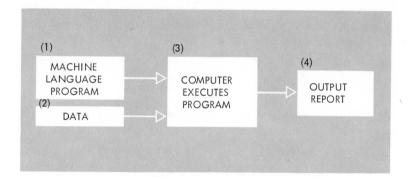

FIGURE 4.21
Machine language
programming.

The human bloodstream can only absorb simple sugars, fatty acids, glycerines, amino acids, and certain other substances like vitamins and salts. Most of these substances are not directly available as food, so the human body is equipped with a digestive system. When food enters the human body, it first goes through the digestive system, which breaks it down into elements which can be absorbed by the bloodstream.

The electronics of the computer can only deal with machine language programs written in bit strings, but for programmers it is extremely inconvenient to write programs in machine language. Thus the computer system comes with a software system which includes the translator. This breaks down the source programs into object programs consisting of bit strings. Thus food corresponds to a source program and amino acids correspond to object programs.

Note that the computer deals with a machine language program in four steps (Figure 4.21.):

1. The program is entered into the computer.
2. The data is entered.
3. The computer executes the program.
4. The output report is printed.

Assembler language programming

When symbolic codes designate both the operations to be performed and the locations in storage for the data, we speak of assembler language programming. Each machine language instruction corresponds to a single assembler language instruction.

In considering how the computer handles an assembler language program, we need to distinguish between two phases of computer operations (Figure 4.22). In Phase 1:

1. The assembler, a machine language program, is entered in the computer.
2. The programmer's program, a source program, is entered in the computer.
3. The computer assembles (translates) the assembler language source program.
4. A machine language (object) program is produced.

In Phase 2, the machine language program and data are entered in the computer, which executes the program and produces an output report.

FIGURE 4.22
Assembler
language
programming.

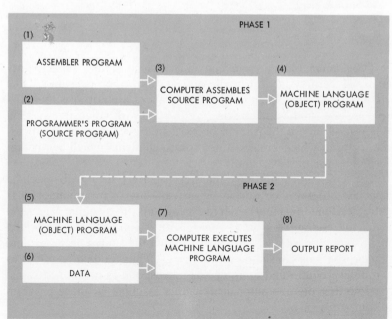

A more detailed explanation of these steps requires more knowledge about computer systems, so it is postponed to later chapters. However, we stress that:

1. A computer can directly execute only a machine language program.
2. The computer assembles an assembler language program independently of any data.
3. Each assembler language instruction is assembled into a single machine language instruction.
4. If the assembler language program is to be used many times, the object program may be stored for later use and executed repeatedly for different sets of data, without the intermediary of the assembler.

Writing assembler language programs is easier than writing machine language programs. Much programming time is saved, fewer errors are made, programs are easier to examine and modify. If errors are made, it is easier to find and correct them. Still, the increased demand for programs brought the need for programming languages more suitable to human programmers. Thus procedure-oriented (high-level) languages were introduced. These can be more conveniently used to express procedures required in the solution of problems.

Procedure-oriented programming

The most commonly used languages are FORTRAN (*FOR*mula *TRAN*slation) and COBOL (*CO*mmon *B*usiness *O*riented *Lan*guage). Programs written in these languages are compiled by a (machine language) program called the compiler into machine language programs. A single source language instruction may be compiled into several object language instructions. Observe in Figure 4.23 that Figure 4.22 holds not only for assembler language programming but also for procedure-oriented languages if you replace the word *assembler* with *compiler* in Box 1 and the word *assembles* with *compiles* in Box 3.

Problems can be solved more easily with procedure-oriented programming than with assembler language programming. Thus much programming time is saved, fewer errors are made, programs are easier to debug and modify. Also, manufacturers provide compilers compatible with procedure-oriented programs, so that a program written in a language such as FORTRAN or COBOL can be run on computers built by different manufacturers. On the other hand, assembler language programming must be tailored to each manufacturer's computer, and adapting an assembler language

FIGURE 4.23
High-level
(procedure-
oriented) language
programming.

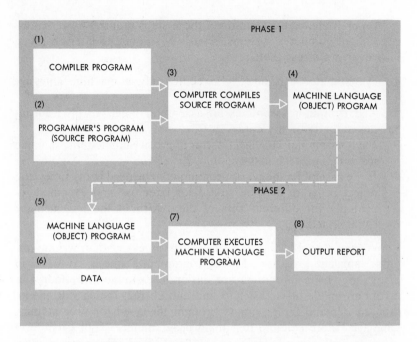

program from one computer to another can be a major undertaking.

Why use assembler language at all? Assembler language programs can be more efficient to execute than procedure-oriented language programs, and some specialized data processing tasks cannot yet be programmed in procedure-oriented languages. Thus before an application is programmed, an analysis must be made to determine whether the program should be written in assembler or procedure-oriented language.

Software development

In the first-generation computers each step in a data processing task had to be programmed by the programmer. Later, software was developed to ease the programmer's burden; manufacturers provided software packages to handle such common data processing tasks as sorting, input, and output. The application programmer was relieved of these routine tasks, and programming time could be reduced.

In the early days of computers each data processing job was also handled on an individual basis. The computer operator took the deck of cards for an application and ran it on the computer. Then the operator looked for the next job to be performed and ran that one. The computer was idle between jobs, and much expensive computer time was wasted.

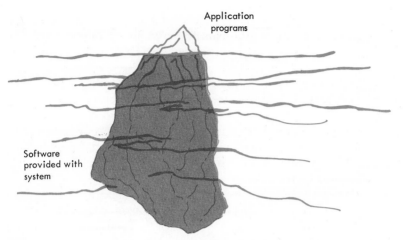

Application
programs

Software
provided with
system

FIGURE 4.24 The
iceberg of
programming.

As the art of automatic computing advanced, the job of operating the computer was automated by software called the operating system (OS), a machine language program provided by the manufacturer of the computer. The application programmer writes the program and a set of special instructions which relate the program to the software, the operating system. Many application programs are submitted to the computer at the same time, and the operating system automatically executes one job after another. This results in considerable saving of computer time.

Thus the application program written by a programmer is only a small fraction of the programs used by the computer. The programs that run the computer can be compared to an iceberg (Figure 4.24). The program written by the application programmer is only the tip of the iceberg of the computer software.

Programming and software were not major issues in the early days of computing, when hardware dominated the field. Today software is fully as important as hardware, and in fact more money is being spent on software than on hardware. The trend toward the growing importance of software is continuing, and in the future software cost will increasingly outweigh hardware cost. Thus the role of the data processing professional will become even more important to future information systems. In Chapters 5 and 9 we will go further into programming and software.

SUMMARY

1. All data and computer programs can be represented by bit strings. A computer operates only with bits represented by media and devices.

2. The classical computer consists of the input unit, the central processing unit (CPU/main frame), and the output unit. The CPU consists of the arithmetic/logic, memory or internal storage, and control units.

3. The control unit issues commands to all other units of the computer and controls the sequencing of actions and the flow of data.

4. It is convenient to discuss computers in terms of generations.

5. Before data can be processed it must be brought into internal storage, which ordinarily consists of magnetic cores and/or semiconductor circuits.

6. Elementary operations (like arithmetic/logic operations) are performed in the register of the computer, which consists of tiny circuits containing transistors, diodes, resistors, and other basic electronic elements.

7. The peripheral units of the computer are the input, output, and external (auxiliary or secondary) storage.

8. External storage units make it possible to process large quantities of data. The most commonly used external units are magnetic disk and tape units where data is stored in the form of tiny magnetized spots.

9. Magnetic tape units can only be accessed sequentially; magnetic disks can be accessed both sequentially and in a random or direct manner.

10. Widely dispersed data processing units can operate together with the aid of communication networks.

11. The classical computer operates in a sequential manner: input, processing, and output. The many peripheral units of a modern large computer system operate simultaneously, and the central processing unit is controlled by an interrupt system.

12. Distributed computer systems have several central processing units and many peripheral units, all operating in a simultaneous manner.

13. A computer program is a set of instructions specifying in a prescribed manner each step of the data processing job to be performed.

14. A computer is a machine capable of executing a program automatically, thereby providing output from input.

15. Programmers write assembler and procedure-oriented source programs. Computers automatically assemble or compile these source programs into machine language or object programs.

16. Software is at least as important as hardware, and the trend is toward devoting an increasing portion of the electronic data processing effort to software.

17. The performance of computers has dramatically improved in

the past 25 years, while costs per unit of processing have decreased. This trend will continue in the foreseeable future, though the total effort expended on computer systems will increase.

18. Figure 4.25 provides a summary of four data processing methods (manual, manual with machine assistance, electro-mechanical, and electronic) and six data processing steps (originating, processing, storing, retrieving, reproducing, communicating).

FIGURE 4.25
Data processing
methods and steps.

Steps in the data processing operation	Data processing methods			
	Manual methods	Manual methods with machine assistance	Electromechanical, punched card methods	Electronic methods
Originating	Handwritten records	Typewriter, cash register	Prepunched cards, keypunched cards, mark-sensed documents	Magnetic and optical character readers, card and tape punches, online terminals
Processing	Hand posting and calculations	Cash register, bookkeeping machine, calculator, accounting machine	Accounting machines, punched card machines	Computer
Storing	Using paper in files, journals, ledgers, etc.		Trays of cards	Magnetizable media and devices, punched media
Retrieving	By file clerk, bookkeeper		Manual tray movement	Online inquiry with direct-access devices, manual movement of storage media
Reproducing	Copying, using carbon paper	Duplicator, addressing machine	Punched card machines	Multiple copies from printers
Communicating	Written reports, hand-carried messages	Documents prepared by machines	Printed documents	Online data transmission, printed output, visual display, voice output, etc.

KEY CONCEPTS AND WORDS

arithmetic/logic unit: the unit of a computing system which contains the circuits that perform arithmetic/logic operations.

assemble: to translate an assembler language program into a machine language program.

assembler: a program which assembles.

assembler language: a symbolic source programming language using mnemonic, symbolic codes to designate both the operations to be performed and the locations in storage for the data.

automatic programming: the method whereby the computer itself is used to translate a higher level program into a machine language program.

binary digit: the numerals 0 or 1 in binary notation.

bit: abbreviation for binary digit.

bit string: a series of binary digits in which the position of each binary digit is considered as an independent unit.

bulk storage: same as *mass storage*.

byte: a string of binary digits, usually eight bits long, operated on as a unit.

calculator: a device capable of performing arithmetic operations with frequent manual intervention.

central computer system: a computer system with a single central processing unit. Contrast with *distributed computer system*.

central processing unit (CPU): a unit of a computer which includes the circuits controlling the interpretation and execution of instructions.

compile: to prepare a machine language program from a procedure-oriented source program.

compiler: a program that compiles.

computer network: a system consisting of two or more interconnected computing units.

control unit: the part of the computer system which directs the sequence of operations, interprets the instructions, and initiates commands to the computer circuits.

data channel: a hardware device which connects a central processing unit and main storage with the input/output control units.

data transfer rate: speed of reading or writing data between a storage medium and the computer.

direct access (random access): (1) refers to the process of obtaining data from or placing data into storage where the time required for such access is independent of the location of the data most recently obtained or placed in storage, (2) pertains to a storage device in which the access time is effectively independent of the location of the data.

distributed computer system: a computer system containing two or more interconnected central processing units. Contrast with *central computer system*.

distributed network: see *computer network*.

electrical or electronic accounting machine (EAM): special-purpose data processing equipment that is electric and/or electronic, capable of performing various data processing functions.

external storage (auxiliary storage): data storage other than main storage. Contrast with *internal storage.*

general-purpose computer: a computer that is designed to handle a wide variety of problems. Compare with *special-purpose computer.*

intelligent terminal: a terminal capable of performing limited data processing functions.

internal storage: storage unit directly controlled by the central processing unit. Contrast with *external storage.*

interrupt: to stop a process in such a way that it can be resumed.

interruption: a break in the normal sequence of execution of instructions.

machine language: a language that is used directly by a machine.

magnetic core: a configuration of magnetic material in which binary data is represented by the direction of magnetization in ring-shaped magnetic material.

magnetic disk: a flat, circular plate with one or two magnetic surfaces on which binary data can be stored by selective magnetization of portions of the surface.

magnetic drum: a circular cylinder with a magnetic surface on which data can be stored by selective magnetization of portions of the surface.

magnetic tape: a tape with a magnetic surface on which data can be stored by the direction of magnetization of portions of the surface.

main frame: same as *central processing unit.*

mass storage: a storage of a large amount of data.

memory unit: same as *storage unit.*

microcomputer: a loose term describing a very small and inexpensive computer. It is usually less powerful than a minicomputer.

microsecond: one millionth of a second.

millisecond: one thousandth of a second.

minicomputer: a loose term describing a small and inexpensive computer. It is usually more powerful than a microcomputer but less powerful than a full-scale computer.

nanosecond: one billionth of a second.

object program: a fully compiled or assembled program that is ready to be loaded into the computer. Contrast with *source program.*

operating system (OS): software which controls the execution of computer programs and which may provide scheduling, debugging, input/output control, accounting, compilation, storage assignment, data management, and related services.

peripheral unit: in a data processing system any equipment distinct from the central processing unit.

procedure-oriented language: a programming language designed for the convenient expression of procedures used in the solution of a wide class of problems.

programmable calculator: a calculator that can be programmed and is designed to handle a variety of problems.

random access: see *direct access*.

register: a device capable of storing a specified amount of data.

remote job entry (RJE): submission of a data processing job from a remote terminal.

sequential: events occurring in time sequence with little or no simultaneity of events. Contrast with *simultaneous*.

simultaneous: the occurrence of two or more events at the same instant in time. Contrast with *sequential*.

source program: a program to be translated into an *object program*.

special-purpose computer: a computer designed to handle a restricted class of problems. Compare with *general-purpose computer*.

storage unit: a device into which data can be inserted, in which it can be retained, and from which it can be retrieved.

target program: same as *object program*.

translator: a program for converting from one language to another without significantly changing the meaning.

DISCUSSION QUESTIONS

1. Report on your collections of newspaper, magazine, television items, cartoons, jokes, and anecdotes.

2. Define and explain in your own words: *calculator, cash register, electrical* and *electronic accounting machines, special purpose* and *general purpose, register*. Give examples. Compare your definitions with those in your dictionary and explain differences, if any.[3]

3. Explain how computations and data processing were performed in the: (*a*) 17th century, (*b*) 18th century, (*c*) 19th century, (*d*) 20th century with punched card machines but before computers. Go to your library or any other source for information.

4. Define the word *automatic,* and compare automatic machines with computers.

5. Give the history, functions, and use of the following devices: (*a*) Jacquard's Loom; (*b*) abacus; (*c*) Pascal's adding machine; (*d*) Leibniz's calculator; (*e*) Babbage's analytic engine; (*f*) the typewriter; (*g*) Hollerith sorter; (*h*) Aiken's computer (Mark I); (*i*) ENIAC; (*j*) EDVAC; (*k*) UNIVAC. Go to your library or any other source for information.

6. Explain how a mechanical wheel compares with an "electronic wheel."

7. Explain and illustrate this statement: All data can be represented by bit strings.

---

[3] In all word problems you need make comparisons only if the word or phrase is in your dictionary.

8. Define and explain in your own words: *binary digit, bit, bit string, byte*. Give examples. Compare your definitions with those in your dictionary and explain differences, if any.

9. Describe the organization of the classical computer.

10. Define and explain in your own words: *peripheral unit, central processing unit, main frame, arithmetic/logic unit, storage memory, control unit*. Give examples. Compare your definitions with those in your dictionary and explain differences, if any.

11. What is meant by generations of computers? State the point of view taken in this book on third- versus fourth-generation computers.

12. Discuss the performance of computers as to size, speed, storage capacity, costs.

13. Define and explain in your own words: *millisecond, microsecond, nanosecond, magnetic drum, data transfer rate, magnetic core*. Give examples. Compare your definitions with those in your dictionary and explain differences, if any.

14. Discuss the performance of peripheral units as to data transfer rate, access method, and costs.

15. Define and explain in your own words: *internal storage, magnetic tape, external, auxiliary, secondary, mass, bulk, storage, direct or random access, magnetic disk pack, minicomputer, microcomputer, programmable calculator*. Give examples. Compare your definitions with those in your dictionary and explain differences, if any.

16. Discuss the seven types of data communication as to possible applications.

17. Define and explain in your own words: *remote job entry, storage and retrieval, interactive, data acquisition and control, data exchange*. Give examples. Compare your definitions with those in your dictionary and explain differences, if any.

18. Why are the resources of the classical computer underutilized?

19. Compare the organization of the classical computer and the modern computer system.

20. Define and explain in your own words: *simultaneous, interruption, interrupt*. Give examples. Compare your definitions with those in your dictionary and explain differences, if any.

21. Discuss the meaning of the statement: Modern computer systems are interrupt driven.

22. Give an everyday example of an interrupt-driven process.

23. Define and explain in your own words: *data channel, central system, distributed system, network, intelligent terminal*. Give examples. Compare your definitions with those in your dictionary and explain differences, if any.

24. What is meant by automatic programming? Describe the meaning of a language *translator* in terms of the *source* and *object* or *target* programs.

25. Describe assembler language programming and compare it with machine language programming.

26. Describe procedure-oriented language programming.

27. Compare assembler and procedure-oriented language programming.

28. What is meant by a *compiler?*

29. What is meant by *software?*

30. What is meant by the *operating system?*

31. Define and explain in your own words: *originating, processing, storing, retrieving, reproducing,* and *communicating* by *manual, manual with machine assistance, electromechanical punched card,* and *electronic* methods. Give examples. Compare your definitions with those in your dictionary and explain differences, if any.

32. Review and update your Personal Summary of this course (see Exercise 28, Chapter 1).

5

Principles of programming development

The principal issue to be faced in programming development is the job data processing professionals do and how they do it. How do they meet the challenge of the development of extremely complex information systems?

Since programming is both an art and a science, we will divide the material into two parts. This chapter presents the principles of programming practices and program development, including the human side of programming and the environment in which the programmer works. It is possible and desirable to discuss such non-technical aspects of programming prior to learning more about the technology of computer systems. In Chapters 6 to 8 we develop this technical knowledge, and in Chapters 9 and 10 we return to advanced concepts of programming and software systems.

PROGRAMMING PRACTICES AND ENVIRONMENT

A computer program was defined in Chapter 1 as a series of instructions or statements in a form acceptable to a computer. The program must achieve desired results, and the programmer is the data processing professional responsible for the program and these results. This section explains what programmers must know, how they do their jobs, and what makes some programmers successful while others fail.

To make a program acceptable to the computer, the rules of

syntax[1] of the computer language must be obeyed (see Chapter 9). The other requirement of the program, that it must achieve results, cannot be dealt with in such precise terms. This aspect of programming is creative, involving problem analysis and problem solving. In Chapter 2, Figure 2.14 gives a simplified set of recommendations to aid in the development of a flowchart. These simple rules can be generalized, and more comprehensive advice as to problem solving can be developed. In fact, philosophers and scientists for hundreds of years have attempted to develop general rules for solving problems.

When you deal with complex programming tasks, however, you need more than the advice in Figure 2.14. The key concept you must develop and master is suggested in Figure 2.2, which illustrates the structure of complex systems. Both the problem and the program are structured, and the two structures must match. Thus a complex computer program, to be successful, must follow a clean, logical approach and exhibit clarity of program structure.

To follow these precepts requires individual creativity and a high standard of excellence. But programmers are not only creative workers; they are also producers of useful products which must achieve desired results. The individual creation of the programmer will be used by others and must meet the test of group requirements and societal needs.

In the early days of computer systems, programmers were solitary workers who analyzed problems, wrote programs, ran them, and also used them. Today they are members of teams. The final product is produced by group effort, and often the programmer's responsibility is to produce a part of a larger whole. The goal is to produce a superior product, a unit that will fit into the total system. Thus today the programmer's responsibility is not only to produce programs but also to make certain that they contribute to the achievement of results. Because the products they deliver will be used by others, programmers must be not only good in the technical aspects of programming but also masters in the art of technical communications.

Ideally, the programmer is a creative but disciplined individual. Programs are written in correct syntax and follow the conventions of a consistent form and style. The programmer is not only knowledgeable in the strictly technical aspects of programming but is also a goal-oriented, productive member of society.

SYSTEM FLOWCHARTS

In working with flowcharts, you have learned how to replace the verbal, narrative descriptions of a simple problem with the

---

[1] Terms printed in color are defined at the end of the chapter.

graphical representation of a flowchart, and then how to translate the flowchart into a computer program. Describing a large data processing task by flowcharting is a more complicated problem.

Why system flowcharts are used

In the typical computer program there is a large number of variables, data items, input, and output. There may be hundreds of data processing jobs to be performed. The outputs of some of these processes will be inputs to some of the other processes. If you tried to make a detailed flowchart of the type used in programming, you would have an enormous number of flowchart boxes to deal with, and you would have great difficulty making progress. Suppose that after you have flowcharted one particular part of the data processing job in great detail, you discover that your solution does not fit in with another part of the data processing job. You need a new type of flowchart describing a total data processing system which can be refined into detailed descriptions of parts of the system. By adding more and more details, you should be able to produce the type of flowchart used in preparing programs and finally proceed to programming itself.

To meet the challenge of difficult and complex data processing jobs, computer people have developed flowcharts called system flowcharts. These are different from the program flowcharts you have used so far in programming.

An example from everyday life is shown in Figure 5.1, which gives instructions on how to call your doctor in an emergency. Observe that the flowchart boxes do not precisely describe how each action is to be carried out.

The difference between a program flowchart and a system flowchart is somewhat blurred. Bear in mind that a system flowchart aims to deal with entire processes, while the program flowchart shows specific steps to be undertaken by the computer. A system flowchart emphasizes input/output and the statement of the process that must be performed between input and output. System flowcharts are made up of IN-PROCESS-OUT loops or modules (see Chapter 2, Figure 2.8). The process part of the module may be just a specification of the process to be performed. In a program flowchart the process part is described in step-by-step detail, so the module can be directly translated into a program. The system flowchart stresses more the *what* than the *how*.

Hierarchical structures and top-down development

To further clarify the use of system flowcharts, we will examine the statement that problems have structures, programs have struc-

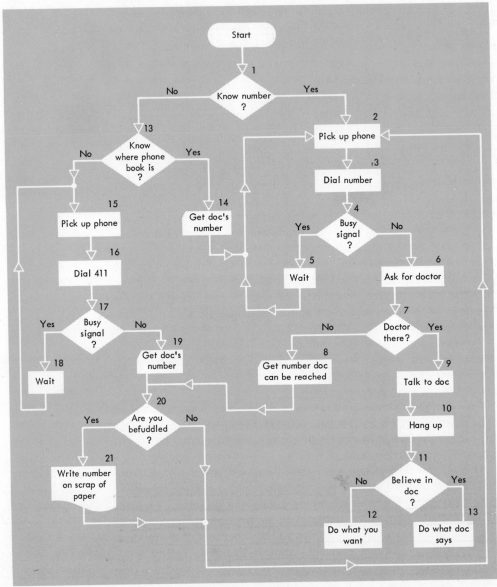

FIGURE 5.1 How
to call your doctor
in case of
emergency.

tures, and a good program must match the problem structure. In
Figure 2.2 we stressed the fact that complexity stems from the
manner in which the modules of the system are linked, or the structure of the system. The concept of hierarchical structures can be
illustrated with examples from everyday life (Figure 5.2).

The human body is an extremely complex structure, but it can
be looked upon as consisting of a few major systems modules —the

circulatory system, digestive system, nervous system, and so on. These modules in turn consist of lower-level modules, since the major systems are made up of organs. Organs in turn are made up of tissues, tissues of cells, cells of molecules, molecules of atoms and atoms of electrons and protons. The human body is a hierarchical structure; and study of the human body can be accomplished by the study of the appropriate modules. Cells, for example, may be studied on the molecular level, but tissues will not be studied on an atomic level, and so on.

A second example of a hierarchical structure is the organization of a large corporation. To simplify, assume that the president has

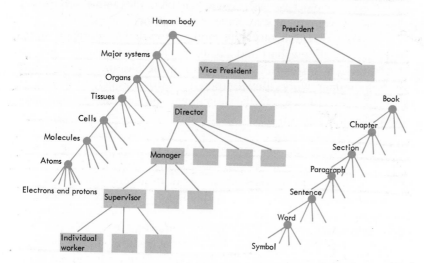

FIGURE 5.2
Examples of
hierarchical
structures.

vice presidents reporting to him; the vice presidents, directors; the directors, managers; the managers, supervisors; and finally the supervisors, individual workers.

An illustration relevant to information systems is a book. A book consists of chapters; chapters are comprised of sections; sections of paragraphs; paragraphs of sentences; sentences of words; words of symbols.

What holds for the human body, a large organization, or a book also holds for a computer program. It must be structured hierarchically to match problem structure. Thus hierarchical structure is necessary for the flowchart. A single, overall flowchart is needed to represent the broadest relationship of the modules; then detailed flowcharts and more detailed flowcharts are needed to show all the relationships. At the bottom of the hierarchy are detailed program flowcharts.

When the programmer or system analyst is faced with the problem of designing a flowchart, two different approaches must be considered. One, the bottom-up approach, starts with the preparation of program flowcharts and then puts these flowcharts together, thereby moving up in the hierarchy. This was the approach in the early days of programming, and even today it is often followed. The advantage of the bottom-up approach is that it is easier to get started and to make progress in the development of flowcharts. There is, however, a serious disadvantage that can make the appearance of progress an illusion. As more and more charts are put together it may very well be that the flowcharts will not fit together and therefore must be redesigned. In fact, the whole process of flowchart development may have to be redone.

To avoid this difficulty, the modern top-down approach starts with an overall flowchart and a general plan for its development. In this approach, instead of climbing up in the hierarchy the analyst or programmer works down from the top, refining the flowchart elements, identifying specific situations, and developing more and more details. The advantage of this approach is the assurance that all parts of the flowchart will fit together and that the program structure will match the problem structure. The top-down approach, characterized by clarity of structure and clean logic, resolves the problem of how to fit together the work of different programmers.

There is, of course, some disadvantage associated with the top-down approach. Considerable planning and forethought are required to carry out the approach; it requires great discipline and patience. For this reason the two approaches are often combined, and an attempt is made to use the advantages of both without being hindered by the disadvantages.

Flowcharting is useful not only in describing data processing jobs but also in providing instructions to perform other types of jobs. As an illustration, we will apply the technique of system flowcharts to the problem of how to prepare a computer program (Figure 5.3).

HOW TO DEVELOP A COMPUTER PROGRAM

The flowchart in the two parts of Figure 5.3 has 20 flowchart boxes. Following standard flowcharting practice (used above and treated later in detail) each input and output is listed in a parallelogram-shaped box   ; each activity in a rectangle   ; and each decision in a diamond-shaped box   .

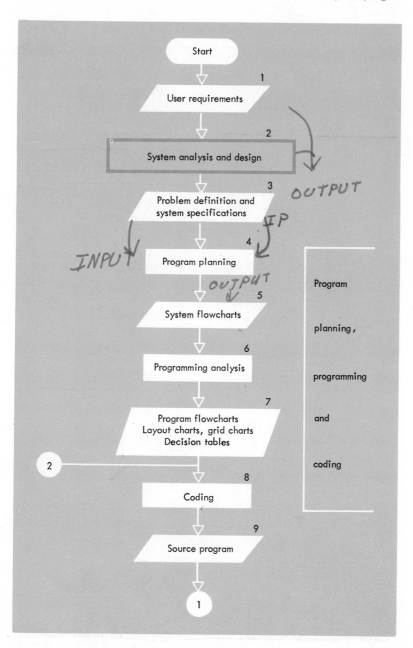

FIGURE 5.3 Flow-chart describing how to prepare a computer program. Each box (shape or form) has a standard, specific meaning.

FIGURE 5.3
(continued)

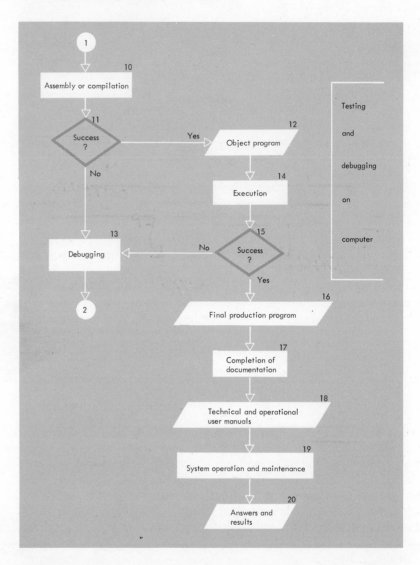

System analysis and design

The fundamental input when using a computer is a statement of user requirements. The best program running on a most advanced computer in the most efficient manner can provide only useless answers unless the requirements of the user are met.

What is the data processing problem? What are the tasks to be performed? What are the objectives of the user? Answers to these questions may appear to be obvious, but the need for them is often overlooked. The process of system analysis and design begins by definition of the objectives. The many facets of the data processing problem are collected, organized, and interpreted. Whether a data processing job is to be performed manually or by a computer, the problem to be solved must be examined and analyzed. A careful review must be made of what is being done, what should be done, and what improvements are possible. Particular emphasis must be put on the benefits that can be realized by introducing a new computerized data processing system.

The output of system analysis and design, as shown in Box 3 of Figure 5.3, is the problem definition and system specifications. These outline the nature and scope of results to be achieved, the form and type of input and output.

The system analysis and design process is, strictly speaking, not a part of program preparation. We will refer to this process again in Chapter 11. For purposes of this discussion, we define programming as the process that uses system specifications as an input and creates usable computer programs as an output.

Program planning, programming, and coding

Box 4 designates the process of program planning which uses as input the system specifications (output of system analysis and design) and creates as output Box 5, the system flowcharts. It is during the program-planning phase of the work that the detailed system specifications stating the various inputs and outputs are developed. Emphasis is still not on how to create output from input, but rather on how to identify and relate the various processes that will create the output.

Box 6 designates programming analysis, whereby detailed system flowcharts are converted into program flowcharts. The specific operations (arithmetic and logical) are all spelled out in detail, so it is known precisely what steps must be followed. As indicated in Box 7, the output of this phase of the work is program flowcharts (with which you are already familiar), as well as layout charts, grid charts, and decision tables. Layout charts state precisely how the input is to be prepared and how the output is to appear. Grid charts define the various data elements of the problem and how they relate to programs and reports. Decision tables supplement flowcharts for problems with complex logical conditions. Layout charts, grid charts, and decision tables are all discussed in some detail later in this chapter because they are important alternatives to flowcharts. The actual writing or coding of programs, that is the process of translating program flowcharts into source programs, is indicated in Box 8 and the resulting source program in Box 9.

Testing and debugging

Boxes 10 to 15 describe the testing and debugging process necessary to produce the final production program (Box 16). The first step is to submit the source program to the computer for assembly or compilation. (Box 10). In real life the first attempt will rarely be successful, and therefore Boxes 11, 12 and 14 will be repeatedly executed. Of course, the most important Boxes are 11 and 15, the decision boxes for determining *success*. One of the measures of the performance of programmers is how many times they go around the loop. An excellent programmer may go around the loop a few times and use limited computer time, whereas a poor programmer may have to go around many times and thus will use up a great deal of computer and programmer time.

Testing and debugging is much more than error finding. Keep in mind that the program must achieve results. Therefore as the **bugs** are removed from the program it may be necessary to revise the programming approach and redefine the problem itself. If original problem definition is poor and the concept of the program is inadequate, errors are compounded during the testing and debugging stage, and much programmer and computer time is wasted.

Documentation

A program cannot possibly achieve desired results unless it can be used by people other than the programmers who wrote it. Therefore, documentation—that is, the result of creating, collecting, organizing, storing, and communicating information necessary to use the program—is a most important product of the program. Box 17 designates the *completion* of the documentation, because good programming practice requires that the activities of documentation be performed during the entire process of program development. Therefore, by the time the final production program is completed, most of the documentation will also be completed, and assembling the existing material and preparing a relatively small amount of missing documentation are all that will be required.

It is useful to distinguish between technical documentation to be used by programmers and the operational documentation used by nonprogrammers. The technical documentation of a program may be used by programmers who did not write it because the programmer who did so may disappear from the scene, and during the long life cycle of the program other programmers will be involved in maintaining and modifying it. The technical documentation should include at least the following items:

1. The complete problem statement.
2. System description, including systems specifications, logic and

structure of flowcharts and programs, data descriptions, input/
output descriptions, systems flowcharts, layout charts, grid
charts, decision tables, and so on.

3. Program description, including a clean, sequence-numbered
program listing with adequate explanations and comments.

4. A definite statement of testing and verification procedures, including listing of test data, program sections tested, verification
descriptions, and so on.

5. Operating instructions or run manual, including input/output
formats; error messages; other abnormal conditions; starting,
running, restarting, terminating procedures, and so on.

System operation and maintenance

Box 19, system operation and maintenance, indicates a continuing activity which must be performed during the entire life cycle of
program development. This operation produces answers and results
(Box 20).

Bear in mind that most programs are not final when they are
apparently debugged. There is such an unthinkably large number
of possibilities in running a program that it is virtually impossible to
test a program for all possible conditions. Often there are a few
bugs lurking in the program which will not be discovered until it
is used under actual conditions. Thus, it is almost certain that the
programmer (or, more likely, another programmer) will make further
corrections to the program.

Moreover, during the long life cycle of a program, requirements
are likely to change, and so program modification will be necessary.
If the original documentation is inadequate, correcting errors or
modifying programs may become almost impossible.

The procedure for program maintenance is essentially the same
as for debugging, except that changes are being made to something
that was thought to be in final form. The following six steps, at
least, are necessary for a properly executed correction of a program:

1. Document the existence of an error.
2. Determine necessary program corrections.
3. Prepare a duplicate program; make the corrections in the duplicate; test and debug the duplicate program.
4. Change the original program and insert comments to show the
history of the changes made.
5. Document the history of the changes made and the new program
itself.
6. Distribute the new program and documentation to users.

This section has reviewed the entire process of program development, with the help of Figure 5.3, an illustrative system flowchart.

Now we will be more specific about how to develop system flow-charts and will describe various tools and techniques available to the programmer and systems analyst.

FLOWCHARTING TECHNIQUES

Standard flowchart symbols

The purpose of flowchart symbols is as an aid in preparing and analyzing flowcharts and to promote communication among programmers and systems analysts. Associations like the International Organization for Standardization (ISO) and the American National Standards Institute (ANSI) have made recommendations with regard to standardization of flowchart symbols. The best way to get accustomed to using these standard symbols is to do your work with a template similar to the one shown in Figure 5.4.

The basic recommended symbols for flowcharts are shown in Figure 5.5. The process form   and the input/output form   were illustrated above. The latter is to be used for any kind of input and output, including cards, documents, magnetic tapes, and disks. Figure 5.6 shows the symbols primarily used in programming, including two already introduced in Chapter 2: the decision and terminal   symbols. The forms in Figure 5.7 are primarily used in system flowcharts. The symbols for punched cards and documents were introduced in Chapter 2 as input and output statement forms.

Figure 5.4
Standard template
for symbols to be
used in making
flowcharts.

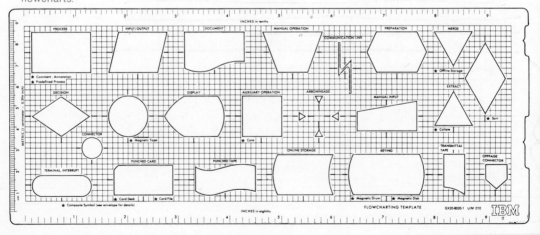

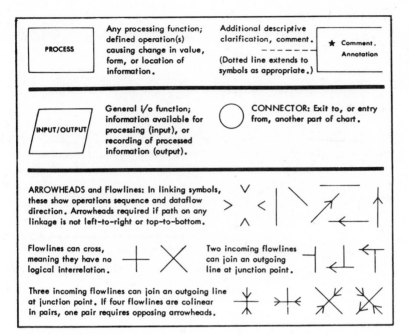

FIGURE 5.5 Basic recommended symbols (forms) to be used in preparing flowcharts.

The star symbol in some of the boxes in Figures 5.4–5.7 indicates that you must combine template forms to draw these boxes.

Flowcharting work sheet

Professional programmers and systems analysts often use standard flowcharting work sheets, as shown in **Figure 5.8.** Such charts

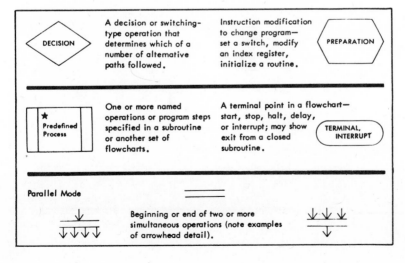

FIGURE 5.6 Flowchart symbols primarily used in program flowcharts.

Figure 5.7
Flowchart symbols
primarily used in
system flowcharts.

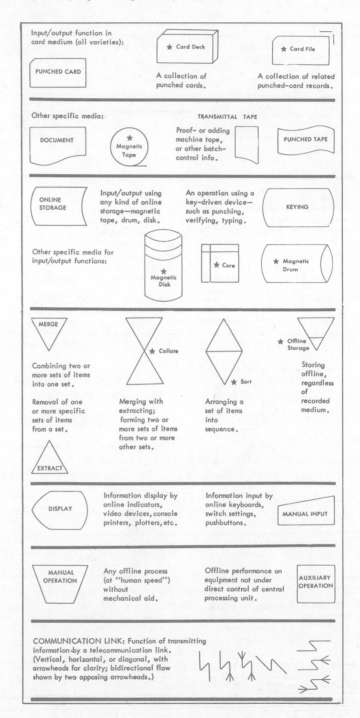

Input/output function in
card medium (all varieties):

PUNCHED CARD

★ Card Deck

A collection of
punched cards.

★ Card File

A collection of related
punched-card records.

Other specific media:

DOCUMENT

★ Magnetic Tape

TRANSMITTAL TAPE

Proof- or adding
machine tape,
or other batch-
control info.

PUNCHED TAPE

ONLINE STORAGE

Input/output using
any kind of online
storage—magnetic
tape, drum, disk.

An operation using a
key-driven device—
such as punching,
verifying, typing.

KEYING

Other specific media for
input/output functions:

★ Magnetic Disk

★ Core

★ Magnetic Drum

MERGE

★ Collate

★ Offline Storage

Combining two or
more sets of items
into one set.

★ Sort

Storing
offline,
regardless
of
recorded
medium.

Removal of one
or more specific
sets of items
from a set.

Merging with
extracting;
forming two or
more sets of items
from two or more
other sets.

Arranging a
set of items
into
sequence.

EXTRACT

DISPLAY

Information display by
online indicators,
video devices, console
printers, plotters, etc.

Information input by
online keyboards,
switch settings,
pushbuttons.

MANUAL INPUT

MANUAL OPERATION

Any offline process
(at "human speed")
without
mechanical aid.

Offline performance on
equipment not under
direct control of central
processing unit.

AUXILIARY OPERATION

COMMUNICATION LINK: Function of transmitting
information by a telecommunication link.
(Vertical, horizontal, or diagonal, with
arrowheads for clarity; bidirectional flow
shown by two opposing arrowheads.)

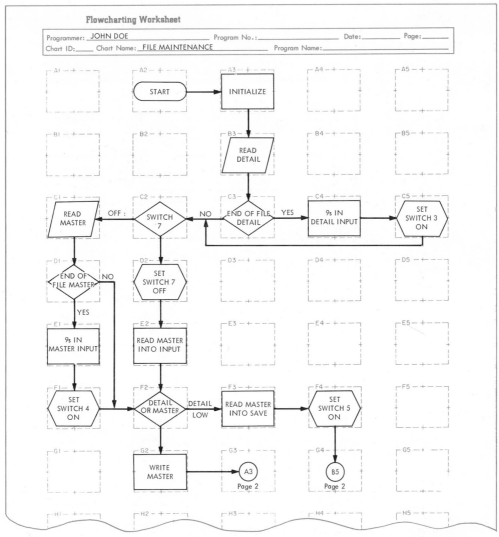

FIGURE 5.8
Flowchart using
standard
flowcharting
work sheet.

promote standardized layouts and thereby simplify the flowcharting
and communication process.

Computer-prepared flowcharts

After a program has been written it can be used as input data for
a software package, and the computer can automatically print a
flowchart using the symbols illustrated in Figure 5.9. This computerized approach to flowcharting saves time, avoids errors, and helps

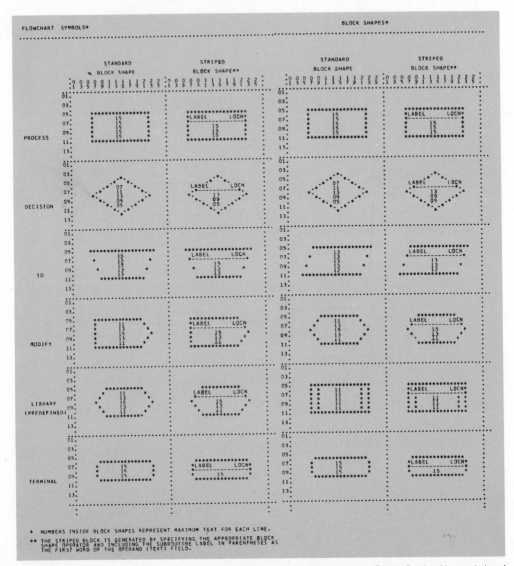

FIGURE 5.9
Computer-
prepared flow-
chart symbols.

R. R. Arnold, H. C. Hill, A. V. Nichols, *Modern Data Processing*, © 1969. Reprinted by permission of John Wiley & Sons, Inc., New York.

in many other ways. Of course, it is necessary to pay for the software and computer usage.

"Blowing up" a flowchart

One of the most important principles in working with systems flowcharts can be illustrated by comparing flowcharts with maps.

Flowcharts provide information necessary to do a data processing job; road maps help people drive from one place to another.

Suppose you lived in Los Angeles and received an invitation from the family living at 1600 Pennsylvania Avenue, Washington, D.C. Naturally you would accept the invitation. If you decide to drive from Los Angeles to Washington, which maps would you need? (See Figure 5.10.)

If you did not know whether Washington is to the north, east, or south, you would need a map of the United States. You would study this map and plan the route to follow. Since the U.S. map would not be detailed enough for driving, you would get state maps along your route. The last of these maps would show Delaware, Maryland, and Virginia. But to drive into Washington, D.C., you would need a detailed map of the capitol city and vicinity, and to find 1600 Pennsylvania Avenue you might need a street map of the city.

Observe that the maps in Figure 5.10 become successively more detailed. Each map shows a "blown up" portion of the previous map. It might be said that you need an overall map and smaller maps to "zoom in" for greater detail. The maps form a hierarchy,

FIGURE 5.10
"Blowing up" a map is like "blowing up" a flowchart. Successive steps produce more detailed, lower-level charts. It is like using a zoom lens on your camera.

Map of United States

Map of Delaware, Maryland, and Virginia

Map of Washington, D.C. and vicinity

Tourist map of Washington

that is, they can be arranged into a graded series of maps, like a pyramid.

The basic principle of system flowchart preparation in data processing is quite similar. First you need top-level system flowcharts. Then you "blow up" parts of these charts again and again until you obtain detailed program flowcharts. You prepare your flowcharts in a hierarchical manner, starting at the top of the pyramid and blowing up the system flowchart as necessary. When you have all these detailed charts you are ready to translate the charts into computer programs; that is, you are ready for coding. The best way to learn to apply this principle is by an example, but first consider the advantages of flowcharts listed below:

Advantages of FLOWCHARTS

1. Quick establishment of the logic of relations between processing elements.
2. Effective analysis and design of data processing systems.
3. Ease of communication between noncomputer people, systems analysts, and programmers.
4. Effective program documentation.
5. Efficient coding, testing, and maintenance of programs.

A CASE STUDY: INVOICE PREPARATION

The principles of flowcharting can be clarified by studying the preparation of invoices under three conditions: (1) manual processing, (2) direct (random) access processing on magnetic disks, and (3) sequential access processing with magnetic tapes.

When merchandise is sold and shipped it is customary to enclose an itemized list of goods shipped, specifying prices in terms of sale. The computerized preparation of these invoices is one of the most common data processing applications. This case study will also be used to illustrate the principles of the top-down approach and show how a hierarchy of IN-PROCESS-OUT modules is constructed. The approach applies equally to manual or computerized data processing.

Hierarchy plus Input-Process-Output (HIPO)

The top-down approach starts with a single IN-PROCESS-OUT module, as illustrated in Figure 5.11. Then, as shown in Figure 5.12, the three flowchart boxes are filled in for the problem being analyzed. So far no structure or detail is shown. The next step is to break down each of the modules into details.

Figure 5.13 shows the flow of information from the salesman to the credit department, to the shipping department, and finally to the sales department where the invoice is prepared. Box 1 indicates

FIGURE 5.11 How
to prepare a
single, overview
IN-PROCESS-OUT
diagram.

that the salesman takes the order, and Box 2 that he prepares a
purchase order (Figure 5.14). The salesman writes in to whom the
sale was made, to whom the product is to be shipped, shipping date,
and shipment method, as well as the buyer number, order number,
and so on.

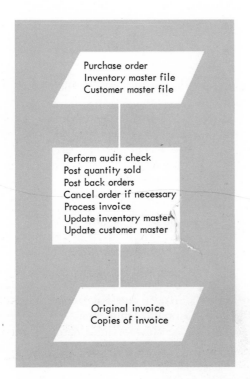

FIGURE 5.12
Filled-in details in
the overview
diagram shown
in Figure 5.11.

FIGURE 5.13
System flowchart
indicating the
processes of
getting a customer
order, making a
credit check,
writing a purchase
order, and
preparing an
invoice.

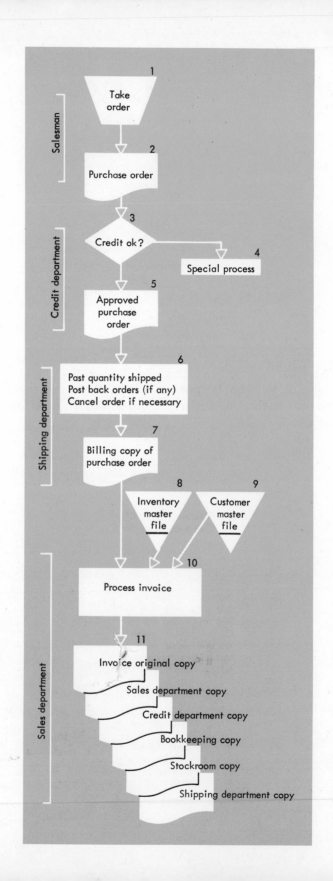

The purchase order goes to the credit department where, as indicated in Box 3, Figure 5.13, a credit check is made. If the credit of the purchaser is unsatisfactory, a special process (Box 4) must be followed to advise the salesman and the customer. If the purchaser's credit is good, an approved purchase order is issued (Box 5). This document now goes to the shipping department.

In the shipping department the goods are shipped and, as in-

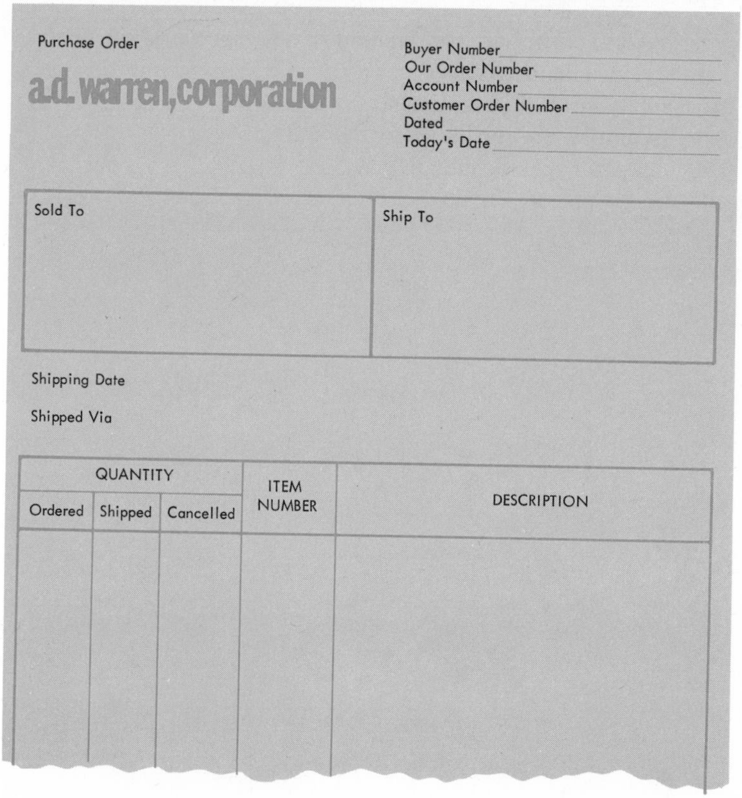
Purchase Order

a.d. warren, corporation

Buyer Number
Our Order Number
Account Number
Customer Order Number
Dated
Today's Date

Sold To

Ship To

Shipping Date

Shipped Via

QUANTITY			ITEM NUMBER	DESCRIPTION
Ordered	Shipped	Cancelled		

FIGURE 5.14 A typical purchase order.

dicated in Box 6, the quantity shipped is posted. If there is not enough of the product in inventory, a partial shipment is made, and back orders are posted. For those customers who do not accept back orders, the orders are cancelled.

The output of this process is the billing copy of the purchase order (Box 7). The billing copy to the sales department includes data on the quantity ordered, shipped, and cancelled, and so on.

The sales department prepares the invoice and five copies. The input is: (1) the billing copy of the purchase order (Box 7), (2) the inventory master file (Box 8), and (3) the customer master file (Box 9). It is assumed that these two files have been created already and are periodically updated and maintained. These three inputs are utilized in the invoice preparation process (Box 10) to prepare the invoice and the various copies (Box 11).

To illustrate the top-down approach further, we will consider the details of processing the invoice. In effect, we will "blow up" Box 10.

Flowcharts for processing invoices manually

The system flowchart for manual invoice preparation is shown in Figure 5.15. The inputs are:

(1) the billing copy of the purchase order (Box 1),

(2) the inventory master file (Box 2), and

(3) the customer master file (Box 4).

FIGURE 5.15
Overall system
flowchart for
manual invoice
preparation.

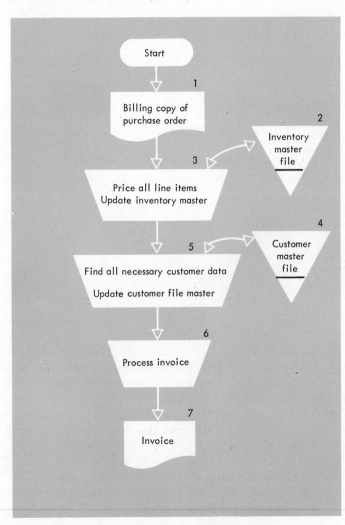

Box 3 indicates that each line item on the purchase order is examined, the price of the item from the inventory master file is retrieved, and the total price for that line item is figured. The quantity in inventory from the inventory master file is also reduced by the quantity shipped; that is, the master inventory file is updated.

Observe the ▽ boxes for manual processing and ▽ boxes for manual files.

Next (Box 5) the customer master file is searched for all necessary information (exact name of customer, address, zip code, applicable discount, etc.). Then all information for this particular purchase is recorded on the customer master file; that is, the file is updated.

Finally the invoice is prepared (Box 6), and the invoice is typed (Box 7).

In Figure 5.16 a more detailed system flowchart for the same manual process is shown. For example, in Box 2 we specifically state that for each line item the quantity shipped and the back order (if any) must be read.

Box 3 makes a more detailed statement as to pricing the line item, updating the inventory master, and figuring the price to be charged. Box 4 explicitly states that the total price must be computed by adding the price for each of the line items. In Box 6 we state that a discount is to be applied if the customer is entitled to it, the tax must be computed, and the invoice must be typed.

In summary, the detailed system flowchart of Figure 5.16 contains more information than the overall flowchart of Figure 5.15. The detailed chart is obtained by "blowing up" elements of the previous higher level system flowchart.

Computerized input and output

To computerize this data processing job, we specify how to enter the data in the computer with the aid of punched header cards, how to store the data in the computer, and how the printed invoice should appear.

Figure 5.17 illustrates the two header cards that are used for each purchase order. For each line item (part ordered) on the invoice we keypunch a detail card (Figure 5.18). Figure 5.19 shows a computer-printed invoice. Figures 5.20 and 5.21 show the layout of the customer master record and the inventory master in the computer.

Direct-access approach

Assume that both the inventory master and the customer master files have already been created on magnetic disks. (We will discuss

FIGURE 5.16
Detailed flowchart
for manual invoice
preparation.

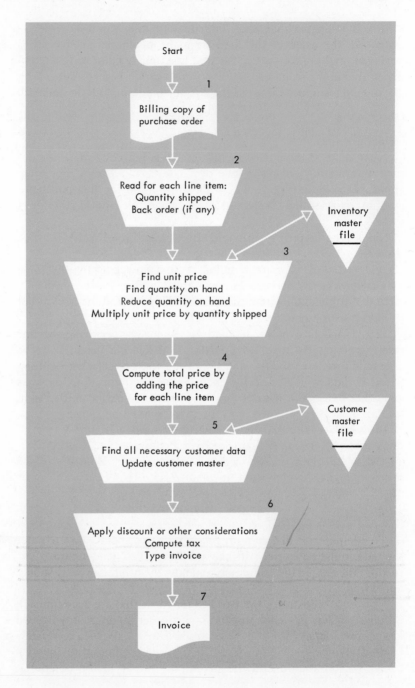

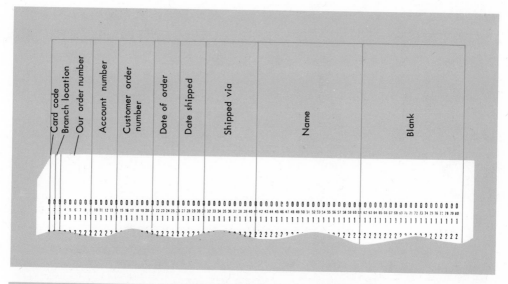

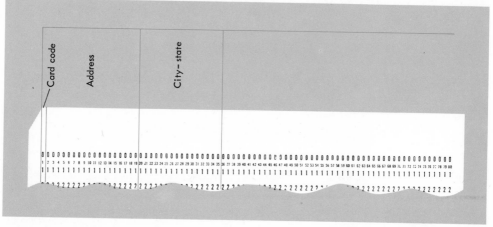

FIGURE 5.17
Header cards for invoice preparation.

magnetic disks in detail later.) Then any inventory master record can be retrieved by part number, and any customer master record can be retrieved by account number.

Box 5 of the system flowchart (Figure 5.22) specifies as input the billing copy of the purchase order. Box 10 indicates keypunching and verification. Box 15 refers to the verified deck of input cards. Box 20 indicates that both master files are on magnetic disks.

The processing itself (Box 25) is so similar to manual processing that hardly any explanation is necessary. Instead of manually retrieving records from the master files, records are retrieved directly by the computer from the magnetic disk files by part number

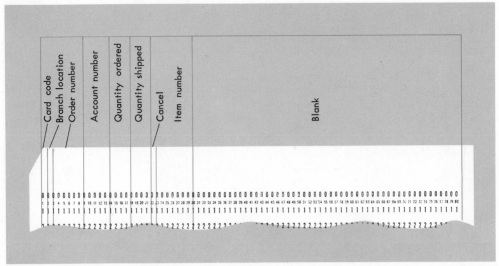

FIGURE 5.18
Sample detail card
for invoice
preparation.

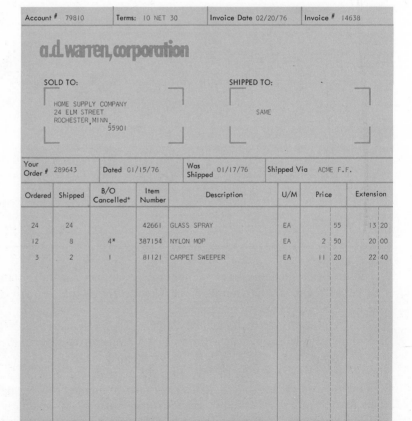

FIGURE 5.19
Computer-printed
invoice
(B/O stands for
back order,
U/M for unit
measure).

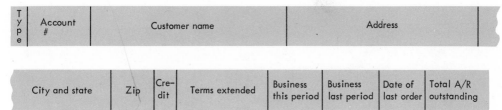

T y p e	Account #	Customer name	Address

City and state	Zip	Cre-dit	Terms extended	Business this period	Business last period	Date of last order	Total A/R outstanding

FIGURE 5.20 Layout of customer record to be used in invoice preparation (A/R stands for accounts receivable).

and account number. The processing itself presents no difficulties at all.

Sequential-processing approach

If both master files are on magnetic tapes (to be discussed more fully later), the records must be processed in sequence, one after the other (Figure 5.23). The computer reads an input record, processes the data, and writes the output on another tape. The computer does not alternately read and write on the same tape. (But the computer can read a record from a disk, process the data, and write on the same disk.)

The principal difficulty of sequential processing is that it is necessary to work with two different files, the inventory master file and the customer master file. The records in these files are in sequence by part number and by account number, respectively. Thus when the invoice is read it is not possible to directly price the line items and update the inventory master file, because these line items are not in part number sequence. The system flowchart in Figure 5.24 shows how the problem is handled in magnetic tape-oriented processing.

Box 5 provides the input, the billing copy of the purchase order. In Box 10 we keypunch the item cards (for the sake of simplicity, assume that a separate card is made for each line item, or part).

FIGURE 5.21 Layout of inventory record to be used in invoice preparation.

T y p e	Part #	Description	Weight	U/M	Vendor codes			Lead time (wks.)
					#1	#2	#3	

Date of last order	Cost of last purchase	% Inc.	Order quantity	Price	Central warehouse inventory and sales					
					On-hand	On-order	Reorder point	Order qty.	Sales this per.	Qty. cancel

		Branch warehouse #1				Branch warehouse #2	
On-hand	On-order	Reorder point	Order qty.	Sales this per.	Qty. cancel	On-hand	On order

FIGURE 5.22
Direct-access
(magnetic disk-
oriented) invoice
preparation.

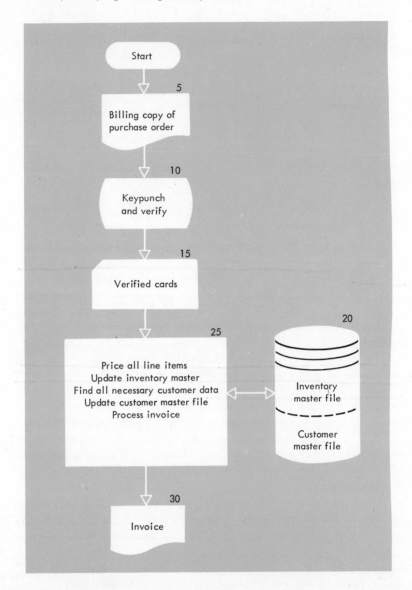

When the punched card is transcribed to the transaction tape, each record will have data on both the customer and the particular line item referenced. Records on the transaction tape will *not* be in part number sequence.

In Box 20 we sort each record on the transaction file by part number. Once the records are in part number sequence we can compare them with the inventory master file sequentially, price our

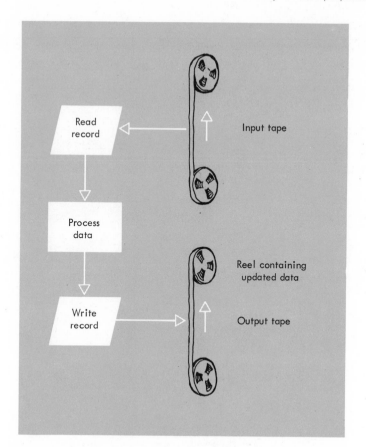

FIGURE 5.23 In sequential processing the computer reads data from the input tape, processes the data, and writes the output on another tape.

Read record

Process data

Write record

Input tape

Reel containing updated data

Output tape

items, and update the inventory master file. Thus the process in Box 20 will result in two files. The first one will be the priced transaction file, showing a complete record for each line item, including the price of the item. The second file will be the updated inventory master file. Both of these files will be in part number sequence.

In Box 30 we sort the priced transaction file into account number sequence. Now that we have the records in account number sequence, we can match them with the customer master file (which is also in account number sequence), update the customer master file and obtain all the data necessary for the invoice. The output of the process in Box 30 will be the updated customer master file and the invoice.

The crux of the difficulty is that the records must be dealt with first in part number sequence, and then in account number sequence. Further details on sequential preparation of an invoice are given in Chapter 10.

FIGURE 5.24
Flowchart for
sequential
(magnetic
tape-oriented)
invoice
preparation.

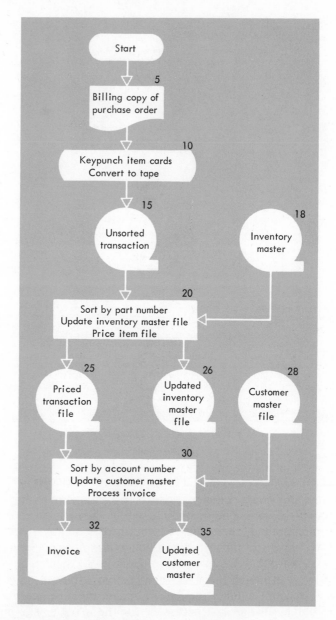

FIGURE 5.24 Flowchart for sequential (magnetic tape-oriented) invoice preparation.

LAYOUT CHARTS AND GRID CHARTS

The second item listed in Box 7 in Figure 5.3, which describes the steps required in preparing computer programs, relates to systematic, formal specifications of data items and records.

Layout charts serve to specify in detail input records, internal records in the computer, and output records. Figure 5.25 illustrates

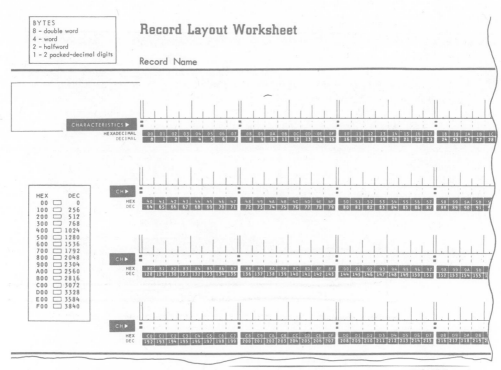

FIGURE 5.25
Typical record layout work sheet.

FIGURE 5.26
Typical printer layout work sheet.

FIGURE 5.27
Typical grid chart
illustrates how
data relates to
programs.

Programs / Data items	Sales analysis	Sales forecast	Sales budget	Salesman evaluation	Warehouse analysis	Product evaluation	Other
Customer name				✔			
Customer address					✔		
Credit code	✔						
Territory code	✔	✔	✔	✔	✔	✔	
Etc.							

how the detailed format of a record is established, and Figure 5.26 shows a printer layout work sheet.

Grid charts serve to establish the relationships between data items, programs, and reports. Some data items appear in many programs and in many reports, and a graphic representation can be of great help. Figure 5.27 illustrates the data items appearing in various programs. Figure 5.28 shows which data items appear in various reports.

DECISION TABLES

There are many data processing problems in which the logic of the flowchart is quite complex because there are many alternate paths for the computer to follow. In such situations flowcharts may be too difficult to draw and can lead to confusion. To handle such problems an alternate approach, the technique of decision tables, has been developed. Decision tables can supplement or

FIGURE 5.28
Typical grid chart
illustrates how
data relates to
output reports.

Reports / Data items	Attendance report	Foreman's production report	Payroll register	FICA quarterly report	Income tax withheld report	W-2 reports	Other
Employee no.	✔	✔	✔				
Employee name			✔	✔	✔	✔	
Employee address						✔	
Social security no.			✔	✔	✔	✔	
Etc.							

possibly replace flowcharting and thus they become part of documentation. To clarify the principles involved, we first illustrate decision tables in a noncomputer problem.

When is a leap year?

What day of the week was February 29, 1900? Do not spend much time trying to answer, as there was no February 29, 1900; 1900 was not a leap year.

You know that years like 1901, 1970, and 1975 are *not* leap years, because if you divide 4 into these numbers you get a remainder of 1, 2, or 3. A year *cannot* be a leap year unless you get a remainder of 0 when you divide it by 4.

Table heading				Decision rules							
				Rule number							
				1	2	3	4	5	6	7	8
Condition	Divide by	400	Is remainder zero?	YES	YES	YES	YES	NO	NO	NO	NO
		100		YES	YES	NO	NO	YES	YES	NO	NO
		4		YES	NO	YES	NO	YES	NO	YES	NO
Decision	It is a leap year?			X						X	
	Check your arithmetic				X	X	X		X		

FIGURE 5.29 Is it a leap year? You can answer the question by using the decision table.

If you divide 4 into 1900 the remainder is 0, so why was 1900 not a leap year? Because years ending in hundreds are not leap years unless they are divisible by 400. How about the year 2000? That will be a leap year, because when you divide it by 400 you get a remainder of 0. Confused?

In problems where there are many conditions, as in this problem, decision tables can be very handy. Figure 5.29 shows a decision table to answer the leap year problem. On the left side of the heavy vertical line are two kinds of table headings: condition and decision. The conditions of the problem are written in the condition stub. The question is whether or not the remainder is 0 after dividing the year by 400, 100, and 4. Under the heavy horizontal line in the decision stub the answers or actions are listed.

Look at the right side of the heavy vertical line and find the decision rule for the year 1900. Does rule 1 apply? Is it a leap year? No, because when you divide by 400 the remainder is 300, not 0.

Rule 2? No, for the same reason. One by one, you try the columns until you get to rule 5. If you divide 1900 by 400 is the remainder 0? No! If you divide 1900 by 100 is the remainder 0? Yes! If you divide 1900 by 4 is the remainder 0? Yes!

You can see that for the year 1900 every one of the condition entries is properly answered in Column 5. So now look at this column below the heavy horizontal line; there is no X or action sign. This means then, that 1900 is *not* a leap year.

Now try the year 2000. All the conditions for rule 1 are satisfied. Below the heavy line you see an X, meaning that the year *is* a leap year. What if you divide 2,000 by 4 and your remainder is 1? You are dealing with rule 2, and your action is to check your arithmetic.

What is the advantage of a decision table over a flowchart? If you have many conditions, tracing through a flowchart is like working through a maze. Each path through the maze corresponds to a column in the decision table. When working with decision tables you are less likely to get confused and omit a logical possibility or to make the wrong decision along one of the logical paths.

A practical data processing application of a decision table is given below.

How to fill out ticket orders

Suppose you are selling tickets by mail order at the prices of $8, $5, and $3. When a request is received and you have a seat. you mail the ticket to the customer. If the seat requested is not available, you may send the customer a lower-priced ticket and a refund, but some customers will not accept lower-priced seats. Figure 5.30 shows the decision table to guide you in your action.

Consider, for example, rule 1. You read in the column above the heavy horizontal line and to the left of the heavy vertical line that rule 1 applies when $8 seats are requested and $8 seats are available. You read below the heavy horizontal line that you should send $8 tickets.

Rule 2 governs when $8 seats are requested but are not available, and the customer will accept lower price seats. So you send a $5 ticket and refund $3.

Advantages and disadvantages of decision tables

The advantages of the use of decision tables are:

1. The programmer is more likely to cover all logical possibilities. The decision table approach forces a discipline on the programmer to think through all possible conditions as a decision table may be easier to construct than a flowchart.
2. Better documentation is provided. Decision tables may be

Table heading	Rule number								
	1	2	3	4	5	6	7	8	9
$8 seats requested	Y	Y	Y	Y	N	N	N	N	N
$5 seats requested	N	N	N	N	Y	Y	Y	N	N
$3 seats requested	N	N	N	N	N	N	N	Y	Y
$8 seats available	Y	N	N	N					
$5 seats available		Y	N		Y	N	N		
$3 seats available			Y			Y		Y	N
Will accept lower priced seats		Y	Y	N		Y	N		
Send $8 tickets	X								
Send $5 tickets		X			X				
Send $3 tickets			X			X		X	
Refund $8 per ticket				X					
Refund $5 per ticket			X				X		
Refund $3 per ticket		X							X

FIGURE 5.30 Decision table showing how to fill ticket orders (Y stands for yes, N for no).

easier to communicate to nontechnical users. Tabular representation may be more compact and workable than flowcharts.
3. Direct conversion into a computer program is possible. Software packages are available which take the statements specifying a decision table and compile it into a program.

There are disadvantages to the use of decision tables:

1. It is an additional tool which may require education and training on the part of both programmers and users. The use of both techniques—flowcharts and decision tables—may impose an additional burden.
2. If there is a large number of alternatives, it may be impractical to list them all in a decision table. On the other hand, even relatively simple flowcharts can represent an unthinkably large number of possibilities.

PRODUCTIVITY AND ECONOMICS OF PROGRAMMING

However challenging and rewarding the task of programming might be, management will judge the programmer by results. Therefore a programmer must be a goal-oriented, creative individual who does the work of programming with the objective of achieving results. The program may be extremely clever and ingenious, and only a high quality program can lead to success. Still the programmer will be judged by how the program performs while in use.

Two main economic factors are involved:

1. Time and cost necessary to develop the program.
2. Time and cost necessary to operate and maintain the program.

These main factors depend on a number of other detailed factors. For example, the number of errors the programmer makes extends the time required to develop the program and increases programming cost. During the testing and debugging phase, in addition to the time of the programmer or analyst there will be computer time when the program is assembled or compiled. Computer runs are expensive; a good programmer can significantly reduce computer costs, but poor programming practices lead to excessively high costs.

In addition to the costs incurred during the development phase, when the final production program is delivered there is also the important cost consideration of the time it takes to execute the program. Poor program structure can lead to excessive execution time, which then penalizes the product during its entire life cycle. Efficiency in the program will reduce costs many times during the many executions of the program.

After the program is delivered, it is very likely there still will be bugs in it. When a program fails in a production run, it will not be possible to obtain results, and time delays will mean increased costs. Therefore there will be a great urgency to debug the program and eliminate errors. If the documentation is inadequate and the description of the program is not easily understandable, time delays and costs will occur. Thus, highly developed communication skills have a potentially large economic benefit.

In addition to developing a program that will achieve desired results, the programmer also plays an important role in the planning phase of program development. Before management makes a commitment whether a system should be developed, estimates as to development time and cost must be obtained. In this phase the programmer is called on to assist in making predictions as to time, cost, and budgets. Later, when the program is developed, these estimates are revised, and the programmer's performance is questioned if large deviations from forecasts occur. Thus programmers are judged not only on the basis of technical skills but also on their ability to visualize the nature of the tasks to be performed and the time and costs necessary to complete the tasks successfully. Thus the task of the programmer depends not only on technical matters but on organization, staffing, management, administrative, and societal aspects.

THE HUMAN SIDE OF PROGRAMMING

The central issue in managing and organizing programming is the necessity for creativity and discipline to coexist in the programming profession. Some of the traditional concepts of supervision, whereby a person in charge tells underlings what to do, cannot be effectively applied to managing data processing groups. The managerial techniques required must encourage the individual creativity of the programmer but still assure that personal excellence is steered to achieve desired goals. Thus the basic principle for the management of programming efforts is based on the concept that the *technological and psychological aspects of programming must be brought into balance.*

Two specific management techniques for achieving this are (1) chief programmer teams and (2) structural walk-throughs.

Chief programmer teams

This organizational approach requires that a specific team of programmers be assigned to each programming project. The three main positions to be described are: (1) the chief programmer, (2) the backup programmer, and (3) the librarian. There are additional programmers and analysts in the team, but their roles are relatively simple to understand. The various functions can be most easily described with illustrations.

Elizabeth Marko is chief programmer of the team. She has 15 years of programming experience, and used to be in charge of a group of programmers. In that position she enjoyed the managerial experience of being the "boss" of programmers but felt frustrated with certain aspects of her position. First she felt that there was really no way to supervise other programmers because each one develops a program in an individual creative manner. She was also disturbed that she could not participate in the creation of new programs and felt that both her education and creative ability were somewhat wasted.

In her new position as chief programmer she feels that all her abilities, both technical and managerial, are used to the fullest. She is fully responsible for the project and the design and development of the system. She writes the main modules of the program and defines the modules to be programmed by other team members. She is responsible for specifying the interface between the modules and reviews the code written by other team members. She also is deeply involved in the testing, debugging, and integration of all programs. Furthermore, she deals with management and resolves conflicts between the desires of management and the possibilities of computer-based information systems. It is particularly gratifying to her that she is involved in program development from the beginning, when systems specifications are agreed upon, to the end, when final testing and debugging is completed.

Ernst Quinn is the backup programmer. He is a senior programmer with 10 years of experience. He works closely with Marko, and when she is absent he assumes the duties of the chief programmer. Marko may call on him to explore alternate design approaches, to perform testing and debugging tasks, or take care of other particularly difficult, special tasks. He is an active participant in all phases of the work, including technical design, coordination of the function of programmers, and dealing with management.

Lenora Mikulski is the librarian of the team. She used to be secretary to the manager of data processing before assuming her new responsibility. She is not a data processing professional, but during her many years of association with programmers and analysts she has learned a great deal about computers, programmers, operations, and the various administrative and clerical tasks involved in program development.

As the interface between the computer and the programmers, Mikulski handles the various machine and office procedures involved in a project. Before the position of librarian was developed, all these functions were performed by programmers, who thus were kept busy on noncreative, administrative tasks. This, of course, detracted from their effectiveness. Now Mikulski maintains all records and documents required for the programming effort, whether these documents are stored outside the computer in filing cabinets or notebooks or inside the computer. Thus she maintains the *Development Support Library* (DSL), (Figure 5.31) including human-readable external records and machine-readable internal records.

Figure 5.31 shows how program development can be described as consisting of two loops. The upper loop describes the functions of the programmers and how they work with the librarian. The lower loop involves the computer and shows how the librarian works with computer operations.

The programmers write programs, make requests for programs to be run, and prepare other documents. These go to the librarian, who then interfaces with computer operations, causes the programs to be executed, collects the printouts and other documents, and files them in the project notebook and other external files. Programmers receive information on their work by consulting these external files created and maintained by the librarian.

While Mikulski performs many administrative and clerical tasks requiring no special computer knowledge, she also performs many computer-oriented functions which require a good knowledge of various computer procedures. Thus, she is an important team member in the program development process.

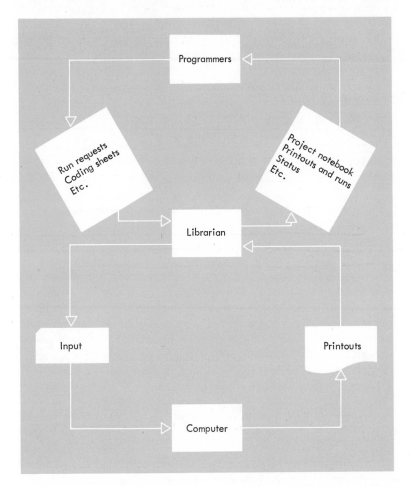

FIGURE 5.31 The librarian is responsible for maintaining the Development Support Library (DSL).

Advantages of chief programmer teams The basic advantage of the use of chief programmer teams from the point of view of management is that the productivity of programmers is increased. There is a reduction in the time and costs necessary to develop, debug, and maintain programs.

These teams require heavy involvement in the process by senior programmers. This leads to better program definition, higher programmer morale and efficiency, more suitable assignment of programming responsibilities, better use of available facilities, and generally better programs.

The importance of the position held by the librarian is that it makes it possible to relieve programmers of routine administrative functions. This leads to better utilization of their time and provides them with opportunities for more professional involvement. Concentration on technical functions creates technical excellence, which promotes faster and more significant professional growth. Thus there is better morale on the programming team.

Team effort also promotes better communication and facilitates the interchange of positions between programmers. The project is performed with more visibility, both to management and team members. Significantly, the private, individual efforts of programmers are integrated into an effective group effort.

Structured walk-throughs

Because the traditional managerial approach of direct supervision is not effective in coordinating the work of programmers, a new management concept has been developed which makes it possible to pool the knowledge and insight of a number of programmers. This is the concept of the structured walk-through.

At appropriate times in program development, the programmer invites colleagues (that is, fellow workers) to review the work so far accomplished. The purpose of these meetings is not to judge the competence of the programmer but to find weaknesses in the program, advance suggestions, and make comments on improvements. With no management participation, the programmer chooses four to six colleagues to review the work in a one- or two-hour meeting.

There are four main steps in such a review:

1. The programmer selects and schedules invitees, sends out review material in advance, and states the specific objectives of the review.
2. Invitees (that is, reviewers) study the material in advance and prepare a list of appropriate questions.
3. Management reviews the advance material and the list of invitees and appoints a moderator to assure that the meeting takes place in an effective manner.
4. The meeting takes place. The moderator assures that the emphasis is on problem detection and not on problem resolution or solution.

The moderator, who is responsible to a large extent for the productivity of the meeting, follows certain specific procedures. There are six steps in an effective meeting:

1. Reviewers comment on the material received and express concern for weaknesses of the work.
2. The programmer gives a brief tutorial presentation on the work performed.
3. The programmer conducts a step-by-step walk-through of the history and rationale of the work.
4. The reviewers comment again in light of the new information received.
5. During the meeting the moderator keeps an "action list" which is distributed at the end of the meeting. This provides final advice and guidance for the programmer on how to improve the work.
6. After the meeting the programmer continues to work on the project, and as the issues and weaknesses of the work are resolved the reviewers are notified on specifics.

Advantages of structured walk-throughs The fundamental advantage again is the increased productivity and effectiveness of the programmers. Specifically, the following five advantages can be listed for structured walk-throughs:

1. Provides broad perspective to the programmer; suggests new techniques and approaches.
2. Detects and removes errors early in the development cycle.
3. Improves communication among team members.
4. Promotes team effort without inhibiting personal excellence.
5. Creates a problem-solving, not a fault-finding environment.

SUMMARY

1. Programming is both an art and a science. It requires creativity and discipline, technical knowledge and problem-solving ability, individual excellence and teamwork.
2. The principle of hierarchical structures of complex systems provides technical guidance to the programmer.
3. Programming starts with broad system specifications and results in computer programs and documentation.
4. The principal steps in programming are: (1) program planning, (2) programming, (3) coding, (4) testing, (5) documentation, and (6) system operation, maintenance, and modification.
5. Flowcharting is one of the most important technical tools of the systems analyst and computer programmer.
6. System flowcharts deal with IN-PROCESS-OUT modules. Program flowcharts describe each programming step in the process part of the module.
7. Flowcharts form a *Hierarchy of In-Process-Out* (HIPO)

modules. Step-by-step "blowing up" of parts of the flowchart proceeds from the top-level system chart to the bottom-level program chart.

8. Layout and grid charts provide a systematic approach to the establishment of the relationship between data items and records.

9. Decision tables can supplement or replace flowcharts for data processing problems involving many conditions, decisions, and actions.

10. Documentation is an indispensable product of the programmer and systems analyst.

11. Programmers' productivity is judged by: (1) achievement of results, (2) time and cost necessary to develop the program, (3) time and cost necessary to maintain and modify the program, (4) efficiency of the program when run on the computer.

12. The principle of balance between technological and psychological aspects of programming provides guidance to the management of programming efforts.

13. The chief programmer team organization leads to high productivity for programmers without impeding their creativity.

14. Structured walk-throughs provide a perspective to the programmer and an environment conducive to efficient and error-free program development.

KEY WORDS AND PHRASES

blowing up a flowchart: replacing a box in a flowchart by a flowchart consisting of several boxes.

bug: a mistake or malfunction.

condition stub: heading on a decision table under which the conditions of the problem are listed.

decision stub: heading on a decision table under which the answers to or actions in a problem are listed.

decision table: a table of all contingencies relating to the definition, analysis, and solution of a problem.

documentation: the result of creating, collecting, organizing, storing, and communicating of information necessary to the use of programs and the computer.

grid chart: tabular representation of the relationship between data items, programs, and reports.

layout chart: pertaining to the detailed specifications for data in records.

operating instructions: instructions for the computer operator.

program flowchart: flowchart for a computer program.

run manual: a document containing all the operating instructions for the computer and programs.

syntax: (1) the structure of expressions in a language, (2) the rules governing the structure of a language.

system flowchart: flowchart pertaining to a data processing system.

DISCUSSION QUESTIONS

1. Report on your collection of newspaper, magazine, and television items, and cartoons, jokes, and anecdotes.

2. Define and explain in your own words: *syntax* and *structure*. Give examples. Compare your definitions with those in your dictionary and explain deviations, if any.[2]

3. Explain the difference between art and science, and how it applies to data processing.

4. What is the purpose of *system flowcharts?* How do they compare with *program flowcharts?* Give illustrations.

5. Design a system flowchart for: (*a*) getting up in the morning, (*b*) fixing a flat tire, (*c*) going to the barber for a haircut.

6. Explain the structure of: (*a*) offices in a modern skyscraper, (*b*) maps of the world, (*c*) the universe, starting from electrons and ascending to the Milky Way.

7. Suppose you are given the assignment of writing an essay on the effective organization of programmers. Describe and contrast a *bottom-up* and a *top-down* approach.

8. Describe and contrast the bottom-up and top-down approaches in computer programming. Give advantages and benefits.

9. Suppose you are in charge of a programming group. Prepare a 200-word directive to instruct your programmer to use the top-down approach.

10. Describe the steps involved in preparing a computer program.

11. Describe system analysis and design. Show how it relates to program preparation.

12. Describe program planning. Why is it important?

13. Describe program testing and debugging. Why do you think this phase of program preparation might be particularly frustrating?

14. Define and explain in your own words: *debugging, bug, technical* and *operational documentation, operating instructions.* Give examples. Compare your definitions with those in your dictionary and explain differences, if any.

15. Describe the importance of *documentation.* Is it easy or difficult to motivate people to prepare documentation? Give your reasons.

16. Describe system operation and maintenance.

---

[2] In all word problems you need make comparisons only if the word or phrase is in your dictionary.

17. Describe and illustrate the various flowchart symbols or boxes.
18. What is meant by *blowing up* a flowchart? Define and explain the word *hierarchy*.
19. Go to your library or any other source and find a: (*a*) program flowchart, (*b*) system flowchart. Copy the chart and describe in your own words the process described by the charts.
20. Describe the meaning of "HIPO." Illustrate with the case study of invoice preparation.
21. Explain and contrast the direct-access and sequential approaches.
22. Describe *layout chart* and *grid chart*.
23. Describe *decision tables,* including their use, advantages, and disadvantages. Give the meaning of *condition stub* and *decision stub*.
24. Rework Figure 5.30 under the assumption that there are $2 seats available.
25. The Soldi Department Store responds in one of three ways to mail orders: (*a*) ships the item ordered, (*b*) rejects the order, or (*c*) back orders. The conditions of the problem are: (*a*) customer's credit is OK, (*b*) quantity ordered is less than or equal to order limit, and (*c*) quantity ordered is less than or equal to quantity on hand. Prepare a decision table.
26. The SWB Airlines responds in one of the following four ways to requests for tickets: (*a*) issues a first-class ticket, (*b*) issues a tourist ticket, (*c*) places customer on a first-class waiting list, or (*d*) places customer on a tourist waiting list. The conditions of the problem are: (*a*) first-class ticket is requested, (*b*) tourist-class ticket is requested, (*c*) first-class seats are available, (*d*) tourist-class seats are available, (*e*) alternate class seats are available. Prepare a decision table.
27. How does economics apply to programming? Why is it important?
28. Discuss the human issues of programming, both psychological and sociological.
29. Describe the organizational approach of using chief programmer teams. What are the advantages?
30. Describe the management concept of structured walk-throughs. What are the advantages?
31. Review and update your Personal Summary of this course (see Exercise 28, Chapter 1).

6

Data representation

The fact that all data in a computer is represented by bit strings was introduced in Chapter 4. When external data is transmitted to the computer it must first be converted into internal data representation[1] (Figure 6.1), so the computer can process the data. When the processing is done the data must be converted back to external data representation, so meaningful answers can be presented to users.

Unless you have a clear understanding of how data is represented internally, computerized data processing will remain a mystery. Therefore this chapter will show how bit strings inside the computer can represent both numeric and nonnumeric data.

NUMBER SYSTEMS

First we briefly review the decimal number system. You may wonder why it is necessary to devote time to the decimal number system since you know how to add, subtract, multiply, and divide. You will find, however, that a better understanding of the decimal number system will help you understand the number systems used by computers.

What is the meaning of the decimal number 62,082? Imagine the string of decimal digits 6, 2, 0, 8, and 2 as representing weights,

[1] Terms printed in color are defined at the end of the chapter.

Note: Much of this chapter can be omitted without loss of continuity.

FIGURE 6.1
Externally coded
data serves for
input, output, and
data transmission;
internally coded
data for
processing
operations.

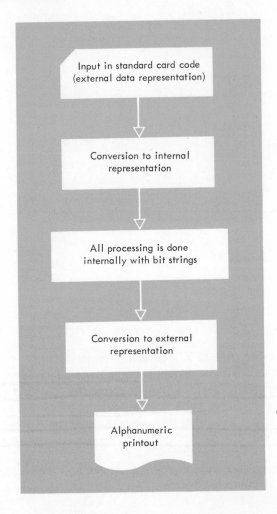

FIGURE 6.1
Externally coded data serves for input, output, and data transmission; internally coded data for processing operations.

as shown in **Figure 6.2.** The digit 6 is in the fifth place (counting from the right) and has a **place value** of 10,000 pounds. Thus the digit 6 in the fifth place represents six 10,000-pound weights, or 60,000 pounds, as shown in the lower left-hand corner of Figure 6.2.

The second digit from the left, the 2 in the fourth place from the right represents 1,000-pound weights: the total is 2,000 pounds. The digit 0, in the third place, represents 100-pound weights: but we don't use any of them. The digit 8, in the second place, represents 10-pound weights: the total is 80 pounds. The digit 2, in the first place, represents 1-pound weights: the total is 2 pounds.

As shown in the lower right-hand corner of Figure 6.2, this example has a total of 62,082 pounds of weight. Observe that the weights in the decimal number system are 1, 10, 100, 1,000, 10,000,

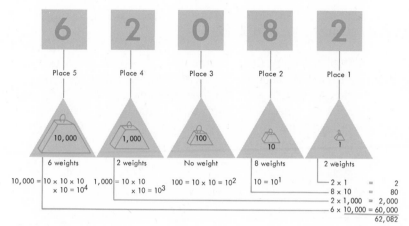

FIGURE 6.2 The meaning of decimal numbers. Each digit has a *place* value or weight attached. The weights in pounds (from right to left) — 1, 10, 100, 1,000, 10,000 — are powers of 10.

and so on. These weights represent powers of 10. (For example, the fourth power of 10, or 10^4 means that 10 must be multiplied by itself four times: $10 \times 10 \times 10 \times 10$.)

The decimal number system is based on the number 10; that is, the base (radix) of the decimal number system is 10. To simplify matters, we have not discussed the decimal point and decimal fractions such as 2.51 or 0.01.

You may wonder why we use the base 10. The Egyptians used the base 60 and some primitive tribes used the base 20. It is believed that we use the base 10 because we have 10 fingers. One could use almost any number for the base, and there have been many suggestions to change from the decimal number system to some other system. Dr. John von Neumann proposed in 1945 that computers use the binary number system.

THE BINARY NUMBER SYSTEM

Figure 6.3 illustrates the binary number 10011001. The digits in a binary number are either 1 or 0, that is, the digits are bits (binary digits). The weights are powers of 2: there is 1, of course, and then 2, 4, 8, 16, 32, 64, 128, and so on. For example, in Figure 6.3 observe that the first digit of the binary number is in the eighth place (from the right) and represents the weight of 128 pounds. To determine the decimal value or decimal equivalent of this binary number, we have to take one of these 128-pound weights. We have nothing in the seventh and sixth places, but we have a 16-pound weight in the fifth place. We also have an 8-pound weight in the fourth place, and finally a 1-pound weight in the first place. This means, as shown in the lower right corner of Figure 6.3, that we have a total of 153 pounds. Thus the decimal equivalent of the binary number 10011001 is 153.

The upper part of Figure 6.3 shows how the binary number is represented internally in core storage. The magnetic cores in the eighth, fifth, fourth, and first places are magnetized in one direction, and in the seventh, sixth, third, and second places in the other direction. This makes internal representation of (true) binary numbers very simple.

FIGURE 6.3 The meaning of binary numbers. Each bit has a place value or weight attached. The weights in pounds (from right to left): $2 \times 1 = 2$; $2 \times 2 = 4$; $2 \times 4 = 8$; $2 \times 8 = 16$; $2 \times 16 = 32$; $2 \times 32 = 64$; $2 \times 64 = 128$; $2 \times 128 = 256$; and so on.

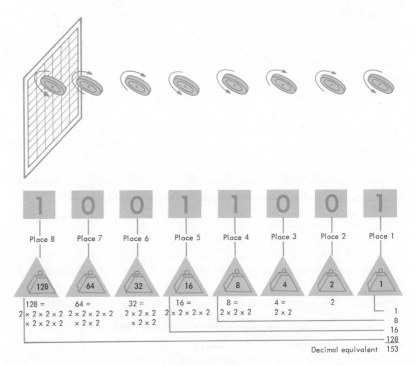

In Figure 6.4, the first column gives a sample of decimal numbers, and the second column gives the binary representation of the decimal numbers. (The third column gives the hexadecimal representation, as discussed below.) By adding the appropriate weights you should have no difficulty in converting any of the binary numbers into decimal equivalents.

Converting a decimal into a binary number

To convert a decimal into a binary number it is first necessary to find the appropriate weights to use. The method can be illustrated with a simple story.

John Richards works in a shipping firm and wants to weigh himself. The scale is not a spring scale but one which uses weights, and the weights available are of the following poundage: 1, 2, 4, 8, 16, 32, 64, 128, 256, 512, 1,024. How should he proceed to weigh himself?

Decimal (base 10)	Binary (base 2)	Hexadecimal (base 16)
0	0	0
1	1	1
2	10	2
3	11	3
4	100	4
5	101	5
6	110	6
7	111	7
8	1000	8
9	1001	9
10	1010	A
11	1011	B
12	1100	C
13	1101	D
14	1110	E
15	1111	F
16	10000	10
17	10001	11
18	10010	12
19	10011	13
20	10100	14
30	11110	1E
40	101000	28
50	110010	32
60	111100	3C
70	1000110	46
80	1010000	50
90	1011010	5A
100	1100100	64

FIGURE 6.4 Comparison of the decimal, binary, and hexadecimal number systems.

Richards has not the vaguest idea of how much he weighs. First he tries the 1,024-pound weight and finds that it is too heavy. So he tries the 512-pound weight and the 256-pound weight, without success. The fourth time he tries the 128-pound weight and discovers that he weighs more than this. So he leaves the 128-pound weight on the scale and adds the 64-pound weight. But this is too much, so he takes off the 64 and adds the 32. This is still too much, so he takes off the 32 and adds the 16. Now he finds that it is not enough, so he leaves the 16 and adds the 8. He discovers that it is still not enough, so he leaves the 8 and adds the 4. This is too much, so he removes the 4 and tries the 2. Still too much, so he takes it off and puts on the 1-pound weight. Now he finds that he has hit upon his exact weight.

Richards now has the following weights on the scale: 128, 16, 8, and 1. Thus he weighs $128 + 16 + 8 + 1 = 153$ pounds. Now look again at Figure 6.3. This weight, the decimal number 153, converts into the binary number 10011001. All that is necessary is to write a 1 when he uses a weight, and a 0 when he does not.

Using the same example, a more formal way to convert this decimal number into a binary number is given in the flowchart of Figure 6.5. Figure 6.6 provides a step-by-step record for converting the decimal number 153.

The first input to the flowchart is the largest WEIGHT to be used in the conversion process, 1,024. Then in Box 2 we read in the DECIMAL NUMBER (153). In Box 3 we introduce a new variable, REMAINDER, and we set its value to the DECIMAL NUMBER (153). In Box 4 we try whether WEIGHT should be used or not.

In Figure 6.6, in the furthest right column of cycle 1, we divide 1,024 into 153. Of course the quotient is 0, and the remainder is 153. So in Box 5 we print the digit 0. The test in Box 6 results in NO, and so in Box 7 we halve the weight (get 512 which we write in the WEIGHT column) and go back to Box 3.

In Cycle 2 we try the weight 512 and in Cycle 3 the weight 256. Neither of these weights is required, so the quotients are 0.

In Cycle 4 we try the weight 128. Now the quotient is 1 and the remainder is 25. So we obtain the first (nonzero) digit of our binary number.

As you can see in the figure, we get 0s in Cycles 5 and 6, and 1s in Cycles 7 and 8. Then again Cycles 9 and 10 give 0s, and finally in Cycle 11 we get the last digit, the 1 of our binary number. Observe also that here the test results in YES, consequently the process terminates.

Advantages and disadvantages of the binary number system

The big advantage of the true binary system is that internal representation is simple and efficient. Binary arithmetic (not covered here) is simple, and consequently circuitry for binary arithmetic is less expensive. Therefore, in scientific and engineering computation, where there is a great deal of computation involved, the true

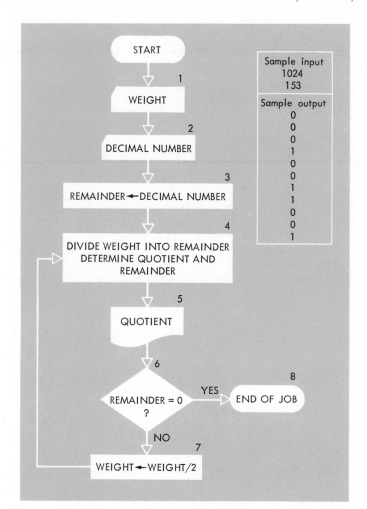

FIGURE 6.5
Flowchart for
converting a
decimal number
into binary.
Sample input: 153;
sample output:
00010011001
(disregard the
leading zeros).

binary number system (or the hexadecimal system, discussed below) is used.

There is, however, one very important disadvantage to the true binary number system. In business we work in decimal fractions, in tenths, hundredths, thousandths, and so on. But the true binary number system works in fractions like $1/2$, $1/4$, $1/8$, $1/16$, and so on. Consequently, when a decimal fraction is expressed as a binary fraction, there may be a small error called a conversion error. For example, when adding the fractions 0.10 and 1.90 in binary you may get an answer of 1.99999 and not 2. In scientific computation this makes no difference, as the answer is accurate enough, but when working with dollars and cents we want absolute precision. So in data processing the binary number system as discussed is rarely used.

Box	Weight	Decimal number	Quotient	Remainder	Print	Test result	Division
1	1,024						
2		153					
3				153			
Cycle 1 4			0	153			0
5					0		$1024\overline{)153}$
6						No	$\underline{0}$
7	512						153
Cycle 2 4			0	153			0
5					0		$512\overline{)153}$
6						No	$\underline{0}$
7	256						153
Cycle 3 4			0	153			0
5					0		$256\overline{)153}$
6						No	$\underline{0}$
7	128						153
Cycle 4 4			1	25			1
5					1		$128\overline{)153}$
6						No	$\underline{128}$
7	64						25
Cycle 5 4			0	25			0
5					0		$64\overline{)25}$
6						No	$\underline{0}$
7	32						25
Cycle 6 4			0	25			0
5					0		$32\overline{)25}$
6						No	$\underline{0}$
7	16						25

FIGURE 6.6
Step-by-step record
for converting
decimal number
153 to binary.
Richards finds
that he weighs
10011001 pounds.

Box	Weight	Decimal number	Quotient	Remainder	Print	Test result	Division
Cycle 7 4 5 6 7	8		1	9	1	No	1 16)25 16 9
Cycle 8 4 5 6 7	4		1	1	1	No	1 8)9 8 1
Cycle 9 4 5 6 7	2		0	1	0	No	0 4)1 0 1
Cycle 10 4 5 6 7	1		0	1	0	No	0 2)1 0 1
Cycle 11 4 5 6 7			1 Stop	0	1	Yes	1 1)1 1 0

FIGURE 6.6
(continued)

The hexadecimal number system

In the hexadecimal number system the base is 16, so the weights to be used are 1, 16, 16 × 16 = 256, 16 × 16 × 16 = 4,096, and so on.

What should we use for digits in a hexadecimal number? Of course we will use 0, 1, 2, 3, 4, 5, 6, 7, 8, and 9. But what about 10, 11, 12, 13, 14, and 15? We need new symbols to designate, for example, the number of 15-pound weights we wish to use. Column 1 of Figure 6.4, in which the hexadecimal number system is illustrated, shows that the decimal number 10 is designated by an A, 11 by B, 12 by C, 13 by D, 14 by E, and 15 by F. For example, in the hexadecimal number system, C means that you must use 12 weights.

The example below shows how the hexadecimal number 2C7 is converted into a decimal number:

$$2C7$$
$$7 \times 1 = 7$$
$$12 \times 16 = 192$$
$$2 \times 256 = \underline{512}$$
$$711$$

Further examples of hexadecimal numbers are given in Figure 6.4, Column 3.

Observe that hexadecimal numbers can be directly converted into binary numbers by changing each hexadecimal digit into a four-digit binary number. For example:

2	C	7	Hexadecimal number
0010	1100	0111	Binary number

Here we simply converted the hexadecimal digit 2 into the binary number 0010, the hexadecimal digit C into the binary number 1100, and the hexadecimal digit 7 into the binary number 0111.

Conversely, we can directly translate a binary number into a hexadecimal number by converting each four-digit binary number into the hexadecimal equivalent. For example:

0010	1100	0111	Binary number
2	C	7	Hexadecimal number

How do we convert a decimal into a hexadecimal number? We can use the method described in the flowchart of Figure 6.5, except we must read in the largest hexadecimal weight in Box 1, and in Box 7 we must divide by 16.

As an example, using the method of the flowchart in Figure 6.5, we can convert the decimal number 1,242 into a hexadecimal number.

$$4 = \text{QUOTIENT} = \boxed{4}$$

Step 1 $256\,)\,\overline{1,242}$ = DECIMAL NUMBER
$$\underline{1,024}$$
$$218 = \text{REMAINDER}$$

$$13 = QUOTIENT = \boxed{D}$$

Step 2   16) 218
                16
                .58
                48
               10 = REMAINDER

$$10 = QUOTIENT = \boxed{A}$$

Step 3   1) 10
               10
               0 = REMAINDER

Final answer: the hexadecimal number 4DA.

BINARY CODED DECIMAL SYSTEMS

So far we have discussed only the coding of numeric data. Now we will consider the coding of both numeric and nonnumeric data.

The four-bit BCD system

The BCD (Binary Coded Decimal) system is used to encode numeric data, decimal digit by decimal digit. Figure 6.7 reproduces (from Figure 6.4) the true binary number representation of the decimal numbers from 0 to 9. In the four-bit BCD system each digit of a decimal number is encoded by using the four bits shown in Figure 6.7. Thus the decimal number 153 is encoded as:

1	5	3	Decimal
0001	0101	0011	Four-bit BCD

(But the true binary form is 10011001.)

Observe that conversion from decimal to four-bit BCD or vice versa is quite simple, as each digit is individually encoded.

If you compare the four-bit BCD system with the true binary number system you observe that in the four-bit BCD system you need many more bits to represent a number. But it can be shown that in the four-bit BCD system decimal fractions are converted precisely, digit by digit, without conversion error. Thus, if you add .10 and 1.90 you will get 2.00. This is the principal reason that in data processing applications the four-bit BCD system is preferred to binary representation.

Could you represent characters in the four-bit BCD system? So long as only four bits are used, there are only 16 possibilities. Ten

FIGURE 6.7 Four-
bit BCD repre-
sentation of
numbers. Each
digit is encoded
individually.

	Four-bit BCD system			
	Place values			
Decimal equivalent	8	4	2	1
0	0	0	0	0
1	0	0	0	1
2	0	0	1	0
3	0	0	1	1
4	0	1	0	0
5	0	1	0	1
6	0	1	1	0
7	0	1	1	1
8	1	0	0	0
9	1	0	0	1

of these are taken for the digits, so there are only six more combinations left. This is clearly not enough to represent alphabetic and other symbols.

The eight-bit EBCDIC system

Figure 6.8 illustrates how the four-bit BCD system was expanded to the eight-bit EBCDIC (Extended Binary Coded Decimal Interchange Code) system.

This last system has four numeric bits and four zone bits. Now there are 256 possibilities, which is more than adequate to meet modern data processing needs. Figure 6.9 illustrates how digits and

FIGURE 6.8
Comparison of the
four-bit BCD and
eight-bit (one
byte) EBCDIC
systems.

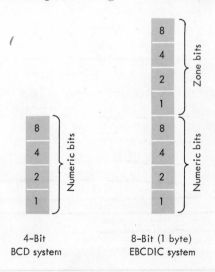

Character	Standard punched card code	EBCDIC		ASCII	
		Binary	Hexa-decimal	Binary	Hexa-decimal
0	0	1111 0000	F0	0101 0000	50
1	1	1111 0001	F1	0101 0001	51
2	2	1111 0010	F2	0101 0010	52
3	3	1111 0011	F3	0101 0011	53
4	4	1111 0100	F4	0101 0100	54
5	5	1111 0101	F5	0101 0101	55
6	6	1111 0110	F6	0101 0110	56
7	7	1111 0111	F7	0101 0111	57
8	8	1111 1000	F8	0101 1000	58
9	9	1111 1001	F9	0101 1001	59
A	12–1	1100 0001	C1	1010 0001	A1
B	12–2	1100 0010	C2	1010 0010	A2
C	12–3	1100 0011	C3	1010 0011	A3
D	12–4	1100 0100	C4	1010 0100	A4
E	12–5	1100 0101	C5	1010 0101	A5
F	12–6	1100 0110	C6	1010 0110	A6
G	12–7	1100 0111	C7	1010 0111	A7
H	12–8	1100 1000	C8	1010 1000	A8
I	12–9	1100 1001	C9	1010 1001	A9
J	11–1	1101 0001	D1	1010 1010	AA
K	11–2	1101 0010	D2	1010 1011	AB
L	11–3	1101 0011	D3	1010 1100	AC
M	11–4	1101 0100	D4	1010 1101	AD
N	11–5	1101 0101	D5	1010 1110	AE
O	11–6	1101 0110	D6	1010 1111	AF
P	11–7	1101 0111	D7	1011 0000	B0
Q	11–8	1101 1000	D8	1011 0001	B1
R	11–9	1101 1001	D9	1011 0010	B2
S	0–2	1110 0010	E2	1011 0011	B3
T	0–3	1110 0011	E3	1011 0100	B4
U	0–4	1110 0100	E4	1011 0101	B5
V	0–5	1110 0101	E5	1011 0110	B6
W	0–6	1110 0110	E6	1011 0111	B7
X	0–7	1110 0111	E7	1011 1000	B8
Y	0–8	1110 1000	E8	1011 1001	B9
Z	0–9	1110 1001	E9	1011 1010	BA

FIGURE 6.9 The 8-bit (1 byte) EBCDIC and the 8-bit ASCII systems (standard punched card code is also shown).

uppercase characters are encoded in the eight-bit EBCDIC system. (Encoding of lowercase characters is not shown.) Figure 6.10 shows special characters.

In internal storage of most modern data processing systems, eight bits are handled as a unit, a byte.

Figure 6.9 also shows how this eight-bit code can be translated

FIGURE 6.10
Special characters
in EBCDIC.

Character	EBCDIC		
	Binary		Hexa-decimal
¢	0100	1010	4A
•	0100	1011	4B
<	0100	1100	4C
(	0100	1101	4D
+	0100	1110	4E
|	0100	1111	4F
!	0101	1010	5A
$	0101	1011	5B
*	0101	1100	5C
)	0101	1101	5D
;	0101	1110	5E
¬	0101	1110	5F
blank	0110	1010	6A
,	0110	1011	6B
%	0110	1100	6C
—	0110	1101	6D
>	0110	1110	6E
?	0110	1111	6F
:	0111	1010	7A
#	0111	1011	7B
@	0111	1100	7C
/	0111	1101	7D
=	0111	1110	7E
"	0111	1111	7F

into hexadecimal form to facilitate reading the code. Consider, for example, the letter K, which is encoded with the zone bits 1101 and numeric bits 0010. The zone bits can be represented by the hexadecimal digit D, and the numeric bits 0010 by the digit 2. Thus the eight-bit code for K can be represented as the hexadecimal number D2.

The ASCII system

Many computer manufacturers use the ASCII (American Standard Code for Information Interchange) eight-bit system, also known as the USCII, instead of the EBCDIC system. This system is illustrated in Figure 6.9 to the right of the heavy vertical line. The last column gives the hexadecimal form of the code. For the letter K, the zone bits are 1010, which is A in the hexadecimal system. The numeric bits are 1011, which stands for the hexadecimal digit B. Thus the code for the letter K in hexadecimal ASCII is AB.

SUMMARY

1. External data representation must be distinguished from internal data representation.
2. The decimal number system uses the base 10, the binary system, 2, and the hexadecimal system, 16.
3. The most commonly used internal data representations are:
   a. The (true) binary number system.
   b. The hexadecimal number system.
   c. The eight-bit (one byte) EBCDIC system.
   d. The eight-bit ASCII system.
   (See Figure 6.11 for examples.)

FIGURE 6.11
Summary and
examples for
coding systems.

Internal data representation		External form	Examples	
			Coded form	
True number systems	Binary	156	1001 1100	
	Hexadecimal	156	9C	
Binary coded systems	Four-bit BCD	156	0001 0101 0110	
	Eight-bit EBCDIC	156	1111 0001 1111 0101 1111 0110	
	Eight-bit EBCDIC	A	1100 0001	
	Eight-bit ASCII	156	0101 0001 0101 0101 0101 0110	
	Eight-bit ASCII	A	1010 0001	

KEY CONCEPTS AND WORDS

ASCII (American Standard Code for Information Interchange): representation of data in which each individual character is represented by a pattern of eight bits or one byte (see Figure 6.11 for examples).

base: base of the decimal system is 10, of the binary system is 2, of the hexadecimal system is 16, etc. See *radix.*

BCD: See *binary coded decimal.*

binary coded decimal: representation of numbers and symbols in which each individual decimal digit is represented by a pattern of four bits (see Figure 6.11 for examples).

binary number (true or straight binary): a number using 2 as the base (radix).

code: a system of symbols for representing data.

decimal number: a number using 10 as the base (radix).

EBCDIC: see *extended binary coded decimal interchange.*

extended binary coded decimal interchange: representation of data in which each individual character is represented by a pattern of eight bits or one byte (see Figure 6.11 for examples).

external data representation: data representation in input, output, and other media outside the computer.

internal data representation: data representation in storage, registers, and other media inside the computer.

hexadecimal number: a number using 16 as the base (radix).

place value: counting from right to left, the place values (*a*) in a decimal number are 1, 10, 100, 1,000, etc., (*b*) in a binary number are 1, 2, 4, 8, 16, etc., (*c*) in a hexadecimal number are 1, 16, 256, etc.

radix: same as *base*.

DISCUSSION QUESTIONS AND EXERCISES

1. Report on your collection of newspaper, magazine, and television items and cartoons, jokes, and anecdotes.

2. Define and explain in your own words: *external* and *internal data representation, decimal number, place value, binary number, hexadecimal number, base, radix.* Give examples. Compare your definitions with those in your dictionary and explain differences, if any.[2]

3. What are the decimal values of the following numbers:

Numbers		Base
10	11	2
15	30	10
53	23	60
24	18	16
21	31	20
22	35	8

4. Convert the following binary numbers into decimal numbers:

101	1011	1111	1000	10010
10101	101011	111111	10000000	1100101

5. Convert the following decimal numbers into true binary numbers:

51   65   91   28   37   48   77   65

6. Convert the following hexadecimal numbers into decimal numbers:

5C   3F   BB   AA   F1   2E   EB   BF   3F   8B

7. Convert the following decimal numbers into hexadecimal numbers:

75   42   127   88   112   48   16   76   100   113

8. Write a column of the decimal numbers 1 to 63 in binary form.

9. Write a column of the decimal numbers 64 to 127 in binary form.

10. Add to Exercise 8, in a third column, the hexadecimal forms of the numbers.

11. In a third column add to Exercise 9 the hexadecimal forms of the numbers.

---

[2] In all word problems you need make comparisons only if the word or phrase is in your dictionary.

12. Define and explain in your own words: *binary coded decimal, extended binary coded decimal interchange code (EBCDIC), ASCII code.* Give examples. Compare your definitions with those in your dictionary and explain differences, if any.

13. Convert the following decimal numbers into four-bit BCD numbers:

     75 42 127 88 67 81

14. Convert the following four-bit BCD coded numbers into decimal numbers:

     0101 0001   0110 0101   1001 0001

15. What is the difference between the true binary representation of numbers and binary coded decimal representation?

16. Explain the difference between internal and external data representation. Give illustrations.

17. Explain and illustrate the eight-bit EBCDIC and ASCII systems.

18. Convert the following words into the (*a*) eight-bit EBCDIC system, (*b*) eight-bit ASCII system:

     DOG HAT 7MZ S2L

    Show also the hexadecimal form.

19. Review and update your Personal Summary of this course (see Exercise 28, Chapter 1). Also present your interim summary covering the first five chapters.

7

Input/output, peripherals, and communications

Following the overview of computer systems and introduction to the principles of programming development presented in preceding chapters, this and the following chapter will concentrate on computer hardware. In specifying what a user, programmer, systems analyst or data processing professional needs to know about hardware, a comparison with the driver of a car may be helpful.

Suppose you find that when you turn the ignition key of your car the motor turns over but the needle on the gas tank indicator is at empty. You will be justified in assuming that there is nothing wrong with the battery, but the car needs gas. On the other hand, if the motor does not turn over and the lights do not go on, you assume that something is wrong with your battery. The point is that you need to know something about the hardware, the machinery under the hood of the car. But there is a limit; you do not need to know technical details such as how the carburetor or the combustion chamber works.

A computer is a complicated machine. You need to know the functions of the various hardware units and how they operate, but you need not know the technological details. For example, knowledge of the mechanical details of high-speed printers or the construction of electronic circuits is not required, but you do need to know what functions a high-speed printer performs.

It is convenient to divide computer hardware into (1) input/output and peripheral units, (2) communication equipment, and

(3) the central processing unit (CPU). This chapter deals with the first two categories and Chapter 8 with the CPU.

The best central processing unit is useless without the appropriate input/output, auxiliary devices, and communication system to tie the units of the computer system together. In fact, today more dollars are spent on peripherals than on CPUs. If a computer system is to be efficient, all these devices must be utilized in the best manner, and the data processing professional and the user must have adequate knowledge of hardware so all resources of the system are allocated in the best way. Assuring this is the principal guideline in learning about computer hardware.

OVERVIEW OF INPUT/OUTPUT AND PERIPHERALS

FIGURE 7.1 Overview of input/output devices and media.

Figure 7.1 shows the input/output and peripheral units grouped according to the principal media used: paper, magnetic, key driven,

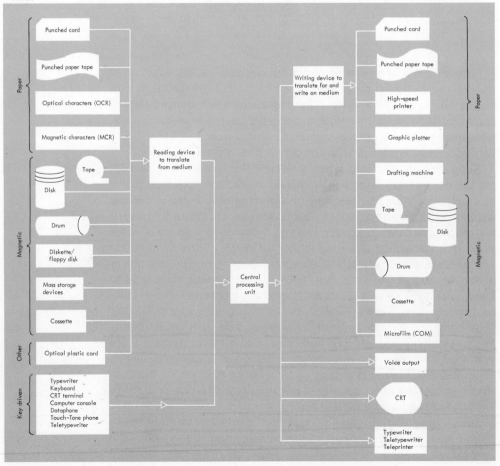

FIGURE 7.2 Summary of performance and applications of input/output devices.

Equipment category	Primary functions	Typical application areas	Data media	
			Input	Output
Keyboard	Key data in card, paper tape, magnetic tape, disk, cassette, etc.	Extensive	Keyboard	Printed document, punched card and paper tape, magnetic tape, disk, cassette
Teletypewriters and tele-printers	Data transmission over narrow or voice band lines	Online communications	Keyboard Punched paper tape	Hard copy Punched paper tape Direct signals to computer
Cathode-ray tube (CRT) devices	Displays via CRT; data received from remote computer or keyboard entry; transmits to computer for storage or other media output	All-embracing	Keyboard Punched paper tape Signals from computer	Video display Punched paper tape Direct signals to computer
Optical character readers (OCR)	Direct reading of printed or handwritten documents	Postal sorting Bank checks Credit cards Billing cards Ticket sales	Printed paper document Printed card Printed journal tape	Punched card Punched paper tape Magnetic tape, disk, cassette Direct signals to computer
Magnetic ink character readers (MICR)	Direct reading of magnetic ink characters or magnetic marks	Banking industry Credit cards Ticketing systems Retail merchandising	Magnetic ink document Magnetic mark card	Punched card Punched paper tape Magnetic tape
Touch-Tone telephone devices	Translate and record data from a Touch-Tone telephone	Extensive	Plastic card Manual Cash register Punched paper tape	Direct signals to computer Magnetic tape, disk, punched paper tape

Equipment category	Data transfer rate	Data volume	Major advantages	Major disadvantages
Keyboard	Up to 15.4 characters/second	Transfer rate limited	Low cost	Low speed
Teletypewriters and tele-printers	5–400 characters/second	Transfer rate limited	Low cost	Low speed
CRT devices	110–40,000 bits/second	Transfer rate limited	Convenient	Limited display capacity
Optical character readers (OCR)	110–2,400 characters/second	180–1,800 documents/minute	No intermediate data preparation required Direct online input	High initial cost Multiple font costs Limitations on input and character sets High volume required
Magnetic ink character readers (MICR)	700–3,200 characters/second	180–1,800 documents/minute	High reliability of reading Reduces forgery possibility	Document must be preprinted and specially prepared Limited character set
Touch-Tone telephone devices	0–2,400 bits/second	Transfer rate limited	Real-time applications Use of common carrier facilities Good low-speed data transmission	Special optional equipment required Limited throughput

FIGURE 7.2
(*continued*)

and other. Observe that the data must be read first in its external form by the appropriate reading device. Then the data must be converted into internal representation to be entered into the computer.

After the data is processed, it must be converted into external representation and transmitted to the writing device. Then the data is presented to the user.

Note the triple role of such media (and devices) as punched cards, magnetic tapes, and disks. These media and devices can be used for input, output, and secondary storage. The two parts of Figure 7.2 summarize the most commonly used devices, their primary functions, the medium used, the data transfer rate (the rate that data can be read or written), and the advantages and disadvantages. Figure 7.3 presents summary information for secondary storage devices. In addition to data transfer rates, the access time (time required to store or retrieve data in a random manner) is given.

As Figure 7.4 shows, for remote processing, data can be transferred at low, intermediate, or high rates between a variety of input/output devices or the computer. The range of respective transmission rates[1] is about 30, 200–400, and 4,000 or more characters per second.

If remote processing is offline, data is transmitted from one peripheral unit to another, as from CRT input to a magnetic tape drive. For online processing, data is directly transmitted under the control of the computer to the CPU.

The use and performance of the most commonly used peripheral media and devices is discussed in the sections below.

PUNCHED CARDS

The punched card is the oldest and most commonly used peripheral medium. It serves a triple purpose:

1. Data can be entered into the computer system.
2. Data can be punched into cards as an output.
3. Punched cards can also be used as an offline, secondary storage medium.

The card reader

Data is entered on cards by the manually operated keypunch machine. Once the data is punched into the cards, the deck is stacked into the hopper of the card reader (Figure 7.5). From the card hopper the cards are moved to the card-feed mechanism (Figure 7.6) past two brush-type or photocell-type reading stations. The brushes or photocells sense the presence or absence of the holes punched into the card and send electric signals to the computer. These signals, which form the external representation of data, are in turn converted by the computer into internal data representation.

Observe the two reading stations in the figure. To avoid errors the signals are compared from the two stations and, if they are not

---

[1] Terms printed in color are defined at the end of the chapter.

Device	Media	Primary storage application	Typical range of storage capacity	Range of transfer rates — thousands of characters per second	Primary advantages	Primary limitations	Typical range of access time
Magnetic core unit	Magnetic core	Internal	From thousands to a million characters	250–2,000	Very fast Random access	Very expensive	.5–40 microseconds
Tape drive	Magnetic tape	Data files	1–20 million characters/tape	15–320	Inexpensive Fast transfer rate	Only sequential access	Only sequential access
Disk pack	Magnetic disk	Data files	2–100 million characters/pack	100–225	Large capacity Random access	Expensive	20–200 milliseconds
Drum storage unit	Magnetic drum	Tables and programs	1–4 million characters/drum	275–1,200	Relatively fast access time	Relatively expensive	10–100 milliseconds
Mass storage devices	Magnetic media	Data files	100 million to 500 billion characters/unit	25–45	Large capacity Inexpensive	Slow access time	.2 to several seconds
Diskette/ floppy disk	Magnetic disk	Data programs	200,000– 500,000 characters/unit	10	Inexpensive	Only sequential access	Only sequential access
Cassette cartridge	Magnetic tape	Data programs	1–2 million characters/unit	3–5	Inexpensive	Only sequential access	Only sequential access

FIGURE 7.3 Summary of performance of secondary storage devices.

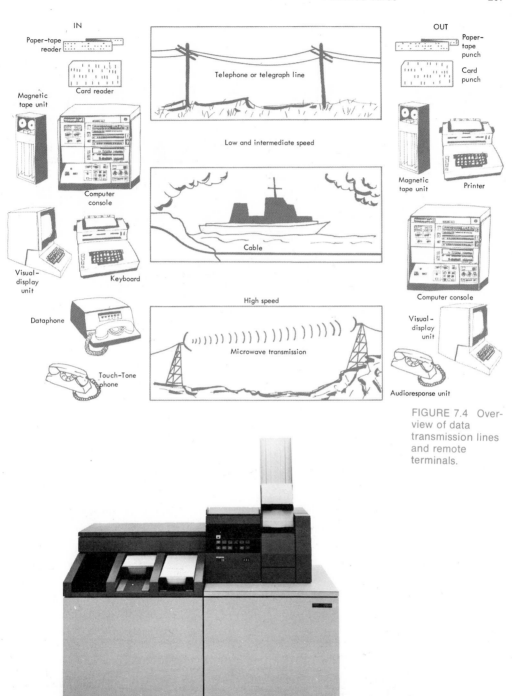

IN

Paper-tape reader

Card reader

Magnetic tape unit

Computer console

Visual-display unit

Keyboard

Dataphone

Touch-Tone phone

Telephone or telegraph line

Low and intermediate speed

Cable

High speed

Microwave transmission

OUT

Paper-tape punch

Card punch

Magnetic tape unit

Printer

Computer console

Visual-display unit

Audioresponse unit

FIGURE 7.4 Overview of data transmission lines and remote terminals.

Courtesy IBM

FIGURE 7.5 Typical card reader.

FIGURE 7.6 Schematic description of card reader.

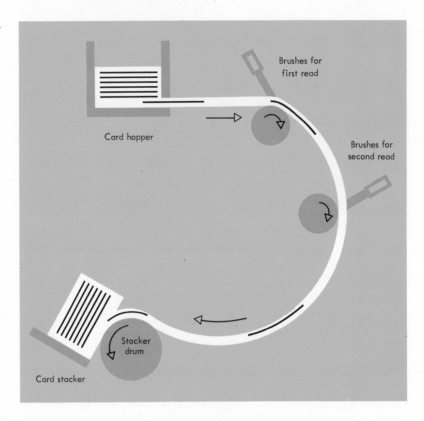

identical, the unit is stopped for corrective action by the operator.

After the cards have been read they are fed into the output hopper. The throughput of cards varies between 100 to 2,000 cards per minute. If 80 columns are punched, for example, this means a maximum of 160,000 characters per minute, or about 2,700 characters per second. This is much faster than a human typing five characters per second but much slower than a magnetic tape drive with a transfer rate of 10,000 to 300,000 characters per second.

The card punch

By computer command, the card punch punches holes into empty cards. Cards are moved one by one through the punch station (Figure 7.7), where the holes are punched. At the read station, the holes are sensed and compared with the required data, and if there is an error, the unit is stopped for corrective action.

Output (punch) speeds are slower than input speeds because the

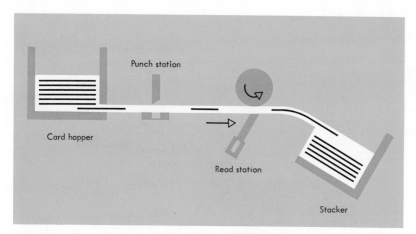

FIGURE 7.7
Schematic
description of
card punch feed
unit.

die punches must be moved. Typical card punch speed is between 100 and 300 cards per minute.

Multifunction card machine (MFCM)

Multifunction card machines (Figure 7.8) combine the various functions of punched card equipment into a single efficient, flexible unit. Cards are stacked into two separate input hoppers which are operated by the computer. Cards are passed one by one under the

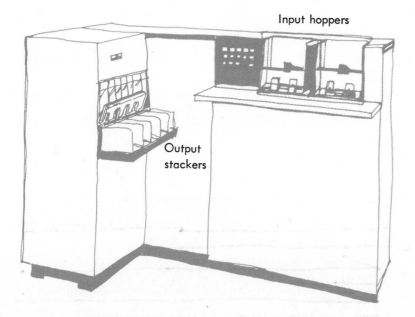

FIGURE 7.8
Multifunction
card machine.

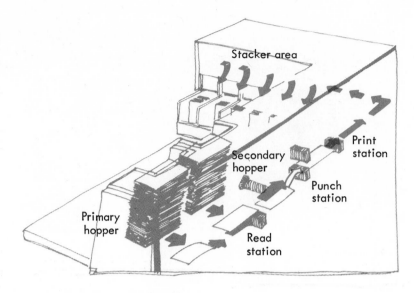

FIGURE 7.9 Card paths through multifunction card unit.

read station (Figure 7.9) in a single merged stream, and data are read and processed by the computer. Data can be punched and printed, and cards can be stacked in four output hoppers. Thus an MFCM unit can merge decks of cards and do file maintenance in a single pass.

Cards may be read up to 10 per second (600 per minute), and columns can be punched up to 160 columns per second.

The IBM 96-column card

In 1969 IBM introduced a 3.25 by 2.63 inch card, the first important innovation since Hollerith and Powers introduced the original punched card. As Figure 7.10 shows, data is punched as circular holes in three sections, each containing 32 characters. All printing is in the upper portion of the card. The IBM 96-column card was especially designed for the IBM System/3, a small-scale business computer system.

Advantages and disadvantages of punched cards

The advantages of punched cards as an input/output and secondary storage device include the following:

1. Each card is a complete record which can be read and understood.
2. Records can be added, deleted, replaced manually, and sorted.
3. Punched cards are a permanent, reliable secondary storage medium.

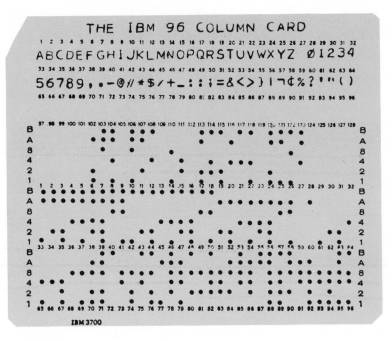

FIGURE 7.10 The IBM 96-column card.

Punched cards also have certain disadvantages:

1. At most 96 and usually only 80 characters can be punched into a card. Thus a record, if it happens to have 100 characters, requires two cards. This leads to wasted space and to a low data density, that is, a low number of characters per card.
2. Punched cards are bulky. A reel of magnetic tape can contain as much data as can be punched into 400,000 cards.
3. The reading and punching of cards is slow. The fastest card reader reads only about 2,500 characters per second. In contrast, a slow magnetic tape drive has a transfer rate of 10,000 characters per second; a fast tape drive can handle 300,000 characters per second.

PUNCHED PAPER TAPE

Punched paper tape, like cards, is a triple-purpose medium. It is used for input, output, and secondary storage. The medium itself is a long, narrow strip of paper, and data is entered in the form of small circular holes (see Figure 7.11).

The most common uses of punched paper tape are:

1. Scientific applications with limited amounts of input and output data.
2. Remote applications for transmission of data.
3. For data generated by adding machines, accounting machines, cash registers, and similar devices.

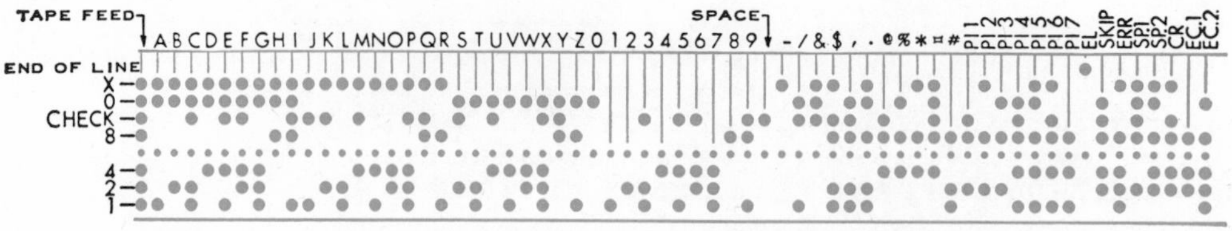

FIGURE 7.11
Eight-track
(channel) punched
paper tape coding.

4. Time-sharing applications with typewriter terminals to store input/output data and computer programs.

Punched paper-tape coding

Figure 7.11 illustrates one of the commonly used punched paper-tape coding systems. Each character is encoded into a frame across the tape, using eight round small punched holes. The rows of holes along the length of the tape are the channels. There are eight rows representing the eight channels, and lengthwise an additional ninth row of tiny holes to move the punched paper tape.

Observe in Figure 7.11 that the bottom four channels have the numeric values 1, 2, 4, and 8. The X and 0 channels are like the zone punches in punched cards. The CHECK channel is used for error checking. A punch in the EL (end-of-the-line) channel indicates the end of a record. (This is not required in punched cards, as each card forms a separate record.)

Input/output equipment

Punched paper-tape readers, like punched card readers, sense the presence or absence of holes and send electric signals to the computer. Reading by brushes is at the rate of 50 to 200 characters per second; photoelectric readers operate at a speed of 200 to 2,000 characters per second. Punching is a slow mechanical operation, performed at a rate of 10 to 300 characters per second.

Advantages and disadvantages of punched paper tape

Unlike punched cards, punched paper tape is not limited to 80 (or 96) characters on records, so records longer than 80 (or 96) characters can be punched one after the other without wasted space. There is no waste for shorter records either. Thus punched paper tape has higher data density than cards.

Punched paper tape is less expensive than cards. Input/output equipment is small, easy to maintain, and relatively less expensive. Thus punched paper-tape units can be attached to other business machines, and the medium of punched paper tape can be auto-matically produced as a by-product.

There are also disadvantages to the use of punched paper tape. The accuracy of data is more difficult to verify for punched paper tape than for punched cards. Correcting errors or changing, adding, or deleting characters or records is difficult, because the punched paper tape must be spliced or entirely repunched. Both punched cards and punched paper tapes have slow data transfer rates when compared with magnetic tapes.

MAGNETIC TAPES

Because they provide high transfer rate and storage capacity (see Figure 7.3), magnetic tapes are a very common medium for input/output and secondary storage for modern computer systems.

Magnetic tape coding

If the medium of the punched paper tape is replaced with mag-netic tape and the punched holes are replaced with magnetized spots on the magnetic tape, this gives the fundamental idea behind magnetic tape coding. The commonly used codes are the seven-track (channel) and the nine-track (channel) codes. Figure 7.12

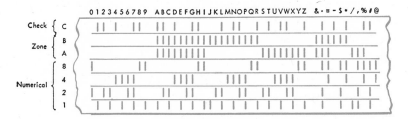

FIGURE 7.12
Seven-track
(channel) magnetic
tape coding.

shows the seven-track (channel) code. You do not need to memo-rize the coding system. All you need know is that the iron oxide particles are magnetized in one direction or the other. By conven-tion, a particle magnetized clockwise represents the binary bit 1, magnetized counterclockwise, the bit 0. In Figure 7.12, only the bits standing for 1s are shown. Bits across the tape form a frame and encode a single character. Each frame includes a bit for error checking.

The tape density is the number of frames per inch of tape. The most common densities are between 800 and 1,600. Typical tape speeds are between 18 and 200 inches per second. Typical transfer rate of data is between 15 and 320 thousand characters per second.

Figure 7.13 illustrates how records are organized on magnetic tape. In the upper part of the figure each record forms an individual block of records separated by blank spaces, the interblock gaps. The computer reads each block one by one, or one record at a time. The tape drive recognizes the end of the block (record) when it reaches the interblock gap and then slows to a halt. At the command to read, the tape drive speeds up, reaches the end of the interblock gap, and starts to read.

In the lower part of the figure several records are grouped into a single block. Thus the computer reads one block consisting of

FIGURE 7.13
Interblock gaps
for single-record
and multiple-
record blocks.

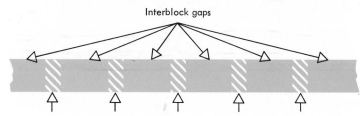

Interblock gaps

Each 80-character record forms a block

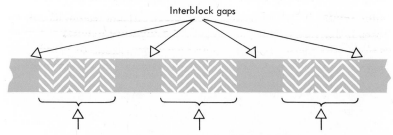

Interblock gaps

Five 80-character records form a block

several records at a time. Each block must be stored in the computer, so when records are blocked more internal storage is required in the computer. On the other hand, there is less blank (waste) space on the tape, and consequently a higher data density is achieved and more records are stored on a reel of tape.

Magnetic tape equipment

Figure 7.14 shows typical magnetic tape units (also called magnetic tape drives, or magnetic tape transports). These units read and write data on magnetic tapes by the use of read-write head assemblies (Figure 7.15). Bear in mind that there are several data channels along the magnetic tape (for example, seven or nine), and

FIGURE 7.14
Typical magnetic
tape units (drives,
transports).

Courtesy Control Data Corporation

therefore there must be a read-write head for each channel. Each read-write head is a small electromagnet. When writing, the computer sends electric pulses to these electromagnets and, as the tape moves, the iron oxide particles on the tape are magnetized in the desired (clockwise or counterclockwise) direction. In reading, the moving magnetized particles induce pulses in the electromagnets, and these electric signals are transmitted to the computer for processing.

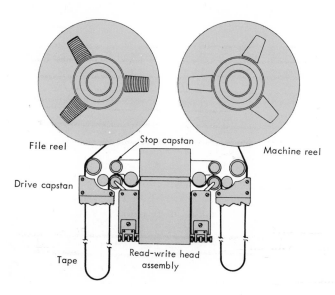

FIGURE 7.15
Schematics of
magnetic tape
feed unit.

Advantages and disadvantages of magnetic tape

Magnetic tape has several advantages as an input/output and storage medium:

1. The data transfer rate is very high, compared to punched cards or punched paper tape. It is comparable to the data transfer rates of magnetic disks. *disk are much faster*

2. Magnetic tape is a compact medium for data storage. It is much more compact than punched cards, punched paper tape, or magnetic disks.

3. Records stored on magnetic tape have essentially unlimited length. Thus magnetic tape is superior in this respect to punched cards but not to punched paper tape.

4. Magnetic tape storage is less expensive per character than punched cards, punched paper tape, or magnetic disks.

5. Magnetic tape (like other magnetic media) can be erased and rewritten, but cards and punched paper tape cannot be erased and rewritten.

The disadvantages of magnetic tape are that:

1. Magnetic tapes cannot be accessed in a random (direct) manner, only sequentially. From this point of view, magnetic tapes are inferior to magnetic disks.

2. Magnetic spots are invisible and cannot be seen or read by people.

MAGNETIC DRUMS

In the early computers, before the introduction of magnetic cores, magnetic drums were used for internal storage. Today drums are used for direct-access secondary storage when the requirement is for intermediate speed in access time and moderate storage capacity, as when storing mathematical tables and programs for software.

A magnetic drum is a metal cylinder coated with a magnetizable surface (Figure 7.16) and housed in a drum storage device. The data is stored on circular channels* grouped into tracks. In a typical drum, a track may consist of four channels corresponding to the four bits of a half byte. Think of each track of a magnetic drum as a small loop of magnetic tape pasted around the cylinder and equipped with a read-write head assembly. Instead of moving the tape, the drum rotates at a high speed past the read/write heads, thousands of times per minute. Thus data is magnetically stored and retrieved.

The data transfer rate of drums is higher than that of magnetic tape drives, because tape drives have only a single read-write head

* Usage is conflicting here. Channels are also called tracks and both channels and tracks are called bands.

assembly, while drums have read-write head assemblies for each track of the cylinder.

The address of data on the drum is specified by the track number and the location along the circumference of the cylinder, that is, the location in the track. Thus when a computer program specifies the track the proper read-write assembly is switched on and the head assembly searches for the data along the track. The head assembly is switched on at electronic speed so, from the point of view of access, this switching time is negligible. Thus the access time depends on the rotational delay, that is, the time required for

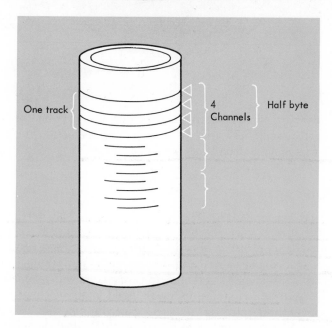

FIGURE 7.16
Typical magnetic
drum.

the drum to rotate the desired data under the head assembly. Typical average rotational delays (half turn of the drum) and access times vary between 10 and 100 milliseconds.

Advantages and disadvantages of magnetic drums

Magnetic drums as direct-access devices compete with magnetic cores and disks. Magnetic cores are more expensive but faster. When millions of data items are required, core storage may be uneconomical. On the other hand, magnetic disks may be more economical than magnetic drums, but the slower access time of magnetic disks may not be acceptable. Under these circumstances magnetic drums offer a good compromise between cost and access

FIGURE 7.17
Typical disk pack.

Courtesy Burroughs

time. However, some modern magnetic disk drives (with fixed read-write head assemblies) are less costly than magnetic drums, and the use of magnetic drums has been decreasing.

MAGNETIC DISKS

Because magnetic disks (Figure 7.17) provide a high data transfer rate, large storage capacity, and random access capability, they are the most common media (together with magnetic tapes) for input/output and secondary storage of modern computer systems.

Magnetic disks, made of thin metal, are coated with magnetizable material, and data is stored as magnetized spots in channels that form concentric circles on the surface of the disk (Figure 7.18a). There are the same number of bits on each channel (Figure 7.18b) so data density along the channel decreases as you move toward the outer edge of the disk.

Figure 7.19 shows a typical disk pack consisting of six disks with

FIGURE 7.18a
Top view of
surface of
magnetic disk.

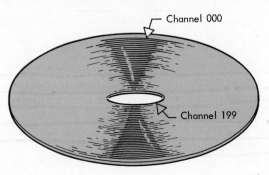

Channel 000

Channel 199

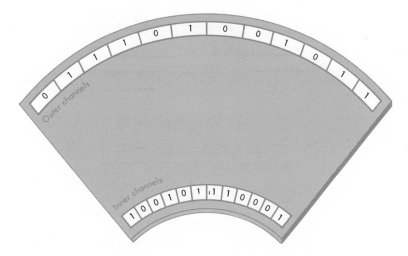

Figure 7.18b How bits are recorded on channels of a magnetic disk. There are the same number of bits on an outer channel as on an inner channel.

ten recording surfaces and the comb-type mechanism holding the read-write head assemblies. Disk packs can be mounted into disk storage units, as illustrated in Figures 7.20 and 7.21. Some disk storage units have built-in disk storage packs, which cannot be removed.

The address of data on the disk pack is specified by the (1) surface number, (2) track number, and (3) location of the data on the track. Thus when the computer program specifies the surface, the proper head assembly of the comb is switched on. When the program specifies the track number, the comb (with all the head assemblies) is made to move and seek the proper track on the surface. Observe that after the head assembly is properly positioned on the track, it will also be positioned on the corresponding tracks on all

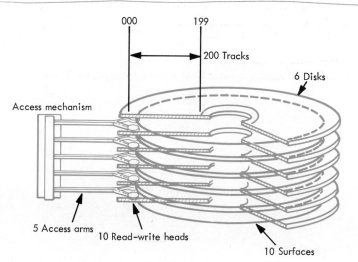

FIGURE 7.19 Typical disk pack and access mechanism.

FIGURE 7.20
Typical disk
storage unit with a
single disk pack.

the surfaces. Once the head assembly is positioned, it will search
the track until the specified data is located under the head assembly.

The access time of a record stored on a magnetic disk is obtained
by adding the seek time, that is the time required to move the head
assembly from one track to another, and the search time, that is the
time required for the disk to turn. Typical figures for seek time are
from 10 to 700 milliseconds, depending upon the equipment and the

FIGURE 7.21
Typical disk
storage unit with
eight disk packs.

Courtesy Control Data Corporation

distance (track to track) the head assembly must travel. Typical search times vary from a fraction of a millisecond to 25 milliseconds.

A typical data transfer rate for read-write is 150,000 characters per second. The storage capacity of disk drives varies from a few million to hundreds of millions of bytes or characters.

DISKETTES OR FLOPPY DISKS

Floppy disks (diskettes) are made of flexible plastic sheets coated with magnetizable material. Storage capacity is typically a few hundred thousand characters. The advantage lies in low cost and easy handling. Floppy disks can be filed and mailed, and data from floppy disks can be entered to the computer through inexpensive input devices.

Advantages and disadvantages of magnetic disks

Magnetic drums have an advantage over magnetic disks in that drums have fixed head assemblies and, therefore, no time is wasted in moving the head assemblies. Thus the access time of magnetic drums is lower than that of magnetic disks. However, there are magnetic disks available with fixed head assemblies, that is, one head for each track. These disks are more expensive but have access times comparable to those of magnetic drums.

Disks have an advantage over magnetic tape drives because they can be accessed directly (randomly), while tapes can be processed only sequentially. Thus when random access is a must (as in online, real-time systems), tapes cannot be used. When there is an alternative, the total cost and efficiency of the data processing system must be evaluated using both disks and tapes. Disk packs are more expensive than reels of magnetic tape, so a library of tapes is less costly than a library of disks. Furthermore, sequential processing of disks may be slower than sequential processing of tapes, but other processing costs may be lower for disk systems requiring random access.

CASSETTE DECKS

Cassette decks use magnetic tape cartridges (Figure 7.22) similar to the cartridges used in everyday cassette recorders. Typical storage capacity is one to two million characters, and data transfer rates are three to five thousand characters per second. Tape drives contain much more data and have a much higher data transfer rate, but cassette decks are much less expensive. Cassette decks are often used as low-priced storage units for data and also for software and program packages.

FIGURE 7.22
A typical cassette
cartridge

MASS STORAGE DEVICES

The devices discussed above can store up to hundreds of millions of characters. However, often there is a need for mass storage devices which can store tens or hundreds of billions of characters. We now discuss several such devices.

Magnetic cards and strips

One of the troubles with punched cards is that only 80 (or 96) characters can be stored on each card. It is possible to overcome this difficulty by attaching magnetizable material to cards; the high-density capability of magnetic materials produces low-cost units with high-storage capacity.

This is the approach taken in devices like the IBM Data Cell and the NCR CRAM (Card Random Access Memory) which use magnetic cards or strips. Data is stored on these materials magnetically and placed into cells or cartridges. Then with the aid of mechanical devices the cards or strips can be randomly accessed or pulled out, and data can be read or written by magnetic heads.

The required mechanical selection and moving of the cards or strips make the access time slow, about .2 to .5 of a second. But many thousands of characters can be stored on each card or strip and accessed at data transfer rates of about 50,000 characters per second. Thus a cartridge or cell containing a few hundred magnetic cards or strips can store many millions of characters, and a device containing many cartridges and cells may contain hundreds of millions or even billions of characters.

When compared with magnetic disk drives, magnetic card and strip devices offer much larger storage capacity at significantly lower cost. However, this high performance is accomplished at the cost of slower access time.

Automated tape libraries

Large users may have thousands of magnetic tapes, and keeping track of tapes and mounting and dismounting them is a problem. There are mechanical devices available which automate this process under the control of the computer. Some of the advantages these devices offer are speed and accurate performance. All operations are performed in a matter of seconds, without human intervention. The wrong tape is never mounted, and physical damage or loss of tapes does not occur. Because tapes have a large data storage capacity, hundreds of billions of characters can be stored online in an automated tape library.

Combining tapes and disks

Inexpensive tapes can be combined with magnetic disks which provide random access. Such an arrangement is used in the IBM 3850 mass storage system.

All data is stored on special tapes contained in cartridges (Figure 7.23). Each of these 2″ × 4″ cartridges contains 50 million characters. The cartridges are mounted in "honeycomb" cells (Figure 7.24), and when data is needed the cartridge is removed from its cell by an automatic mechanism and temporarily transferred to a disk storage unit for computer use. This mass storage system (Figure 7.25) can store up to 472 billion characters, all online to the computer.

FIGURE 7.23
Data cartridge holding magnetic tape with 50 million characters of data for IBM 3850 storage system.

FIGURE 7.24
Cartridges are
stored in a
"honeycomb"
of cells.

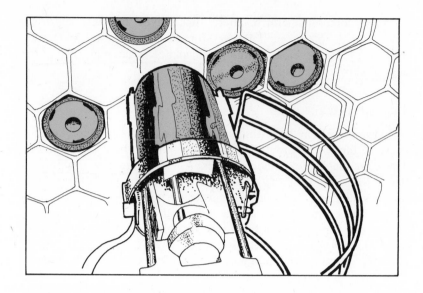

MAGNETIC INK CHARACTER RECOGNITION (MICR)

If you take a good look at a typical bank check (Figure 7.26), you might wonder about those odd-looking numbers at the bottom. They are printed with a special ink containing tiny iron oxide magnetizable particles. When the bank receives the check, the clerk prints the amount on the check with a device using a special font of type (Figure 7.27) and magnetic ink. The check now can be processed automatically on the magnetic ink character reader-sorter unit (Figure 7.28). This process is called magnetic ink character recognition (MICR).

As a first step of processing, the iron oxide particles are magnetized. Then the read heads recognize the characters and produce appropriate electric signals. The signals are transmitted to the computer or are recorded on magnetic tape. The checks themselves are dropped into the appropriate sorting pockets.

FIGURE 7.25 The
IBM 3850 mass
storage system
can hold 472
billion characters
of data online to
the computer.

Courtesy IBM

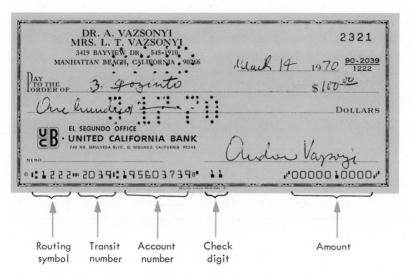

FIGURE 7.26
Check illustrating
the use of
magnetic ink
characters.

Routing
symbol

Transit
number

Account
number

Check
digit

Amount

Typical throughput of the magnetic ink character reader-sorter unit is 750 to 1,500 checks or documents per minute.

Advantages and disadvantages of MICR

MICR has certain advantages:

1. It provides automated, reliable source data entry.
2. The data can be read by people.

The disadvantages of MICR are that:

1. It is not fully automatic; the amount of the check (or other data) must be added manually.
2. Damaged or incompletely encoded documents must be handled manually.
3. Only a small number of characters (14) is available.

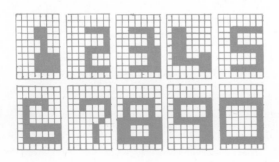

FIGURE 7.27
Patterns of font
used for MICR
(magnetic ink
character
recognition) digits.

FIGURE 7.28
Typical MICR
(magnetic ink
character
recognition)
reader-sorter.

Courtesy IBM

OPTICAL CHARACTER RECOGNITION (OCR)

Optical character recognition (OCR) devices can directly read data printed or written on documents. Therefore OCR is used widely for the input of source data.

For example, when you make a purchase with your credit card, the clerk prints information with your card, and the sales slip (Figure 7.29) can be read automatically by an optical character reader. Or when your water or gas meter is read, the form has your name,

FIGURE 7.29
Typical sales slip
to be used with
optical character
recognition (OCR)
devices. The
upper-left portion
of the slip is
produced by a
plastic credit card.

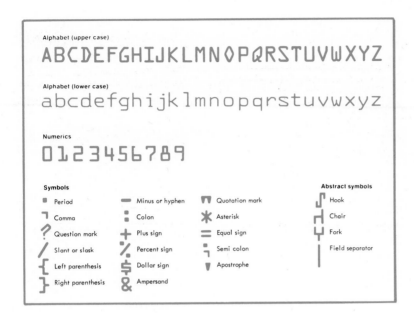

FIGURE 7.30
Typical characters
recognized by
OCR readers.

account number, and other information in optically readable form. Other applications of OCR are utility company billings, insurance premium notices, sales invoices, automatic sorting of mail.

There are many types of optical character readers on the market. All use photoelectric devices to recognize characters. **Figure 7.30** shows some of the typical printed characters recognized by OCR readers. Some of the machines also recognize hand-printed characters, others only **mark-sensing** symbols (**Figures 7.31, 7.32**).

FIGURE 7.31
Mark-sense
punched cards.
The marks are
made by pencil,
and the reader
converts the
marks into electric
signals.

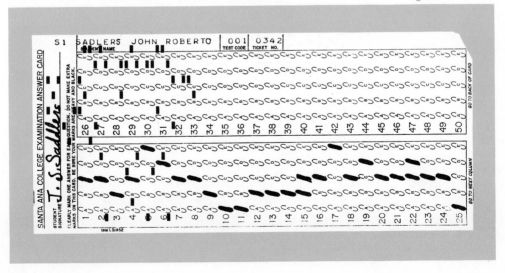

FIGURE 7.32
College grading
report for optical
readers. The
instructor marks
the grades, and
the machine
converts the
marks into electric
signals.

UNIVERSITY OF SOUTHERN CALIFORNIA
Office of the Registrar
GRADE REPORT

MARK GRADES IN CORRECT COLUMN
BELOW WITH ENCLOSED PENCIL
SEE INSTRUCTIONS
DO NOT WRITE HERE

	DEPT.	COURSE		SESSION TITLE
	QBA	531		FALL SEMESTER 197–
	SESS 410	DIV 1	CLASS 21331	

COURSE TITLE
INTRO COMPUTERS FOR BUS

INSTRUCTOR
VAZSONYI

PRINT GRADE HERE (OPTIONAL)

	N A M E	SOC. SEC. NO.	GRADE
1.	BLANK STEPHEN	228561689	A B C D F V W IN CR –
2.	CHRISTMAN DAVID	496492854	A B C D F V W IN CR –
3.	CORRELL NELL	112901953	A B C D F V W IN CR –
4.	FREEMAN WILLIAM JAMES	182774512	A B C D F V W IN CR –
5.	GRAVES DEBORAH ANN	726849293	A B C D F V W IN CR –
6.	HALL EUGENE RAY	898584460	A B C D F V W IN CR –
7.	KENNEDY JONATHAN	530570533	A B C D F V W IN CR –
8.	KRAMER JAMES EDWARD	911579745	A B C D F V W IN CR –
9.	MILLAR MICHAEL DAVIS	328460152	A B C D F V W IN CR –

Figure 7.33 shows how an OCR system operates, and **Figure 7.34** illustrates a typical optical reader-sorter.

The performance of OCR is measured by the rate that:

1. Characters are read.
2. Documents are rejected, that is, the number of documents that must be handled manually.
3. Errors are made.

Typical reading speeds range from 70 to 2,500 characters per second. Reject rate is about 2 to 10 percent of documents handled, and the error rate is about 1 percent.

FIGURE 7.33 How
an OCR (optical
character
recognition)
system operates.

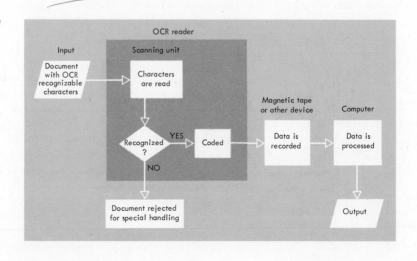

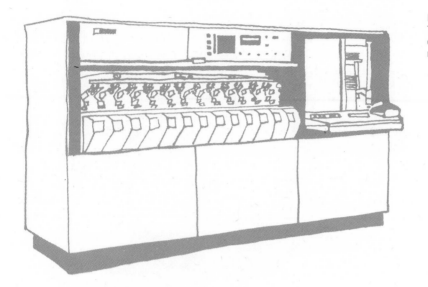

FIGURE 7.34
Typical optical
character
read-sort unit.

Advantages and disadvantages of OCR

OCR provides these advantages:

1. Automated source data entry.
2. Data that can be read by people.
3. Wide applicability.

OCR also has disadvantages, including these:

1. Only certain types of printed or handwritten characters can be read.
2. Printing for OCR must meet high standards, and this is expensive.
3. The reject and/or error rate may exceed user requirements.
4. Relatively high-priced equipment is required, so OCR is economical only when a large number of documents are to be processed.

However, OCR is relatively new and is continuously being improved. Increasing usage can be expected.

HIGH-SPEED PRINTERS

Impact printers

The most common printing device is the high-speed impact printer (Figure 7.35). In an impact printer a character is generated by using mechanical pressure to transfer ink from ribbon to paper.

You need not know the mechanical details of the printer, only that there is no moving carriage, as in a typewriter, and that with a line printer entire lines are printed (one at a time) at speeds as high as 2,000 lines per minute.

How long would it take to print a typical book? Assuming a standard of 40 lines per page, a high-speed printer can print the equivalent of 50 book pages per minute. Thus a 250-page book could be printed in 5 minutes.

How many characters to a line? The typical printer has 120 to 132 characters per line. There are various character sets available, with sizes of sets ranging from a very limited choice of 13 characters up to 240. The EBCDIC system (see Chapter 6) permits using up

FIGURE 7.35
Typical high-speed
line-by-line impact
printer.

Courtesy Honeywell

to 254 different characters, including upper and lower case alphabetic, numeric, and special characters. The mechanical design of printers is such that the more limited the character set, the higher the printing rate. For example, using a reduced character set may allow the printing of 2,500 lines per minute.

Laser electrophotographic printer

Electrophotographic printing is a process that uses a special surface on which the shape of a character that is to be printed is formed by light. Black plastic particles are attracted to those spots on the special surface that have been exposed to light. The black plastic particles are then transferred to paper and fused into the fibers of the paper to create the printed output. The required intense and precise light source is a laser device.

FIGURE 7.36
Electrophoto-
graphic printer
can print over ten
thousand lines
per minute.

Courtesy IBM

The advantages of the electrophotographic printer (Figure 7.36) are in its great speed and flexibility of format, font, and so on. Speeds over ten thousand lines per minute are possible, and thus a typical book could be printed in one minute.

An electrophotographic printer can provide a much larger variety of printing types and sizes than an impact printer. It is also possible to create simultaneously a business form and its content. This is done by inserting an overlay of the desired form into the printer.

Electrophotographic printers, due to their very high speed, flexibility, and scope, turn the computer into a device that is competitive with a printing shop.

FIGURE 7.37
Typical
typewriterlike
input/output
device.

Courtesy IBM

Key-driven input/output devices

Key-driven input/output devices are typewriterlike or simple keyboard-type devices used for input and output messages (Figure 7.37). Key-driven devices may be close to or remote from the main frame of the computer.

A key-driven device commonly used is the computer-console (Figure 7.38), which enables the computer operator and the computer to communicate. The operator can enter data, programs, or program modifications, and the computer can request the operator to perform certain tasks, such as stopping the computer system or mounting a required tape of a specified tape drive.

FIGURE 7.38
Typical computer
console terminal.

Courtesy IBM

Remote key-driven devices may be used for data collection or as transaction recording stations for all manner of business applications. Key-driven devices also enter data directly to magnetic tape, disk, or cassette. Point-of-sale devices are key-driven; some also allow the use of plastic cards and permit optical code recognition with the aid of the "magic wand" (Figure 7.39). Typewriterlike devices also serve as time-sharing terminals.

Key-driven devices provide immediate, direct, and inexpensive two-way communication between the user and the computer.

CATHODE-RAY TUBE (CRT) VISUAL DISPLAYS

Because typewriterlike devices are electromechanical, they print answers slowly. If much data is to be provided by the com-

FIGURE 7.39
Point-of-sale
device. The
"magic wand" is
on the left side.

Courtesy IBM

puter, the user communicating with the computer may be held up in his work. To improve user-computer interaction, manufacturers provide a cathode-ray tube, CRT (televisionlike tube) terminals (Figure 7.40).

With CRT devices, users see what they type and can make immediate corrections. Computer messages appear on the face of the tube rapidly. Typical CRT tubes display 6 to 12 lines, each line with 40 to 80 characters.

Optional equipment is available, so the operator can direct the computer system to print the message appearing on the tube with a high-speed printer or to have the message photographed automatically on film by a camera. Wall-sized projections of the CRT tube also can be obtained. Color displays are an optional feature.

FIGURE 7.40
Typical CRT–
equipped display
station with
alphanumeric
keyboard.

Courtesy Honeywell

FIGURE 7.41   CRT
display showing
graphics and
alphanumeric
characters.

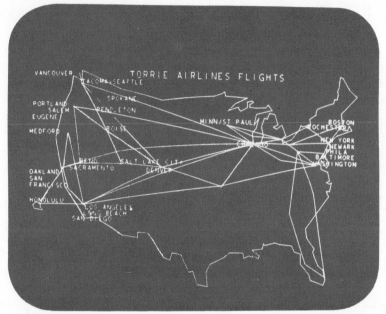

Reprinted by permission from *GA22–7001–IBM s/370*, p. 7.14 © 1970 by International Business Machines Corporation.

Graphic display CRT tubes

Graphic display CRT devices are much more expensive and provide not only alphanumeric data but enable the user to display, manipulate, and update drawings and pictures (Figures 7.41, 7.42). In addition to the typewriterlike keyboard, special keys and a fiber optics light pen can be used for input.

If an engineering drawing is sketched and specific points are designated by the light pen, the computer can make perfect straight lines, triangles, circles, and so on, from the rough sketches provided by the user. The light pen is operated with the aid of a photocell. The screen can detect the light from the pen, and electric pulses can be transmitted to the computer. Thus the user can "write" on the surface of the CRT tube.

CRT-equipped terminals provide the most convenient and direct two-way communication between user and computer.

COMPUTER OUTPUT TO MICROFILM (COM)

In computer output to microfilm, a recorder accepts digital data either directly from the computer (online operation) or from a magnetic tape (offline operation), transforms the data into char-

FIGURE 7.42
CRT–equipped
graphic display
unit with light pen.

Courtesy Control Data Corporation

acters and graphics, and records it with the aid of a photographic
camera on 16, 35, 70, and 105 millimeter film.

Figure 7.43 shows how COM works:

1. The data is converted into a form acceptable to the CRT.
2. The pictures appear on the CRT.
3. The camera photographs the face of the tube on film.
4. The film is developed and processed for later handling and
    storage.

A "forms overlay" can also be photographed by the camera, so
business forms and graphics (not stored in the computer) will be
recorded on the film and produced as output.

FIGURE 7.43 How
computer output
microfilm (COM)
systems work.

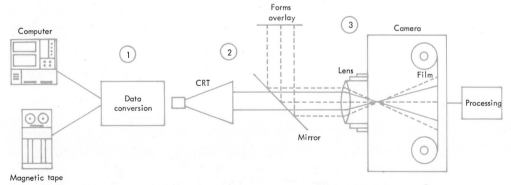

After the microfilm is developed it can be reproduced if desired, and used as a film reel, a strip, cut into frames and mounted in an aperture card, or photographed on some other media (Figure 7.44). Thus microfilm can be used as a unit record, like a punched card. Or, as an alternate, the CRT can be photographed on a small portion of a microfiche, and thus on one single card hundreds or even thousands of printed pages can be stored.

Figure 7.45 shows typical graphical COM outputs, a bar graph and a trend chart. COM provides extremely high-speed output. Typical equipment can produce up to 60,000 lines per minute, and 1,000 lines per second, or up to 500,000 characters per second. This is 50 times faster than a high-speed printer. It almost matches

FIGURE 7.44 How COM–produced output is used

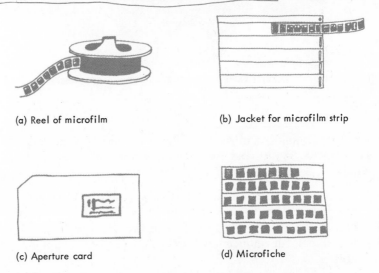

(a) Reel of microfilm

(b) Jacket for microfilm strip

(c) Aperture card

(d) Microfiche

the character transfer rate capability of a modern computer system. A typical 250-page book can be displayed in 10 seconds.

After microfilm or microfiche records are produced, they are stored and organized into files. Thus COM-based files provide an alternate means for the storage and retrieval of large amounts of data. Users can retrieve information in fractions of a second from files containing hundreds of millions of data items, review information through optical devices, or produce "hard copy" by photographic means.

Advantages and disadvantages of COM

Computer output to microfilm provides the following advantages:

1. Very high-speed output.
2. High-resolution graphics.

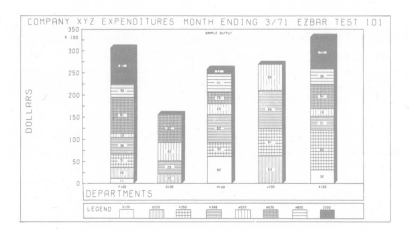

FIGURE 7.45 Bar graph and trend charts produced by COM

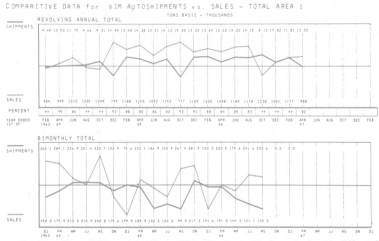

Courtesy of Kenneth Shostack and Charles Eddy, "Management by Computer Graphics," *Harvard Business Review*, Vol. 49, No. 6 (November–December), 1971.

3. Microfilm-based files that are compact, convenient, and permit rapid information storage and retrieval.
4. Economy.

The disadvantages of COM are:

1. COM recorders and associated equipment are expensive and require a large investment. Consequently, COM is applicable only for large work loads.
2. COM provides limited flexibility with regard to input format.

DATA COMMUNICATIONS

Figure 7.4 shown earlier illustrates the wide variety of transmission lines and terminals used for remote data communications. The

FIGURE 7.46 The modulator (modem) changes the electric signals from an input device into an electric wave (tone).

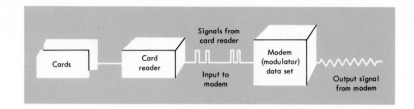

most commonly used equipment and services are discussed in this section.

Data sets or modems

Suppose a deck of punched cards is read by a card reader. The brushes (or photocells) in the card reader sense the holes and generate electric signals. Or suppose some other input device (tape drive, keyboard, CRT) generates electric signals (Figure 7.46). Transmission lines (Figure 7.47) transmit only electric waves or tones, so the signals from the input device cannot be transmitted directly through the lines. There is a need for a device, a modem (or data set) to modulate the digital signals generated by the input devices into waves or tones (see Figure 7.46). Such a device, the Dataphone, is illustrated in Figure 7.48.

FIGURE 7.47 How data is communicated between remote locations. The modulator converts the signal from the input device into an electric wave or tone. The demodulator converts the electric wave into signals acceptable to the computer system.

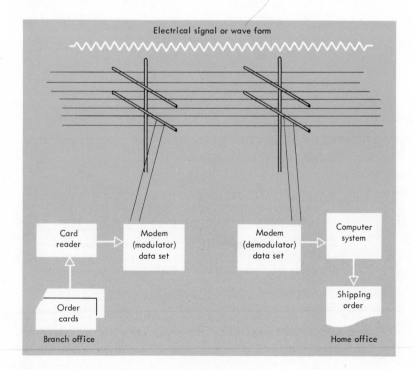

FIGURE 7.48 A modem or data set—the Dataphone

Similarly, the electric waves (tones) from the transmission lines cannot be fed directly into a computer unit (card reader, printer, magnetic tape drive). First the electric waves must be demodulated by a device. Modems (or data sets) perform both the modulation and demodulation functions; the word modem is the combination of the initial five letters of these two words. There must be a modem between every input/output device (or the computer) and the transmission line or channel to be used (Figure 7.49).

Multiplexing

It is possible to use the same communication channel to send many messages simultaneously between several devices. You may

FIGURE 7.49 Typical communication system for real-time remote application.

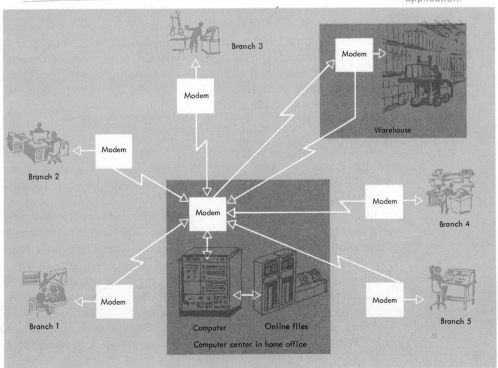

FIGURE 7.50
Your ear may
transmit three or
more signals
simultaneously to
you: (1) the
lecture, (2) the
overhead jet, (3)
the fire engine
siren.

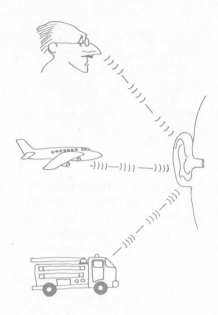

be listening to your instructor, and at the same time hear a jet flying overhead and then the siren of a fire engine (Figure 7.50). Your ears represent a single communication channel to your brain, but several messages can be carried simultaneously through the channel.

In the communication industry, a device, the multiplexer, makes it possible to have hundreds or even thousands of communications transmitted through the same transmission facility. With the aid of multiplexer devices, it is possible for many input/output devices to communicate among themselves and the computer, using the same communication channels (Figure 7.51).

Dataphone and voice response

The Dataphone (see Figure 7.48) is not only a modulator/demodulator (data set) but also a device on which you can dial and establish communications.

In a Touch-Tone telephone the dial is replaced by buttons which generate tones to be transmitted through the wires to establish connections between the users of the system. After the connections are made, you can transmit data to the computer or to peripheral devices by touching the buttons and generating tones. Some of these devices are also equipped with punched card input capability (Figure 7.52).

Touch-Tone terminals are also commonly used as audioresponse units. With the aid of the buttons you can generate tones and enter

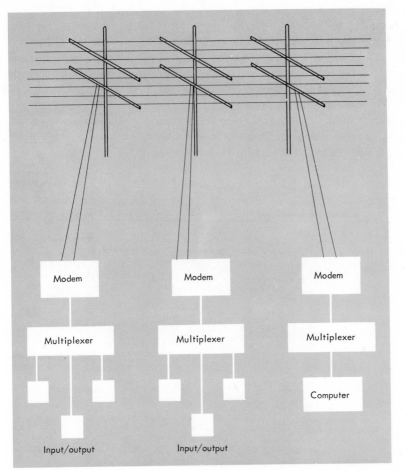

FIGURE 7.51
Multiplexing
makes it possible
to transmit many
messages on the
same transmission
line.

FIGURE 7.52
Touch-Tone
terminal with
keyboard and
punched card
input.

inquiries in the computer, and you can receive answers in the form of a spoken voice from the computer. Parts of speech are prerecorded and stored on a magnetic disk. On a query by a remote user, the computer retrieves and activates the proper sounds and words and generates an audio (voice) response.

In areas where no Touch-Tone devices are available, inexpensive and portable attachments can be obtained so the computer is no farther away than the nearest telephone or telephone booth (Figure 7.53). If there is no standard telephone near you, you can obtain a

FIGURE 7.53 The computer is no farther away than the nearest telephone booth or a portable unit in a suitcase.

Courtesy IBM

mobile telephone in your car, or you can carry a portable telephone in a suitcase. Computers equipped with these devices can be used whenever you have access to a fixed or mobile telephone.

Can you input data to the computer by talking to it? Not yet! Computer recognition of human speech is a difficult technical problem, and only experimental research equipment has been developed.

Teletype and typewriterlike terminals

The Teletype terminal (Figure 7.54) is one of the commonly used inexpensive communication sets. Higher performance more costly typewriterlike terminals also can be obtained. These can provide output at a higher typing rate and with better printing quality. There are also keyboard devices which do not type messages but use a CRT device.

Paper Tape
Attachment

FIGURE 7.54
Typical Teletype
send/receiver set.

Courtesy IBM

Other communication equipment

There is a great variety of further communication equipment, but you need to learn only about those that are widely used.

Facsimile machines are capable of transmitting copies of printed or handwritten documents. Punched paper tape, card, or magnetic tape transmission terminals transmit data between input/output devices and the computer itself. With the aid of these terminals, you can remotely enter jobs to the computer and receive printed answers through character-at-a-time printers or line printers. There are also devices available so you can transmit data directly from computer to computer.

Communication facilities

The terminal devices used in communications utilize certain communication channels. The Federal Communications Commission (FCC) regulates radio, television, and interstate communication services. Figure 7.55 shows the most important communication services.

Figure 7.4 shows that there are three levels of transmission speed or band width:

1. Low-speed narrow band width transmission of about ten characters per second. Narrow band width is inadequate for human voice communication, but satisfactory for teletype messages. Narrow band width lines are the least expensive.
2. Intermediate-speed or voice grade transmission of about 500 characters per second. This band width is adequate for voice

Designation	Carrier	Description
Public telephone network Dataphone	American Telephone and Telegraph Company	Voice grade, switched network, measured rate DDD (Direct Distance Dialing)
WATS (Wide Area Telephone Service)	American Telephone and Telegraph Company	Voice grade, switched network, flat monthly rate, unlimited service
Leased voice-grade lines Leased low-speed lines	American Telephone and Telegraph Company Western Union	Dedicated lines between users
TWX and Telex Teletype Exchange Service	Western Union	Low-grade switched network
Datacom	Western Union	Multiple low-speed lines between two or more users
Broad Band Switching Exchange	Western Union	High-speed network
Series 5000 Channels Telpak Series 8000 Wide Band Data Channels	American Telephone and Telegraph Company Western Union	High-speed, but can be used as multiple channels for lower capacity
Packet-switched service	Telenet System Graphnet System	Computer-switched packets of digital data

FIGURE 7.55 The most important communication services.

communication and is used for ordinary telephone communications. The costs involved are the same as for voice telephone communication.

3. High-speed or wide band width transmission, from 4,000 to millions of characters per second. Ordinarily microwave (radio wave) channels are used. These wide band width channels can also be partitioned into many medium band width channels and, by multiplexing, can handle many low-speed messages.

The design of communication systems varies. In a switched network (as in your telephone) there are more subscribers than telephone lines. When you dial, your call is routed to the other party through the network. If no line is available, you get a busy signal. The communication system arrangement is different in a point-to-point communication system. Here there is a dedicated line from one party to another, like the hot line from the White House to the Kremlin. You can always get through your communication line, but only to the party at the other end of the line. Only people located at the two ends of the line can use the system and, therefore, they must pay the total cost. In a switched network, costs are shared by the subscribers and therefore are lower.

In a packet-switched communication system, packets of data (usually 1,000 bits long) are routed from the user site via dedicated line to a nearby switching computer. From there they are routed via wide band lines or satellite to another switching computer near the destination site, and then to the destination computer. By very efficiently sharing the high-speed circuits and eliminating the long switching times of the regular phone network, inexpensive high-speed data transmission is provided.

The subscriber, of course, is interested not only in the performance of the system but also in what he must pay. He may pay a flat monthly charge (as with local calls on the telephone) or subscribe to measured service, in which the length of calls is measured in minutes or hours (as with toll calls). The charge also depends on the distance between the subscriber and the other party (as for long distance calls). However, in a satellite communication system the distance between users does not matter, and so the charge may be independent of the distance between users.

How to choose a communication service

The cost of the communication service must be balanced against requirements, performance and benefits. Here are some of the important factors to be considered:

1. The number and location of the input/output devices and the location of the computer.
2. The volume of data to be transmitted.
3. The speed and timing of transmission required.

SUMMARY

1. The most widely used input medium is the punched card.
2. Magnetic tapes have very large storage capacity and a fast data transfer rate but can be used only for sequential processing.
3. Magnetic disks have large storage capacity and fast data transfer rates and can be used either for direct (random) access or sequential processing.

4. Combining tapes and disks results in very large online storage capacity with good direct (random) access and sequential processing ability.

5. High-speed impact printers are the most commonly used output devices.

6. Magnetic ink character recognition (MICR) is used primarily in financial institutions; optical character recognition (OCR) in many industries.

7. Optical character recognition and mark sensing are used widely in all walks of life.

8. Key-driven devices, CRT devices, and audioresponse units provide direct and remote communication between man and the computer.

9. A wide variety of transmission facilities provides data transfer between input/output devices and the computer.

10. The modern computer, with its many distant devices, is made possible only by the combination of two powerful electronic systems: communication and computer systems.

11. Figures 7.1 through 7.4 present a summary of the peripheral devices discussed in this chapter.

KEY CONCEPTS AND WORDS

address: an identification, as represented by a name, label, or number, for a register or location in storage.

alphanumeric (or alphameric): a letter, digit, or other character, like a punctuation mark.

band: (1) see *track*, (2) the communication frequency spectrum between two defined limits.

band width: a group of consecutive communication frequencies constituting a band which exists between stated limits.

block of records: a group of records on a magnetic medium, separated from another group by an interblock gap.

cassette deck: magnetic storage device similar to the cartridge in everyday cassette recorders.

channel: (1) a path along which signals can be sent, (2) See *track*.

computer output to microfilm (COM): a device which converts a computer output to a photographic image on microfilm.

Dataphone: a data set (*modem*) to establish communication between man and the computer.

data set: see *modem*.

diskette: see *floppy disk*.

electrophotographic printer: printer using laser beam to generate characters from black plastic particles.

floppy disk: plastic sheet coated with magnetizable material. Same as *diskette.*

impact printer: device using mechanical pressure for the printing of characters.

interblock gap: an area on a data medium used to indicate the end of a block.

line printer: a device that prints all characters of a line as a unit.

magnetic ink: ink that contains magnetizable particles.

magnetic ink character recognition (MICR): machine recognition of characters printed with magnetic ink.

mark sensing: electrical sensing of manually recorded data.

modem: device to modulate and demodulate electronic digital signals into electrical waves.

multifunction card machine (MFCM): a device to combine the functions of various punched card equipment.

multiplexer: device for transmitting simultaneously two or more messages on a single channel.

optical character recognition (OCR): recognition of printed characters through the use of light-sensitive devices.

search: examine a set of items for any that have a specified property.

seek: pertaining to storage on magnetic disks—the motion of the head assembly from one track to another.

switched network: a communication system with more subscribers than lines.

track: the portion of a moving storage medium, such as a drum, tape, or disk, that is accessible to a given reading/writing head position.

transmission rate: the number of symbols (bits, characters, etc.) sent through a line per unit of time.

wide band width transmission: utilizes a communication line with a transmission rate of more than 4,000 characters per second.

DISCUSSION QUESTIONS

1. Report on your collection of newspaper, magazine, and television items and cartoons, jokes, and anecdotes.

2. Explain why you need to learn about hardware. What level of knowledge of hardware detail must the user of a computer system have?

3. Discuss the performance of various input/output media and devices as to applications, data transfer rate, advantages, and disadvantages.

4. Discuss the performance of various secondary storage devices as to advantages and disadvantages, applications, data transfer rate, storage capacity, access time.

5. Discuss the performance of transmission lines as to transmission rates.

6. Describe what steps the card reader and card punch unit go through in performing operations.

7. Compare the traditional punched card system with the multifunction card machine (MFCM).

8. Describe the IBM 96-column card and compare it with the 80-column card. What are the advantages and disadvantages?

9. What are the advantages and disadvantages of punched cards?

10. Describe punched paper tape, and state its advantages and disadvantages.

11. Describe magnetic tape media and devices. How is data read and written? List advantages and disadvantages.

12. Define and explain in your own words: *data density, tape density, frame, channel, transfer rate, interblock gap, block of records, transmission rate, alphanumeric.* Give examples. Compare your definitions with those in your dictionary and explain differences, if any.[2]

13. Describe magnetic drums. What factors determine direct-access time? List advantages and disadvantages.

14. Describe magnetic disks. What factors determine direct-access time? List advantages and disadvantages.

15. Define and explain in your own words: *band, address, rotational delay, track, seek, search.* Give examples. Compare your definitions with those in your dictionary and explain differences, if any.

16. Describe floppy disks or diskettes. List advantages and disadvantages.

17. Describe cassettes and their advantages and disadvantages.

18. Describe magnetic cards and strips and their advantages and disadvantages.

19. Describe automated tape libraries and their advantages and disadvantages.

20. Describe systems which combine magnetic tapes and disks and give their advantages and disadvantages.

21. Compare MICR and OCR mark sensing and discuss their uses. List advantages and disadvantages.

22. Describe high-speed printers and their use.

23. Describe key-driven input/output devices, CRT-equipped devices, the use of a light pen and COM. Give examples of how each of these devices is used. List advantages and disadvantages.

24. What is a modem? What does it do? What is multiplexing?

25. What is a dataphone? What is voice response? How are these devices used?

26. Can you input information to a computer by voice?

27. Describe the three classes of communication facilities and their uses.

28. Discuss why communication systems are important to modern computer systems.

29. Review and update your Personal Summary of this course (see Exercise 28, Chapter 1).

---

[2] In all word problems you need make comparisons only if the word or phrase is in your dictionary.

8

The central processing unit and programming concepts

The previous chapter covered input/output, peripherals, and communications; now we proceed to the central processing unit (CPU). But first we must determine what we need to know about the CPU and clarify our approach to hardware.

THE APPROACH TO HARDWARE

The user views a computer system principally through software, and the best way to understand the functions of hardware is through software. In fact, we could construct a ladder of software leading to hardware: (1) flowcharts, (2) procedure-oriented languages, (3) symbolic languages, (4) assembler languages, and (5) machine languages. The ground floor, that is, the flowchart, is totally hardware independent, but as we climb the ladder we get closer and closer to hardware.

You are already familiar with flowcharts and probably know something about procedure-oriented languages (see Chapter 4 and the Language Supplement, Appendix one). In this chapter we translate flowcharts directly into symbolic language[1] instructions, that is, instructions in which addresses are represented by symbols, and we proceed directly from symbolic to machine language. Detailed discussion of procedure-oriented and assembler language programming is postponed to Chapter 9.

---

[1] Terms printed in color are defined at the end of the chapter.

This chapter also discusses how the central processing unit (CPU) operates to process the data and instructions specified by the programming. The operations of the CPU can be understood by learning how it:

1. Represents data and instructions.
2. Stores data and instructions.
3. Moves data and instructions.
4. Interprets and executes instructions.
5. Controls peripheral units.

The CPU performs these functions with the aid of the memory (primary storage unit), the arithmetic/logic unit, and the control unit. To clarify how these three units perform the various functions, we return to the account-balancing problem dealt with in Chapter 2. Specifically, we show how the operations required for the account-balancing problem (see the flowchart in Chapter 2, Figure 2.6) can be described by programming instructions and then how these instructions are performed by the units of the CPU.

SYMBOLIC LANGUAGE PROGRAMMING

To start, it would be too difficult to explain how the units of the CPU perform the functions described by the boxes of the flowchart in Figure 2.6. First we must replace the flowchart by a set of instructions—a symbolic language program.

The input unit

The task of the input unit is simplified by specifying that only a single, whole (integer) number can be written on an input card. In Figure 8.1 the first flowchart box in the account-balancing computation is replaced by three boxes containing three symbolic instructions:

> READ OLD
> READ DEP
> READ CHECK

Observe that each symbolic instruction has two parts: the *operation* and the *operand*. In the three instructions shown in Figure 8.1 READ is the operation. The operands are: OLD, DEP, and CHECK.

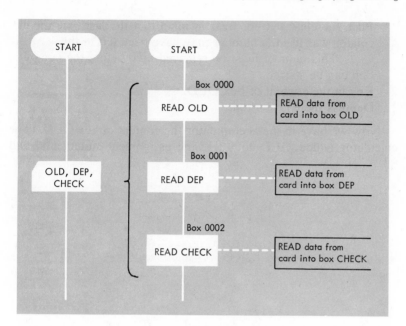

FIGURE 8.1 Three
symbolic
instructions are
required to read
the three data
items for the
account-balancing
problem.

In flowcharts we number each box, and in discussing the charts we refer to the flowchart boxes. To refer to symbolic instructions we name the instructions. For example, in

B0000 READ OLD
B0001 READ DEP
B0002 READ CHECK

B0000, B0001, and B0002 are instruction names. Instruction names may be omitted; they are used only if we wish to refer to them.

The arithmetic/logic unit

The arithmetic/logic unit can be compared with an electronic calculator operated by a human (Figure 8.2). In our analysis of the account-balancing problem, Figure 8.3 indicates that the assignment statement of the account-balancing calculation is translated into four separate symbolic instructions. The first symbolic instruction, in Box 0003:

LOAD   OLD

requires the following actions:

1. Push the clear button. Bear in mind that the last time the cal-
    culator was used, a number may have been left in the accumu-
    lator. This number must be replaced by 0 before the computa-
    tion can be started.
2. Key in the content of box OLD.
3. Depress the ⊕ button.

Now we have in the accumulator the content of box OLD. (The
calculator added OLD to 0.) Using assignment statements, and

FIGURE 8.2
Electronic
calculator,
representing the
arithmetic/logic
unit of the
computer.

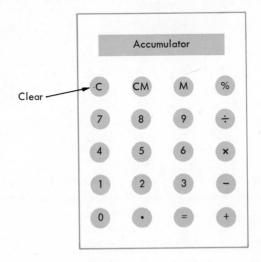

FIGURE 8.3
Computation of
BAL requires only
a single
assignment
statement, but four
symbolic
instructions.

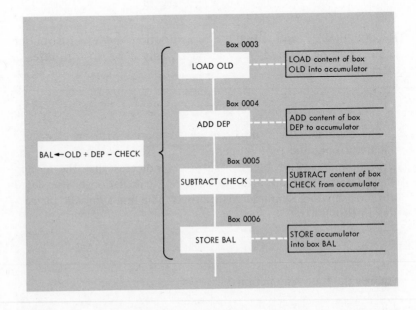

designating the content of the accumulator by ACC, we can say that our first symbolic instruction means:

$$\boxed{\text{ACC} \leftarrow \text{OLD}}$$

The second symbolic instruction, in Box 0004, in Figure 8.3 requires the following action:

1. Key in the content of box DEP.
2. Depress the ⊕ button.

Now DEP is added to the content of the accumulator, and we have OLD + DEP in the accumulator. Observe that the ADD symbolic instruction accomplishes the assignment statement:

$$\boxed{\text{ACC} \leftarrow \text{ACC} + \text{DEP}}$$

The third symbolic instruction, in Box 0005, requires the following actions:

1. Key in the content of box CHECK.
2. Depress the ⊖ button.

Now the amount of the check is subtracted from the content of the accumulator, and we have OLD + DEP − CHECK, or BAL, in the accumulator. Observe that the SUBTRACT symbolic instruction accomplishes the assignment statement:

$$\boxed{\text{ACC} \leftarrow \text{ACC} - \text{CHECK}}$$

The fourth and last symbolic instruction, in Box 0006, stores the content of the accumulator at memory location BAL:

$$\boxed{\text{BAL} \leftarrow \text{ACC}}$$

Note the difference between STORE and LOAD. Namely:

$$\boxed{\text{STORE BAL}}$$

means

$$\boxed{\text{STORE content of accumulator into BAL}}$$

but

LOAD OLD

means

LOAD into accumulator content of OLD

The output unit

Figure 8.4 shows how the single output flowchart box is translated into four symbolic instructions:

WRITE OLD
WRITE DEP
WRITE CHECK
WRITE BAL

What about the last symbolic instruction in Box 0011 in Figure 8.4? We are eliminating the flowchart, so we do not have flow lines

FIGURE 8.4
Printing four
numbers requires
four symbolic
instructions. The
BRANCH
instruction
replaces the
reverse flow
line of the
flowchart.

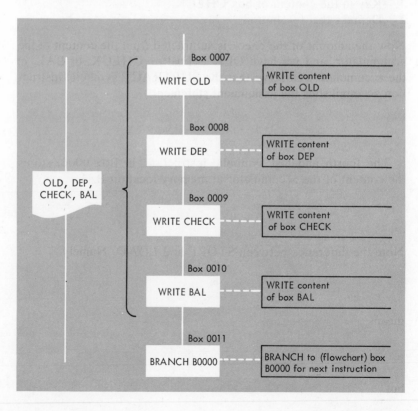

and arrows, and we must replace the reversed flow lines by a symbolic instruction. So by writing

BRANCH B0000

we tell the computer to branch unconditionally to the symbolic instruction which has the name B0000. Be sure to remember that the operand in an unconditional branch instruction is the name of an instruction, and not the name of data. Note that if an instruction is the target of a BRANCH instruction it must have a name.

Review of symbolic language programming

Figure 8.5 repeats, to the left of the first heavy vertical line, the symbolic language program for the account-balancing calculation. This is, then, the sheet that replaces the flowchart. To the right of this line the figure shows what happens in the accumulator and the storage boxes as the program is executed. On the far right are listed the actions caused by execution of instructions in the program. Amounts are in pennies because all data is in whole numbers.

Figure 8.6 summarizes the seven instructions discussed. If you want to write programs for more complicated flowcharts you need more instructions to perform operations like multiplication, division, and conditional branching, corresponding to Box 5 in Figure 2.10. However, it can be shown that a total of 12 symbolic instructions is sufficient to perform all calculations.

To clarify the meaning of the symbolic instructions discussed here, Figure 8.7 provides a comparison between symbolic,

FIGURE 8.5
Complete symbolic language program for account-balancing problem.

Assembly Language Program			Contents of Cells					Action
Name	Operation	Operand	Acc	OLD	DEP	CHECK	BAL	
B0000	READ	OLD	?	500	?	?	?	Read value of OLD from card
	READ	DEP			800			Read value of DEP from card
	READ	CHECK				400		Read value of CHECK from card
	LOAD	OLD	500					ACC ← OLD
	ADD	DEP	1300					ACC ← ACC + DEP
	SUBTRACT	CHECK	900					ACC ← ACC - CHECK
	STORE	BAL					900	BAL ← ACC
	WRITE	OLD						Print OLD
	WRITE	DEP						Print DEP
	WRITE	CHECK						Print CHECK
	WRITE	BAL						Print BAL
	BRANCH	B0000						Pick next instruction from B0000.

FIGURE 8.6
Summary of the
seven instructions
used.

THIS IS NOT A PROGRAM!

Operation	Operand	Comments
READ	A	Read the value of A from a card
WRITE	B	Write the value of B on output
LOAD*	C	ACC ← C
STORE†	D	D ← ACC
ADD	E	ACC ← ACC + E
SUBTRACT	F	ACC ← ACC − F
BRANCH	B7	Pick next instruction from B7

* LOAD into accumulator content of C
† STORE content of accumulator into D

FORTRAN, and COBOL language instructions. To write a program in symbolic language usually requires many more instructions than are necessary to write one in either FORTRAN or COBOL.

MACHINE LANGUAGE PROGRAMMING

In developing an understanding of the functions of hardware through an examination of software we progress from symbolic language programming to machine language programming.

The memory unit is a storage device having 10,000 pigeonholes or cells (Figure 8.8). Each of these cells can store a string of ten characters (letters or digits) preceded by the sign + or −, and each has an address of a four-digit number written directly above the cell. The data is kept in the cells of the storage device and referred to by the address of the cell in which the data is stored. In addition, operations are referred to by the three-letter alphabetic operation codes listed in Figure 8.9.

How do we translate or assemble a symbolic language program into a machine language program? All we need do is to specify where to keep the data, that is, provide each data element with an address, and then in each instruction, line by line, replace the opera-

FIGURE 8.7
Comparing
symbolic
instructions with
FORTRAN and
COBOL.

Symbolic		FORTRAN	COBOL
LOAD	C	ACC = C	MOVE C TO ACC
STORE	D	D = ACC	MOVE ACC TO D
ADD	E	ACC = ACC + E	ADD E TO ACC
SUBTRACT	F	ACC = ACC − F	SUBTRACT F FROM ACC
BRANCH	B0007	GO TO 0007	GO TO B0007

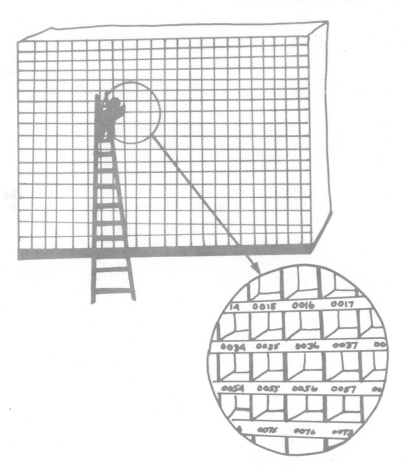

FIGURE 8.8 The memory is like a device used in a post office. Each of the 10,000 pigeonholes or cells has an address (like the number of the post office box) and holds a single data item.

Operation	Operation code
READ	RWD*
WRITE	WWD†
LOAD	LDA
STORE	STO
ADD	ADD
SUBTRACT	SUB
BRANCH	BRU‡

* Read a WorD
† Write a WorD
‡ BRanch Unconditionally

FIGURE 8.9 Operations are designated by an abbreviated three-letter operation code.

tion by the operation code and the name of the data by the cell address.

This process can be illustrated with the aid of the account-balancing problem. Let us arbitrarily agree that the values of OLD, DEP, CHECK, and BAL will be kept in cells with addresses 0100, 0101, 0102, and 0103. Now we can translate, line by line, the symbolic program of Figure 8.5 into the machine-language-oriented program shown left of the first heavy vertical line in Figure 8.10. Observe under the location column that now we simply number our instructions starting with 0000.

To the right of the first heavy line in Figure 8.10 it is shown how the contents of the cells change as the program is executed, and to the right of the second heavy line what actions are taken. The parentheses indicate the content of the referenced storage cell. Thus (0100), (0101), (0102), and (0103) indicate the values of OLD, DEP, CHECK, and BAL.

HOW THE COMPUTER SYSTEM OPERATES

The operations of the computer system can be illustrated by continuing the discussion of the account-balancing problem. The control unit first examines instruction 0000 (Figure 8.10) and tells the input unit to read one number from the input card and to store the number in the cell with address 0100.

Figure 8.11 illustrates the storage of sample values of OLD, DEP, and CHECK, following the reading of the first three data cards. After the third card is read cells 0100, 0101, and 0102 hold data; the rest of the cells hold *garbage,* that is, data of no use.

Note the difference between the *address* and the *content of a cell.* In Figure 8.11 cell 0100 does not contain the number 0100! It contains the number 500 encoded as + 000 000 0500.

The first three instructions in Figure 8.10 are already executed. Now the control unit examines the LOAD instruction, 0003, and tells the arithmetic unit to execute it. The arithmetic unit fetches the content of cell 0100 and follows this sequence of steps:

1. Clears the accumulator.
2. Keys in the number.
3. Depresses the (+) button.

that is, executes the LOAD instruction. And so on.

Storing the program in the computer and executing instructions

Finally the instructions are stored one by one in the memory, starting at location (address) 0000 so the instructions can be exe-

Machine language program / Contents of cells / Action

Location	Operation		Address	ACC	0100	0101	0102	0103	Print	For sample data	In general
0000	+RWD	000	0100	?	500	?	?	?		(0100)* ← 500	(0100) ← OLD
0001	+RWD	000	0101			800				(0101) ← 800	(0101) ← DEP
0002	+RWD	000	0102				400			(0102) ← 400	(0102) ← CHECK
0003	+LDA	000	0100	500						ACC ← 500	ACC ← OLD
0004	+ADD	000	0101	1300						ACC ← 1300	ACC ← ACC + DEP
0005	+SUB	000	0102	900						ACC ← 900	ACC ← ACC − CHECK
0006	+STO	000	0103					900		(0103) ← 900	(0103) ← BAL
0007	+WWD	000	0100						500	Print 500	Print OLD
0008	+WWD	000	0101						800	Print 800	Print DEP
0009	+WWD	000	0102						400	Print 400	Print CHECK
0010	+WWD	000	0103						900	Print 900	Print BAL
0011	+BRU	000	0000							Go to cell 0000	Go to cell 0000

* (0100) designates the content of cell 0100.

FIGURE 8.10
Machine language program for account-balancing problem.

FIGURE 8.11 How
storage cells are
filled with data.

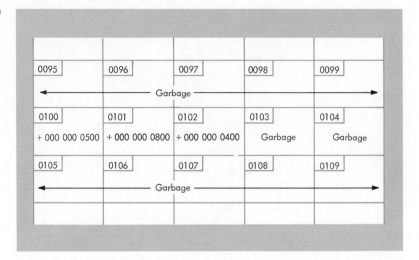

cuted. As shown in Figure 8.12, the machine language program will
be stored in cells 0000 to 0011.

The instructions of the program are in a dormant state in the
memory. The control unit activates the instructions one by one and
brings them to a live state. Two cycles of operation should be
distinguished:

1. The instruction cycle.
    a. The control unit fetches the instruction from memory and
        brings it alive by placing it into one of the registers of the
        CPU.
    b. The control unit examines and decodes the instruction to
        determine what action to take.
2. The execution cycle. The input, output, arithmetic/logic units
    perform all necessary actions, that is, execute the machine
    language oriented instructions.

FIGURE 8.12
Internal storage
of program for
account-balancing
calculation. Cells
0000 to 0011 hold
the machine
language
program.

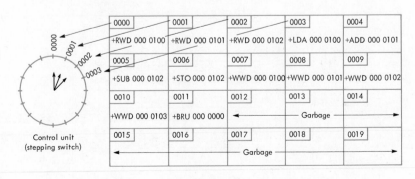

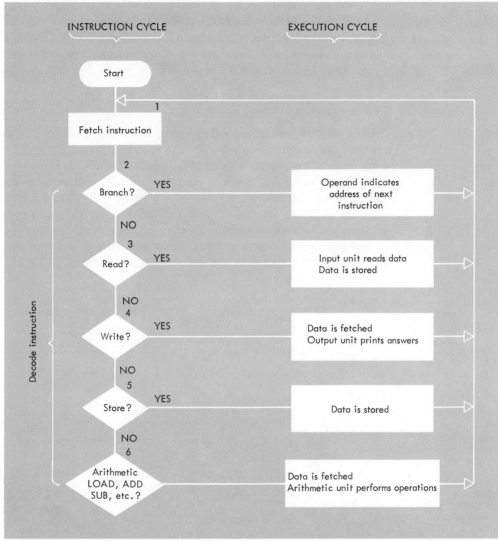

FIGURE 8.13 The instruction and execution cycles.

Figure 8.13 provides a flowchart which describes how the operations are broken up into subinstructions and then performed. First the control unit fetches the instruction from cell 0000. This is the fetch phase of the instruction cycle. The second phase is the decode phase of the instruction cycle, which involves a series of tests to determine what action is to be taken.

If the operation is an unconditional BRANCH (Box 2), the operand indicates the address of the next instruction. If it is not a BRANCH instruction the program drops through to Box 3 to test for READ. Then Box 4 tests for WRITE, Box 5 for STORE, and

Box 6 for the various arithmetic instructions (LOAD, ADD, SUB-TRACT, MULTIPLY, and DIVIDE).

You can think of the control action as performed by a clocklike switch which activates the sequence of instructions residing in the storage cells (see Figure 8.12, left side).

Alternate operations codes

Observe that we can use a three-letter alphabetic code for operations, as we assumed that the cells can hold ten characters and the signs + or −. If we assume that the cells hold only decimal numbers, we must replace the alphabetic operation codes by decimal codes (Figure 8.14). As an example, Figure 8.15 shows that the machine language program for the account-balancing program becomes a sequence of decimal numbers.

If storage is restricted to binary numbers, we can use the four-digit binary code shown in the last column of Figure 8.14 for the

FIGURE 8.14
Operation codes
may be alphabetic,
decimal, or binary.

Operation	Alphabetic code	Decimal code	Binary code
READ	RWD	01	0001
WRITE	WWD	02	0010
LOAD	LDA	03	0011
STORE	STO	04	0100
ADD	ADD	05	0101
SUBTRACT	SUB	06	0110
BRANCH	BRU	10	1010

FIGURE 8.15
Machine language
program for
account-balancing
problem using
decimal operation
code.

Location	Alphabetic code	Decimal code
0000	+RWD 000 0100	+01 0000 0100
0001	+RWD 000 0101	+01 0000 0101
0002	+RWD 000 0102	+01 0000 0102
0003	+LDA 000 0100	+03 0000 0100
0004	+ADD 000 0101	+05 0000 0101
0005	+SUB 000 0102	+06 0000 0102
0006	+STO 000 0103	+04 0000 0103
0007	+WWD 000 0100	+02 0000 0100
0008	+WWD 000 0101	+02 0000 0101
0009	+WWD 000 0102	+02 0000 0102
0010	+WWD 000 0103	+02 0000 0103
0011	+BRU 000 0000	+10 0000 0000

operations. But now we must also change the addresses into binary numbers. As an illustration, the symbolic instruction

+ ADD 000 8192

appears in decimal form as

+ 05 000 8192

and in binary form as

+ 0101 000 10000000000000

Symbolic language instructions cannot directly control the operations of a computer; only machine language instructions can do this. A high-level or symbolic language program must first be compiled or assembled into a machine language program before it can be executed by the computer.

The three components of the CPU

Data is processed by the three hardware components:

1. The memory unit.
2. The arithmetic/logic unit.
3. The control unit.

We discuss these units below.

MEMORY UNITS

Magnetic cores

A magnetic core is molded from iron powder into a tiny doughnut-shaped ring. Typical cores may be the size of the head of a pin or smaller. Each core is strung on four different wires, like beads, to form core planes (Figure 8.16). Several core planes are stacked one above each other to form a core stack (Figure 8.17).

If a sufficiently strong current is sent through the wire, the core will be magnetized (Figure 8.18) and stay magnetized even after the current is cut off. When the core is magnetized clockwise it is said to be turned "on," to represent the binary bit 1. If magnetized counterclockwise, the core is "off," to represent the binary bit 0. Thus by sending electric signals, cores can be turned on and off to

FIGURE 8.16
Magnetic cores
are first
organized into
planes. Four
wires are threaded
through each
core.

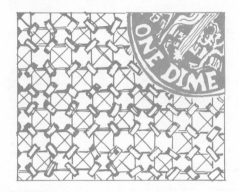

store bits, and the nine bits in "columns" in Figure 8.17 can represent characters in EBCDIC.

Magnetic cores were first introduced in the second-generation
computers, and by their fast, random-access capability made computers reliable, economical, and practical. Typical access times are
fractions of microseconds in fast cores and microseconds in slow
cores. However, today magnetic cores are being replaced in computers by semiconductor storage devices which are also called core
storage.

FIGURE 8.17 A
stack of magnetic
core planes. Each
column of cores
encodes a
character (byte).

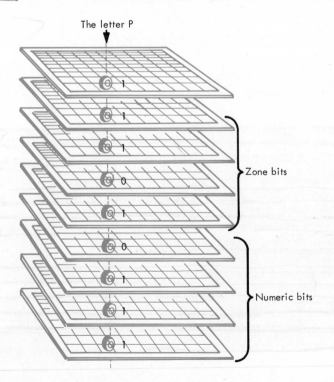

FIGURE 8.18 A strong electric current flowing from right to left magnetizes the core in a clockwise direction.

Semiconductor storage devices

Semiconductors are electronic devices (circuits, transistors, etc.) deposited on a base material consisting of a thin silicon chip sliced from a pure crystal. A single chip may contain thousands of storage and supporting circuits. The advantage of semiconductor storage devices is in short access time and small size. The access times are tens of nanoseconds and a single chip, .2 by .2 inches, may contain 10,000 circuits (Figure 8.19), implying that hundreds of thousands of circuits can be deposited per square inch of surface.

The storage is volatile, that is, if the current is interrupted, the bit is lost. This contrasts with nonvolatile magnetic storage, which depends on the magnetization of particles and not on the flow of electricity.

A storage bit is represented in a semiconductor circuit by the direction of the flow of electricity.

Virtual memory and storage hierarchies

In this chapter we have discussed semiconductor memories, which operate at speeds of tens of nanoseconds, and slow and fast cores, which operate in fractions or multiples of microseconds. In

FIGURE 8.19 A tiny semiconductor storage unit can contain many thousands of electronic circuits and can store many thousands of bits. The illustration is magnified about five times.

Courtesy Rockwell International

Chapter 7 we discussed mass storage units like magnetic disks, drums, and tapes and combinations of tapes and disks which have much slower access times. High performance systems can be obtained by combining various storage devices into a hierarchy of units. The combination can be effected by wiring or by software. The advantage of these combined units is that, on the average, shorter access time at lower costs are obtained.

When internal memory and auxiliary mass storage is combined by software, the storage system which results is called virtual storage. In virtual systems computer programs are divided into pages. Programs are stored in auxiliary devices like magnetic disks, but the programmer may not be aware of this situation. When a particular instruction is needed the appropriate page is transferred from the hibernating state in the auxiliary storage to the memory of the computer. When programmers write or study programs, they read the program sheet by sheet; the computer works with the program page by page. The advantage of virtual storage is that the programmer and the computer can use millions of bytes of effective storage, though the physical memory of the system is only a fraction of this amount.

THE ARITHMETIC/LOGIC UNIT

The arithmetic/logic unit was compared previously with an electronic calculator. In a computer, the calculator keyboard is replaced by an electronic register, so data can be fetched from storage and entered into the arithmetic/logic unit. The $\oplus$, $\ominus$, $\otimes$ keys (and so on) are replaced by electronic switches so all operations can be performed automatically and electronically. After an arithmetic operation is performed, the results are held briefly in one of the registers of the arithmetic/logic unit, and then the register releases electric signals so that data can be stored in the storage unit.

Connection between the arithmetic/logic unit, the storage unit, and the control unit is through a switching network similar to that of a telephone system.

THE CONTROL UNIT

The control unit is made up of electronic circuits and registers. The operations of the control unit are similar to the instruction and execution cycles described in Figure 8.13.

During the fetch phase of the instruction cycle the control unit establishes connections between the storage cell, where the instruction is stored, and the instruction register (Figure 8.20) of the control unit and transfers the instruction from storage to the instruction register. This is like dialing a telephone number and transmitting data.

Now the instruction is alive. The control unit also stores in the sequence register of the control unit the address of the instruction being worked on. This is necessary so the next instruction can be fetched from storage after the current instruction is executed.

It is of great importance to understand the role of the instruction register. A dormant instruction from storage is fetched and must

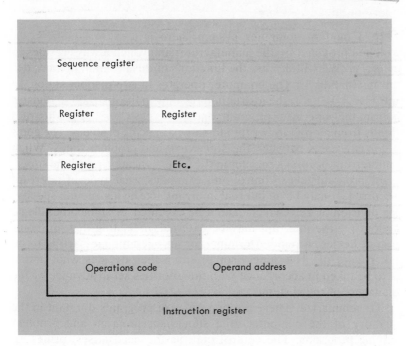

Sequence register

Register   Register

Register   Etc.

Operations code   Operand address

Instruction register

CONTROL UNIT

FIGURE 8.20   The control unit is made of several electronic registers, but the heart of the unit is the instruction register.

be held alive in the instruction register so the instruction can be decoded and executed. A source program instruction (FORTRAN, COBOL, etc.) or a symbolic instruction cannot be placed in the instruction register. Thus source programs must first be assembled or compiled. Only machine language instructions can be brought alive, placed into the instruction register, and handled by the CPU.

During the decode phase of the instruction cycle the decoder, a device of the control unit, examines the operation code. During the execution cycle, the decoder causes the circuits to perform the detailed steps implied by the operation code.

The control unit moves from instruction to instruction. In a classical computer there is only one program in execution, and the control unit moves from one instruction to the next unless there is a branch instruction, in which case the operand may be the address of the next instruction. If the instruction is not a branch instruction, the number in the sequence register is increased by 1, and thereby the address of the next instruction is obtained.

Thus, by alternating between the instruction cycle and the execution cycle, the program stored in the computer is executed.

Interrupt-driven systems

In a modern computer system there is a supervisor program which is provided by the manufacturer and which always resides in memory. (We will discuss the functions of this program in more detail in Chapter 9.) The computer operates in two distinct states: In the supervisor state the instruction residing in the instruction register is from the supervisor program; and in the problem state the instruction is from a program written to solve a specific problem. The computer alternates between the supervisor and problem states. When an interrupt occurs, a register in the CPU indicates it, and the supervisor program takes control and examines what type of interrupt occurred. It may be an internal interrupt, like an instruction specifying division by zero which cannot be executed, or some other illegal action. Or the interrupt may be external, indicating that an input/output device, a remote terminal, or an operator message is to be taken care of. The supervisor program then decides what action is to be taken in accordance with the priorities set in advance by the managers of the system.

To summarize: There are two types of programs dormant in the memory of the computer—the supervisor program and problem solving programs. The control unit, as the need arises, brings an instruction from these two types of programs alive by placing it into the instruction register.

Reliability control

The control unit also deals with malfunctions of the system which can cause interrupts. In a classical computer if failure occurs, the computer stops and the operator fixes the system and starts the computer again. Most likely the operator must start to run the program from the beginning.

In a modern computer system the possibility of failure must be dealt with in an automatic and efficient manner. To avoid the possible need for starting programs over again, the system has checkpoints at which the contents of all registers are moved into nonvolatile storage. If failure occurs the system can perform a restart by retrieving the lost contents of registers from the non-volatile storage.

Suppose, for example, a power loss occurs. This does not happen instantaneously, and there are instruments in the system which detect the drop in the power level. The computer automatically takes action: the contents of registers are stored in nonvolatile storage for use when restarting. If an auxiliary power supply is available, it is switched in automatically and there is no interruption in the operation of the system.

THE COMPUTER CONSOLE

The computer itself may be completely automatic, but who runs the computer? Who starts and stops it? And how? It is the computer operator, with the aid of the computer console panel (see Figure 7.38 in Chapter 7), which may be equipped with a CRT device.

The console, the typewriter, and the CRT device tell the operator:

1. The status of the computer system.
2. The status of the peripheral equipment.
3. Contents of the registers of the computer.

For example, the operator may be told that a printer needs paper, that a particular magnetic tape reel is to be mounted on a designated tape drive, that a particular disk drive is overheating and the system is to be shut down.

Several actions are available to the operator, who can:

1. Start and stop the computer.
2. Manually instruct the computer to perform certain operations.
3. Change the operations of the computer.
4. Enter data into registers and storage.
5. Enter instructions into registers and storage.
6. Find out what is wrong with the computer by diagnosing malfunctionings.

The operation of the computer system is highly automatic, because of the software (to be discussed in detail in Chapter 9) stored in the system. Once the computer is started, it will run on its own, supported and monitored by the human operator.

SIMULTANEOUS PERIPHERAL OPERATIONS

The discussion so far has assumed that the input, arithmetic/logic, and output units work serially, one after the other. Figure 8.21 illustrates the timing of events in such a computer system. To be

FIGURE 8.21 In
serial (unbuffered)
processing, only
one unit of the
computer system
works at a time;
the others are idle.

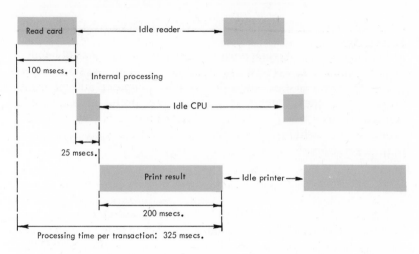

Processing time per transaction: 325 msecs.

specific, assume that the card reader reads 600 cards per minute (10 cards per second), and that one card must be read for each transaction. Thus the input time for one card is 100 milliseconds. Assume that the CPU takes 25 milliseconds to process the data, and finally that the printer prints 300 lines per minute (5 per second), and that only a single output line is required. Thus, output will take 200 milliseconds per transaction. The total time to process a transaction will be:

$$100 + 25 + 200 = 325 \text{ milliseconds}$$

This system is said to be input/output bound; the CPU is idle more than 90 percent of the time. Why not keep the CPU busy by making the units work simultaneously? Why not overlap operations to reduce the time to process a transaction? In modern computer systems this is possible by spooling (Simultaneous Peripheral Operations On Line,) and by the use of buffers and channels. Such devices and techniques, under the control of the CPU, serve to decrease the wait or idle time of the CPU and increase the efficiency of computer operations.

Buffer storage

Buffer storage devices are high-speed storage units incorporated either into input/output devices or the CPU, or housed separately as peripheral devices. Instead of wiring the input/output devices directly to the CPU, input/output devices are wired to the buffer storage, which in turn is wired to the CPU (Figure 8.22). Once the CPU issues a command to the input buffer, it will continue with its own work and the input buffer will, independently from the CPU, accept data from an input device. It can accept data at a slow rate, if required, and also release data at an electronic speed to the internal storage unit when commanded to do so by the CPU. The output buffer can accept data at electronic speed from the storage unit and can release data at slow speed if required to an output device.

The result of inserting the buffer between the slow input/output unit and the internal storage unit is that the CPU needs to devote only a limited amount of its time to input/output, and the components of the computer system will essentially operate simultaneously. Observe in Figure 8.23 that it still takes 325 milliseconds to process a transaction, but due to an overlap of 125 milliseconds, one transaction is completed each 200 milliseconds. Thus buffers can increase the throughput of computer systems, although this system is still output bound.

FIGURE 8.22
Input/output units communicate with the CPU through buffers. The CPU needs to spend only a limited time on input/output operations.

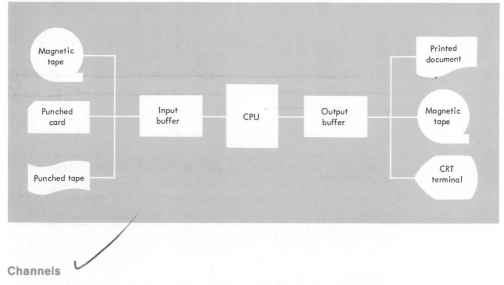

Channels

To further increase the data processing capacity and speed of modern large-scale computer systems, tens and even hundreds of input/output units can be placed under the control of a single CPU. Buffers are inadequate to handle the complexity and high-speed requirement of such systems, and therefore they are replaced by self-contained computers called channels, which are housed separately from the CPU. Channels are special-purpose computers, that is, they are input/output processors inserted between the main storage and the other peripheral units.

A channel, under command from the CPU, handles the opera-

FIGURE 8.23.
When processing
is buffered, the
various units of
the computer
system essentially
work
simultaneously.

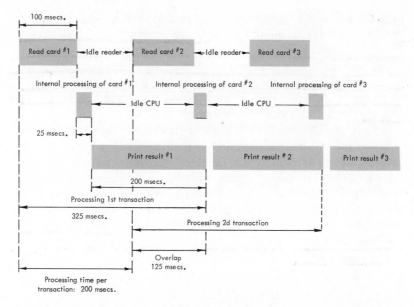

tions required to transmit data between input/output units and the CPU. As a result, the CPU spends practically no time on input/output, and peripheral units appear to operate simultaneously, for all practical purposes.

MODERN COMPUTER SYSTEMS

As the performance and complexity of computer systems increase, the problem of sharing and allocating resources and facilities in the best way becomes more severe. Providing high performance at low cost requires the introduction of new techniques, such as the three we discuss below.

Multiprogramming

In *time sharing* many users share the same computer system. Each user controls the computer during different time intervals. In multiprogramming two or more programs share the memory of the computer within the same time interval, that is concurrently. Thus several programs control the system. Note that there is only one instruction register, so at the same instant only one of the programs is in control.

As an example, consider a computer system which operates in a time-sharing mode and concurrently executes programs in a batch mode. The memory of the computer is divided into partitions. One of these partitions is assigned to foreground processing of time-sharing programs. However, time sharing is only a part-time function for the system, so when there is no time-sharing program to execute, the system performs a switching operation from foreground to background processing to execute batch programs. When requirements for the execution of time-sharing programs arise, the system switches back to foreground operation.

To provide efficient operations, programs are divided into smaller units of work, or tasks. The system contains a software item called a scheduler which takes care of the tasks accomplished according to the established priorities. Some systems operate in multiprogramming with a given or fixed number of tasks (MFT) and others with a variable number of tasks (MVT). Multitasking means concurrent execution of one main task and one or more subtasks in the same partition of the memory.

The utilization of internal storage can be further increased by the use of overlays. With overlays the same area in internal storage can be used for different program segments at different times. Thus when one program is no longer needed in storage, another program can replace all or part of it.

Multiprocessing

In time sharing or multiprogramming the computer system operates in a concurrent but not simultaneous mode. In a multiprocessing system there are several processors working together in a simultaneous manner.

Consider, for example, the situation when a computer is connected to a large number of remote terminals and a great many interrupts occur. To relieve the CPU of the work of taking care of interrupts, a separate front-end processor is provided. The advent of inexpensive minicomputers makes such an approach particularly desirable from the economic point of view, and the simultaneous operation of the two computers produces a highly efficient system.

Another example is a large user who operates two or more computer systems. When a program is to be executed, the human operator must decide which of the computers should be allocated to the program. Often programs can be broken into separate parts, such as input/output or computation. To provide efficient operation, the human operator may assign the input of one program to one machine and, later, the computations to another machine. Multiprocessing provides the capability to wire the computers together and to automate the operations of the computers in an efficient manner.

When a computer system operates with a large number of remote terminals, there is the possibility that processing can be performed where the terminals are located. With the aid of inexpensive mini-computers, or intelligent terminals, it becomes possible to distribute data processing between the central computer and remote computers. This results in simultaneous processing at remote locations.

Microprogramming

Computer systems differ in their manner of operation, and in general, a machine language suitable to one computer system cannot be operated on a different system. In discussing Figure 8.20 we noted the registers of the control unit, in particular the role of the instruction register. Such a computer is inflexible and is wired to operate with a fixed set of instructions.

Figure 8.13 showed how the traditional computer decodes and executes instructions. Because instructions are broken up into sub-instructions or microinstructions and then executed, some computers are wired only to execute microinstructions. Such computers execute programs with the aid of microprogramming. When such a computer is manufactured it would be incapable of executing instructions, except that it is provided with read-only memory. The read-only memory is loaded by the microprogram stored on an auxiliary storage device like a floppy disk or diskette, and then the computer is ready for the user. After the content of the read-only memory is stored in the computer, it becomes similar to a traditional computer.

This kind of computer can be loaded with various microprograms, can execute different kinds of instructions, and, in fact, can operate in a different manner for different users. Once the computer is loaded and delivered, it can be changed to perform new instructions by loading a new microprogram. Thus microprogramming allows a great deal of additional flexibility.

A computer can execute an assembler language program written for another computer. Likewise, a small microprogrammed computer can have the capability of executing a large number of instructions available otherwise only to large computers. Thus, small computers can execute programs written for large computer systems. It is also possible to provide specialized control instructions to increase the efficiency of input/output devices.

Hardware versus software

In the classical computer there is a clear distinction between hardware and software. With microprogramming the line between hardware and software becomes blurred, and data processing functions performed by hardware can become software functions, and vice versa.

The idea that functions can be performed either by hardware or software is not new. For example, early computers performed floating-point operations (scientific computations with numbers to the base 10) with software, that is with programming. Later, circuits were built to perform floating-point operations with hardware. Today, in some families of computers small models perform floating-point operations through software, and larger models through hardware. However, the machines are compatible, and the programmer does not see the difference; the programmer writes a program which runs on either a small computer or a large one. Thus machine language instructions may be executed in some models by software and in others by hardware.

We have considered the function of compiling a program as a software function. However, in an online system there is a need for high-speed response, and therefore many systems operate in an interpretive mode. This means that each time an instruction is written, it is translated immediately into machine language instructions.

In most systems the translation, that is, interpretation, is done by software, which results in relatively slow operations. In some computers (like the IBM 5100), however, the interpretation is done not by software but by read-only memory, that is, by hardware. Thus high-speed interpretation results.

Hardware costs have been rapidly decreasing and will continue to do so in the future. Therefore it is predicted that many software functions will be taken over by hardware.

Computer configurations

From the various components of the computer system, an essentially infinite variety of computer configurations can be built. In fact, a large variety of computer systems is available; there is a practically continuous size range, from very small to very large. There is no need to go into the details of different computer configurations, but a rough classification of systems is useful.

The smallest of the computers are the microcomputers, which we discussed in Chapter 4. These computers are used mostly in controlling processes.

The next level of computer is the programmable calculator (Figure 8.24). These are very much like the classical computer and have become popular because of their low cost. Some of these programmable calculators operate only with keys; the operator carries out a data processing task by depressing a sequence of keys. The

FIGURE 8.24
Typical
programmable
calculator.

Courtesy Hewlett-Packard

memory of the calculator stores the sequence of keys, and from then on the same task can be accomplished automatically. Other programmable calculators accept magnetic cards, cassettes, or other input media, and data and programs can thus be entered. Some of the calculators display answers in registers, and some are equipped with printers.

FIGURE   8.25
Typical small
minicomputer.

Courtesy IBM

	1950	1955	1960	1965	1970	Present & future
Number of components/cubic feet	1,000	10,000	100,000	1,000,000	10,000,000	300,000,000
Internal time to add	250	15	4	.5	30	10
		——— in microseconds ———			——— in nanoseconds ———	
Access time to internal storage	300	12	4	.5	100	30
		——— in microseconds ———			——— in nanoseconds ———	
Core storage capacity in bytes	100	150,000	150,000	500,000	1,000,000	billion
			——— bytes ———			
Cost in dollars per bytes of core storage	25	20	10	2	1 to .5	.05
			——— dollars/bytes ———			
Cost in dollars per bytes of external magnetic storage	7 to 3	5 to 1	5 to .01	1 to .01	.01 to .001	.0001
			——— dollars/bytes ———			
Cost in dollars to execute one million instructions	1.5 to 10	5 to 1	1 to .5	.2 to .05	.05 to .01	.001
			——— dollars/one million instructions ———			

FIGURE 8.26 Performance of past and present computers.

These calculators are relatively easy to program, and manufacturers also provide specialized programs to aid the user. Programmable calculators are suitable for small data processing jobs and provide inexpensive ways to solve simple problems.

The next level of computer configuration is the class of minicomputers (Figure 8.25). These are small computers capable of performing small-scale or limited data processing operations. They are also useful as parts of distributed computer systems to perform specialized operations and are therefore widely used. Medium-size computers are larger, faster, and have more general data processing capabilities than minicomputers.

At the highest level are the large, general-purpose, comprehensive data processors. These excel in general capability and are suitable to performing large data processing jobs. However, the cost of such processors is high.

Future hardware systems

Because of rapid changes in this field it is hard to predict what the performance of future hardware systems will be, but it is certain that the trend to improvement in computer hardware and software will continue.

Figure 8.26 summarizes the performance of past and present computers. It is predicted that computers will perform billions of instructions per second and occupy a space comparable to that needed for a shoe box. Circuits will perform in a few nanoseconds. Internal memories will have access times measured in tens of nanoseconds and storage capacities measured in hundreds of millions of bytes. Mass memories will have access time measured in microseconds and capacities measured in trillions of bytes. We can also predict that the dramatic decrease in cost of hardware will continue.

SUMMARY

1. For the user the best approach to hardware is through software and programming.
2. The CPU represents, stores, and moves both data and instructions. It interprets and executes instructions and controls peripheral devices.
3. Symbolic and machine language instructions consist of two parts: the operation and the operand.
4. In symbolic programming instruction operands are represented by symbols, in machine language programming by addresses (numbers).
5. Only machine language instructions can be used directly by

the registers of a computer. High-level and symbolic language programs must first be compiled or assembled into machine language programs.

6. Storage units contain both data and programs.
7. The most commonly used memory units consist of magnetic cores and semiconductor devices.
8. The arithmetic/logic unit, an electronic calculatorlike device, performs all arithmetic and logical operations.
9. The control unit performs its functions in two cycles:
   a. the instruction cycle (fetch and decode phases).
   b. the execution cycle.
10. The control unit alternates between executing instructions of the supervisor program and of the problem (application) programs.
11. The simultaneous operation of the peripheral units of the computer system is accomplished by buffers and channels under the control of the CPU.
12. Multiprogramming and multiprocessing greatly increase the efficiency and flexibility of computer systems.
13. Microprogramming allows modification of the instruction set of the computer system through the use of read-only memory.
14. As new hardware techniques are developed, the distinction between hardware and software functions becomes blurred.
15. There is an enormous variety of configurations of computer systems.
16. A large-scale modern distributed computer system is a combination of CPUs, channels, internal storage units, and peripheral units, integrated into an efficient high-performance data processing system.
17. The future of hardware can be summarized in four statements: more powerful, faster, smaller, and less expensive.

KEY CONCEPTS AND WORDS

accumulator: a register in which the result of an arithmetic or logic operation is formed.

background processing: the automatic execution of lower priority computer programs when higher priority programs are not using the system resources.

buffer: storage used to compensate for a difference in rate of flow of data or time of occurrence of events when transmitting data from one device to another.

channel: a hardware device that connects the CPU and main storage with the control unit of input/output.

checkpoint: (1) a place in a program where a check or a recording of data for restart purposes is performed, (2) a point at which information about the status of a job and a system can be recorded so that the job can later be restarted.

concurrent: pertaining to the occurrence of two or more events or activities within the same specified interval of time.

configuration: the interconnected group of machines, devices, and programs that makes up a data processing system.

current instruction: the instruction on which the CPU is working at the instant.

decode phase: the phase of the instruction cycle during which the instruction is examined, identified, and executed.

execution cycle: the second of the two cycles of operations required for the execution of an instruction, that is, the time interval when the control unit carries out the detailed steps implied by the operation code of an instruction.

fetch phase: the phase of the instruction cycle when an instruction is transferred from memory to the instruction register.

foreground: in multiprogramming, the environment in which high-priority programs are executed.

front-end processor: a computer which relieves the CPU of a number of functions caused by interrupts and other requirements.

input/output bound: situation when throughput in a computer system is limited by input or output capacity.

instruction cycle: the first of the two cycles of operation required for the execution of an instruction.

instruction register: the register into which an instruction is transferred from memory.

interpretive mode: a method of operation in which each source language statement is translated and executed before translating and executing the next source language statement.

microprogramming: a method of operation in which each complete instruction starts the execution of a sequence of microinstructions which are generally at a more elementary level.

multiprocessing system: a computer system employing two or more interconnected processing units to execute programs simultaneously.

multiprogramming: the concurrent execution of two or more programs by a computer.

multiprogramming with fixed number of tasks (MFT): multiprogramming system allowing a fixed number of tasks in main storage.

multiprogramming with variable number of tasks (MVT): multiprogramming system in which the number of tasks in main storage can be changed by the operating system.

multitasking: the concurrent execution of one main task and one or more subtasks in the same partition or region of memory.

operation code: a code that represents a specific operation.

overlap operations: to do something at the same time that something else is being done.

overlay: the technique of repeatedly using the same regions of internal storage during different stages of a program.

page: a set of instructions in virtual storage; data that can be transferred between memory and external storage.

partition: an assigned section of the memory used in multiprogramming.

problem state: a state during which the central processing unit executes instructions from a problem or application program.

read-only memory: storage in which contents are not directly alterable by programs written by the user.

restart: to reestablish the execution of a program using the data recorded at an earlier time.

scheduler: a program which schedules jobs for processing.

semiconductor: solid material whose capacity for carrying an electric current is between that of a conductor and an insulator.

semiconductor storage: storage units using semiconductors as circuit elements.

sequence register: register in the control unit where the address of an instruction is held while the instruction is being executed.

spooling: simultaneous operation of the peripheral units of a computer system.

supervisor program: program which coordinates the use of resources and maintains the flow of CPU operations.

supervisor state: state during which the CPU can execute instructions of the supervisor program.

symbolic language: computer language in which addresses are represented by symbols.

task: a unit of work for the CPU in multiprogramming.

virtual storage: an area in auxiliary storage where programs can be stored and transferred to memory.

volatile storage: a storage device in which stored data is lost when electric power is removed.

DISCUSSION QUESTIONS

1. Report on your collection of newspaper, magazine, and television items, and cartoons, jokes, and anecdotes.

2. Prepare a flowchart to describe our approach of going from software to hardware.

3. Describe and illustrate the five functions of the CPU.

4. What are the two parts of a computer instruction in symbolic language programming? Illustrate.

5. Describe in your own words what we mean by symbolic programming.

6. Define and explain in your own words: *accumulator, unconditional,*

transfer, target, branch. Give examples. Compare your definitions with those in your dictionary and explain differences, if any.[2]

7. Change the account-balancing program in the text, assuming that two deposits are made, DEP1 and DEP2. For this new problem modify Figures 8.1, 8.3, 8.4 and 8.5.

8. Write a symbolic language program which: (*a*) reads a sequence of pairs of numbers, A and B, (*b*) prints a sequence of numbers, B and A.

9. Repeat Exercise 8, but also print A + B.

10. How do you accomplish branching (transfer of control) in symbolic language programming?

11. What is the difference between the *address* of a cell and the *content* of a cell?

12. What is the difference between a symbolic and a machine language instruction?

13. For the problem given in Exercise 7, prepare an illustration similar to Figure 8.10.

14. For the problem in Exercise 7, prepare an illustration similar to Figure 8.11.

15. For the problem in Exercise 7, prepare an illustration similar to Figure 8.12.

16. Describe how a computer executes a program. Where are the instructions stored? What are the operation cycles?

17. Define and explain in your own words: *fetch, dormant, live.* Give examples. Compare your definitions with those in your dictionary and explain differences, if any.

18. What is a subinstruction?

19. How can a machine language instruction be encoded into decimal form? Binary form? Illustrate.

20. In Figure 8.15 replace the operation code with binary code.

21. Prepare a machine language program similar to the one shown in Figure 8.15 for the problem given in Exercise 7. Use an alphabetic code.

22. Repeat Exercise 21, but use a decimal code.

23. Define and explain in your own words: *operation code, alphabetic, decimal, binary.* Give examples. Compare your definitions with those in your dictionary and explain differences, if any.

24. What is the difference between the memory (internal storage) and external storage? Compare the use of both. Provide illustrations.

25. What are magnetic cores? Core planes and stacks? What is stored in cores? Describe the advantages and disadvantages of magnetic cores.

---

[2] In all word problems you need make comparisons only if the word or phrase is in your dictionary.

26. Describe semiconductor storage. Compare semiconductor and magnetic core storage. Describe advantages and disadvantages.

27. What is volatile storage?

28. What is virtual memory?

29. Define and explain in your own words: *virtual, page, hibernate.* Give examples. Compare your definitions with those in your dictionary and explain differences, if any.

30. What is meant by a hierarchy of storage units?

31. Describe the arithmetic/logic unit of the computer.

32. Describe the control unit—its operation, cycles, phases, and registers.

33. Define and explain in your own words: *instruction register, dormant, alive, sequence register, current instruction, fetch phase, decoder.* Give examples. Compare your definitions with those in your dictionary and explain differences, if any.

34. Describe a computer driven by interrupts.

35. Define and explain in your own words: *supervisor program, supervisory state, problem state, internal and external interrupt, priority.* Give examples. Compare your definitions with those in your dictionary and explain differences, if any.

36. How is reliability dealt with in a modern computer?

37. Define and explain in your own words: *checkpoint, restart.* Give examples. Compare your definitions with those in your dictionary and explain differences, if any.

38. Describe the functions of the computer console and computer operator.

39. Describe how *spooling* is performed in a modern computer system.

40. Prepare an illustration similar to Figure 8.21, assuming that it takes: (*a*) 150 milliseconds to read a card, (*b*) 15 milliseconds to perform internal processing, (*c*) 250 milliseconds to print the results. What is the total processing time per transaction?

41. Compare *buffers* and *data channels.* How are they used? Why are they important?

42. Prepare an illustration similar to Figure 8.23 for the problem given in Exercise 40. What is the processing time per transaction?

43. Describe and compare the meaning of the words: *multiprogramming, multiprocessing,* and *microprogramming.*

44. Define and explain in your own words: *concurrent, partition, foreground, background, task, scheduler, MFT, MVT, multitasking, overlay, front-end processing.* Give examples. Compare your definitions with those in your dictionary and explain differences, if any.

45. Compare the technique of microprogramming with the use of subinstructions in Figure 8.13. What is a microinstruction?

46. Compare the functions performed by computer hardware and software.

47. What is meant by *interpretation?*
48. Describe various configurations of computer systems with which you are familiar.
49. Describe programmable calculators.
50. Describe predictions as to future hardware systems.
51. Review and update your Personal Summary of this course (see Exercise 28, Chapter 1).

9

Programming and
software systems

Y ou now have the necessary background to go more deeply into programming and software systems: Chapter 5 discussed the job of the data processing professional and the principles of programming development; Chapter 6 discussed data representation, and Chapters 7 and 8, hardware systems. To perform their functions, programmers and systems analysts need two types of knowledge. One is technical; it involves better programming languages and more automation in program preparation. The second is the approach to programming; this is more art than science. You need to acquire both of these types of knowledge.

The introduction of procedure-oriented languages was perhaps the greatest boon to the programming profession. Even today much advanced work is being done to improve these languages. Over 100 procedure-oriented languages are now in existence, forming a veritable Tower of Babel of computer-programming languages (Figure 9.1). Fortunately, most procedure-oriented language programming is done in one of four languages: COBOL, FORTRAN, BASIC, and PL/I. The first three of these are topics of chapters in the Language Supplement (Appendix one), and in this chapter we present only an overview of them. The fourth language, PL/I, is not as widely used, so a brief introduction suffices. We also present an introduction to assembler language programming, input/output control systems (IOCS), and the report program generator (RPG). Thus you will have the necessary foundation for further study of any of these languages.

An improved approach to the art of programming is provided by structured programming, which is based on the principle of hierarchical structures introduced in Chapter 5. It offers programmers a valuable tool with which to improve their performance.

FIGURE 9.1 The Tower of Babel of programming languages.*

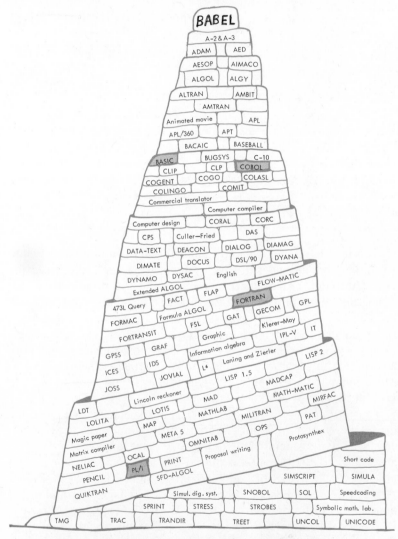

And the LORD said, . . . let us go down, and there confound
their language, that they may not understand
one another's speech (Genesis, 11: 6–7)

* Concept of the Tower of BABEL to represent a large set of programming languages is attributable to the *Communications of the ACM*, a publication of the Association for Computing Machinery, Inc. The illustration appears on the front endpaper of *Programming Languages: History and Fundamentals* by Jean E. Sammet © 1969 Prentice-Hall, Inc., Englewood Cliffs, N.J.

PROCEDURE-ORIENTED LANGUAGES

FORTRAN

The history of the development of FORTRAN[1] (*FOR*mula *TRAN*slation) closely parallels the history of programming. By 1954 there was widespread dissatisfaction with assembler language programming, and the concept emerged that the computer could produce machine language programs automatically. FORTRAN was conceived as a language to be used in solving numerical computations with the aid of mathematically oriented notation. FORTRAN was not oriented toward business data processing, though it has found some applications in business. By 1963 substantially all manufacturers offered FORTRAN compilers.

The language has been considerably standardized and extended, and it has become the most popular language used in education. A significant contribution to the teaching of FORTRAN was made when the University of Waterloo in Canada introduced *WAT*erloo *FORTRAN*, WATFOR, and later WATFIV ("the one after WATFOR"). These versions of FORTRAN are particularly suitable for educational applications.

Advantages and disadvantages of FORTRAN FORTRAN has a number of advantages as a programming language:

1. Outstanding capability for mathematical calculations.
2. Highly standardized.
3. Available on most computer systems.
4. Relatively easy to learn.

FORTRAN also has disadvantages:

1. Not oriented to business data processing.
2. Limited capability to manipulate data, files, data bases, and non-numeric processing.
3. Limited input/output capability.
4. Only six characters allowed for names of variables, thus offering little mnemonic capability.
5. Limited capability to take full advantage of modern hardware and software.

COBOL

In 1959 a meeting was held at the Pentagon by the Department of Defense to suggest that a *CO*mmon *B*usiness *O*riented *L*anguage, COBOL, be developed. The underlying philosophy of the development of a common business language was to provide a natural, Englishlike language that is readable by nonprogrammers. The

---

[1] Terms printed in color are defined at the end of the chapter.

mathematically oriented notation of FORTRAN programmers was specifically excluded from COBOL.

COBOL is a frustrating language for students to master. A significant educational contribution was the University of Waterloo's introduction of *WAT*erloo C*OBOL,* or WATBOL.

Advantages and disadvantages of COBOL   COBOL has these advantages:

1. Business data processing oriented.
2. Good capability for data, files, and data base manipulation.
3. Good input/output and edit capability.
4. Englishlike, easy to read and to understand.
5. Full mnemonic notation and practically self-documenting.

Disadvantages of COBOL include:

1. Requires a great deal of writing.
2. Calculations are difficult to perform.
3. Hardware dependent; often difficult to make versions from different computers compatible.
4. Relatively hard to learn.

BASIC

BASIC (*B*eginners' *A*ll-purpose *S*ymbolic *I*nstruction *C*ode) was developed in a time-sharing environment at Dartmouth College in 1965. It was conceived as an easy-to-learn, calculations-oriented language which could serve as a stepping stone in learning FORTRAN.

Advantages and disadvantages of BASIC   The advantages of BASIC are:

1. It is easy to learn.
2. It has a good capability for numerical calculations.
3. It is tailored to a time-sharing environment.

The disadvantages of BASIC are:

1. It is not business oriented.
2. Names of variables are one letter followed by a digit, providing no mnemonic capability.
3. Limited instruction set provides modest programming power and requires many programming instructions.
4. It has limited data, file, data base, input/output, and nonnumeric capability.

PL/I   *TEST*

By 1963 many people recognized the need for a language which would combine and replace both FORTRAN and COBOL, so an effort was begun to develop *Programming Language I* (PL/I). The aims of PL/I are very ambitious; it is supposed to have the advantages of all popular programming languages without any of their disadvantages. Not surprisingly, therefore, PL/I is an extremely comprehensive language with large capability, many features, and numerous complications.

The future of PL/I is still uncertain, however, as most manufacturers do not provide compilers. To facilitate the acceptance of PL/I a subset with more modest capability, PL/C, was developed at Cornell University. The elements of PL/I can be illustrated with programs for the commission calculation problem (Chapter 2, Figure 2.10).

The commission calculation in PL/I   PL/I programs are written in segments called procedures which later are put together to form a complete program. Figure 9.2 shows an extremely simple procedure for handling the commission calculation.

The first line indicates that the program is a MAIN PROCEDURE. The name of the procedure happens to be VAZSONY. Every PL/I program must start with a MAIN PROCEDURE statement.

Observe that the coding form has no special headings. Programmers write statements in a free form wherever they want to in Columns 2 to 72. To let the compiler know the end of a statement each statement in PL/1 must end in a semicolon. The programmer can write several statements on the same line in the coding sheet or continue a statement on the next line.

Statements can be labeled in PL/I; this program has three labels: B1, B10, and B55. The compiler knows that these are labels because there is a colon after each label.

The statement labeled B1 reads the value of the amount. This is one of the ways to input data in PL/I; there are several other ways not covered in this text. The next statement is a branch instruction. If the amount is less than or equal to 150, control is transferred to B10. Otherwise, the program drops through to the next statement, where C, the commission, is computed. Then there is an unconditional transfer, the GO TO B55.

The statement labeled B55 is the output statement. This is only

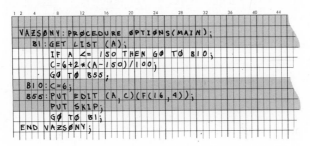

FIGURE 9.2
Commission
calculation in
PL/I (FORTRAN-
like).

one of the statements used in PL/I for printing; several others used for output are not covered in this text. The next statement advances the paper in the printer, and then there is an unconditional transfer to B1 to read another data item.

All procedures must end with an END statement.

Does this program look like a FORTRAN program?[2] We have mentioned that PL/I contains the features of both FORTRAN and COBOL, and much more. The program we have just discussed is indeed much like a FORTRAN program and will compile into an object program quite similar to a FORTRAN program.

What about the COBOL-like or data processing features of PL/I? Figure 9.3 shows the commission program rewritten in a somewhat different manner. First we use mnemonic names for the variables, as is customary in data processing. In addition, we use a DECLARE statement, which makes the program perform calculations with decimal numbers. Both the amount and the commis-

FIGURE 9.3
Commission
calculation, in
PL/I (COBOL-
like).

```
COMSION: PROCEDURE OPTIONS(MAIN);
    DECLARE (AMOUNT,COMMISSION) FIXED DECIMAL ((10,2));
    INPUT: GET LIST (AMOUNT);
    IF AMOUNT <= 150 THEN COMMISSION = 6;
        ELSE COMMISSION = 6 + 2*(AMOUNT-150)/100;
    OUTPUT: PUT EDIT (AMOUNT,COMMISSION)(F(15,2));
    PUT SKIP;
    GO TO INPUT
END COMSION;
```

sion are decimal numbers with an allowance for ten decimal digits, including two digits after the decimal point. This program compiles into an object code much more like a COBOL program, and it provides answers more accurate and satisfactory for data processing purposes.

How to choose a programming language

The first step in choosing a programming language is to determine your alternatives. Often you have no other choice than one of the popular languages, namely assembler language, FORTRAN or COBOL, or some of the special-purpose languages. The decision in choosing a language must depend upon such factors as suitability to the problem at hand, compatibility with people and hardware available, and the economic analysis of the total cost incurred. Here are some of the points to watch:

---

[2] These comments are for students who have covered Language Supplements B and C.

1. Are programmers available with good working knowledge of the language? If not, how easily and quickly can the new language be learned?
2. How easy is it to use the language?
3. Which language is most suitable for the application?
4. Is the problem dominated by computations or the management of data?
5. Does the application to be programmed relate to other applications? You may find that a scientifically oriented language is more suitable, but the application must relate to other programs already written in a business-oriented language. Even if the single application could be written better in the scientifically oriented language, you may be better off using a business-oriented language.
6. Evaluate the time necessary to compile and to execute. If it is a production program which will be run many times, execution time is more important. In such a case you may use assembler language programming. If the application is to be run only once or a few times, then compile time may be more important. *not very important*
7. Consider problems related to program conversion. If related programs must be converted, you need to determine the effort and cost involved in converting the other programs. If the application is likely to be modified or changed, you need to know the problems related to reprogramming. If there is a possibility of a change in the hardware system, you need to determine how easy it will be to convert your program. You also need to know whether the programming language itself is finalized or is subject to change. If it changes, what will be involved in modifying your program?
8. Consider the total cost involved in preparing the program, running it, and the possibility of reprogramming.

Bear in mind that costs associated with using a programming language and, in general, the cost of software cannot be separated from the cost of hardware. Thus language selection must be considered simultaneously with hardware selection.

TEST SPECIAL-PURPOSE PROGRAMMING LANGUAGES ⟋ *unique applications*

The procedure-oriented languages discussed above are all general-purpose languages; a large variety of problems can be solved with them. There are also a great many specialized languages which can be applied only to a narrow class of problems. The advantage of these languages is that much programming time can be saved. The disadvantages are that the programmer must learn the language, a special-language processor must be purchased or rented, and compile and execution time may be relatively slow. Some of these languages are discussed below, briefly.

Machine tool control languages, such as APT (*A*utomatically *P*rogrammed *T*ools) automate the cutting of pieces of metal by machine tools. Machine tools can be controlled either manually or by means of a punched paper tape. Punched paper tape is preferable for many reasons, though the preparation of such punched paper tapes is time-consuming. Machine tool control languages serve to automate or partially automate the preparation of such punched paper tapes.

Civil engineering-oriented languages such as COGO (*CO*ordinate *Ge*O*metry) and STRESS (*STR*uctural *E*ngineering *S*ystems *S*olver) allow engineers to solve problems without learning a general-purpose computer language. For example, a problem in surveying land can be stated by engineers in a form which is natural and logical to them, and then the computer can solve the problem. Surveying problems can be solved in COGO, for example, and the analysis of framed structures in STRESS.

Computer design can be aided by a number of special-purpose languages such as LOTIS (*LO*gic, *TI*ming, *S*equencing), and LDT (*L*ogic *D*esign *T*ranslator). One advantage of these languages is that the design of a computer can be debugged before it is built by studying the design on another computer. These languages also help in the description of computers.

Query languages such as COLINGO (*C*ompile *O*n *L*I*N*e and *GO*) and ADAM (*A* *DA*ta *M*anagement system) make it possible for users not familiar with programming to retrieve information from data bases. These languages are easy to learn. Either forms to be filled out by the user or special Englishlike languages are used.

Text editing and processing languages such as ATS (*A*dministrative *T*erminal *S*ystem) make it possible for users to compose and modify text as presented in books, magazines, and journals. Operations such as deletion, insertion, replacement, and movement of a unit of a text to a different place can be easily done. The advantage of these systems is that much typing or typesetting is saved in automating these simple jobs by computer, and the user does not need to learn a programming language. Text editing by computers is one of the fastest growing fields of data processing.

Simulation languages

Simulation is one of the important fields of application of computers (see Chapter 3). It is possible to write simulation programs in any of the general-purpose computer languages, but to save programmers' time special-purpose languages have been developed. An example follows.

A machine tool in a manufacturing shop is turning out parts at the rate of one every 5 minutes. As they are finished, the parts go to an inspector, who may take 1, 2, 3, 4, 5, 6, or 7 minutes to examine each of the parts. You know that he rejects about 10 percent. Suppose 1,000 parts are made. How long will it take to inspect the parts, and how many will be rejected?

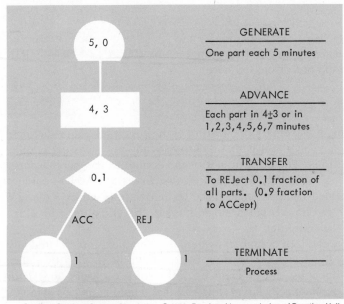

FIGURE 9.4 GPSS block diagram for manufacturing simulation.

GENERATE

One part each 5 minutes

ADVANCE

Each part in 4±3 or in 1,2,3,4,5,6,7 minutes

TRANSFER

To REJect 0.1 fraction of all parts. (0.9 fraction to ACCept)

TERMINATE

Process

Geoffrey Gordon, *System Simulation,* © 1969. Reprinted by permission of Prentice-Hall, Inc., Englewood Cliffs, N.J.

We show how to solve this problem in GPSS (General Purpose Simulation System). First prepare a graphical representation, that is a block diagram, of the problem, as illustrated in Figure 9.4. The shapes and words (GENERATE, ADVANCE, TRANSFER, TERMINATE) have specific meanings in GPSS. The second step in preparing the program is filling out the GPSS coding form (Figure 9.5) in accordance with the block diagram. With the aid of the GPSS compiler you can compile and run the program and thus obtain the answers to your problem.

Of course, GPSS can solve much more complicated problems, and it uses many more forms and words (like SEIZE, RELEASE, ENTER, LEAVE). GPSS can be learned in a matter of hours and can save much programming time. There are many other simulation

FIGURE 9.5 GPSS
program for
manufacturing
simulation.

GPSS III – CODING FORM

LOCATION	OPERATION	A,B,C,D,E,F		
*		MANUFACTURING SHOP – MODEL 1	
*			
	GENERATE	5,	CREATE PARTS
	ADVANCE	4,3	INSPECT
	TRANSFER	.1,ACC,REJ	SELECT REJECTS
ACC	TERMINATE	1	ACCEPTED PARTS
REJ	TERMINATE	1	REJECTED PARTS
	START	1,000	

Goeffrey Gordon, *System Simulation,* © 1969. Reprinted by permission of Prentice-Hall, Inc., Englewood Cliffs, N.J.

languages, but the most popular are GPSS and SIMSCRIPT (a language not discussed here).

OPERATING SYSTEMS

The most remarkable feature of the computer which distinguishes it from a calculator is that it automatically performs data processing operations. The control unit of the computer has been discussed in Chapters 4 and 8. We have shown that the classical computer is controlled by this single piece of hardware (Figures 4.6 and 4.13), and have noted that a single human, the computer operator, controls the computer.

The modern computer system is a complex, interrelated network of machines which operates in real time, controlled by interrupts. Simultaneous and efficient operation of processors and sharing of various resources (as in time sharing) would be impossible with the classical control arrangement of a single control unit and a single human operator. The modern computer system is controlled automatically by the operating system (OS), software consisting of many thousands of computer instructions. (Operating systems residing on disks are called disk operating systems, or DOS.)

The purpose of operating systems is to control the resources of a computer system efficiently and to serve as an interface between humans and the computer system. The operating system (Figure 9.6) optimizes the allocation and sharing of hardware and software resources, obeys users' established priorities, or establishes priorities of its own.

Figure 9.7 diagrams the components of the operating system (which we will discuss later) and indicates how the operating system interacts with other software. The heart of the operating system, the supervisor program (also called the executive or monitor), is a program we have already mentioned, in Chapter 8. The importance of this program is comparable to the hardware control unit of the

FIGURE 9.6 User
or programmer
commands the
operating system,
which controls
the computer
system.

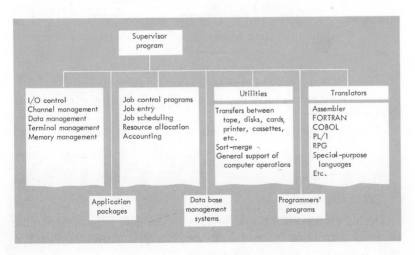

FIGURE 9.7
Software and
operating system
(OS) components.

Supervisor program			
I/O control	Job control programs	Utilities	Translators
Channel management	Job entry	Transfers between	Assembler
Data management	Job scheduling	tape, disks, cards,	FORTRAN
Terminal management	Resource allocation	printer, cassettes,	COBOL
Memory management	Accounting	etc.	PL/1
		Sort-merge	RPG
		General support of	Special-purpose
		computer operations	languages
			Etc.
Application packages	Data base management systems	Programmers' programs	

classical computer. The supervisor program must be in the memory permanently, because when interrupts occur it is the supervisor program that handles them. Other software programs may reside on disks, because the supervisor can load them or call them in memory when needed.

The operating system originally was conceived to assist computer operators and to perform many of their functions automatically. Therefore this is a good starting point in the study of operating systems.

The operator and the operating system *skip*

To illustrate the functions of the operating system, we describe the steps an operator has to follow to run a program written in COBOL.

Step 1   Operator examines the submitted deck and determines that it is a COBOL program.

Step 2   Operator records start time and program name in logbook.

Step 3   Operator loads deck of cards into card reader.

Step 4   Operator finds magnetic tape containing COBOL compiler.

Step 5   Operator loads COBOL compiler into storage.

Step 6   Operator starts COBOL compilation of program.

Step 7   At completion of compilation operator examines program printout.

Step 8a   If compilation is successful, operator loads into memory the object program created by the COBOL compiler.

Step 8b   If compilation is not successful, operator follows instructions specified by run manual.

Step 9   Operator determines if all peripheral equipment is ready.

Step 10   Operator starts execution of object program.

Step 11   Computer completes execution of program.

Step 12   When execution is completed, operator decides if the run was successful.

Step 13   Operator writes time of completion on computer logbook.

Step 14   Operator stops the computer.

Step 15   Operator examines decks to be run and selects the next one to work on.

In this discussion we assume that all the data is furnished in the deck. If data is to be read from tapes or disk packs the operator must also mount and dismount these.

This describes a system controlled manually by the operator. In a modern computer system, under the automatic control of the operating system, which is given the same COBOL program to run, a different procedure is followed.

Stacked-job processing *≠ TEST*

In a modern system, the programmer must submit the program, the data, and the job control cards (Figure 9.8). These cards contain the instructions in the job control language (JCL). This is the way the programmer communicates with the operating system.

Figure 9.9 illustrates a stack of five jobs to be processed. For each job, the job control cards in the stack tell the operating system what to do. For example, the job control cards specify which input and output units are to be used, which reels of tapes must be mounted, and on which tape drives. The stack of cards contains both programs and data.

The operating system handles the stack of jobs to be processed as follows. When the computer is running, the supervisor program is in core storage. The job control program reads the job control cards and executes the instructions contained in them. Utilizing appropriate software as listed in Figure 9.7, the computer goes through the following 11 steps:

FIGURE 9.8
Examples of job control cards to compile and execute a COBOL program.

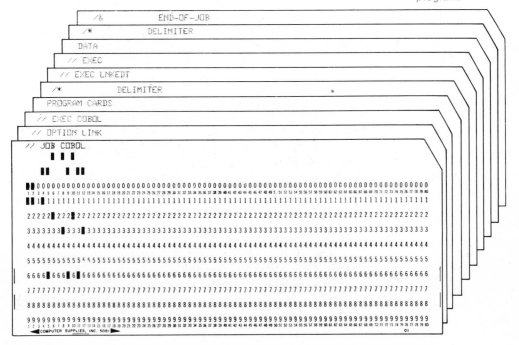

FIGURE 9.9 A
stack of five jobs
to be processed.

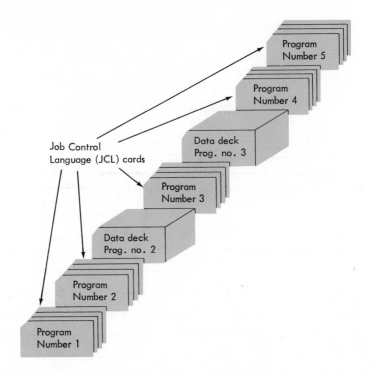

Step 1   The supervisor program calls in the job control program, which executes the job control cards.

Step 2   The system determines that the program to be compiled
is in COBOL.

Step 3   The system loads the COBOL compiler and starts
compilation.

Step 4   The system checks for successful compilation. If compilation is successful, system proceeds to Step 5; otherwise it provides appropriate error messages and proceeds to next program.

Step 5   The system loads into memory the object program
created by the COBOL compiler.

Step 6   The system calls in the appropriate utility program to
read the data.

Step 7   The system starts execution.

Step 8   The system calls the appropriate utility program to take
care of output.

Step 9   The system prepares reports on the various time elements required for administrative and charging purposes.

Step 10   The system completes execution.

Step 11   At successful completion of the job, the control program returns control to the supervisor program.

Then the system proceeds automatically to the next job in the stack, and so on. Thus the operation of the computer is automated.

Summary of functions of the operating system

In summary, the operating system performs the following functions:

1. Loads and calls in programs.
2. Handles interrupts.
3. Schedules and controls input/output operations and jobs.
4. Measures and times operations, prepares data for accounting and charges to user.
5. Communicates control and error messages to operator.

We have only highlighted here some of the intricate functions of the operating system, without going into detail about the complications that are caused by such techniques as multiprogramming, multiprocessing, and teleprocessing. Our aim is to establish a foundation on which, if required, further studies can be built.

SOFTWARE PACKAGES

In addition to the software systems discussed so far, there are hundreds of other software packages available. Figure 9.10 provides an overall review of how software helps the user and the programmer and automates some of the programming functions in the several computer generations.

In the first generation of computers, programs were written in machine language. Then programming aids like assembler language programming, input/output control systems, and macroinstructions

FIGURE 9.10 Automation of programming in the various generations of computers.

DEGREE OF AUTOMATION			
First generation: None	*Second generation: Low*	*Third generation: Medium*	*Current and future: High*
Machine language programming	Assembler language programming Input/output control systems (IOCS) Macroinstructions	Application packages Procedure-oriented languages Operating systems Direct-access methods	Application packages Software enhancement Hardware enhancement System design Data base management systems

were introduced (all of these will be discussed below). Later, procedure-oriented languages, operating systems, and direct-access methods of storage control were introduced. The right side of Figure 9.10 lists some new software packages which are becoming increasingly important.

Application packages are sets of application programs which are written for or by users to apply to their own work. These application programs, also called canned programs, perform data processing tasks in practically all functions of management, such as accounting, payroll and pension, finance, engineering, inventory control, marketing, manufacturing, mailing activities, property management, project management, operations research, and management science. Application programs are also available to do data processing for specific industries, such as banking, construction, insurance, and supermarkets. The advantage of these application packages is that the cost of writing application programs decreases or may be eliminated.

The usefulness of software packages goes further. There are program packages that enhance the operations of the operating system, taking over and augmenting some of its functions. This results in better allocation and management of the resources of the computer system. There are also software packages that do not influence the operating system but directly improve the efficiency of hardware; and others that aid system designers in fulfilling their functions (see Chapter 11). Data base management systems (DBMS), a most important type of software, is the topic of Chapter 10.

STRUCTURED PROGRAMMING

The challenges and difficulties facing programmers in their assignments were introduced in Chapter 5. A new development to help programmers make their jobs more interesting and more productive is called structured programming.

If you turn back to Figure 2.11, which illustrates the power of branching instructions, you see how intricate this diagram is. Imagine how difficult it is to keep a program in good order following such a flowchart, and how difficult it is for a person who has not developed it to read, modify, or maintain a program of this sort. The complexity arises not from the individual flowchart boxes but from the relationships among the boxes. These difficulties can be avoided by providing structure to the diagram. This is the aim of structured programming.

Structured programming recognizes three elementary flowchart structures and shows that all flowcharts can be conceived as combinations of these three. One is the relationship between flowchart boxes 28 and 60 in Figure 2.11; in structured programming this is called a simple sequence. Figure 9.11 shows all three basic control structures: (a) the *simple sequence,* (b) the *selection,* and (c) the *repetition.* To help identify such structures, the flowchart box numbers that were used in Figure 2.11 are repeated here.

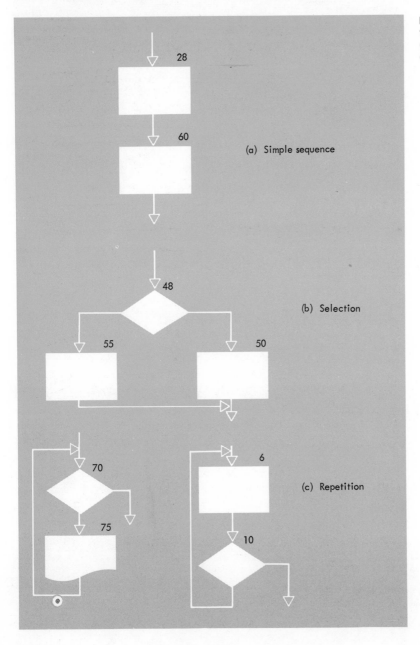

FIGURE 9.11 The three elementary control structures of programming.

FIGURE 9.12a
Combination of
selection, simple
sequence, and
repetition
structures.

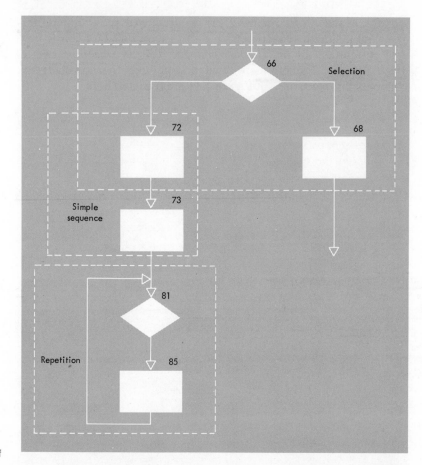

FIGURE 9.12b
Four-way branch
as combination of
three selection
structures.

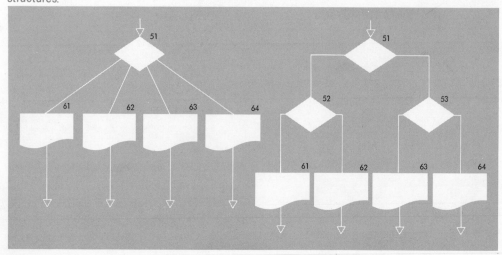

The principle underlying structured programming, that all programs and flowcharts are combinations of these three basic structures, is illustrated in Figure 9.12. Figure 9.12a shows a flowchart which is a combination of a selection structure, a simple sequence structure, and a repetition structure, and Figure 9.12b shows a multiple-choice structure which can be replaced by a combination of three selection structures.

It may not be immediately clear to you how every flowchart can be comprised of combinations of three basic structures. The instructions in the flowchart in Figure 9.13, for example, would have to be examined in detail before the flowchart could be rewritten in a form satisfying structured programming requirements.

GOTO-less programming[3]

The immense degree of confusion and frustration caused by the complexity of large programs is often due to the large number of GOTO statements. There is hardly a programmer who has not fallen at some time into the trap of forgetting a GOTO or putting it in the wrong place. Therefore in structured programming the programmer is asked to eliminate or at least minimize the number of GOTO statements. To illustrate, consider the commission problem (Figure 2.10, Chapter 2). The structured programming approach is satisfied by doing the computations the following way in FORTRAN:

```
IF(AMNT.LE.150.00)   COM = 6.00
IF(AMNT.GT.150.00)   COM = 6.00 + .02 * (AMNT−150.00)
```

The same purpose can also be accomplished in COBOL:

```
IF AMNT IS LESS THAN 150 THEN COM = 6
   ELSE COM = 6 + .02 * (AMNT−150)
```

As a further illustration consider the tax problem shown in Figure E-14 (Appendix two). The structured programming approach in FORTRAN is accomplished by writing:

```
IF(AMNT.LE.4000.0) TAX = 0.16 * AMNT
IF((4000.0.LE.AMNT).AND.(AMNT.LE.8000.0))
                   TAX = 640.0 + 0.20 * (AMNT−4000.0)
IF(8000.0.LE.AMNT) TAX = 1440.0 + 0.25 * (AMNT−8000.0)
```

---

[3] Most languages take either GO TO or GOTO. Since the advent of structured programming it is becoming more popular to use the single word GOTO and the expression GOTO-less programming.

FIGURE 9.13
Example of a
flowchart which is
not "structured."

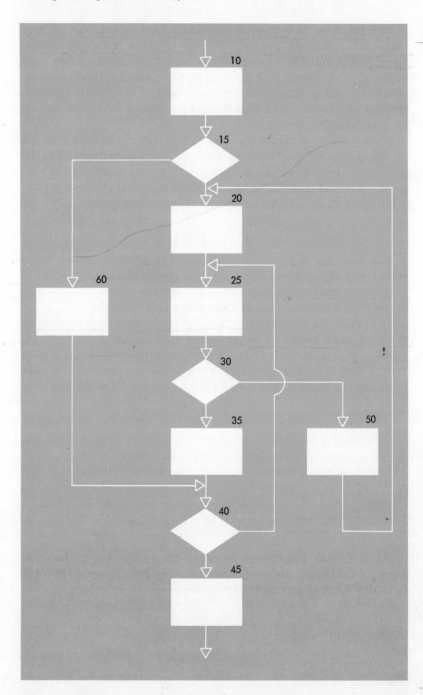

The same approach can be easily applied in COBOL.

PL/I is particularly suitable for structured programming because of its rich capability to perform branching and repetitions. For example, the problem of sorting three numbers shown in Figure E-15 (Appendix two) can be accomplished by the following three statements:

> IF A > B THEN DO; X = A, A = B, B = X; END;
> IF A > C THEN DO; X = C, C = A, A = X; END;
> IF B > C THEN DO; X = C, C = B, B = X; END;

Note that in all these assignment statements there are no GOTO statements.

The principles discussed here form the strict scientific basis of structured programming. They provide a foundation for further study and the practice of structured programming.

Advantages of structured programming

Structured programming has numerous advantages, including the following:

1. Reduces cost and time of program development.
2. Reduces cost and time of program maintenance.
3. Makes programs more adaptable to change.
4. Increases the productivity of the programmer.
5. Provides more challenge to the programmer.
6. Forces programmers to think carefully through the functions to be accomplished by the program.
7. Aids in matching program and problem structure.

ASSEMBLER LANGUAGE PROGRAMMING[4]

In spite of the advantages of procedure-oriented languages, a fair percentage of data processing problems still require assembler language programming. Furthermore, assembler language programming provides a good insight to hardware. The brief introduction to assembler language programming which follows is presented as a foundation for further study.

The simplified symbolic programming language discussed in Chapter 8 uses only 12 instructions. (You should review at this time the simplified symbolic language program for the account-balancing problem in Figure 8.5.) In a real computer over 100 in-

---

[4] Much of this section may be omitted without loss of continuity.

structions may be available. As you have already learned, symbolic language instructions are hardware dependent; different computers require different instructions. In what follows we discuss a typical third-generation computer programming system, the symbolic programming language or assembler language (BAL–Basic Assembler Language) used in the IBM System/360 and IBM System/370 computers.

Before describing assembler language programming, a few words about input/output instructions are in order, although handling input/output is not ordinarily done with the aid of strictly assembler language instructions.

Input/output and operation instructions

Input/output instructions are used for simple input/output requirements. They replace the READ and WRITE instructions used in the simplified symbolic programming system. Input/output instructions specify:

1. The device to be used.
2. Whether to read or write.
3. The channel to be used.
4. The storage locations to be used.
5. Various control operations—back-spacing, rewinding, positioning.
6. Sensing for errors or unusual conditions, and transfer to error routines.

There are only four input/output instructions for the IBM System/360. The normal input/output uses the single instruction:

> START I/O

The IBM System/360 assembler language has three types of instruction:

1. Fixed-point (no decimal point allowed) operations.
2. Decimal operations.
3. Floating-point operations.

Floating-point operations use numbers in powers of 10 and are used for scientific and engineering problems. This type of operation is rarely used in business data processing and will not be discussed further in this book. Fixed-point operations only are considered here, using the illustration of the commission calculation (Figure 2.10, Chapter 2).

The commission calculation in fixed-point operations

Figure 9.14 shows the program for the fixed-point operation. Because we want to illustrate only assembler language instructions, input/output instructions and some other auxiliary instructions are omitted. Observe that all programs must be written on coding forms similar to the one shown in Figure 9.14. The headings referring to *Name, Operation,* and *Operand* are all familiar concepts from the simplified programming system discussed in Chapter 8.

FIGURE 9.14 IBM System/360 fixed-point assembler language program for the commission calculation.

Name	Operation	Operand		
		Introductory routine omitted		
		Input routine omitted		
	L	3, AMNT	#1	
	C	3, =F'15000'	#2	
	BC	12, JUMP	#3	IF AMNT <= 15000 BRANCH TØ JUMP
	S	3, =F'15000'	#4	
	M	2, =F'2'	#5	
	D	2, =F'100'	#6	
	A	3, =F'600'	#7	
	BC	15, FINISH	#8	BRANCH TØ FINISH
JUMP	L	3, =F'600'	#9	
FINISH	ST	3, CØM	#10	
		Output and edit routine omitted		
AMNT	DS	F	#11	
CØM	DS	F	#12	

The IBM System/360 has many registers, out of which 16 general registers (Figure 9.15) are of particular importance. Each of these registers can be compared with the accumulator used in our simplified symbolic programming system. But we cannot say

> LOAD AMNT

as the computer would not know into which of the general registers to put AMNT. We can arbitrarily select register #3 as our accumulator. The operation code for LOAD is abbreviated simply to L, so our first instruction is:

> L   3, AMNT

where we have two operands. The first operand, the #3, designates the register to be used as an accumulator; and the second operand

FIGURE 9.15
Registers of the
IBM System/360
CPU.

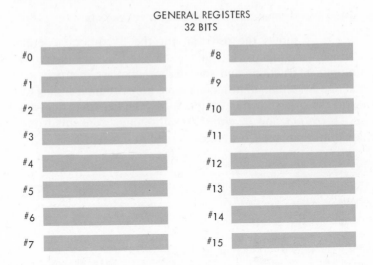

GENERAL REGISTERS
32 BITS

#0   #8
#1   #9
#2   #10
#3   #11
#4   #12
#5   #13
#6   #14
#7   #15

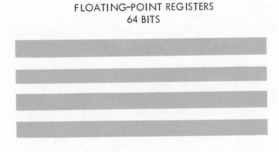

FLOATING-POINT REGISTERS
64 BITS

PROGRAM STATUS WORD
64 BITS

is, of course, AMNT for the variable. We skip for the moment the second and third instructions in Figure 9.14 and concentrate on the four arithmetic instructions with operation codes S, M, D, and A.

The fourth instruction in the program:

$$S \qquad 3, = F'15000'$$

subtracts the literal (constant) 15000 from the content of register #3. The quote marks, the = sign, and the F specify that we are referring to a literal, a fixed point constant. You can check in Figure

9.16, which lists some of the fixed-point instructions that the subtract instruction has the form:

$$\boxed{\text{S} \qquad 5,\text{P}}$$

where the action is to subtract the value of P from the content of register #5.

Instruction	Operation	Operands	Action
Load	L	5,P	(5) ← P
Add	A	5,P	(5) ← (5) + P
Subtract	S	5,P	(5) ← (5) − P
Multiply	M	4,P	(4) & (5) ← (5) * P
Divide	D	4,P	(5) ← (4) & (5) / P
Store	ST	4,P	P ← (4)
Compare	C	4,X	⎰Compare (4) and (X) ⎱Set condition code
Branch on condition	BC	mask JUMP	⎧Transfer control to ⎱JUMP depending on ⎱value of "mask" and ⎱condition code

FIGURE 9.16
Some IBM System/360 fixed-point assembler language instructions.

The fifth instruction in Figure 9.14

$$\boxed{\text{M} \qquad 2, = \text{F}'2'}$$

which multiplies the content of register #3 by #2, needs some explanation.

In Figure 9.16 the multiply instruction:

$$\boxed{\text{M} \qquad 4,\text{P}}$$

will multiply the content of register #5 by P, and the product will appear in the combined registers #4 and #5. If the numbers are small, the product will not overflow into register #4, and the answer will be in register #5. To simplify matters we always assume that the numbers are sufficiently small so that there will not be an overflow into the even-numbered register, and the product will be in the odd-numbered register. Thus, going back to the commission calculation, the content of register #3 is multiplied by 2 by writing

$$\boxed{\text{M} \qquad 2, = \text{F}'2'}$$

and the answer will be in register #3 (no overflow).

Remember that we are working in pennies, so to get 2 percent we must divide the content of register #3 by 100. We write the sixth instruction:

$$D \qquad 2, = F'100'$$

and the answer will be in register #3. (There is an assembler language instruction to *shift* a number, but we will not discuss this instruction here.)

In general, as you can check in Figure 9.16, the instruction

$$D \qquad 4,P$$

will divide by P the content of the combined registers #4 and #5, and the quotient will appear in register #5. (Ordinarily you must clear register #4 to get rid of the garbage, but in our case, when we multiply, register #5 is automatically cleared.)

The seventh instruction:

$$A \qquad 3, = F'600'$$

adds the literal 600 to the content of register #3.

The form of the add instruction, as you can easily check in Figure 9.16, is:

$$A \qquad 5,P$$

The next, or eighth instruction, in the commission problem in Figure 9.14 is a branch instruction.

Branching[5]

Unconditional branching is simple. In the eighth instruction we write:

$$BC \qquad 15, FINISH$$

and control is transferred to the instruction with the name (label) FINISH. The 15 is the mask value; it designates an unconditional branch. To branch conditionally we would have to use another value for the mask and also make a comparison first. For example, the instruction:

---

[5] Knowledge of details of branching is not required elsewhere in the text.

```
C       7,P
```

compares the content of the register designated by the first operand (#7) and the value of the second operand (P). On the basis of the comparison, a special register containing the condition code is set to a specific value.

The compare instruction is followed by a BC (branch on condition) instruction which tests the value of the condition code with the aid of a mask. Figure 9.17 shows what value of the mask is to be used for each condition. For example, in the commission calculation we want to branch if AMNT ≤ 15000. So we need to make a comparison to set the condition code, and then use the mask 12 (second and third instructions in Figure 9.14):

```
C       3,=F'15000'
BC      12, JUMP
```

FIGURE 9.17 How to branch in IBM System/360 assembler language.

Instruction	Operation	First operand	Second operand	Action
Compare	C	4	X	Compare (4) and (X) and set condition code
Branch on condition	BC	mask	JUMP	Transfer control to JUMP if condition is met

Condition		Use mask
First operand is less than	second operand	4
First operand is less than or equal to	second operand	12
First operand is greater than	second operand	2
First operand is greater than or equal to	second operand	10
First operand is equal to	second operand	8
Unconditional transfer		15

Now you should understand the logic of the program in Figure 9.14. The first instruction loads AMNT into register #3. Then we make a comparison between the content of register #3 and the literal 15000 (Box 5 in Figure 2.10). This compare instruction sets the condition code. The next BC instruction tests the condition code with the mask 12. If the amount is less than or equal to 15000 we branch to JUMP. Here the literal 600 is loaded into register #3, and the next instruction assigns the proper value to the commission

(Box 30 in Figure 2.10). On the other hand, if the test in the conditional branch fails, we drop through, the commission is properly computed (Box 10 in Figure 2.10), and we branch to FINISH.

Defining storage operations

In IBM System/360 assembler programming we must tell the assembler to reserve storage space for our variables. Thus we must us the define storage (DS) instruction for each variable. (These are the last two instructions in Figure 9.14.) We must also define the type of storage to be used (fixed point, decimal, floating point, length of storage, and so forth). In our program we use fixed-point operations, so we list the letter F in the operand column.

Advantages and disadvantages of assembler language programming

The advantages of assembler language programming include the following:

1. The programmer has absolute control of the computer.
2. All capabilities of the computer can be fully exploited.
3. The program can be directly assembled into a machine language program without the use of a compiler.
4. Efficient object programs can be obtained.

Disadvantages of assembler language programming include:

1. Learning assembler language programming is relatively difficult and time-consuming.
2. Program preparation is laborious.
3. Assembler language programs can be run only on specific computer hardware.
4. Program documentation, debugging, and modification of programs are difficult.

Emulation

Some qualification of the statement above, that assembler language programs are limited to the computer hardware for which they are written, is in order. Manufacturers provide special hardware, an emulator, to emulate computers. Thus an assembler language program written for the IBM System/360 can be run on another computer if the emulator hardware is available.

INPUT/OUTPUT CONTROL SYSTEMS (IOCS)

We have touched upon the problem of input/output only briefly, but not because it is unimportant. In fact, 40 percent of all assembler language instructions in a typical program refer to input/output. Precisely for this reason the programmer is provided with assistance in the form of an input/output control system (IOCS). With the aid of a few specialized instructions the programmer is relieved of such drudgery as specifying in detail from which devices data must be read, or with which devices output must be provided.

What IOCS does ✗ Important

Suppose the programmer needs to read records from a magnetic tape drive or wants to write records on a magnetic tape. Records are blocked into physical blocks for efficient storage on magnetic tape. It would be quite a time-consuming job for a programmer to write programs to read records when the equipment is designed to read physical blocks. The functions of deblocking physical blocks from magnetic tape, and again blocking records into physical blocks for writing on magnetic tape are automatically performed by IOCS.

If a programmer is reading from a magnetic tape, and for some reason there is an error and the reading is unsuccessful, it is necessary to backspace on the tape and try to read again. In fact, the programmer may try to read it ten times before the computer provides an error message. The programmer need not be concerned about writing such an error correction program, because IOCS automatically handles it.

When data is read from an input device, it is not immediately transferred to the central processing unit. The computer system may be using buffers or channels or may be operating simultaneously a large number of peripheral devices. How could a programmer write a program in such an environment? The programmer would have to take care of a great deal of detail and know precisely the complete input/output hardware configuration of the computer system. The fact is, programmers do not need to be concerned about these problems, as the IOCS relieves them from incorporating into programs the solving of these problems.

Suppose a new input/output device is added or removed. Or suppose one of the devices is not operational. If the programmer writes a program specifying which input/output devices are to be used, under such a changed condition the program could not be run. With IOCS, the operator could take appropriate measures and run the program on the modified input/output system.

Macroinstructions ✗ TST large instructions

An assembler language instruction is assembled into a single machine language instruction and the computer is capable of executing such an instruction. In addition to assembler language instructions, programmers can also be provided with macroinstructions, or macros. These macroinstructions will be assembled into a whole set of machine language instructions. Therefore, when a programmer writes a macro, a whole set of machine language instructions is created. Programming systems include many types of macroinstructions, but those most frequently used serve to handle input/output.

Consider, for instance, a typical IOCS macro "OPEN file name." When the programmer writes such a macro and the program is assembled into machine language instructions, all the steps will be generated to handle the problem of opening a file. Similarly, the macro "CLOSE file name" will take care of closing a file. A record can be obtained from a file by simply writing GET and the file name, and a record can be written on a file by writing the macro PUT and the file name. Another important macro performs control (often designated by CNTRL), which specifies the file name and control code.

Using IOCS offers many advantages and much flexibility. It eases the burden of the programmer and thereby saves effort, time, and money. It cuts down the idle time of the computer system and also helps the operator by providing him with standard messages.

REPORT PROGRAM GENERATOR (RPG)   TEST

COBOL is the most commonly used business data processing language. However, small computers and minicomputers often lack the memory capacity needed to store the COBOL compiler, so manufacturers offer alternate programming languages. The Report Program Generator (RPG) is such a business-oriented language, particularly suited to perform simple data processing tasks such as billing, payroll, accounting, and inventory.

Report Program Generator is a language which is halfway between assembler language programming and higher level language programming. It uses a set of specification forms which must be filled out according to the rules of RPG. It can be illustrated by writing a program for the commission calculation in the Report Program Generator language for IBM System/360.

The commission calculation in RPG   To write a program in RPG we begin by filling out the file description specifications form shown in Figure 9.18. We will be using two files in our program—DECK, our input file, and DOCUMENT, our output file.

Observe in the *File Type* column that the codes I and O designate input and output. The code F refers to fixed field lengths of 80 and 120 characters. A card reader is specified for input, and a printer is specified for output. If we had more than two files, of course there would be more entries in Figure 9.18.

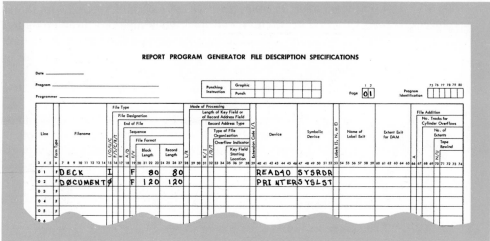

FIGURE 9.18
Commission
calculation in
RPG—file
description
specifications.

Figure 9.19 shows the input specifications. We have only one file, DECK, and we happen to have only one record on this file, AMOUNT. We have to tell the computer where in the card AMOUNT will be punched, and so in the *Field Location* column we specify that AMOUNT will be punched in columns 1–10. We also specify that there are two digits after the decimal point. Bear in mind that if we have several files there will be an entry for each of them in the *File Name* column, and for each record on each file there will be an entry in the *Field Name* column.

Figure 9.20 shows the calculation specifications. It is here that all the calculations and the processing are performed. Before we discuss Figure 9.20 in detail, we will describe how to branch in RPG.

FIGURE 9.19
Commission
calculation in
RPG—input
specifications.

In assembler language first we set a condition code with the aid of a compare instruction, and then we branch on condition by testing the condition code with the aid of a mask. In RPG first we make a comparison which sets an indicator, and then we branch by testing the indicator.

In the calculations for the commission problem in Figure 9.20 we arbitrarily decide to use indicator 02 for branching. So in Line 1 we "turn off" this indicator by writing in the *Operation* column the

FIGURE 9.20
Commission
calculation in
RPG—calculation
specifications.

REPORT PROGRAM, GENERATOR   CALCULATION SPECIFICATIONS

Line	Form Type	Control Level (0-19, LR)	Indicators And Not	And Not	And Not	Factor 1	Operation	Factor 2	Result Field	Field Length	Decimal Positions	Half Adjust (H)	Resulting Indicators Plus / Minus / Zero or Blank — Compare High 1>2 / Low 1<2 / Equal 1=2	Comments
0 1	C						SETOF						02	
0 2	C					AMOUNT	COMP	150.00					02	
0 3	C		02				GOTO	JUMP						IF INDICATOR
0 4	C						MOVE	6.00	COM	1	0	2		02 IS ON
0 5	C						GOTO	WRAPUP						
0 6	C					JUMP	TAG							
0 7	C					AMOUNT	SUB	150.00	OVER	1	0	2		
0 8	C					OVER	MULT	0.02	BONUS	1	0	2		
0 9	C					6.00	ADD	BONUS	COM	1	0	2		
1 0	C					WRAPUP	TAG							
1 1	C													
1 2	C													
1 3	C													
4	C													

operation code SETOF and then we write 02 in the *Indicator* column. In Line 2 we compare the AMOUNT with 150.00. AMOUNT is written in the *Factor 1* column, COMP in the *Operation 1* column, and the literal 150.00 in the *Factor 2* column. If Factor 1 is higher than Factor 2, we want to turn on the indicator 02. For this reason we wrote 02 in the *High* column.

In Line 3 we branch to JUMP, provided the indicator 02 is ON. Observe in Line 6 JUMP is written in *Factor 1* column. TAG is written in the *Operation* column. This is the way to branch in RPG. Line 3 also shows what happens if AMOUNT is no higher than 150.00 and indicator 02 is not ON; we drop through directly to Line 4. Here we MOVE Factor 2, that is 6.00, to the *Result Field,* designated COM. As you know, under this condition this will be the value of the commission. We also specify 10 in the *Field Length* column, to get two digits after the decimal point.

Line 5 illustrates an unconditional branch. In Lines 7, 8, and 9 the commission is computed when the amount is over 150.00 and a bonus must be included. Line 10 is needed so the statement in Line 5 has a place to branch to. The fourth form, the output-format specifications, is illustrated in Figure 9.21. We have only a single output file, DOCUMENT. (Compare with Figure 9.18.) We have only two data items, AMOUNT and COM, in our output. We allow 15 positions, including the decimal point, for each of these

FIGURE 9.21
Commission
calculation in RPG
—output-format
specifications.

REPORT PROGRAM GENERATOR OUTPUT-FORMAT SPECIFICATIONS

Form X24-3352-1 U/M 025
Printed in U.S.A.

Date _____
Program _____
Programmer _____

Punching Instruction: Graphic / Punch

Page: 04   Program Identification

Line	Form Type	Filename	Type (H/D/T)	Stacker Select	Space Before	Space After	Skip Before	Skip After	Output Indicators And / And Not / Not	Field Name	Zero Suppress (Z) / Blank After (B)	End Position in Output Record	Packed Field (P)	Constant or Edit Word	Sterling Sign Position
0 1	0	DOCUMENT													
0 2	0									AMOUNT	Z	15			
0 3	0									COM	Z	30			
0 4	0														
0 5	0														
0 6	0														

data items, and specify two digits after the decimal point. Thus in the output field AMOUNT will end in position 15 and COM in position 30. The code Z stands for zero suppression; we do not want the computer to print the leading zeros.

Where are the READ and WRITE commands? Nowhere! The RPG coding forms are designed such that when the program is translated into machine language form, the input/output statements are automatically taken care of.

Observe that RPG will always read an input record, do the processing, and print the output. Then the cycle will be repeated over and over automatically. So RPG represents a perfect embodiment of the IN-PROCESS-OUT structure of data processing which was illustrated in Chapter 2, Figure 2.8.

Advantages and disadvantages of RPG   The advantages of RPG are:

TEST

1. It is available on small computers.
2. It is business data processing oriented.
3. It is easy to learn.
4. It has good output capability.
5. It creates efficient object programs.

RPG has these disadvantages:

1. Applicable only to limited types of business data processing problems.
2. Can be run only on a limited class of computer hardware.
3. There is no standard version of RPG, and therefore programs are not interchangeable for different hardware.

applicable most types
not True

SUMMARY

1. The most widely used languages are the procedure-oriented languages.
2. FORTRAN is the most widely used language for mathematical computations, and COBOL for business data processing.
3. BASIC is an easy-to-learn time-sharing language.
4. PL/I combines and extends the capabilities of FORTRAN and COBOL.
5. The choice of a computer language must be based on an economic analysis.
6. Special-purpose computer languages solve specific classes of problems at substantial savings in programming effort.
7. The operating system (*a*) provides the interface between the human user and the computer system (hardware and software); (*b*) assures the efficient automatic operation of the computer system.
8. There is a wide variety of software packages available to help the user and to increase the productivity of the programmer and the computer system.
9. Structured programming is an important technique to improve the art of programming.
10. Assembler language programming provides most complete control of the computer system and capability for efficient object programs. But programming in assembler language must be tailored to specific hardware and is time-consuming.
11. Assembler language programming also provides a unique insight into computer systems hardware.
12. Input/output control systems (IOCS) save a great deal of programming time, help the computer operator, and cut the idle time of the computer.

13. The report program generator (RPG) is a language partic-
     ularly useful for simple business data processing problems.

KEY CONCEPTS AND WORDS

BASIC: *B*eginners *A*ll-purpose *S*ymbolic *I*nstruction *C*ode language.

blocking: grouping records into blocks.

call: to transfer control to a specified program.

COBOL: *CO*mmon *B*usiness *O*riented *L*anguage.

condition code: the code contained in a special register of a control unit
     serving to perform branching.

data base management systems (DBMS): a data processing system serving
     as the interface between humans and the data base.[6]

deblocking: separating blocks into records.

decimal operations: operations in a computer using a number system with
     the base 10.

emulator: a device that enables a computer to execute instructions written
     for another computer of dissimilar design.

fixed-point operations: operations in a computer using whole numbers.

floating-point operations: computational system used in scientific and engi-
     neering problems in which each number is represented by a pair of
     numerals.

FORTRAN: *FOR*mula *TRAN*slating language.

input/output control system (IOCS): that part of the operating system which
     deals with input/output operations.

job: a specified group of tasks prescribed as a unit of work for the computer.

job control language (JCL): computer language used to tell the operating
     system the identification of a job and the description of its requirements.

literal: a data item which is designated character by character by the data
     itself.

load: to enter data or a program into storage or registers.

macroinstruction or macro: an instruction in a source language that is
     equivalent to a specified sequence of machine instruction.

mask: a pattern of characters that is used to control the retention or elimina-
     tion of portions of another pattern of characters.

mnemonic: symbolism chosen to assist human memory.

PL/I: *P*rogramming *L*anguage *I*.

Report Program Generator (RPG): *R*eport *P*rogram *G*enerator language.

software package: a collection of computer programs which are applicable
     to a broad class of data processing problems.

structured programming: a style of programming in which programs are
     written so that they can be read from top to bottom without branching
     back to something written earlier.

---

[6] A more complete definition is given in Chapter 10.

utility program: a program in general support of the operation of a computer, such as input/output, diagnostic, etc.

DISCUSSION QUESTIONS AND EXERCISES

1. Report on your collection of newspaper, magazine, and television items and cartoons, jokes, and anecdotes.

2. Describe the two types of knowledge required by programmers and systems analysts.

3. What are procedure-oriented languages? Why are they used?

4. Give a brief description, including objectives, advantages, and disadvantages, of FORTRAN, COBOL, BASIC, and PL/I. Compare some of the simplest instructions in the four languages.

5. Describe the factors involved in choosing a programming language.

6. What are special-purpose programming languages? Review the ones discussed in the text.

7. Can you write a simulation program in procedure-oriented languages like FORTRAN or BASIC? Why are simulation languages used?

8. Describe what the OS (DOS) does. Describe its purpose and main components, and provide illustrations. Use Figure 9.7 as a guide.

9. Define and explain in your own words: *mnemonic, load, call.* Give examples. Compare your definitions with those in your dictionary and explain differences, if any.[7]

10. Compare the steps a human operator takes with the functions of the operating system when a COBOL program is executed.

11. Describe stacked-job processing. What is a job?

12. Describe and compare various software packages. Include discussion of degree of automation and benefits.

13. Define and explain in your own words: *application package, canned program, software,* and *hardware enhancement.* Give examples. Compare your definitions with those in your dictionary and explain differences, if any.

14. Describe in your own words what structured programming is, including the basic principles involved. Describe the three basic structures and the advantages of structured programming.

15. Define and describe GOTO-less programming. Discuss advantages.

16. *This exercise is only for students already familiar with procedure-oriented languages:* Replace the FORTRAN program given in the text for the tax problem with a procedure-oriented program which does not use structured programming.

17. *This exercise is only for students already familiar with procedure-oriented programming:* Replace the PL/I program given in the text for sorting three numbers with a procedure-oriented program not using structured programming.

---

[7] In all word problems you need make comparisons only if the word or phrase is in your dictionary.

18. What is assembler language programming?

19. What do I/O instructions specify?

20. What are the types of operations available in IBM System/360 assembler language?

21. List and explain the simplest IBM System/360 assembler language instructions.

22. Write an IBM System/360 assembler language program for the account-balancing problem (Figure 2.6).

23. Repeat Exercise 22 for the problem in Exercise 8, Chapter 8.

24. Repeat Exercise 22 for the problem in Exercise 9, Chapter 8.

25. How do you branch (transfer control) in IBM System/360 fixed-point assembler language?

26. The input to this program is a pair of numbers; the output is the larger of the two numbers. Write an IBM System/360 fixed-point assembler language program.

27. Repeat Exercise 26, but provide output for the smaller of the two numbers.

28. Compare assembler language programming with high-level programming and describe advantages and disadvantages.

29. What are the functions of IOCS? How are they used? What are the advantages?

30. Define and explain in your own words: *emulate, blocking, deblocking, literal.* Give examples. Compare your definitions with those in your dictionary and explain differences, if any.

31. What are macros? Illustrate.

32. Describe RPG. List advantages and disadvantages.

33. Go to your library and find a FORTRAN program which has at least 50 statements and at least one IF statement. Prepare a flowchart of the program. Describe in words what the program does.

34. Repeat Exercise 33 for a BASIC program.

35. Repeat Exercise 33 for a COBOL program which has at least 50 statements in the PROCEDURE DIVISION.

36. Review and update your Personal Summary of this course (see Exercise 28, Chapter 1).

ch⁸ 12,15,21

Data base management
systems

I n the discussion of programming and software systems in the preceding chapter, we presented techniques whereby the productivity of the programmer and the systems analyst can be enhanced. Figure 9.10 shows how the degree of automation of programming increased as new generations of computers appeared. In the righthand column, under the heading Degree of Automation, *Current and future: High*, is data base management systems (DBMS)[1], a topic that is becoming increasingly important to the data processing profession. Before proceeding to study DBMS, we reflect on the functions of data processing.

DATA VERSUS PROCESSING

As developed in this book, the data processing professional creates the new resource, information. And in this development, we show that data processing is concerned with converting data into information. The key words are *data* and *processing*. In the past, processing was stressed; today both data and processing are given equal emphasis, an approach that will continue in the future.

As the functions of data processing increase and the computer is applied to more problems, large amounts of data and files are

---

[1] Terms printed in color are defined at the end of the chapter.

Note: This chapter contains some advanced material and may be omitted without loss of continuity.

amassed. Many organizations find that they spend millions of dollars on data and realize that data itself is a *resource* which must be *managed*. The management of data also becomes critical as immense technological advances in computer hardware are made, such as the emergence of online storage devices for trillions of bytes of data. Thus a great deal of attention must be paid to data as a resource.

To meet this challenge, during the past few years a host of new software techniques and packages has appeared. The traditional approach to data is inadequate, and the new data base concept offers techniques to remedy some of the existing shortcomings. This chapter examines the advantages and implications of data base management for the user, management, and the data processing professional.

There are a number of different approaches and concepts to data base management and over a hundred software packages dealing with problems of data base management. The subject, being new and under continuous change and expansion, has not yet settled down to uniform concepts and definitions. In this chapter we provide a foundation on which further study and practice can be built and a framework into which future developments can be fitted.

PROCESS ORIENTATION: THE TRADITIONAL APPROACH

The traditional approach to data processing is an evolutionary one. Starting with such bread-and-butter applications as payroll, accounting, and billing, more and more complex data processing systems are established. This approach leads to a preoccupation with processes and programs, and each data processing system is designed and operated independently, each with its own input and output (Figure 10.1). As long as computers used only magnetic tapes, the process-oriented approach was the only one available. Later, when magnetic disks were introduced, the tradition of using specialized programs with separate input/output files continued. This approach leads to hundreds of files and processes, each independent of the other. What is wrong with this approach?

Several examples from the illustration of the Warren Corporation can be used to point out the difficulties. Take for example the data describing annual gross sales at the Warren Corporation. In some of the accounting systems the sales are recorded with penny accuracy. The system producing data for the annual report contains the same gross sales rounded to the dollar. The marketing system generates sales reports in thousands of dollars. So not only are sales recorded many times in a redundant manner, the figures are also inconsistent. Suppose there is a requirement for monthly sales.

Depending on where the data is obtained, different answers may result: the accounting system will say $1,056,500.55; the annual report will say $1,056,501; and the marketing system will say one million fifty-six thousand dollars.

As a second illustration, consider how the departments are coded in the Warren Corporation. When the corporation was small there were only six departments, so a single digit as the department code was used in the records. Later the corporation grew, and data

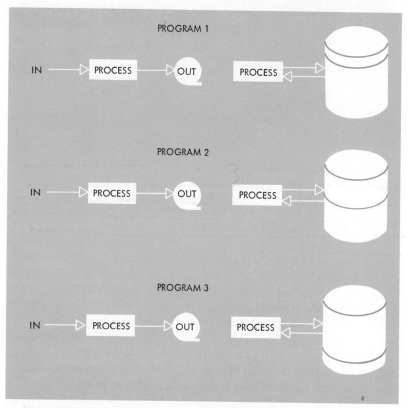

PROGRAM 1

IN → PROCESS → OUT   PROCESS

PROGRAM 2

IN → PROCESS → OUT   PROCESS

PROGRAM 3

IN → PROCESS → OUT   PROCESS

FIGURE 10.1
The process orientation means that each program is provided with a separate data input file.

processing had to deal with 15 different departments. This required a two-digit code for departments, and all programs using this code had to be modified. The problem could have been easily solved if programs and data had independence, meaning that either programs or data could be changed without the need for changing the other.

The same idea applied to the storage of data on disks. As the business grows there are more parts manufactured, and more storage space on disks is required. Should storage space be reserved for future contingencies? If so how much? Too little may require modifying the system, and too much may lead to waste and excessive cost in storage.

FIGURE 10.2
Process
orientation leads
to excessive
maintenance work
and cost.

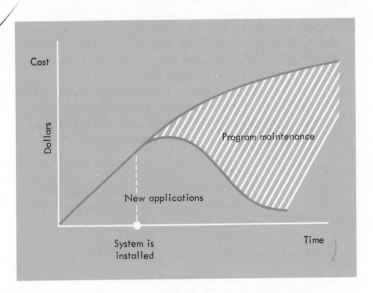

If a new application involving data from several functional areas of the business (such as finance, marketing, and production) requires data from many files, writing the program and preparing new data files will be time-consuming and expensive. The problem could be solved easily if related data could be retrieved, that is, if the system provides data relatability.

It has been noted that programs and systems are not just completed and delivered but must be continually modified and maintained. The process-oriented approach involves increasing difficulties with the maintenance of programs and systems. It leads to a situation in which an excessive proportion of the data processing budget must be spent on program maintenance, and little is left for new applications (Figure 10.2). The process-oriented approach leads to a dead end, inhibiting increase in the scope of data processing and preventing the full utilization of technological advancements.

To summarize, the process-oriented approach consists of five steps: (1) prepare program to create file, (2) prepare program to generate reports, (3) collect data for input, (4) create file, and (5) generate report. To increase the productivity of computer systems, there is a need to automate the various data management functions: better ways are needed to create files; retrieve and access data; add, delete, update, and store data; generate and format reports; control peripheral units; manage storage space, and so on.

DATA BASE ORIENTATION

The central concept of data base management is to pool data for many programs and store the data in data bases (Figure 10.3).

Data is entered only once in the system, and as little redundancy as possible is allowed. The five-step process-oriented approach to program preparation discussed above is replaced by a two-phase task specialization (Figure 10.4). *First, the data base must be created and maintained.* The activity of the creation, modification, deletion, and updating of data is controlled in a formal and centralized manner, independent from program writing. *Second, programs must be prepared and reports generated.*

Perhaps the most important single concept in data base management systems is the separation of the physical and logical organization of data. The significance of this all-encompassing concept can be indicated by comparison with an everyday example.

Take the situation where you want to find a book in your college

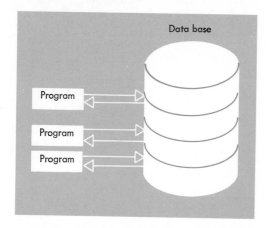

FIGURE 10.3 Data base orientation means that programs operate on pools of data, the data bases of the system.

library (Figure 10.5); books can be compared with data and the process of getting a book with the process of getting data for an application program. Assume that you, as a user of the library, are not allowed to go to the stacks and search for the book you want. Not only would this take a lot of your time, but it could also lead to confusion, as you might mix up the books on the shelves. Your approach is to search the card index, find the call number of the book, and ask the librarian to get it for you. Either the librarian or the clerk supporting the librarian, gets the book for you. You yourself probably do not know the physical location of the book, but this does not concern you, because the librarian is the human interface between the user and the library.

In the library the books are independent of the index; the books in the stacks can be rearranged without changing the index. There are two separate forms of organization: the physical organization of the books in the stacks and the logical organization used in the index cards. Suppose, for example, you are going through the author's index and find this textbook under the author's name, Vazsonyi. The next index card refers to an author, Vazzana (Figure 10.6). But if you go to the stacks and find Vazsonyi's book you would not see the book by Vazzana next to it because that is a book on culinary art, stacked in an entirely different location.

FIGURE 10.4 Data base orientation leads to separation of functions into two phases: creation and maintenance of data bases, and operation of programs.

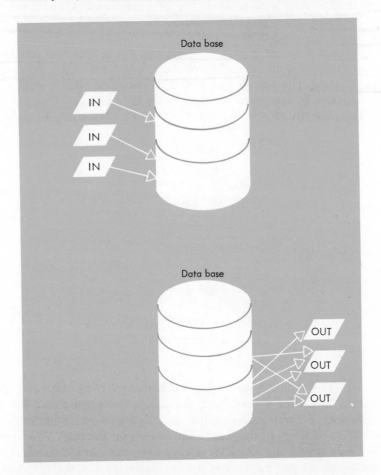

The librarian in the example, the human interface, corresponds to the data base administrator (DBA) discussed in Chapter 1. The actual manner in which the librarian retrieves the book from the stacks (including the possibility of using assistants) corresponds to the programs and software used in data base management systems.

Searching for books in a library provides one illustration of the difference between physical and logical organization. In everyday life we encounter such a distinction quite often. The records at a radio station must be cataloged; the logical organization of the

Index

FIGURE 10.5 Data base management system compared with central desk of library. The user need not be concerned with the physical location of books.

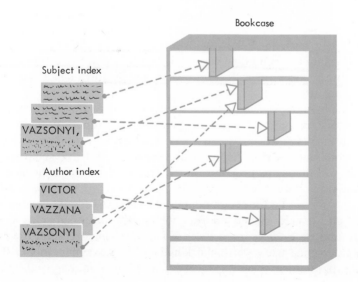

Bookcase

Subject index

VAZSONYI,

Author index

VICTOR

VAZZANA

VAZSONYI

FIGURE 10.6 Subject and author indexes show how physical and logical relationships are separated, due to data independence.

catalog is different from the physical storage of records. The logical organization of the classified section of the telephone book is different from the physical location of the subscribers.

DATA STRUCTURES   *TEST*

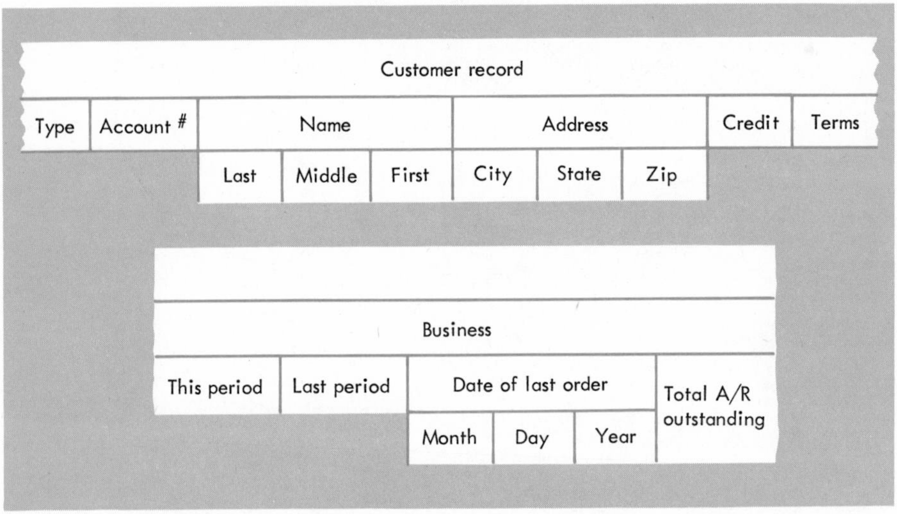

FIGURE 10.7
Hierarchical data
structure for
invoice
preparation.

If the function of a data base were merely to store data, its design, organization, and maintenance would be simple. Most of the difficulty arises from the fact that the data base must also show the relationship between the various items of data, records, and files. Thus, in addition to storing data, the data base must show how

characters form fields, how fields form files, how the characters and fields relate to each other within files or between two or more files, how the records relate to each other, and so forth (see Chapter 2, Figure 2.16).

To illustrate, consider the physical layout of the customer and inventory records used in the problem of preparing an invoice (Chapter 5, Figures 5.20 and 5.21). The fields in these records are adjoining and form a simple, fixed sequence. But this sequence of fields within the record does not correspond to the point of view of the programmer, who visualizes a tree structure or a hierarchical data structure. To the programmer the customer record contains, for example, a field named *address* which has three subfields—*city, state* and *zip code* (Figure 10.7). To specify the structure, the programmer must use a particular language. For example, in COBOL the programmer specifies records, as shown in Figure 10.8. In traditional data processing the fields are stored physically next to each other, and so implementing the structured view of the programmer is relatively simple. In a data base environment, where physical and logical views are separated, the problem of establishing the relationship between the two views becomes more involved.

In Figure 10.9 the hardware or physical data base is represented by magnetic disks. The view for humans, that is, the logical view, is provided by the data base management system.

The data base administrator has a logical view called the schema. The programmer's view, which is logical and corresponds to Figures

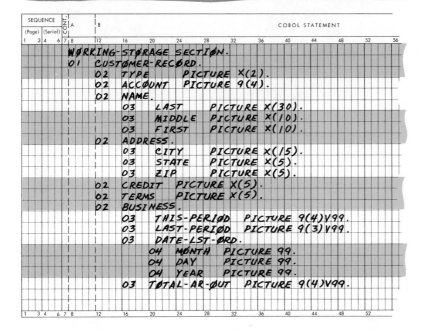

FIGURE 10.8 COBOL specification of hierarchical data structure for invoice preparation.

10.7 and 10.8, is called a subschema: different application programmers will consider different subschemas. The relationships between schema, subschema, and the physical structure are provided by software. The application programmer may not even know what the global or total schema is, or what the physical structure is.

At first it may appear strange that different views of the same thing are possible. In fact, it is not surprising that things are not always what they seem (Figure 10.10). Examples should clarify the point.

When you look through a magnifying glass (Figure 10.10b) you see what in physics is called a virtual image. In your camera the lens produces a real image (Figure 10.10c), which can be recorded photographically. Users of a time-sharing system (Figure 10.10d)

have the illusion of working with a private computer, but in reality they have access to the computer only for short time periods. A programmer may write a program to operate on data stored in virtual memory (Figure 10.10e), and, so far as the programmer is concerned, there is no distinction between real, physical, or vitural storage. The logical structure of data, like beauty, is in the eyes of the beholder (Figure 10.10f).

FIGURE 10.9 Physical layout refers to hardware. Logical view refers to the minds of the data base administrator, users, and programmers.

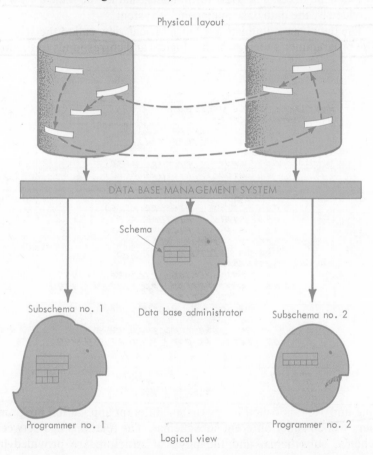

Physical layout

DATA BASE MANAGEMENT SYSTEM

Schema

Subschema no. 1   Data base administrator   Subschema no. 2

Programmer no. 1   Programmer no. 2

Logical view

The separation of physical and logical concepts requires changing our way of thinking and describing data. Therefore, data processing professionals have created a set of specific names to deal with logical concepts of data.

According to CODASYL (*CO*mmittee on *DA*ta *SY*stems Languages) Data Base Task Group, one influential professional group, a data item is the smallest named unit in a data base. A *record* is a collection of one or more data items. A *data set* is a named collection of records and relationships between two or more

FIGURE 10.10
The physical versus logical point of view in everyday life and in the computer world.

(a) Do you see a vase or profiles?

(b) A magnifying glass creates a virtual image.

(c) A camera creates a real image on film.

(d) A user of time-sharing has the illusion of having a private computer.

(e) A programmer uses virtual memory.

(f) Beauty is in the eyes of the beholder.

records; this is the basic building block to form data structures. A data set has only one owner but may have any number of members (Figure 10.11). For example, in Figure 10.7 the field *address* owns three members: *city, state,* and *zip code.* An area is a named, logical subdivision of the data base. The schema is a complete logical description of all data items in the data base, and the sub-schema is a logical part of the schema.

FIGURE 10.11
Graphical
representation of
how logical
relationships are
established.

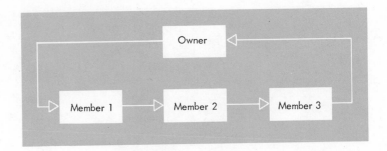

Another influential data processing group, the Joint Guide and Share Data Base Requirements Group, makes different recommendations and uses different words. When you consult other books and publications, you must be certain that you understand the definitions of the words. We will use the definitions provided at the end of this chapter.

DATA BASE MANAGEMENT SYSTEMS   *TEST*

There are over a hundred generalized software systems available to aid the user, programmer, and systems analyst in such operations as file generation and maintenance and report generation. Some of these have been developed by software firms, some by manufacturers, some by large organizations for their own use. Many of these systems are a natural outgrowth of the efforts of programmers to deal with data management problems in a generalized manner. For example, application programmers have not written sorting programs for a long time because generalized sorting programs are available. Formerly these programming packages were called information retrieval systems, file processors, file processing systems, reporting systems, and so on. Today most of them are called data base management systems.

Characteristics of data base management systems

A data base management system (DBMS) is a set of software programs which is characterized by these facts:

1. It is independent from the particular set of programs or files which will use it.
2. It references data by name and not by physical location.
3. It provides means to operate on data for data definition, storage, maintenance, retrieval, and so on.
4. It provides means to deal with logical relationships between data items, records, sets, and so on.

A legitimate point of view for application programmers is that compilers, operation systems, and data base management systems are software packages to facilitate their work. To the application programmer the processor of the data base management system may look like a compiler, but to the operating system it appears more like an application program.

Types of data base management systems   *TEST - 2 types*

In a *self-contained* data base management system, users need not know any other programming language. They can do all their work with the DBMS. In the class of self-contained systems there is a distinction between *forms-controlled* and *data-management-language-controlled* systems.

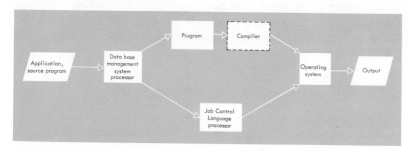

FIGURE 10.12
How a self-contained DBMS operates.

The simplest self-contained DBMS is forms controlled. The user is provided with instructions on how to complete a set of forms, and this is all the user has to do. Thus the user of such a system need not be a programmer, and some of the forms-controlled systems can be mastered in a matter of hours. Later we will illustrate such systems with the Mark IV File Management System.

A language-controlled, self-contained DBMS is more complex to use because the user must master the specific source language of the system. However, the user need not know other programming languages.

In a self-contained DBMS the user writes the program in the language of the system, and then the DBMS takes over (Figure 10.12). The DBMS processor generates a program and the job control language statements. The program generated may be in machine language or in a procedure-oriented language. If it is in the latter, there is a need for a compiler to generate the machine language program. The operating system provides the interface between the programs and the hardware.

Another type is called a procedure-oriented, language-embedded

FIGURE 10.13
How a
language-
embedded DBMS
operates.

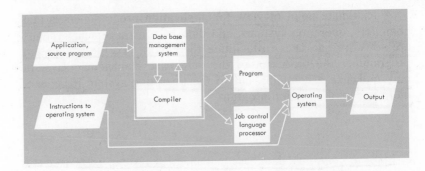

DBMS. Users write their programs in the host language, such as COBOL, and in the DBMS-provided source language, which is consistent with the host language. Users must also provide instructions to the operating system (Figure 10.13). The DBMS and the compiler of the host language jointly generate the object program and the job control language statements. Output is generated by the operating system.

Components of data base management systems

The most important components of a DBMS for the user are the various source languages provided. If it is a self-contained system, all instructions must be written in the DBMS languages. If it is a host-language-embedded system, both languages must be used. If it is a forms-controlled system, the user masters only the technique of filling out the form.

The two most important languages provided are the data description/definition language (DDL) which, as the name implies, provides a formal and precise definition of data, how it is stored, and how it is related, and the data manipulation language (DML), which is a source language to enable the application program to give instructions to the data base management system. If there is a perfect separation of physical and logical organization of data, the user need know only the forms or languages of the DBMS. However, in most systems the programmer also needs to be familiar with the data accessing–addressing techniques used, to be discussed below.

The six steps of data transfer

There are six steps in the process whereby the DBMS transfers data to the application program:

1. The application program requests the DBMS for a record.
2. The DBMS compares the schema, the subschema, and the physical data base description.
3. The DBMS requests the operating system for the record.
4. The operating system makes the record available to the DBMS.
5. The DBMS compares the schema and subschema and transforms the data into the logical record needed.
6. The DBMS transfers the logical record to the application program.

IMPLICATIONS OF DATA BASE MANAGEMENT SYSTEMS   *TEST*

There is hardly any facet of data processing not influenced by the introduction of modern data base management systems. The broad implications are increases in system performance and flexibility, decreases in the various costs associated with data processing, and the cost and time required for system development. These systems increase the productivity of programmers, decrease software and computer costs, ease problems of system design, improve operations, increase throughput, and decrease response time. More specifically, the following advantages hold:

1. Reduction of data redundancy. The proliferation of data unavoidable in the process-oriented approach is eliminated, and redundant data is maintained only when it is required or economically beneficial. Independent files are eliminated, so storage requirements are reduced. Costs are reduced because data is stored and maintained only once.
2. Increased capability to relate associated data. This allows the production of reports for multiple, interrelated files, a requirement difficult to meet in the process-oriented approach.
3. Creation of data and program independence. The application programmer need not know the entire record or the physical location of the data. Physical data location and application programs can be changed independently. This gives a high degree of flexibility.
4. Increased data integrity. The application programmer has no direct way to change physical data bases, so it is almost impossible to destroy data, alter relationships between data, add duplicate records, lose records, and so on. To protect the data base against accidental loss, procedures to backup, recovery and restart can be provided.
5. Security of data. Access to data can be easily limited by passwords to authorized users, so data privacy can be assured.

6. Adaptability and flexibility. Physical data can be viewed as logically different by different users. This permits multiple use of the same data.

7. Reduction of physical storage requirements. The separation of physical and logical organization allows higher storage space utilization, in particular for variable length records, because there is no need to provide unused space for future use.

Managerial implications

We have noted the decrease in overall cost of data processing and time required for development which is one of the most important consequences of the use of data based management systems. There are, however, some other features which lead to increased value and benefits.

The use of a self-contained, forms-controlled DBMS opens the door to the use of computers by nonprogrammers. This increases the entire scope of data processing, and the number of personnel who can directly benefit is multiplied.

One of the serious impediments to wider use of data processing systems is the time and cost involved in developing custom-tailored systems which are used only once or infrequently. For example, the marketing department of a corporation may want to make a market survey for a specific group of products and class of customers. In such ad hoc applications the execution time or the efficiency of the program becomes secondary to the time and cost it takes to develop programs. Such needs are particularly difficult to meet with the process-oriented approach, while data based management systems are well suited to the task.

Another closely associated problem which causes a great deal of frustration to management is the difficulty of solving problems which require data from various systems. In the process-oriented approach, for example, it may become prohibitively expensive in dollars and time to make a top-management study involving the combined use of data from marketing, production, and finance, because there are many independent files to meet the needs of each of these systems. In the data base environment all data is integrated and easily accessible, so such top-management requirements can be met with much greater ease.

Costs and disadvantages

When a data base management system is introduced, new software costs associated with it are incurred. There may also be an increased need for physical storage of data, since the software must be stored. There are always educational and learning costs when a new system is introduced, and some productive personnel time must be assigned to these tasks, which do not lead to immediate economic benefits.

When a new DBMS is introduced there is the risk of obsolescence because it is dealing with innovative approaches. Some systems are limited in scope, and users may discover only after a DBMS has been introduced that benefits are not as significant as expected. If a DBMS is not completely tested, it may have bugs in the documentation and in operational procedures.

On the human side, the personnel problems necessary to operate such systems can become severe. If there is a lack of competent personnel to work with the data base environment, even the most ingenious and sophisticated system will bring only limited benefits.

The computer time required to run application programs may be increased, at least temporarily, in the data base environment. Programs may be slow when processed by the language processor— slow to compile and slow to execute.

However, it must be recognized that the introduction of any innovative approach can lead to problem areas and additional costs. This may be true when a DBMS is introduced, though in the long run its benefits outweigh costs and disadvantages.

AN EXAMPLE: THE MARK IV FILE MANAGEMENT SYSTEM

The Mark IV File Management System produced by Informatics, Inc., is a forms-controlled DBMS which can be used without any specific knowledge of programming languages. Mark IV has a source language of its own for description of files to be processed, files to be maintained, selection logic for information retrieval, formats for output, and instructions needed by the operating system. Instead of writing instructions in FORTRAN or COBOL or another procedure-oriented language, the user of Mark IV fills out a variety of forms containing descriptions of data and the processing to be performed.

For purposes of illustration, in Figure 10.14 we show the Mark IV program to solve the following problem:

1. Search the personnel/payroll file and produce a salary survey.
2. Select all personnel with a salary greater than $450 *and* who have been with the company since 1960.
3. Sort the selected data by department, within the department by group and within the group by salary. Sort by salary in descending order.
4. Start a new page for each new department.

MARK IV FILE MANAGEMENT SYSTEM®

INFORMATION REQUEST

informatics inc.®

PAGE ____ OF ____

DECK I.D.

REQUEST NAME: SALSURVY

REPORT DATE: I R TODAY

REQUESTORS NAME: I. V. MARK TELEPHONE/EXT. 360 DIVISION/DEPT. 30

REPORT FORMAT — SUMMARY REPORT ONLY? | VERTICAL SPACING | FORMS CONTROL | WIDTH OF PAGE | HEIGHT OF PAGE | LINE NUMBERS?

RECORD SELECTION / REPORT SPECIFICATION

SEQ. NO.	LOGIC LEVEL	CONNECTOR	FIELD NAME A	OPERATION	BLANK, C OR D	FIELD NAME B OR CONSTANT		SEQ. NO.	NO. OF SPACES BEFORE COLUMN	FIELD NAME	SEQUENCE	DESC.?	CONTROL	SUBTITLE	TOTAL	CUM	COUNT	MAX.	MIN.	AVG.
P R			SALARY	GE	D	$450.00		R 1	20	GROUP	2		2							
P R		A	HIREYEAR	GE	C	60		R 1	10	DEPT	1			P						
P R								R 1	30	SALARY	3	Y			2	1	2	2	2	2
P R								R 1	40	EMPNAME										
P R								R 1												
P R								R 1												
P R								R 1												
P R								R 1												
P R								R 1												
P R								R 1												
P R								R 1												
P R								R 1												
P R								R 1												
P R								R 1												
P R								R 1												

TITLE

T 1 0 0 1 SALARY SURVEY - BY GROUP WITHIN DEPARTMENT.

MK IV IR02 COPYRIGHT 1968 INFORMATICS INC   *KEYPUNCHING NOTE: THIS NAME MUST APPEAR IN COLS 1-8 OF ALL CARDS PUNCHED FROM THIS FORM.

John A. Postley, *"General Purpose Systems: The Mark IV File Management System"* in Critical Factors in Data Management, *Fred Gruenberger, Ed.* © 1969, p. 121. Reprinted by permission of Prentice-Hall, Inc., Englewood Cliffs, N.J.

FIGURE 10.14 A simple MARK IV program to prepare a salary survey.

5. For each group within a department produce a total salary, and a count of the number of persons selected in the group.
6. Compute and print the maximum, minimum, and average salaries in the group. Whenever a change is made in a department, produce the cumulative total of salaries.
7. Print the report on $8\frac{1}{2}'' \times 11''$ paper, displaying the date on which the program is executed.

Observe how simple it is to fill out the information request form. Figure 10.15 shows a partial printout.

SEQUENTIAL ACCESS METHOD

In the early days of computers, when only magnetic tapes were available, the sequential access method was the only possible approach. Even today the sequential approach can compete successfully with other approaches, though it must be kept in mind that maintenance and modification of sequential files can be costly.

Sequential processing is illustrated by discussing again the problem of invoice preparation. To simplify, sequential processing

FIGURE 10.15
Printout produced
by MARK IV salary
survey program.

FEB. 31, 1984   PAGE 1

SALARY SURVEY - BY GROUP WITHIN DEPARTMENT

101

		GROUP	SALARY	NAME
		20	$1120.00	SIEGAL, M. C.
			805.00	SMITH, C. H.
			600.00	JONES, T. L.
			580.00	WILSON, W. C.
			535.00	KENT, L. F.
GROUP	TOTAL		$3640.00	
GROUP	COUNT		5	
GROUP	MAX.		$1120.00	
GROUP	MIN.		$535.00	
GROUP	AVG.		$728.00	
		21	$1250.00	TONAI, M. M.
			905.00	KEITHLEY, L. J.
			600.00	WILLIAMS, J. G.
			550.00	MARTIN, T. D.
			525.00	JENSON, J. J.
			480.00	LEE, F. C.
			475.00	YOKUM, L. A.
GROUP	TOTAL		$4785.00	
GROUP	COUNT		7	
GROUP	MAX.		$1250.00	
GROUP	MIN.		$475.00	
GROUP	AVG.		$683.57	
DEPT.	TOTAL		$8425.00	
DEPT.	CUM.		$8425.00	
DEPT.	COUNT		12	
DEPT.	MAX.		$1250.00	
DEPT.	MIN.		$475.00	
DEPT.	AVG.		$702.08	

John A. Postley, "General Purpose Systems: The Mark IV File Management System" in Critical Factors in Data Management, Fred Gruenberger, Ed., © 1969, p. 123. Reprinted by permission of Prentice-Hall, Inc., Englewood Cliffs, N.J.

is discussed in terms of magnetic tapes, with a more detailed description of the system flowchart in Figure 5.24 (Chapter 5). The discussion applies equally well to the sequential processing of magnetic disks, however.

Sequential approach to invoice preparation

Figure 10.16 shows in more detail the sequential invoice calculation. The five processes of the operation are discussed below.

FIGURE 10.16
Detailed flowchart
for sequential
invoice
preparation.

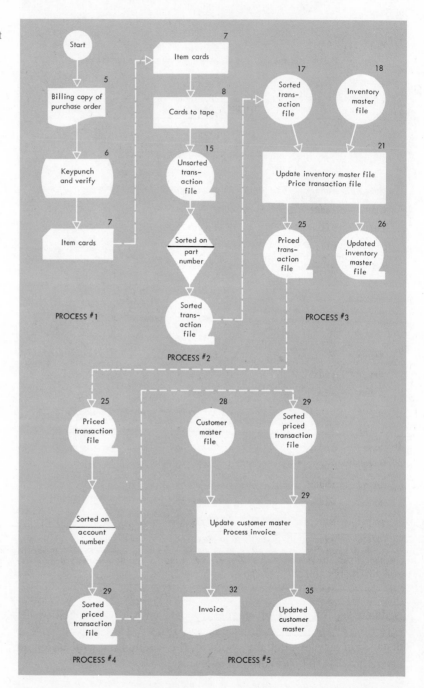

Process #1. The input is the billing copy of the purchase order (Box 5). The data is keypunched and verified, and then the item cards are produced (Box 7).

Process #2. The input to this process is the deck of item cards. First, the deck is converted to tape, and the unsorted transaction file is obtained. This file is in turn sorted by part number, and the sorted transaction file is obtained.

Process #3. The inputs are the sorted transaction file and inventory master file, both of which are in part number sequence. As Box 21 indicates, the inventory master file is updated and the price is included in the transaction file. Thus the output is the priced transaction file and the updated inventory master file, both in part number sequence.

Process #4. The input is the priced transaction file, which is in part number sequence. The file is sorted by account number and a priced transaction file in account number sequence is obtained.

Process #5. The inputs are the customer master file and the sorted priced transaction file, which are both in account number sequence. Now the customer file can be updated and the invoice processed. The outputs are the invoice and the updated customer master file.

Before we leave the problem of invoice preparation we should point out a simplification used in discussing the processing of two input files. The computer must be told what to do the first time the end of a file is reached. There may be special records at the end of the files, or there may be other approaches available to the programmer. Resolution of this *end-of-file condition* depends on the system used by the particular installation. This can be easily learned, so it will not be discussed here.

Information retrieval

Assume there is a single input personnel file and the problem is to retrieve and print first the personnel records of males and then the records of females. Figure 10.17 shows the flowchart to accomplish this task.

For the moment, ignore the test in Box 5 and look at the test in Box 15. If sex is male, the personnel record is printed in Box 20. If it is female, the personnel record is written on a scratch tape. Going back to Box 10 (through Box 5), the next personnel record is read. Thus the records will be read one by one. The personnel records of the males will be printed, and the scratch tape will contain the records of females.

After all the records have been read, the test in Box 5 comes into action. When there are no more records the tape is rewound

FIGURE 10.17
Flowchart
showing how to
print personnel
records first of
males, then of
females.

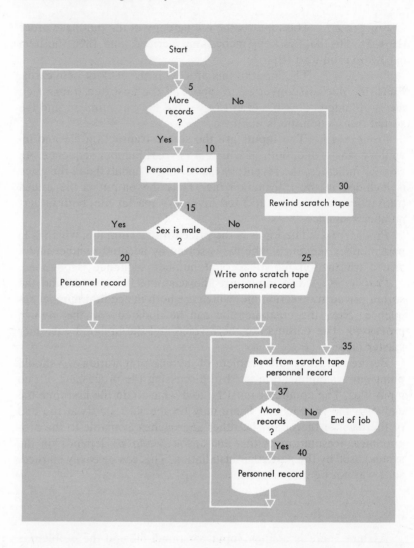

(Box 30), and the records from the scratch file are read and printed (Boxes 35 and 40).

Thus it takes *two passes* of the input file to generate the output.

Updating a master file

Figure 10.18 shows how, in the invoice preparation problem, the inventory master file is updated with the aid of the transaction file. (Both these files are in part number sequence.)

Box 2 indicates that one line item record from the transaction file is read, and a test is made to terminate the processing after all the cards have been read (Box 10). Then a record is read from the inventory master file (Box 15).

Observe that there are now two records in memory: the line item record and the record from the inventory master file. Depending on whether the two part numbers agree, it may be necessary to do two types of processing.

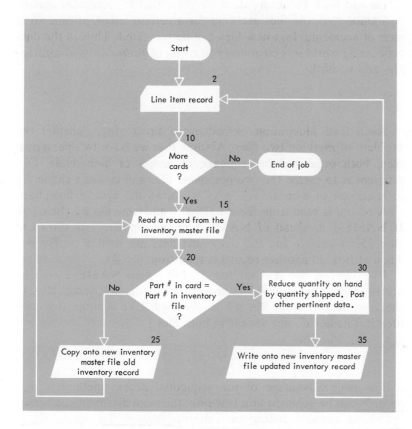

FIGURE 10.18
Flowchart showing how to update an inventory master file by sequential processing.

If the part numbers agree, it means that the item is on the transaction file. If it has been shipped, the quantity on hand in inventory is reduced by the quantity shipped and other data is posted (Box 30). Then the updated master inventory record is written (Box 35).

If the part numbers do not agree, it means that the particular item is not on the transaction file. So the record obtained previously from the master inventory file is copied on the new master inventory file (Box 25). Then (Box 15) the next record from the inventory master file is read in.

Observe, on the other hand, that if the item is shipped, control moves from Box 35 back to Box 2 to read the next line item record.

To summarize: (1) when there is an agreement in part numbers, the inventory on hand must be reduced and the next record from the transaction file must be read; (2) if the part numbers do not agree, the inventory record is simply copied, and the next record from the inventory master is read.

After a file is updated, that is, a new file is created, what happens to the old file? To assure data integrity, that is protection against accidental loss, old files are kept for a certain length of time so in case of accidental loss new files can be recreated. Thus in the data processing world it is customary to speak of *father file, grandfather file,* and so forth.

Merging two files

As a final illustration of sequential processing, consider the problem of merging two files. Assume that we have two personnel files, both organized in sequence of names of individuals. Our problem is to merge the two personnel files and create a single file in sequence of names. Figure 10.19 shows the system flowchart.

A record is read from file #1 (Box 5) and from file #2 (Box 10). If NAME-1 is ahead of NAME-2 in the alphabet, as shown in Box 25, NAME-1 and the personnel data are written on file #3. Then at Box 30 another record is read from file #1.

If, however, the text in Box 15 fails, then NAME-2 and the corresponding personnel data are written on file #3, and at Box 10 the next record from file #2 is obtained. (We assume that two identical names do not appear in both files.)

INDEXED SEQUENTIAL ACCESS METHOD

The main advantage of the sequential access method is that records can be scanned at a fast rate; the main disadvantage is that individual records cannot be retrieved unless the whole file is scanned. This leads to unacceptable delays when records must be retrieved quickly, but magnetic disks provide the capability of quick retrieval of records from large files. The approach described here, the indexed sequential access method (ISAM), maintains the advantages of the sequential approach, such as the ability to scan quickly, but also provides the capability of quick retrieval of individual records. The approach is based on the concept of using an index to retrieve records by key, such as social security number, payroll number, or some other identifying code.

In discussing magnetic disks we noted that this storage medium has the capability of retrieving records by addressing, that is by

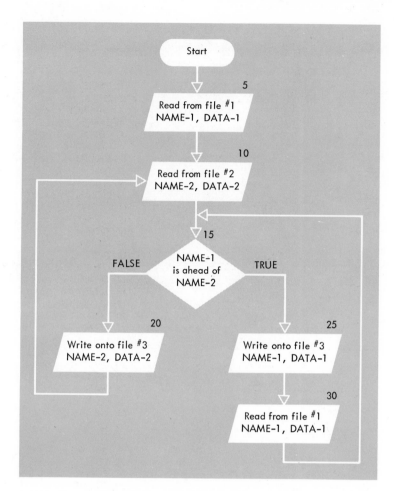

FIGURE 10.19
Flowchart
showing how to
merge two
sequential files.

specifying the track and surface numbers. If an index is kept of the key of the record and its address the address of the record can be found by searching the index, and so the record can be retrieved.

A familiar example of using indexes is the example given above of finding books in a library. You do not search the stacks; you consult the files of index cards for a call number for each book. You provide the librarian with the number, and this helps locate the book in the stacks. Similarly, the computer could keep an index for disk addresses by the keys of the records. This would require that the key and address of each record appear on the index, however, and the indexing methods used in data processing are somewhat different.

FIGURE 10.20
Single-stage
indexed sequential
access method
(ISAM).

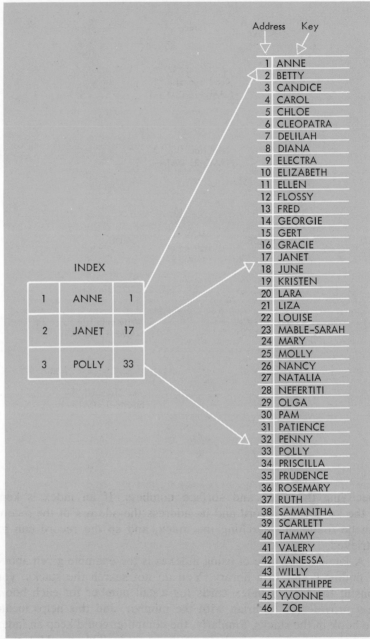

James Martin, Computer Data-Base Organization, © 1975. Reprinted by permission of Prentice-Hall, Inc., Englewood Cliffs, N.J.

In Figure 10.20, the keys of 46 records are shown on the right side. On the left side an index listing only three keys and addresses from the file are shown.

If we want to find Mary's record in the file, we read the first key in the index Anne. The index shows that this record is stored at address 1. We know that the records are in alphabetic order, so Mary will be somewhere after Anne. Now we read the second key in the index, Janet, which is stored at address 17. Mary also follows Janet in the alphabet, so we proceed to read the third key, Polly. We know that Mary is somewhere between Janet and Polly. So we go to address 17, where Janet's record is stored, and scan the records until we find Mary's record.

With ISAM (Indexed Sequential Access Method), the first search is of the index, which gives an approximate location for the record, and then of the file itself. This significantly cuts down the requirement for scanning the file. For example, suppose we have 10,000 records and the index contains 100 keys. The index containing only 100 items, each with only a few characters, can be searched quickly. Therefore the time required to find the record is not much more than the time it takes to search 100 records, not 10,000.

Even greater savings in time can be achieved by replacing the single-stage indexed sequential access method described so far with a two-stage approach. Figure 10.21 shows that in the first-level index, on the left, there still are three keys. However, the second-level index further narrows the storage area to be searched. Suppose we want to retrieve Mary's record again. Searching the first-level index tells us that Mary's record is between Janet's and Polly's, so we proceed to the second-level index starting with Janet. Here we find the names Janet, Liza, Molly, and Olga, and we conclude that Mary is between Liza and Molly. Now we go to location 21 in the file and search the records until we find Mary's record.

To appreciate the time savings resulting from a two-stage indexed sequential file, assume that (1) we have one million records, (2) the first-level index has 100 keys, and (3) there are 100 second-level indexes, each with 100 keys. The indexes, being short records, can be searched quickly, and so only 100 records in the file will have to be searched to find the desired record.

To make it easy to understand how the system actually works with magnetic disk storage, it can be compared with the everyday problem of finding the phone number of a person in the phone book.

Figure 10.22 shows how the telephone book search can be described with the aid of the indexed sequential access method. On the left side is a *page* index, a listing of the first subscriber named on each page of the telephone book and the corresponding page num-

10 / Data base management systems

FIGURE 10.21
Two-stage
indexed sequential
access method
(ISAM).

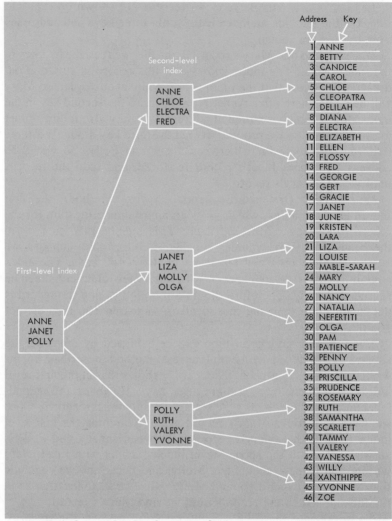

James Martin, Computer Data-Base Organization, © 1975. Reprinted by permission of Prentice-Hall, Inc., Englewood Cliffs, N.J.

ber. The *column* indexes, one for each page of the phone book, show the name of the person at the top of each column.

Suppose we want to find the phone number of Miles Aberbach in the Rochester phone book. The page index shows that the first entry on page 15 of the book is A J's Bakery; the first entry on page 16 is Aaragon, the first entry on page 17 is Ackerman, and so on. When we search the page index, therefore, we find that Aberbach must be after Aaragon but before Ackerman. So we know that Aberbach is on page 16 of the phone book, which leads to the column indexes, in which the names correspond to the names at the top of each column of the phone book. By searching the index for page 16 we conclude that Aberbach must be between Abelove and Abrams. So we go to the third column of names on page 16 and search until we find Aberbach and the corresponding phone number.

Bear in mind that the page and column indexes can be searched

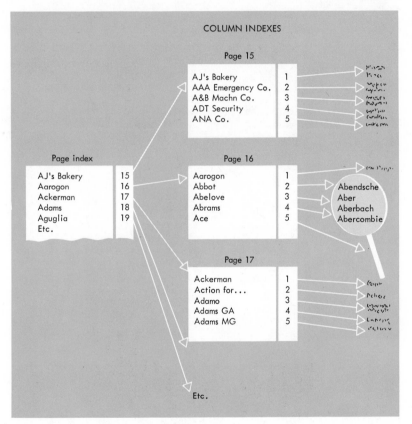

FIGURE 10.22
Indexed sequential access method for telephone book.

quickly. As for searching the records, only those in a single column need to be searched.

Before we show the relationship between the phone book example and an indexed sequential file on a magnetic disk, we need to introduce the concept of the cylinder. The first tracks on the surfaces from the first cylinder; the second tracks the second, and so forth. Observe that when searching records on the same cylinder, there is no need to move the read/write head. Now Figure 10.23 shows that *if the page of the phone book is wrapped around the cylinder of the disk,* each column in the phone book corresponds to a track on the surface of the magnetic disk. The page of the phone book corresponds to a cylinder on the magnetic disk, and the page index compares to the so-called *cylinder index*. Since the column of the phone book corresponds to a track on the magnetic disk, the column index of the phone book corresponds to the *track index*. Searching a column of names in the phone book corresponds to scanning a track on the disk.

FIGURE 10.23
Telephone book pages wrapped around the cylinders of a disk pack.

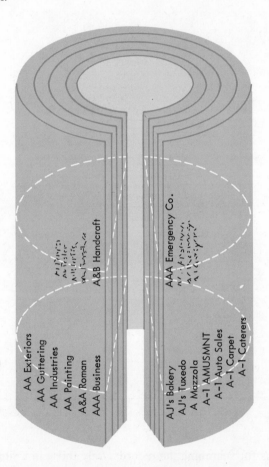

To summarize, in a phone book we find the name of a person by searching (1) the page index, (2) the column index, and (3) a column of names. On the magnetic disk the computer searches (1) the cylinder index, (2) the track index, and (3) the track itself.

Where the cylinder and track indexes are stored is a matter of the particular system design. It is customary, however, to store these indexes on the magnetic disk at strategic locations which can be found quickly on the disk.

Note that the approach consists of searching indexes and files of records. Because the records are kept in sequence, a sequential access method is also available.

This simplified description of the Indexed Sequential Access Method (ISAM) provides general knowledge and a basis for further studies. A more complete discussion should include problems of how records are deleted and added.

DIRECT-ACCESS METHODS   *Test*

Some data processing applications require extremely fast retrieval capability but no sequential access. For such situations direct-access methods, in which there is a specific technique to determine the address of a record if the key is specified, are available. We illustrate here only one of the methods, which relies on a computational technique.

Suppose a company wants to control access of employees to buildings and offices by a computerized badge system. To simplify matters, assume the goal is to store information on 700 employees in such a manner that random access can be achieved very quickly. Assume that the data is stored in an area of a magnetic disk where 1,000 locations are available. Suppose, furthermore, that the key for each employee is the social security number and that the problem is to determine from the social security number the address on the disk. How is a nine-digit social security number converted into a three-digit address corresponding to the 1,000 locations?

One approach, the hashing or randomizing method, is the following: We take a number less than 1,000 but close to 1,000, like 997. When we divide each social security number by 997 we obtain a quotient and remainder. The record is stored at the address equal to the remainder.

For example, assume that the social security number of the employee is 185–22–9188. This number is 185,229,188. If we divide this number by 997 the remainder is 546, and we store the record at address 546.

So far so good. But suppose two employees have social security numbers which lead to the same storage address, 546. What is to be done then? Such keys for records are called *synonyms*. The dilemma is resolved by storing in the record of the first employee a code indicating the address of the synonym. The first record contains the address of the second record; the second record of the third record, and so forth.

In more technical language, we would say that the problem of synonyms is handled by having a field reserved in each record to contain a pointer which *points* to the location of the next synonym.

In the next section we will discuss in more detail what pointers are and how they are used.

NETWORK STRUCTURES AND ACCESS METHODS

So far we have discussed three access methods: sequential, indexed sequential, and direct. There are more sophisticated data processing problems in which none of these approaches provide satisfactory solutions.

Suppose we want to know the names and phone numbers of people living on a particular street; ordinarily we would have to search the entire phone book to find the correct people and numbers. In a corporation, suppose invoices are stored in sequence of invoice numbers. If we want to find, for example, the unpaid invoices for the Empire Graphic Foundation, we would have to search the entire file. Solutions to such complex problems are obtained by network structures and access methods.

To help you understand these methods, consider the family tree of some of the English kings (Figure 10.24). Suppose the name of each king and information about him are stored on a magnetic disk. The key to each record is the name of the king, and assuming that the names are in alphabetic order using an indexed or direct-access approach, the record of each king and its content can be retrieved by key.

Suppose now that it is desired to list the kings in their order of succession to the throne. A graphical solution to the problem is also shown in Figure 10.24, where a chain (or list) is drawn to link the records of the kings in their order of succession to the throne. How can this linking of records be accomplished in storage?

In each record we include a field where a pointer showing the address of the next record is stored. Note that each record contains three types of data: (1) the name of the king, that is, the key, (2) the special field containing the pointer, and finally, (3) the content of the record, that is information such as date and manner of death. Observe that the structure of the data is stored in the pointers which indicate the next king in succession.

In the example described, the pointers are stored in fields in the records. An alternate approach is to provide multiple indexes for the records. This corresponds to the subject and author indexes provided in the library (see Figure 10.6).

As to the kings of England, we need two indexes. In the first, the name of the king is the key and the index is in alphabetic order. In the second, the date of succession is the key; this index is kept in chronological order. With the aid of these two indexes the kings can be retrieved either in alphabetic order or in order of succession. This second alternate approach uses *external* pointers, to be contrasted with the technique discussed first, which uses *internal* or *embedded* pointers.

Now suppose we want to retrieve the names of the individuals who died a violent death (Figure 10.25). The solution to this problem

FIGURE 10.24 In this network structure the kings of England are linked by a chain in their order of succession to the throne.

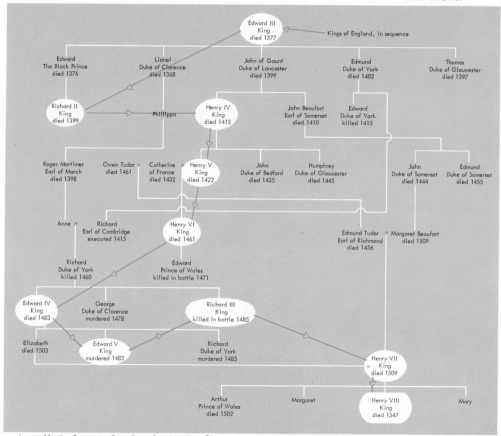

James Martin, Computer Data-Base Organization, © 1975. Reprinted by permission of Prentice-Hall, Inc., Englewood Cliffs, N.J.

can be obtained by establishing a second field in the record for a second set of pointers which will chain the kings who died violent deaths. Or, as an alternative, a third index could be established.

We are dealing here with advanced classes of data structures, in which pointers link records into various chains and records contain several fields with pointers. In fact, records are processed by programs *chasing* pointers in the data base (Figure 10.26).

Many types of chains are used in network data structures; we

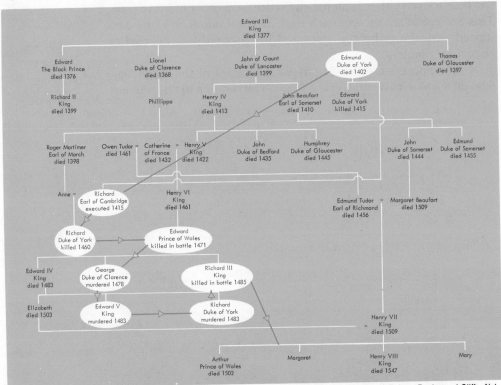

Edward III
King
died 1377

Edward
The Black Prince
died 1376

Lionel
Duke of Clarence
died 1368

John of Gaunt
Duke of Lancaster
died 1399

Edmund
Duke of York
died 1402

Thomas
Duke of Gloucester
died 1397

Richard II
King
died 1399

Phillippa

Henry IV
King
died 1413

John Beaufort
Earl of Somerset
died 1410

Edward
Duke of York
killed 1415

Roger Mortimer
Earl of March
died 1398

Owen Tudor =
died 1461

Catherine
of France
died 1432

= Henry V
King
died 1422

John
Duke of Bedford
died 1435

Humphrey
Duke of Gloucester
died 1445

John
Duke of Somerset
died 1444

Edmund
Duke of Somerset
died 1455

Anne =

Richard
Earl of Cambridge
executed 1415

Henry VI
King
died 1461

Edmund Tudor =
Earl of Richmond
died 1456

Margaret Beaufort
died 1509

Richard
Duke of York
killed 1460

Edward
Prince of Wales
killed in battle 1471

Edward IV
King
died 1483

George
Duke of Clarence
murdered 1478

Richard III
King
killed in battle 1485

Elizabeth
died 1503

Edward V
King
murdered 1483

Richard
Duke of York
murdered 1483

Henry VII
= King
died 1509

Arthur
Prince of Wales
died 1502

Margaret

Henry VIII
King
died 1547

Mary

James Martin, Computer Data-Base Organization, © 1975. *Reprinted by permission of Prentice-Hall, Inc., Englewood Cliffs, N.J.*

FIGURE 10.25
Chain linking
British kings who
died violent
deaths.

have discussed only a few. For example, **Figure 10.27** shows a *ring* structure, in which each record has a predecessor and successor and thus forms a **cycle**. **Figure 10.28** shows a *list* structure, in which the chain has a single *head* and a single *tail*.

This discussion of advanced types of data structures provides

FIGURE 10.26
The program
chases pointers in
the data base as
children chase
clues in a
treasure hunt.

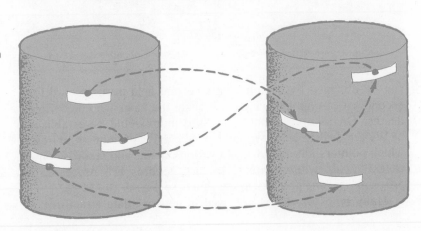

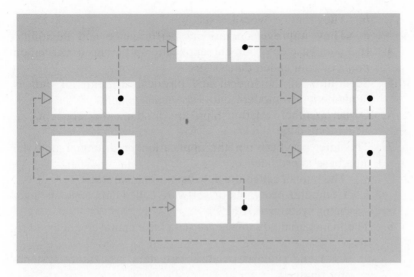

FIGURE 10.27
Diagram of ring structure.

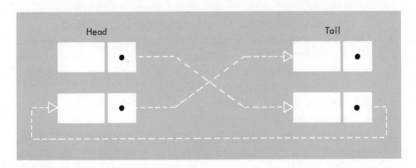

FIGURE 10.28
Diagram of list structure.

general knowledge and a foundation for further study of this sophisticated subject matter.

SUMMARY

1. The functions of data management are the generation, storing, retrieving, addition, deletion, updating, and sorting of data, the generation of reports, and the management of storage space.
2. The data base, the hierarchical collection of data, is a resource in itself which must be designed, organized, implemented, and managed.
3. Data base management systems provide many advantages, such as:
   a. They increase the productivity of the programmer by automating data management functions previously performed manually.

     b. They reduce overall costs.

     c. They improve operational performance and flexibility.

4. In a data base environment, application programs use common pools of data called data bases.

5. Separation of the logical and physical structure of data is fundamental to modern data base management.

6. Owner/member relationships are fundamental concepts in structuring data.

7. The interface between the application programmer and the data base is provided by:

     a. The human called the data base administrator.

     b. Computer programs or software called data base management systems (DBMS).

8. The managerial advantages of data base management systems are:

     a. Cost and time associated with data processing systems are reduced.

     b. Use of computers by nonprogrammers is promoted.

     c. Answers to ad hoc requirements can be provided.

9. Detailed advantages of data base management systems are:

     a. Reduction of data redundancy.

     b. Provision of associative relations.

     c. Creation of data independence.

     d. Improved data integrity.

     e. Improved data security.

10. The three major categories of data base management systems are:

     a. Self-contained, with own data management language.

     b. Procedure-oriented, language-embedded systems.

     c. Self-contained and forms-controlled systems.

11. The three most commonly used data access methods are the sequential, direct, and indexed sequential access method (ISAM).

12. The processing of records by content can be facilitated by structuring data hierarchically or by networks containing chains.

13. Structuring of data can be accomplished either by external pointers or pointers embedded in records which link records into chains.

KEY CONCEPTS AND WORDS

access method: technique for moving data between memory storage and input/output devices.

area: a named subdivision of logical address space in a data base.

chain: a technique which uses linkages between items to derive a logical organization of data items from a physical organization. Same as *list*.

cylinder: the tracks of a disk storage device that can be accessed without repositioning the access mechanism.

cycle: a data structure of two or more elements forming a closed loop.

data base administrator (DBA): a person responsible for the definition, organization, control, protection, and efficiency of the data base.

data base management systems (DBMS): a software data processing system to control and process all requests for data in support of the user and the data base administrator.

data description/definition language: a language whose statements provide a formal and precise definition of data, how it is stored, and how it is related.

data manipulation language (DML): a computer language to convey information between the application program and the data base management system.

data set: a named collection of stored records and logical relationships between two or more record types.

hashing (randomizing): an address calculation technique in which the record's key is converted into a near random number to be used as the address of the record to be stored.

hierarchical data structure: a set of directed relationships between two or more items, such that some items are considered *owners* while others are *members*. An owner may have one or more members. Same as *tree structure*.

host language: a standard procedure-oriented language tied to the data base management system to perform the functions of data base management. Contrast with *self-contained* data base management systems, which use no host languages.

independence: data independence means the separation of logical and physical data so that application programs and physical location of data can each be changed independently.

index: a table to permit access to stored data. The input to the table is the key of the record sought, and the output is the address of the record.

indexed sequential access method (ISAM): an access method used to retrieve or update data on a direct-access device using an index to locate the data.

integrity: (1) protection of data against accidental invalidation or loss, (2) preservation of content and relationships between data.

key: one or more characters within an item of data used to identify with or control its use.

list: see *chain*.

logical organization: the organization of data as viewed by the data base administrator, the application programmer, and the user. Contrast with *physical organization*.

member: one of the records in a *data set*. A data set has one owner and may have one or more members.

network structure: a set of directed relationships between two or more data items, such that some data items are considered *owners* while others are *members*. Each member may have one or more owners.

owner: a record in a data set. Each data set has a single owner.

physical organization: the organization and layout of data in a storage unit. Contrast with *logical organization*.

pointer: an address or other indication of the location of data.

recovery: recovery from data loss implies a procedure which will reconstruct data if it is accidentally destroyed.

redundant: the same data stored more than once.

relatability: the ability to relate data.

schema: a complete description of all data items, record types, data set types, and areas that exist in a data base.

subschema: a logical subset of *schema* which names only those record types, data set types, and areas that are accessed by one or more specific application programs.

tree structure: see *hierarchical structure*.

DISCUSSION QUESTIONS

1. Report on your collection of newspaper, magazine, and television items and cartoons, jokes, and anecdotes.

2. Describe the difference in emphasis between the traditional process-oriented and the modern data-oriented approach. Why is data a resource? Provide illustrations.

3. Describe the five steps involved in the process-oriented approach. Provide illustrations. Describe disadvantages of the traditional approach.

4. Define and explain in your own words: *redundant, independence, relatability, data base management system*. Give examples. Compare your definitions with those in your dictionary and explain differences, if any.[2]

5. Describe the two phases of the data base management approach. What are the advantages?

6. Describe in your own words the distinction between the physical and logical views of a library.

7. Go to your library and find an atlas of the world. There will be a map of the physical world and other maps describing how humans view the world. List five of these nonphysical maps of the world. Compare this with our specifications of physical and logical views.

---

[2] In all word problems you need make comparisons only if the word or phrase is in your dictionary.

8. Describe the difference between the programmer's view and the data base administrator's view of the data base.

9. Describe the structure of a data base.

10. Define and explain in your own words: *tree structure, hierarchical data structure, schema, subschema, data item, data set, record, owner, member, area, recovery.* Give examples. Compare your definitions with those in your dictionary and explain differences, if any.

11. Describe the characteristics of a data base management system. Give illustrations.

12. Describe the types of data base management systems available. Discuss relative advantages.

13. Describe the components of data base management systems.

14. Describe the six steps involved in data transfer.

15. Describe the seven implications of data base management systems.

16. Discuss the managerial implications of data base management systems.

17. Describe the Mark IV File Management System. Why can this be considered a data base management system?

18. The text provides a study of the sequential approach to invoice preparation. Replace this entire study by the preparation of cost accounting reports for a factory. Assume that two files are maintained. One of these is in project number sequence and accumulates costs by project numbers. The other is in payroll number sequence and accumulates credits for each employee. For example, when an employee works a certain number of hours, there will be a charge made by project number to the project on which he worked, and a credit made to the individual in the personnel file by his payroll number. Assume that transactions are received by the data processing department, containing the payroll number of the individual, the project number on which he worked, and the number of hours he worked. Sort the transactions by payroll number, and then, with the aid of the payroll master file, determine the dollar amount involved in the transaction. Update the personnel file. Then sort the transactions which already contain the dollar amounts by project number and update the project file.

19. Replace the information retrieval problem described in Figure 10.17 by a problem in which sales information is required in an international firm. Assume that a master file contains all sales records. The problem is to print a sales record first for the United States, then for Canada, and finally for the rest of the foreign sales.

20. Develop a flowchart similar to the one shown in Figure 10.18 for exercise 19.

21. In the problem of merging two files described in Figure 10.19, it was assume that it is impossible to have the same individual appear in both files. Modify the flowchart to take care of the possibility of an error. Design the flowchart so that if two identical names appear, the computer will stop processing and print an error message.

22. Define and explain in your own words: *access method, data, integrity, father file, grandfather file*. Give examples. Compare your definitions with those in your dictionary and explain differences, if any.

23. Using Figure 10.20, describe how Scarlett's record is retrieved.

24. Using Figure 10.21, show how Scarlett's record is retrieved.

25. Replace Figures 10.22 and 10.23, using the phone book available to you.

26. Explain ISAM with the aid of your own phone book.

27. Define and explain in your own words: *index, key, synonym, hashing*. Give examples. Compare your definitions with those in your dictionary and explain differences, if any.

28. Explain how direct-access methods and hashing or randomizing work. Using the system described in the chapter, determine the address of a record with the social security number 185–22–4188.

29. Describe in your own words what network structures and access methods are. Describe the advantages of such structures.

30. Define and explain in your own words: *pointer, chain, list, ring, cycle, head and tail*. Give examples. Compare your definitions with those in your dictionary and explain differences, if any.

31. Review and update your Personal Summary of this course (see exercise 28, Chapter 1).

11

The selection, design, and use of computer systems

Certain steps are required in selecting and designing a computer system to make it of maximum benefit to the user. The decision to obtain or change a computer system is a major one because large sums of money are involved, and the use of a computer system influences the entire management of the organization. Consequently, studies leading to computer decisions are usually conducted by a team of personnel from various organizational units and levels. The final decision is made by high-level management, since economic, operational, and other organizational benefits must be evaluated.

While the team conducting the feasibility study must have a high degree of expertise in computers and data processing, such knowledge in itself is not adequate; expertise in other areas of the business such as finance, production, and marketing, is also required. This chapter differs from the others because it discusses topics other than those directly related to computers and data processing. The main concern is to summarize principles and practices relating to computers and data processing which are required of a team conducting such a study. First we develop a general principle relating to the conduct of these studies, and then we show, through a hypothetical case study, how the problem of selecting, designing, acquiring, and using computer systems can be accomplished.

A PRINCIPLE OF COMPUTER SYSTEM DEVELOPMENT

Problems involved in new-product development and computer system development are similar. Both must be solved by the application of sound management theory and practice.

To illustrate this principle, Figure 11.1 draws a parallel between the steps required for new-product development and computer system development. The left side shows the eight steps involved in new-product development; the right side, the steps in computer system development.

FIGURE 11.1 New-product development compared with computer system development.

New-product development	*Computer systems development*
1. Identification of market requirements.	1. Establishment of user requirements.
2. Financial and engineering analysis is performed to determine whether a profit can be made and whether the product can be manufactured.	2. Systems analysis is performed to determine whether system is economically advantageous and technically possible.
3. Engineering and manufacturing design is done.	3. System design is completed, and system flowcharts are prepared.
4. Tools, jigs, and dies are designed.	4. Program flowcharts are prepared.
5. Tools are built.	5. Programs and documentation are prepared.
6. Pilot operation is carried out.	6. Programs and documentation are tested on a computer.
7. Goods are produced.	7. Information is produced.
8. Production technique improvements are made.	8. System improvements are made.

The best way to learn about computer system development and the application of this principle is by considering a simplified, realistic case study. In this chapter we describe the process of selection, design, and use of computer systems at the Marshall Corporation when the chairman of the board, president, and majority stockholder, Sydney E. Marshall, decides to convert the manual data processing installation into a modern computerized system.

THE MARSHALL CORPORATION: A CASE STUDY

The Marshall Corporation, a small manufacturer and distributor of lawnmowers, small gas engines, garden tractors, and associated

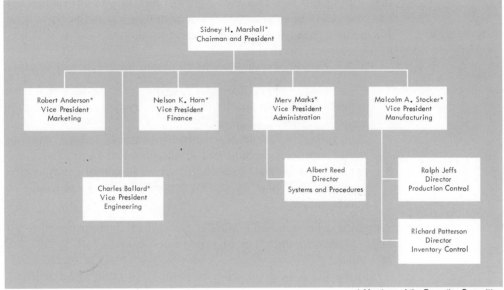

* Members of the Executive Committee.

FIGURE 11.2
Organization chart
of the Marshall
Corporation.

equipment, has been in business for 15 years, during which period it has undergone a steady growth. All manufacturing facilities are in Rochester, New York, but salespeople, who travel throughout the United States, sell to wholesalers. Figure 11.2 shows the relevant part of the organization chart, including all members of the Executive Committee.

To provide background and insight to the narrative, the principal executives of the corporation and their outlook toward computer systems are described below.

Sidney H. Marshall, chairman of the board and president

Sidney Marshall has just returned from a data processing conference held for presidents of small and medium-sized corporations. He is convinced that his manual data processing practices are obsolete and that there is great opportunity in introducing a computer system to his company. He is also aware of the various pitfalls for corporations installing computer systems, but he believes that with the aid of careful planning he will be able to avoid them. He is determined to introduce computers, not for the sake of having one, but for the economic benefits and competitive advantages he believes can be obtained.

As entrepreneur Marshall realizes that any new undertaking and investment involves risk he aims to take all necessary steps to minimize the risks involved in installing a computer system. He considers that his corporation is making a fair profit but is concerned that during the last two years growth has slowed to a standstill, and he would like to reinstate his company as a growth corporation. He believes that installing a modern computer system will help in this respect.

To summarize, Marshall wants to obtain three types of benefits:

1. *Cost displacement*—decrease operating cost through reduction in personnel and in space utilization; increase production equipment utilization, and so on.
2. *Operational efficiencies*—reduce inventory, reduce ordering cycle, improve scheduling of production, and so on.
3. *Intangible benefits*—benefits for which it is hard or impossible to provide a dollar figure, such as improved morale and corporate image.

Uppermost in Marshall's mind is growth. He is determined to put his company in the class of growth companies, both in fact and reputation.

During the data processing conference in which Marshall participated, it became apparent to him that to install a successful computer system four conditions must be satisfied. There must be:

1. Top-management participation and support.
2. Careful planning and control.
3. Competent technical performance.
4. Careful consideration of the human element.

Marshall is determined to meet the first condition by personal participation and insistence that his top executives do likewise. He will meet the second, the planning and control condition, by frequent reviews through his Executive Committee and heavy reliance on Nelson Horn, vice president, finance, and Merv Marks, vice president, administration. He is not overly concerned about the third item, the technical considerations, as he trusts Marks and Albert Reed, director of systems and procedures. On the other hand, he is much concerned about the fourth item, consideration of the human element. He realizes that the installation of a computer causes many personality problems, organizational changes, and other difficult stresses in the working environment. He realizes that people have a strong resistance to change and that the introduction of a new computer inevitably causes disruption in the organization.

Nelson K. Horn, vice president, finance

Nelson Horn believes in computer systems and is an excellent planner. He thinks in dollars and cents and knows about many computer system installations that have been essentially failures. He is suspicious of all cost estimates and believes that most of the time costs are underestimated and savings overstated. He believes that tight management control is a must in connection with computer systems.

Horn is particularly suspicious of intangible benefits, which cannot be translated into dollars and cents. Statements that the computer can provide better information to enable managers to make better decisions or can free managers from routine tasks so that they can work on complex problems make no impression on Horn. He wants to see standards of performance against which he can measure actual performance and take corrective action when necessary.

However, his rigorous attitude does not mean that he does not believe in computer systems. In addition, he is a good friend of Merv Marks and so would support the computer effort with all his capabilities and resources.

Merv Marks, vice president, administration

Systems and procedures are supervised by Merv Marks. He has been with the corporation for only three years, but he had a great deal of experience with computers in his previous job. He would like very much to replace his obsolete manual operations with a modern computer system. However, he knows that top-management support is a must, and he did not push Sidney Marshall until Marshall himself saw computers as an opportunity for the corporation. He knows that in the long run he will get the credit or blame for the success or failure of the computer system.

Now that Marshall is convinced and enthused, Marks wants to go ahead at full speed. In fact, he has anticipated that eventually the Marshall Corporation will have to convert to the computer system and has taken preliminary steps to prepare his organization for the transition. Marks's most important move in getting ready was to hire Albert Reed to head systems and procedures.

Albert Reed, director of systems and procedures

Albert Reed is a young computer professional who had an important managerial job before coming to Marshall. The only reason he accepted being director of systems and procedures was that he saw the handwriting on the wall; Marshall eventually would have to convert to computers. Reed believes that heading up systems and procedures will establish him as a respected member of the management team of the corporation, and with his knowledge of computers

FIGURE 11.3 List of activities required to carry out a successful computer system development and acquisition effort.

Feasibility study	Objectives of feasibility study
	Costs vs. benefits
	EDP or not EDP?
	Plan effort for EDP
System study	System objectives
	System description
	Input/output and processing requirements
	Preliminary system specification
System justification	Evaluation of vendor proposals
	Vendor and computer selection
	Financial conclusions
	Management justification
	Executive authorization to order equipment
System design	Consider alternate solutions
	Evaluate alternatives
	Choose best solution
	Establish final system specifications
	Prepare system flowcharts
System implementation and operation	Implementation plan
	Organize and educate computer staff
	Write application programs
	Install computer
	Test programs
	Convert to computerized operation
	Systems shakedown and regular operation
Maintenance and modification	Establish benefits and performance
	Improve all operations
	Plan future applications and growth

he is the natural person to lead Marshall to the new world of computers. Reed is right!

When Reed hears that Marshall is proceeding with a computer study, he pulls out his old files from his previous employment and reviews the steps required to install a computer. He prepares a list of activities (Figure 11.3) required to carry out a successful computer system development and acquisition effort.

Malcolm A. Stocker, vice president, manufacturing

Malcolm Stocker is the person who keeps the factory humming. He is an old-line, hard-headed production executive who hates paper work and does not believe in any newfangled stuff like computers or the systems approach. He says he has enough trouble without trying to change things, and that there is no substitute for hard work.

But Stocker has great difficulty in keeping up with the growth of the Marshall Corporation. His production records are inadequate, and he often misses prescribed schedules. He also has troubles with purchasing. Often raw materials and purchased parts are missing, resulting in expensive production stoppages.

Stocker also has trouble with Horn, vice president, finance, who thinks that the inventory of raw materials, purchased parts, and in-process inventory is too high but cannot prove his point. Horn is convinced that a computerized system could help if only Stocker would let the computer help him.

Stocker's main concern is to keep his people busy and the factory running smoothly. He is bothered by the fact that Marshall's business is seasonal items (such as lawnmowers), and so he cannot keep a steady work force. He must train and retrain his factory hands and has a high turnover of labor. He finds it difficult to reconcile the production manager's desire for steady employment with the Marshall Corporation's high seasonal business. He feels that Robert Anderson, vice president, marketing, is doing a very poor job of forecasting needs. If only Anderson could tell him in advance what he needed, expensive rush ordering and expediting could be eliminated, and the factory could be run in a smooth manner.

Stocker does not believe in the computer system at all. He will do everything in his power to discredit and stall the effort to introduce the computer.

Robert Anderson, vice president, marketing

Anderson's concern is to keep the customer happy. He fights Stocker because the schedules for his rush orders are not met. He feels that the 90-day cycle for delivery is much too slow. If only the cycle could be dramatically cut he thinks he could sweep the market.

He is also dissatisfied with manual data processing operations. The catalogs are never kept up to date. Records for the salespeople are inaccurate, and he feels that salespeople are spending too much time on paper work instead of the "creative" work of selling. He is much in favor of using computers to at least lessen the need for pencil pushing and paper shuffling.

THE FEASIBILITY STUDY

Soon after his return from the data processing conference, Marshall tells the Executive Committee that he wants to look into the possibility of acquiring a computer system. He outlines the benefits he expects to get from the computer and the way he thinks the effort should be organized. Specifically, he assigns the job to Merv Marks and asks him to conduct a feasibility study to determine whether a computer should be used, and if so what resources will be required to carry out the effort. He also asks Marks to set up a study team with a chairman.

In the next meeting of the Executive Committee Marks presents his plan to carry out the feasibility study. He proposes that Reed be designated as the chairman of the study and asks for participation from each of the functional units. He also proposes to retain Gary Reeves, a data processing consultant, for general advice and guidance.

The Executive Committee agrees on the membership of the committee and assigns the chairmanship to Albert Reed.

First meeting of the study team

At the first meeting of the team Reed outlines his views on how to start the feasibility study. Before the new computer system can be designed, the study team must establish the information requirements of the Marshall Corporation. Thus the team must understand what the manual system does, and it must interview personnel to find out what information is needed. In particular, the team must specify the input/output requirements and what processing must be done.

Reed suggests that promising application areas will have the following characteristics:

1. High volume of transaction.
2. Repetitive type of transaction.
3. Need for greater speed.
4. Need for greater accuracy.
5. Complex processing task.
6. Demand for quick turn-around time.

Reed emphasizes that it is not enough just to convert manual data processing operations. It is also necessary to know what is needed. Reed presents a list of typical areas of applications (see Chapter 3, Figure 3.1) and proposes that company personnel be interviewed to gather data, uncover facts, and develop requirements.

Cost estimates   / tangible & intangible

After completion of the interviews, the study team settles down to earnest work. An overall system description is prepared for each

---

[1] Terms printed in color are defined at the end of the chapter.

computer application, including input/output requirements, types of processing to be performed, and so on. Now the team faces up to the problem of how to translate these systems descriptions and requirements into costs when using a computer system.

It is, of course, impossible to determine precisely what the cost of processing will be. However, there is a great deal of experience in professional computer circles to make possible reasonable estimates of the cost of processing. This is where advantage can be taken of the experience of the consultant, Gary Reeves. Reeves has a wide variety of rules-of-thumb for estimating costs. He recommends considering such factors as:

1. Input/output requirements.
2. Processing and storage requirements.
3. Computer rental.
4. Salaries of programmers and operators.
5. Cost of supplies.
6. Floor space and building requirements, including air conditioning.
7. Experience level of computer staff.

After all these cost estimates are made and added, the total estimated operating cost of the computer system is projected.

The next step in the analysis is to establish the cost of the current manual data processing system. The difference between the projected and current costs gives the cost displacement (saving) generated by the computer system.

However, it is not enough to consider operating costs, that is, recurring costs only, as there are certain types of nonrecurring costs associated with installing the new computing system. These costs include training and education of the computer staff, preparation of the programs, conversion of data, preparation of the facility, simultaneous or parallel operation of the manual and computer systems.

Once the nonrecurring costs and the cost displacement are established, the question arises as to whether it is worthwhile for the Marshall Corporation to lay out this initial expense (investment) to pay for the yearly operating cost displacement. The problem is complicated by the fact that all estimates are subject to uncertainty.

Converting benefits to dollars is further complicated by the difficulty of evaluating the importance of reduction in inventory and in the order cycle. The study team decides that at the presentation to the Executive Committee, the prediction of a 20 percent cut in inventory and the reduction of the order cycle from 90 to 60 days will be presented as separate items.

Intangibles

The study team also decides to present a narrative description of such intangible benefits as:

1. New reports and information.
2. More timely reports.
3. How the new reports will support management decisions.
4. Advantages of creating a more progressive and better corporate image.

Executive briefing

At the study team's initial briefing for the Executive Committee, first Reed and then other members of the team present their general findings. The list of applications reviewed (Figure 11.4) is presented, and comments on each of the applications are made. Then Reed proceeds to present his findings with regard to costs. In particular, he claims that in two years the operating cost displacement saving will make up for the nonrecurring costs. But Horn, vice president, finance, is skeptical of these figures. He claims that nonrecurring costs have been underestimated, and the cost displacements have been overestimated. He ventures that the company will be lucky if it gets its money back in four years.

Sidney Marshall begins to question whether this is the right way to make the financial analysis. Shouldn't they use return on investment? In fact, are there not better opportunities for the corporation to use this money? At this point a detailed discussion takes place

FIGURE 11.4
Applications
reviewed. by study
team.

Accounting	Payroll checks and reports
	Customer billing
	Accounts receivable and payable
	General accounting
	Cost accounting
Sales	Sales forecasting
	Sales analysis
	Expediting
Inventory control	Inventory status reporting
	Order control system
	Purchase order writing
Production control	Bills of material
	Factory labor and machine loading
	Dispatching
	Work-in-process control

between Marshall and Horn, while the study team idles. Then Marshall tells Horn to look into the matter personally and give him a private report.

In the meantime Stocker, vice president, manufacturing, has the time to think things over, and when the presentation of the study team continues, he begins to raise all sorts of objections. Then Marshall again gets into the act. What about the growth potential of the system? Suppose the corporation doubles its size in five years? What would happen then?

Marshall recalls that he has a luncheon date and asks for a second briefing at the next meeting of the Executive Committee. The meeting ends abruptly.

Second executive briefing

By the second executive briefing Reed has reworked his figures and has discussed the matter in detail with Horn. They have agreed that cost displacement will make up for nonrecurring costs in three years. Horn already has had his private discussion with Marshall about return on investment, so Marshall makes no particular objections.

The study team reports that the proposed system can indeed very well accommodate a significant growth in the corporation's business. They present figures to show that if the corporation doubles its sales, then only a 20 percent additional cost in nonrecurring expenses will occur, and recurring operational costs will increase by only 35 percent. Marshall is much interested in these figures and presses hard to test their validity. Finally, he is convinced about the growth potential and agrees to proceed with the effort.

Milestones	Months to complete from start date
Executive decisions to authorize effort	0
Release preliminary systems specifications to vendors	6
Receive vendor bids	8
Order equipment	9
Complete flowcharts	10
Complete application programs	15
Receive equipment	15
Test and debug programs	18
Phase out old equipment and convert to new	18

FIGURE 11.5 Schedule of times required to complete major milestones. All times measured in months from authorization date.

As the last item in the discussion, Reed presents his proposed schedule of time required to complete major milestones (Figure 11.5).

SYSTEM STUDY

The output of the system study will be the preliminary system specifications, which will be sent to vendors so they can propose a hardware system to do the job. Consequently, it is of great importance that the data processing job be clearly defined in the system study.

The study team agrees to the following six objectives for the system:

1.   Reduce processing costs.
2.   Improve accuracy of all records.
3.   Reduce order cycle from 90 to 60 days.
4.   Reduce out-of-stock conditions.
5.   Reduce inventory levels by at least 20 percent.
6.   Provide for growth in number of transactions.

To provide a system description, it is decided that four subsystems must be considered: (1) accounting, (2) sales forecast, (3) order processing, and (4) production and inventory control.

In Figure 11.6, which shows the top-level (overall) system flowchart for the system, the lower part of the diagram depicts the material flow through the corporation. As shown in the box on the extreme right, raw materials and finished parts move from the suppliers to the factory and warehouse of the Marshall Corporation. Then (left) the finished products move to the wholesalers.

The study team also prepares a more detailed system flowchart for each of the subsystems. The system flowchart for order processing is shown in Figure 11.7. Descriptions of each of the records and files, including input/output layouts, are also prepared. Among others, the following data volumes are specified:

1.   Number of orders received per day.
2.   Average number of items per order.
3.   Number of salespeople and sales territories.
4.   Number of finished goods and items carried in stock.

Finally, the study team makes run-time estimates for each of the jobs to be performed. Both sequential and direct (random) access, are considered. However, the study team soon is convinced that order processing will have to be done through a remote direct-access system to meet the requirement for shortening the order cycle.

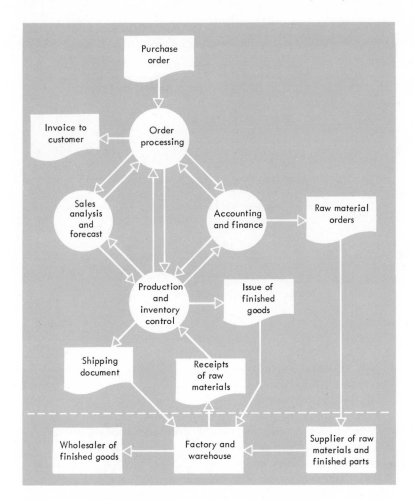

FIGURE 11.6 Top-
level system chart.
The information
flow is above the
broken line, the
material flow is
below.

On the other hand, it is found that accounting can be done sequentially in batches.

Executive briefing

After the team completes its study, Reed makes a brief presentation to the executive committee, and invitations for bids on the computer system are sent out to the vendors.

SYSTEM JUSTIFICATION

After proposals are received from vendors A, B, and C, the study team proceeds to the evaluation of the bids. For each proposal the following eight criteria for selection are considered:

FIGURE 11.7
Order-processing
subsystem.

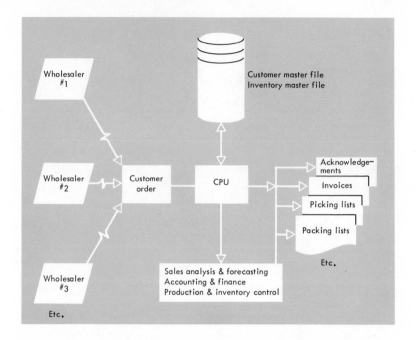

1. Nonrecurring and recurring costs.
2. Availability and quality of software.
3. Hardware performance.
4. Vendor support to Marshall Corporation.
5. Compatibility among the various computer models offered.
6. Capability of system growth.
7. Delivery reliability.
8. Availability of application programs.

After the study team evaluates each of the vendors for each of the selection criteria (Figure 11.8), the real dilemma arises. Vendor A is best (lowest) on nonrecurring costs, but worst (highest) on recurring (operating) costs. Vendor A is best on availability and quality of software, but worst on hardware performance. None of the vendors is superior on all of the selection criteria. How can the study team decide?

After much discussion, the vendors are ranked, and it is decided that vendor B is best, vendor A is in the middle, and vendor C is the worst.

Is there a more reliable technique of evaluation? Reeves, the consultant, recommends the use of a point system. For each of the selection criteria a maximum number of points is allotted. For example (Figure 11.8), availability and quality of software is worth 30 points to the best vendor, that is, to vendor A. Hardware per-

Selection criteria		Vendors						Maximum points
		A		B		C		
1. Nonrecurring costs		$ xxx best		$ xxx middle		$ xxx worst		
			5		4		3	5
Recurring costs		$ xxx worst		$ xxx middle		$ xxx best		
			3		4		5	5
2. Availability and quality of software		best	30	middle	25	worst	10	30
3. Hardware performance		worst	5	middle	15	best	20	20
4. Vendor support		worst	5	best	15	middle	10	15
5. Compatibility of computer models		middle	9	worst	5	best	10	10
6. Capability of system growth		best	5	middle	4	worst	3	5
7. Delivery reliability		best	5	worst	1	middle	3	5
8. Availability of application programs		tie	1	tie	1	tie	1	5
Overall ranking		middle		best		worst		
			68		74		65	100

FIGURE 11.8
Rating of vendors.

formance is worth the maximum of 20 points to vendor C. Thus each vendor is evaluated on each of the selection criteria, and finally the points are added together.

After much discussion and several revisions of the point system, the study team still finds vendor B best, A second, and C third.

Executive briefing

Recommendation that the equipment be ordered from Vendor B is favorably received by the Executive Committee without too much discussion or probing.

SYSTEM DESIGN

Once the study team knows which computer system will be used, the design of the system can be undertaken. Requirements for input, output, and storage are established (Figure 11.9), and a number of alternate system solutions are assumed. After various comparisons, the most promising approach is selected.

Transaction	Characters per transaction	Number of transactions per month	Total characters	Growth factor	Input capacity required
Sales order	X	X	X	X	X
Time card	X	X	X	X	X
Requisition	X	X	X	X	X
Job completion	X	X	X	X	X
Move ticket	X	X	X	X	X
Total	X	X	X	X	X

Output document	Number of forms/month	Lines per form	Lines of print	Growth factor	Output capacity required
Customer invoice	X	X	X	X	X
Sales analysis	X	X	X	X	X
Inventory status	X	X	X	X	X
Payroll register	X	X	X	X	X
Paychecks	X	X	X	X	X
Purchase orders	X	X	X	X	X
Total	X	X	X	X	X

File	Characters per item	Number of items	Total characters	Growth factor	Storage capacity required
Customer	X	X	X	X	X
Sales history	X	X	X	X	X
Product master	X	X	X	X	X
Work in process	X	X	X	X	X
Vendor	X	X	X	X	X
Personnel	X	X	X	X	X
Total	X	X	X	X	X

FIGURE 11.9
Input, output, and storage requirements. To avoid listing nonrepresentative data, all actual figures are replaced by an X sign.

Then final system specifications are established and system flowcharts are developed. During the flowcharting phase of the effort, the application programmers take a very active part in the work, and the final system flowcharts are accepted only after agreement with the programmers is reached.

Executive briefing

The presentation of the system design to the Executive Committee takes very little time, and no objections are raised. In reality, members of the committee do not have adequate technical education

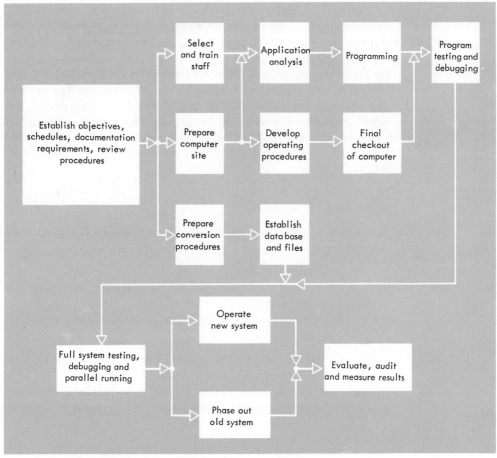

FIGURE 11.10
Implementation
plan

to follow the details of the design. Neither do they have much interest in the subject of design. The committee does show some interest in the implementation and operations plan presented by Reed (**Figure 11.10.**)

SYSTEM IMPLEMENTATION AND OPERATION

After the successful briefing of the Executive Committee, Reed suddenly realizes that he is fully in charge and responsible for introducing the computer to the Marshall Corporation. All the preliminary work—the planning, evaluation—is complete, and now action must follow. Reed realizes that the phase of *decision* is over, and now *doing* is necessary. He ponders the things that must be done (Figure 11.10).

During the entire effort, Reed has somewhat neglected the management of systems and procedures. Now he is back again as a manager but on a much bigger scale. He must reorient his thinking, begin to delegate technical matters to his staff, and concentrate on the tasks of management. When he discusses his new problem with Marks, Marks suggests that the time has come for Reed to broaden and reassess his knowledge of management. So they decide that Reed should take a week off and attend an executive seminar on problems of managing computer installations. Some of the things that Reed learns about the theory of management are discussed below.

Management functions

Figure 11.11 diagrams the three main managerial functions. Bear in mind that:

1. **Planning** means to decide what to do.
2. **Organizing** and **staffing** means to group people and teams into units to carry out plans.
3. **Controlling** means to assure that tasks are performed efficiently and standards are met.

Information processing in the company must support each of the management functions.

Reed knows that he must apply management theory to the operation of the data processing organization, but he must also under-

FIGURE 11.11
How management functions are supported by information processing.

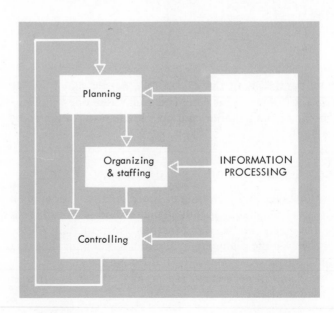

stand how management functions are carried out in the Marshall Corporation so he can support management with the computer system.

With respect to the first function, planning the data processing operations, Reed feels quite confident. A tremendous effort has been devoted to prepare the plan. With respect to organization and staffing of the data processing group, he is confronted with several problems. He must phase out the manual installation and introduce the computer. He needs to retrain the staff of the operation so they can perform the tasks necessary to run the computer system. He sees no difficulty in training the computer operators, but with respect to programming he does have a problem. The decision was made that problem originators (users) will not do their own programming, that is, all programming will be done in the data processing department. As the computer professionals say, Reed will run a closed shop, not an open shop. Thus he needs more programmers.

Controlling data processing operations

Reed's first problem is phasing in the new computer and phasing out the manual operation. The greatest problem, of course, is the problem of preparation of the computer programs. Figure 11.12 shows some of the events that must be taken care of for each application.

Reed realizes that one aspect of program preparation will be particularly difficult; he is thinking of the problem of documentation.

Program narrative
Top level flowchart
Input/output layouts
File design
Control techniques
Volume and timing estimates
Detailed flowcharts
Programming
Keypunching
Compilation
Debugging
Preparation of sample test data
Machine testing
Documentation
Preparation of production data
Production checkout
Establishment of maintenance procedures

FIGURE 11.12
Activities to be completed for each application program.

Programmers dislike preparing documentation. Preparing programs is challenging, but there is great resistance to documentation. How can Reed overcome this resistance? How can he motivate the programmers to do documentation? He must prove to his programmers that:

1. To create adequate documentation is not only useful but a must.
2. The programmers who do a good job on documentation will be recognized for their achievement.
3. Documentation can be just as interesting and meaningful as programming.
4. A sure way for programmers to advance in the organization is to create top-notch documentation.

To prove to the staff that he really means what he says, Reed decides to emphasize documentation in the staff meetings and to personally evaluate and control performance.

With respect to site preparation, Reed feels quite relaxed. Facilities management of the company has been very competent and cooperative. Reed reviews the layout drawings of the site, the floor loading proposed, the location and type of power source, the air-conditioning installation, and so on. He also reviews the installation schedules and feels that facilities management will come through with the necessary action.

Reed also feels that the plan for parallel operation and conversion is sound. True, it will be a tremendous job to convert the records and files, and an extraordinary load will be placed on the keypunch operators. (In fact, there may be a need to contract out some of the keypunching.) However, the problem which gives the greatest concern to Reed is the conversion steps the users must take.

User conversion and resistance to change

Reed realizes that the real problem in regard to user conversion is that he has no control at all over users. In fact, not even his boss, Marks, vice president, administration, has control. If a real difficulty arises with the users, an appeal would have to be made to Marshall, and that might turn out to be very difficult. Let us review how Reed feels about the four subsystems shown in Figure 11.6: order processing, accounting and finance, production inventory and control, and sales analysis and forecast.

The order processing system, which worried him at the beginning a great deal, is coming along fine. The terminals are arriving on schedule, and personnel in the sales offices are picking up the operational procedures quite easily. The key is that Anderson, vice president, marketing, is completely behind the project.

The subsystem on accounting and finance is in the best shape of all. The computer system will replace the manual data processing system, and in this subsystem the people are used to the rigors required for computerized processing. Also Horn, vice president, Finance, and Marks get along very well, and Horn provides complete support.

The sales analysis and forecasting subsystem is not too complex and presents no significant problem.

However, the situation with production and inventory control is completely different. Stocker was never in favor of the computer and has been showing great resistance to change. His key employee, Ralph Jeffs, director of production control, strictly follows the example set by Stocker and does not cooperate. There is, however, one bright spot in this subsystem. Richard Patterson, director of inventory control, is much impressed by the capability of the computer and the work it has done so far. He supports the project and does whatever he can within his own sphere of influence.

Parallel operation

Finally the day has come; the computer arrives! Program testing and debugging are followed by parallel operation. But everything conceivable goes wrong, in accordance with certain unwritten rules (Figure 11.13).

As the dust begins to settle, however, the hidden bugs are found and corrected, and slowly things begin to improve. The accounting and finance subsystem is operational on schedule. The sales analysis and forecasting and the order processing subsystems are delayed, but not too much. However, as Reed and Marks have feared for some time, serious difficulties develop with respect to the produc-

---

1. Anything that can go wrong will go wrong.
2. Things always go from bad to worse.
3. If several things can go wrong, the one that goes wrong is the one that causes disaster.
4. Mother Nature:
   a. Hates computers.
   b. Sides with the bug.
   c. Always adds one more bug.
5. If by some miracle everything is going well:
   a. The specifications are changed.
   b. The test data is nothing like the real data.
   c. The project is cancelled.
   d. You didn't "really" understand the requirements.

FIGURE 11.13 The five unwritten rules of data processing.

tion and inventory control system. It is now that the degree of resistance, bordering on sabotage, becomes apparent.

Some employees have withheld information and turned in data late. Other employees have knowingly provided inaccurate data. As a result, even employees sympathetic to the computerized system have begun to doubt the validity of the reports. Stocker has taken advantage of the situation and has spread rumors that the computer installation, so far as manufacturing is concerned, is a complete failure and in fact is undermining the morale and productivity of the division.

After several lengthy discussions between Reed and his boss, Marks, it is decided that it would be poor politics to appeal to Marshall for support. What could Marshall do? The corporation is going through a phase of high production, and it is the wrong time to have Mr. Marshall overrule Stocker. Marks decides to postpone implementation of the new production and inventory control system and to continue parallel operation with the manual system until the computer can at least replace the reports produced by the manual installation.

Marks knows that the time will soon come when the seasonal demand for production will slacken, and this will be a more opportune time to deal with Stocker. However, Marks asks Reed to call a series of meetings with employees of manufacturing to provide them with more information about the computerized system and have them participate more intensely in the effort. Marks feels that this is the best strategy to follow.

Then an unexpected event completely changes the situation. Stocker gets an excellent offer from the MLS Corporation to be executive vice president and decides to leave the Marshall Corporation. Now the question comes up as to who gets Stocker's job. It is Mr. Marshall's policy to promote from within whenever possible. The two serious candidates are Jeffs, director of production control, and Patterson, director of inventory control. Marks, of course, knows that Patterson is much in favor of the computerized system, but Jeffs is opposed. So for Marks the issue is how to convince Marshall to promote Patterson to Stocker's job.

At the next Executive Committee meeting the problem of replacing Stocker comes up. Marks states his preference for Patterson and details his reasons. Anderson and Horn are both in favor of the computerized approach; so, after relatively little discussion, Marshall agrees to promote Patterson.

After Patterson's promotion to vice president, manufacturing, there is a dramatic improvement in the production and inventory control subsystem. Improvements are due to a considerable extent to the efforts and changed attitude of Jeffs, who now also becomes a computer enthusiast.

Executive briefing

Presentation to the Executive Committee on the progress of system implementation and operation is uneventful. It is recognized that implementation and operations are behind schedule and that some problems still must be solved. However, the committee feels that progress is satisfactory.

SYSTEM MAINTENANCE AND MODIFICATION

A computer system needs continuous attention, maintenance, and modification; there is always room for improvement. Troubles in many areas may occur. The list presented in Figure 11.14 pinpoints some of the most important performance areas to watch.

Are computer reports useful, on time, and reliable?
Is the computer system reliable, well utilized, properly controlled?
Does documentation meet standards?
Are data processing procedures efficient?
Are budgets being observed?
Is the programming shop well run?
Is the computer center well run?
Are new applications developed on schedule?

FIGURE 11.14
Data processing performance checklist.

During the maintenance and modification phase, or more correctly, during the entire operation of a computer system, periodic briefings must be made to management. These usually do at least the following:

1. Compare performance with stated objectives.
2. Compare operating costs with projected standards.
3. Present suggestions for improvements and extensions.

Executive briefing

At a management briefing after six months of computer systems operation, it is reported that:

1. Only 20 percent of the projected cost reduction in data processing has been realized.

2. The order cycle has been reduced from 90 to 70 days, but not to 60 days as predicted.
3. Out-of-stock conditions have been reduced by 70 percent.
4. Inventory levels have been reduced by 20 percent as predicted.

In addition to these specific comparisons between performance objectives and accomplishment, other matters, such as improvement in the accuracy and timeliness of reports, are discussed. Reed also presents some of the problem areas with which data processing is faced. These include shortages of skilled personnel, equipment downtime, and bugs in software provided by the manufacturer.

After covering all these matters, a general discussion on the scope of the applications handled by the computer system follows. Anderson proposes that new marketing applications be placed on the computer. Charles Ballard, vice president, engineering, complains that his operations have not been significantly aided by the computer and proposes that a feasibility study be made as to how engineering could use it.

At this point Marks takes a cautious position and explains that in practically every case the effort required to create a new application is larger than anticipated. Horn also suggests caution and proposes that instead of taking up new applications, at least in the near future, data processing should continue to eliminate problem areas and to improve efficiency. Marshall asks questions about the capability of the system to take care of growth. In particular, he wants to know whether going after new applications would impair the growth potential of the system.

There is general agreement that if growth potential is the dominant requirement for the system, it is better to forego expanding the scope of data processing and concentrate on improving efficiency.

POSTSCRIPT

One year after installation of the computer system, most of the operational difficulties have been eliminated and the Marshall Corporation is considered to be a leader in their industry in the efficient use of computers. In an Executive Committee meeting, Marshall reveals that he has decided to merge with Hammond and Carlson, a corporation manufacturing and distributing marine engines and motors. Marshall also states that the successful and advantageous merger deal was influenced by the fact that the major stockholders were greatly impressed by the Marshall Corporation's leadership in the modern use of computer systems. They were particularly impressed by the fact that the information system was designed for a changing environment and therefore could easily be adapted to the new, merged situation.

SUMMARY

1. The principles of new-product development and computer system development are similar.
2. Executives of a corporation expect various and possibly conflicting benefits from the installation of a computer system.
3. Some of the most important problems in introducing a computer system relate, not to the technical aspects of the computer, but to management, organization and people.
4. Acquisition of a computer system comprises six activities shown in Figure 11.3.
5. The feasibility study establishes whether the computer can help to resolve problems and take advantage of opportunities.
6. The system study results in system description and preliminary system specifications.
7. System justification results in equipment ordering.
8. System design establishes final system specifications and system flowcharts.
9. System implementation includes programming, documentation and initial computer operation.
10. Maintenance and modification are unending efforts associated with any data processing operation.
11. The principal functions of management are: planning, organizing, staffing, and controlling.

KEY CONCEPTS AND WORDS

closed shop: operation of a programming group in which problem originators do not do their own programming.

compatibility: the characteristics of computers by which the output from one computer may be used as input to another without conversion or modification.

controlling: to assure that tasks are performed efficiently and plans and standards are met.

feasibility study: study conducted to determine whether a computer should be used and, if so, what resources should be used.

maintenance: any activity aimed to keep a system in satisfactory working condition.

nonrecurring costs: costs that are incurred only once.

open shop: operation of a programming group in which problem originators are permitted to do their own programming.

organizing: to group people and teams into units to carry out plans.

parallel operation: introducing a new system as the old system is being phased out.

planning: to decide what to do.

recurring costs: costs that are incurred periodically.

staffing: to make people available for organizations.

DISCUSSION QUESTIONS

1. Report on your collection of newspaper, magazine, and television items, and cartoons, jokes, and anecdotes.

2. Define and explain in your own words: *market requirements, financial and engineering analysis, tools, jigs and disks, pilot operation, production techniques.* Give examples. Compare your definitions with those in your dictionary and explain differences, if any.[2]

3. Describe in your own words the principle of computer system development used in the text. Discuss the points shown in Figure 11.1 and provide illustrations.

4. Describe the Marshall Corporation, including the organization chart and the principal executives. What did the executives expect from the computer? What were they afraid of?

5. List conditions necessary for successful computer acquisition.

6. Compare tangible and intangible benefits of information systems. Illustrate both.

7. Review the computer acquisition effort (Figure 11.3) and explain and illustrate why and how each of the six phases is carried out. Discuss possible traps and pitfalls.

8. Discuss the feasibility study.

9. Review the applications listed in Figure 11.4 and explain and illustrate each.

10. List and discuss characteristics of jobs that can be done well (*a*) by computer processing, (*b*) by manual processing.

11. How would you interview company personnel during the feasibility study? What questions would you ask, of whom?

12. List the various costs of introducing a computer system which must be estimated. Explain recurring and nonrecurring costs.

13. To make a financial analysis it is not enough to consider costs alone. Explain and illustrate.

14. Review and explain the milestones chart (Figure 11.5).

15. Describe the system study, including objectives, system and subsystem charts.

16. Describe system justification, including vendor evaluation (Figure 11.8).

---

[2] In all word problems you need make comparisons only if the word or phrase is in your dictionary.

17. Describe system design and review. Explain and illustrate.

18. Discuss system implementation and operation. How does this phase differ from the others? Explain Figure 11.10.

19. Describe the steps in programming and application.

20. What is management? What are the three principal functions of management? Illustrate.

21. What is meant by planning the computer acquisition process? What are the problems involved?

22. What are the problems related to organizing and staffing a data processing group? What is meant by open and closed shops?

23. What are the problems related to controlling data processing operations?

24. What steps must be taken to assure that users will indeed accept and use computer outputs? Describe resistance to the computer. How do you overcome these people problems?

25. What steps must be taken during the maintenance and modification phase?

26. How do you check the performance of a computer system?

27. The Cupid Personal Dating Service is losing business because clients do not consider their manual data processing service to be modern. Assume that you are retained as a consultant to design a computer-based information system to support the dating service. Find out how computerized dating services operate in your city, and propose an information system for your client. Develop a flowchart to show how a computer can recognize the compatibility and chemistry so important to a personal relationship. Compare a manual with a computer-based system and indicate benefits. Include your personal opinion of the usefulness of computers in support of a dating service.

28. Review and update your Personal Summary of this course (see Exercise 28, Chapter 1).

Epilog: Your stake in the future

Your purpose in seeking higher education is to stimulate and guide your self-development. While you study today, you are concerned with the future, and the future is a moving target. You are also concerned with the living world about you, not with dead knowledge. There is no practical field which is faster changing or more alive than the field of computer systems technology and applications.

We began this course by considering the social implications of computer use, stressing the always-present human element, the challenge to mankind, and our faith in a positive future. The computer field cannot be conceived independently of people; society and people are central to the subject. At the end of the first chapter we stated that we are dealing with a craft and described the joys of that craft.

Joy is an emotion that comes with the fulfillment of our potential. Fulfillment brings us the feeling that we can cope with the environment, a sense of confidence in ourselves as significant, competent, likable persons, fully capable and free to express our feelings; in short, a feeling of maturity. Joy results from self-contentment, successful relations to society, and excellence in accomplishments.

Competence will take you a long way in the field of computers. However, the greatest joy of the craft comes from excellence, and there is no practical field of knowledge which offers a higher opportunity in the pursuit of excellence than the computer field.

THE LAST DISCUSSION QUESTION

Suppose that all current technical problems of computers and communications have been solved. A computer with a trillion-byte memory can be put into a shoe box, can execute instructions in nanoseconds, and costs less than $1,000. You have a wristwatch computer that cost $10. You have a picture phone and a two-way wristwatch telephone. A one-hour call across the country costs 10 cents. For $100 you can buy a wall-size color TV unit on which you can watch motion pictures, theater presentations, sport events. You also can selectively scan a newspaper, Congressional hearings, court trials. You can take a college course on your two-way TV set and can browse through books in a library.

Using the technical knowledge you have learned in this book, assume that such progress (fantastic today, but foreseeable in the future) has been made on all technological problems of computers. But assume that human nature has been at a standstill, and you are dealing with today's society. Let your imagination take hold, and discuss the kind of society we would have under such circumstances.

For example, every inhabitant of the United States could have a national identification number, such as the social security number, so that purchasing, banking, and all other transactions could be performed instantaneously at negligible cost. Should a system of this nature be installed? What societal dangers would be involved?

Review the first chapter of this book and prepare a detailed

Your stake is in the future, but the future is a moving target.

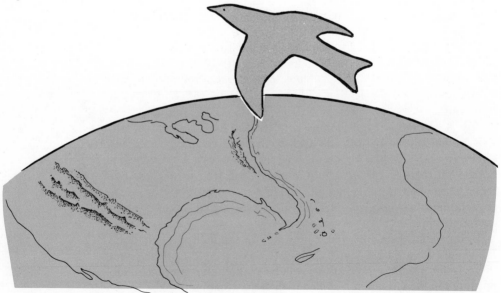

discussion of how a society of this sort could operate. What would be its advantages and disadvantages?

THE LAST ASSIGNMENT

Present your 550-word Personal Summary of this course. (See Exercise 28, Chapter 1).

appendix one

Language supplement

INTRODUCTION

While a data processing job can be described both in words and
with flowcharts, if a computer is to carry out the data processing
job we cannot use words and flowcharts directly, because the
computer does not understand such instructions. We must translate
the flowchart into a computer program written in a language suited
to the computer. The purpose of this Language Supplement is to
introduce you to the fundamentals of the three most commonly
used languages, FORTRAN, COBOL, and BASIC, and to teach
you how to translate flowcharts into computer programs.

FORTRAN, COBOL, and BASIC are computer languages
with a large number of instructions, and to master these languages
you must have special courses beyond the scope of this introductory
data processing course. Therefore we will introduce only the basic
elements of these languages, so you will have an introductory
knowledge of the subject. Later, if you wish, you can expand this
knowledge to a more complete mastery of the language.

We make the learning of these languages easy by using only a
specific *subset* of the instructions of the language.[1] This subset
does not provide the full power of the language, and this makes
limitations and restrictions necessary. Thus, for the advantages of

---

[1] Our COBOL–SUBSET is also a subset of WATBOL (see Chapter 9).

quick learning and the ability to get on the computer fast, we sacrifice the generality and power of the complete language. *If you write your programs following the rules presented in this text, your programs will run.* However, the opposite does not hold, because by using features of the full language you may violate the rules for the subset given here and still obtain valid programs. Some students may already have some knowledge of these languages or may want to go deeper into the subject and consult books on the full language. This Language Supplement does not preclude such an approach, though a careful distinction between the rules of the subsets presented here and the rules of the full language must be made.

You will learn programming by translating flowcharts into computer programs. Appendix two, the Data Processing Applications and Flowcharting Supplement, presents a number of simplified case studies and flowcharts.

There are two principal ways computer programs can be presented to a computer. If you operate in a time-sharing mode you can type your programs directly on a terminal. If not in a time-sharing mode, you most likely will have to keypunch your program into a deck of punched cards. Chapter A describes punched cards and the keypunch machine for those who must use punched card input.

The punched card and
the keypunch machine

The punched card[1] (Figure A-1) is a piece of high-quality paper $7\frac{3}{8}$ inches long and $3\frac{1}{4}$ inches wide. This card is divided into 80 vertical columns. In each column holes can be punched to represent a character, digit, or a special symbol. The card is also divided into 12 rows. The illustration shows the holes for digits, letters, and some special characters.

Observe that a single hole is used for digits, two holes are used for letters, and special characters may use one, two, or three holes.

Card columns are laid out in groups called *fields*. The width of a field is the number of columns in the field. Figure A-2 shows a card used in an invoice preparation problem. Observe that columns 1-6 are used for customer number, columns 7-36 for customer name, and so on. Only the holes are read by machines; the printed matter serves the people who work with the cards.

The most common way of recording data in punched cards is with the aid of the keypunch machine, a typewriterlike device (Figure A-3). The keyboard and corresponding holes punched are shown in Figure A-4. Here is a description of what happens if you push the keys.

Keys 1-29, 33, and 40-43 These keys work like typewriter keys. The character on the lower half of the key is punched and printed

---

[1] We are not discussing here the IBM 96-column card.

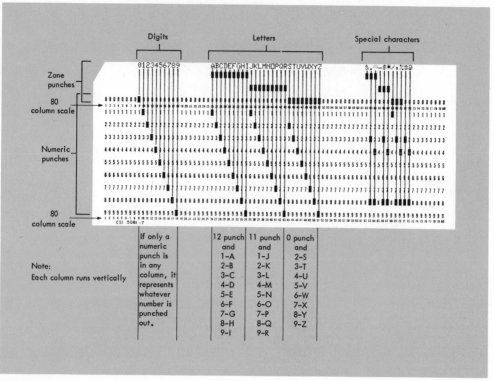

FIGURE A–1 The punched card and code.

FIGURE A–2 Punched card used in invoice preparation program.

Note: Br stands for branch

FIGURE A–3
The keypunch
machine.

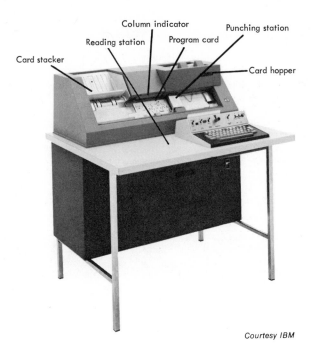

Column indicator
Reading station
Card stacker
Program card
Punching station
Card hopper

Courtesy IBM

unless the NUMERIC key is held down. If the NUMERIC key is held down, the character on the upper half of the keys will be punched and printed. Observe that there is no character on the upper half of keys 7 and 13; these keys will not operate when the NUMERIC key is held down. Key 33 punches and prints the − (minus sign), whether the NUMERIC key is held down or not.

Key 30   NUMERIC (numeric shift). As long as this key is held down, the keyboard shifts into NUMERIC position.

Key 32   DUP (duplicate). When this key is held down, data on the card in the reading station (Figure A–3) is duplicated on the card in the punching station.

Key 34   REL (release). This key advances the cards at the punching station and the reading station.

Key 35   FEED (card feed). This key places the cards at the punching station and reading station, and it feeds the card released from the reading station into the stacker.

Key 37   REG (card register). This key registers (positions) the cards at the punching station and reading station and feeds the card released from the reading station into the stacker.

SPACE bar   The SPACE bar advances the cards at the punching station and reading station by one column. No characters are printed, and no holes are punched.

FIGURE A–4
The keyboard
and card code
of the keypunch
machine.

Key Number	ALPHABETIC		NUMERIC	
	Card Code	Graphic	Card Code	Graphic
1	11–8	Q	12–8–6	+
2	0–6	W	0–8–5	_
3	12–5	E	11–8–5	)
4	11–9	R	12–8–2	¢
5	0–3	T	0–8–2	0–8–2*
6	0–8	Y	12–8–7	|
7	12–1	A	none	none
8	0–2	S	0–8–6	>
9	12–4	D	8–2	:
10	12–6	F	11–8–6	;
11	12–7	G	11–8–7	¬
12	12–8	H	8–5	'
13	0–9	Z	none	none
14	0–7	X	0–8–7	?
15	12–3	C	8–7	"
16	0–5	V	8–6	=
17	12–2	B	11–8–2	!
18	11–5	N	12–8–5	(
19	11–7	P	12	&
20	0–1	/	0	0
21	0–4	U	1	1
22	12–9	I	2	2
23	11–6	O	3	3
24	11–1	J	4	4
25	11–2	K	5	5
26	11–3	L	6	6
27	11–4	M	7	7
28	0–8–3	,	8	8
29	12–8–3	.	9	9
33	11	–	11	–
40	8–4	@	8–3	#
41	0–8–4	%	0–8–3	,
42	11–8–4	*	11–8–3	$
43	12–8–4	<	12–8–3	.

The remaining keys, numbers 30–32, 34–39, and 44–48 control the various functions of the card punch as follows:

    30. NUMERIC (numeric shift)
    31. ALPHA (alphabetic shift)
    32. DUP (duplicate)
    34. REL (release)
    35. FEED (card feed)
    36. SKIP
    37. REG (card register)
    38. AUX DUP (auxiliary duplicate)
    39. PROG TWO (program two)
    44. MULT PCH (multiple punch)
    45. PROG ONE (program one)
    46. MC (master card)
    47. ERROR RESET
    48. LEFT ZERO

* Blank

Photo courtesy IBM

HOW TO OPERATE A KEYPUNCH MACHINE

Step 1   Turn on the main line switch on the front right side under the keyboard.

Step 2   Load the blank deck of cards into the card hopper with the cards facing you and the printed side up.

Step 3   Turn on the functional control switches, *Autofeed* and *Print*. Turn the program control level to the right to make inoperative the other three functional control switches.

Step 4   Press the FEED key to feed the first card in the card hopper. Press the FEED key to feed another card from the card hopper and to feed the first card into the punching station.

Step 5   Punch the required data into the card at the punching station. Watch the column indicator, which shows the number of the column currently in the punching station.

How to punch cards one at a time

Turn off the *Autofeed* switch. Push the REL key to clear a card out of the punching station or the reading station. To feed a new card press the FEED key. To position it in the punch station, push the REG key. Punch the required data. After the punching is completed, push the REL key, to release the card from the punching station. Pushing the REG key will now place the card in the reading station, and pushing the REL key will release the card from the reading station. Pushing the REG and FEED keys will feed the card which was released from the reading station into the card stacker.

Additional information

The BACK SPACE key moves the cards at the reading station and the punching station to a back space. You must not use this key after column 78 has been passed. You cannot backspace for more than 20 consecutive columns.

The *Clear* switch advances all cards to the stacker without feeding new cards from the hopper.

This brief summary of features of the punched card machine describes only the most commonly used keys. Consult your manual for further information.

ASSIGNMENTS

1.   Keypunch the FORTRAN program for the account-balancing problem (see Figure B–3 in Chapter B).
2.   Keypunch the PROCEDURE DIVISION of the COBOL program for the account-balancing problem (Figure C–4 in Chapter C).

Introduction to FORTRAN programming

This chapter covers the elements of FORTRAN (*FOR*mula *TRAN*slation), one of the most widely used computer languages.[1] We concentrate on the fundamental aspects of FORTRAN, and, to help you get started quickly, we use a special FORTRAN-SUBSET. All the programs presented are written in FORTRAN-SUBSET. Only at the end of the chapter will we describe some of the features of full FORTRAN.

AN EXAMPLE: THE ACCOUNT-BALANCING PROBLEM

First we present the FORTRAN-SUBSET program for the account-balancing problem. Figure B–1 shows how some flowchart statements can be translated into FORTRAN. Figure B–2 shows a complete FORTRAN program for the account-balancing problem, written on a *coding form*. Figure B–3 shows the complete program, the data, and the location of the *job control* cards required to submit the program to a computer system. These job control cards automate the scheduling and handling of programs on the computer system. Usage of job control cards varies from installation to installation, and you must find out from your computer center what cards to use. Job control cards will not be discussed any further here.

---

[1] The history and use of FORTRAN are discussed in Chapter 9.

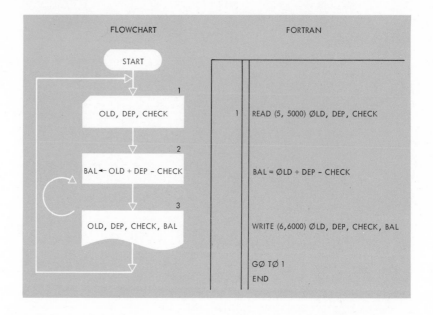

Figure B–4 shows a FORTRAN statement keypunched into a card. Figure B–5 shows a data card. Figure B–6 shows the complete FORTRAN deck that must be submitted to the computer system. Finally, Figure B–7a and Figure B–7b show part of the printout produced by the computer. The first of the printouts (Figure B–7a) is a *listing* of the program and is included only for your convenience.

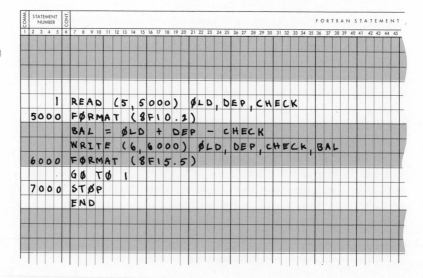

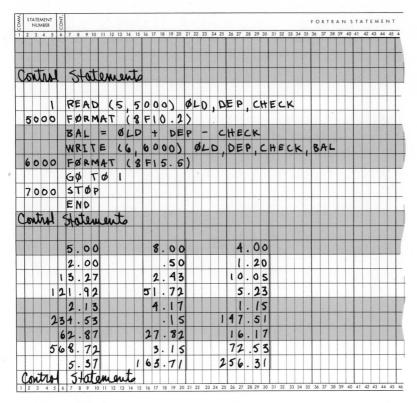

FIGURE B–3
Complete
FORTRAN
program including
control cards and
data for
account-balancing
problem.

The second part of the printout (Figure B–7b), gives your answers.[2] (Note 568.72 prints as 568.71997, 51.72 as 51.71999. Such inaccuracies are unimportant and are difficult to avoid in FORTRAN.)

Before discussing in detail the FORTRAN language, we want to point out the following:

1. Each *character* of the program is written on a separate "cell" of the coding sheet.
2. Each line of the coding sheet is keypunched into a single card, line by line, character by character (Figure B–8). Thus, the 80 columns of the coding form correspond to the 80 columns of the punched card.
3. Each FORTRAN statement in the program goes on a separate card. Statements must be in columns 7–72.
4. There are no lowercase characters. The letter O (Oh) is written as Ø.

---

[2] You should be warned that in most systems this program will result in an error message, because there is no statement in the program to indicate which is the last card in the input. The beginner should ignore this error message. Later, you will learn how to avoid it.

FIGURE B–4
Sample FORTRAN
program card.

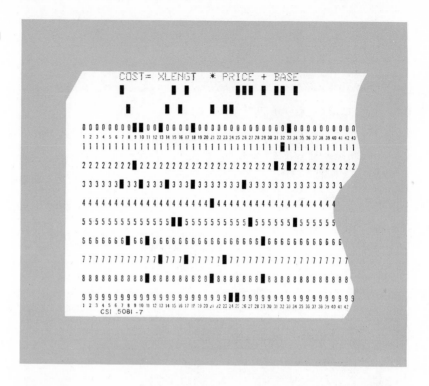

FIGURE B–5
Sample FORTRAN
data card.

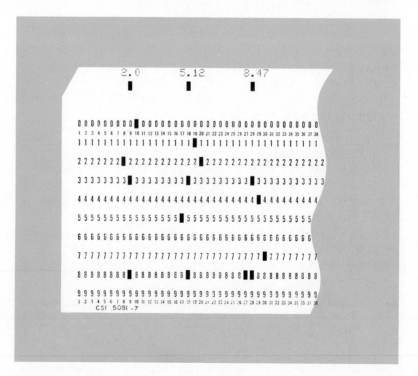

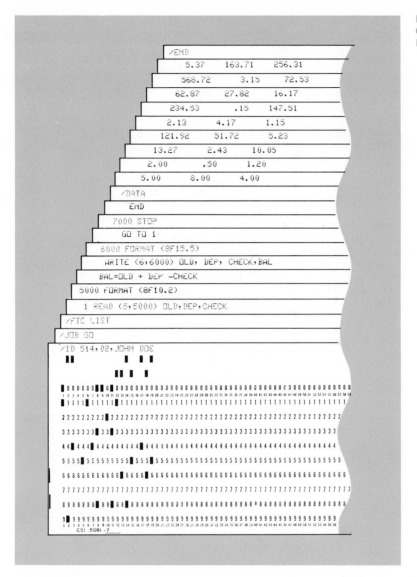

FIGURE B-6
Complete
FORTRAN deck.

5. A statement may be *labeled* by a *statement number* up to five digits. (In Figure B-2 there are four statement numbers: 1, 5000, 6000, 7000.)

6. The names of variables have six or fewer characters, and the first character cannot be a digit.

7. The *assignment* symbol of the left arrow (←) used in flow-charts is replaced by the equals (=) sign.

8. GO TO statements change the normal sequence of logic of the program. These are *jump* or *transfer* commands.

```
/ID  514,C2,JOHN DOE
/JOB GO
/FTC LIST
BPS FORTRAN D COMPILER
    S.0001          1 READ (5,5000) OLD,DEF,CHECK
    S.0002       5000 FORMAT (8F10.2)
    S.0003            BAL=OLD + DEP -CHECK
    S.0004            WRITE (6,6000) OLD, DEP, CHECK,BAL
    S.0005       6000 FORMAT (8F15.5)
    S.0006            GO TO 1
    S.0007       7000 STOP
    S.0008            END
                 SIZE OF COMMON   00000      PROGRAM   00264
  END OF COMPILATION   MAIN
```

FIGURE B-7a
Partial computer
printout for
account-balancing
problem.

```
/DATA
         5.00000          8.00000          4.00000          9.00000
         2.00000          0.50000          1.20000          1.30000
        13.27000          2.43000         10.05000          5.65000
       121.92000         51.71999          5.23000        168.40997
         2.13000          4.17000          1.15000          5.15000
       234.53000          0.15000        147.50999         87.17000
        62.87000         27.81999         16.17000         74.51999
       568.71997          3.15000         72.53000        499.33984
         5.37000        163.70999        256.30981        -87.22983
```

FIGURE B-7b
Partial computer
printout for
account-balancing
problem.

9. Some of the numbers and statements in the program have no counterparts in the flowcharts and will have to be explained in detail (for example, in Figure B-2 the 5 and 5000 in the READ statement; the 6 and 6000 in the WRITE statement; the FORMAT statements).

10. Every FORTRAN program must terminate in an END statement.

11. FORTRAN decks are put together in the following sequence:
    a. Job control cards.
    b. Program.
    c. Job control cards.
    d. Data.
    e. Job control cards.

SOME RULES OF FORTRAN–SUBSET

FORTRAN uses two types of numbers: integers and floating-point numbers. *Integers,* that is whole numbers like 2, 17, 3, −2, do not have fractional parts. *Floating-point,* that is, *real* numbers like 2.71, 3.025, −7.1782 do have fractional parts. Most calculations are carried out with floating-point numbers, so in our FORTRAN–SUBSET we allow only floating-point numbers. Ac-

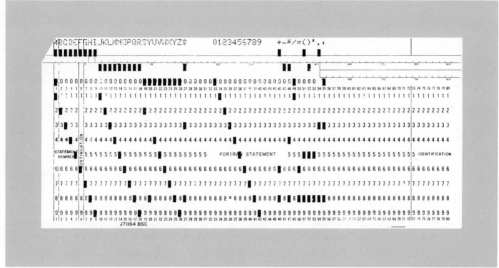

FIGURE B–8 The characters used in writing FORTRAN statements.

cording to the rules of FORTRAN, the names of floating-point variables must *not* start with the letters I, J, K, L, M, or N, unless special statements are made in the program. In order to follow this *I–N convention* in the FORTRAN–SUBSET, we do not use variable names starting with these letters.

Examples of acceptable variables:

RØBERT
DØG52
A31
F1000T
X

Examples of unacceptable variables:

ØLDBALANCE — more than six letters

5NEW — starts with a digit

A*B — contains the symbol*

NEWBAL — in full FORTRAN, this is an integer variable. In the FORTRAN–SUBSET we forbid the use of such a name.

Because we exclude integers from the FORTRAN–SUBSET, we will write all our constants (numbers) and data with the decimal point included. For example, we will use:

2.0, 0.0, 157.0

instead of

2, 0, 157

Note, however, that a statement number (label) must not contain a decimal point, and in the SUBSET an exponent will not contain a decimal point.

THE WRITE STATEMENT

In FORTRAN programs the word **WRITE** is followed by two integers in parentheses. The first of these numbers in the FORTRAN–SUBSET is 6; this number tells the computer to use the printer for output. The second number is the statement number of the FORMAT statement referenced in the WRITE statement. The FORMAT statement tells the computer how to print the answers.

We can use any whole number up to five digits to *label* FORMAT statements, but in order to simplify matters in our FORTRAN-SUBSET we will mostly use 6000. So we will have:

WRITE (6,6000)

followed by the *list of variables* to be printed.

FORMAT statements

Figure B-9 illustrates **WRITE** statements and referenced FORMAT statements.

FIGURE B-9
Sample WRITE and FORMAT statements. FORMAT statement 5 will mostly be used in FORTRAN-SUBSET.

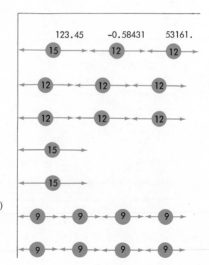

1.   WRITE   (6, 6000) A, B, C
      6000 FØRMAT (F15.2, F12.5, F12.0)

2.   WRITE   (6, 17) A, B, C
      17 FØRMAT (F12.2, F12.2, F12.2)

3.   WRITE   (6, 6000) A, B, C
      6000 FØRMAT (3F12.2)

4.   WRITE   (6, 100) A
      100 FØRMAT (F15.5, F15.5, F15.5)

5.   WRITE   (6, 6000) A
      6000 FØRMAT (8F15.5)

6.   WRITE   (6, 6000) A, B, C, C
      6000 FØRMAT (F9.1, F9.0, F9.0, F9.1)

7.   WRITE   (6, 6000) A, B, C, C
      6000 FØRMAT (F9.2, 2F9.0, F9.1)

Example 1   The list of variables is: A, B, and C. The *matching* format list also has three items: F15.2, F12.5, F12.0. So the output field widths will be 15, 12 and 12, and the number of digits printed after the decimal point will be 2, 5, and 0 (none).

Example 2   Self-explanatory.

Example 3   Same as Example 2.

Example 4   Additional items in the FORMAT list are disregarded.

Example 5   Provides the same printout as Example 4. The extra seven elements in the FORMAT list are disregarded. We will mostly use this FORMAT statement in our FORTRAN–SUBSET. It allows us to print up to eight variables, each with a field width of 15, and 5 digits after the decimal point. (Most printers allow up to 132 characters.)

Example 6   Self-explanatory.

Example 7   Provides the same printout as Example 6.

Printing literals and headers

Suppose you compute the average of a column of numbers, and you want to print:

THE AVERAGE IS: 2.53

Here the character string "THE AVERAGE IS" is called a *literal*. You want the computer to print *literally* what you write. You can accomplish this printout by writing:

```
      WRITE(6,1234) A
 1234 FORMAT (' THE AVERAGE IS : ',F5.2)
```

You can insert literals anywhere between items of your FORMAT list by the use of quote marks.

Some FORTRAN systems do not allow the use of quote marks for literals. You would rather have to write:

```
 1234 FORMAT (18H THE AVERAGE IS : ,F5.2)
```

where H stands for Hollerith (the inventor of the punched card machine) and the number 18 designates that there are 18 symbols in the literal.

Observe the blank at the beginning of each literal. The first character in the string is never printed; it serves to control the movement of the paper. You have the option to use a blank, 0, 1, or +. This is the printer action that follows:

Character in first position	Printer action
blank	single space
0	double space
1	skip to top of next page
+	suppress spacing

If in the program you want to skip a line (that is, leave an empty line) you can use FØRMAT ('b') or FØRMAT (1Hb), where b stands for *blank*.

Suppose in the account-balancing problem you want to print the headers OLDBALANCE, DEPOSIT, CHECK, NEW-BALANCE for the columns. You can accomplish this by writing

or by using the H(Hollerith) option. (The X in column 6 of the coding form serves to indicate line continuation.)

THE READ STATEMENT

The READ statement is much like the WRITE statement. The first number in the parentheses following the word "READ," the number 5, tells the computer to use the card reader for input. The second number is the statement number of the FORMAT statement referenced in the WRITE statement.

In our FORTRAN–SUBSET we mostly use:

> READ(5,5000) *list of variables*
> 5000 FØRMAT (8F10.2)

This statement allows the input of up to eight data items, each written in field widths of ten. If we wish to use other field widths we must specify the widths by the integer part of the number after the F. For example, F15.3 and F8.2 mean field widths of 15 and 8.

What about the digit after the decimal point? What is the difference between F10.2, F10.0, and F10.5? In our FORTRAN-SUBSET we always use data with the decimal point, like 7.2, 3.0, or 6.52. The computer will interpret the data as punched and ignore the difference between F10.2, F10.0, and F10.5.

What if the READ statement cannot find data because all data cards have been used up? FORTRAN systems are designed so that execution of the program will immediately stop. Some systems provide an error message, too. In our FORTRAN-SUBSET we rely on this system capability and take no special measures to deal with the problem of the last data card. If we receive an error message, we disregard it.

SUMMARY OF RULES FOR FORTRAN-SUBSET

For convenience, Figure B-10 summarizes these rules. We stress again that these rules assure that any program you write using these rules will run. However, in full FORTRAN many of these rules need not be observed.

HOW TO PREPARE A FORTRAN PROGRAM

The steps to take in preparing a FORTRAN program are as follows:

Step 1 Translate the flowchart into FORTRAN.
    a. Introduce suitable names for the variables.
    b. Each input statement requires a READ statement.
    c. Each output statement requires a WRITE statement.
    d. Assignment statements are directly translatable into FORTRAN statements.
    e. READ and WRITE statements need FORMAT statements. The same FORMAT statement may serve several READ or WRITE statements.

Step 2 Write in the data.
Step 3 Insert the job control statements.
Step 4 Keypunch the coding sheet.
Step 5 Submit the punched card deck to the computer for execution of your program.

FIGURE B–10
Summary of rules
of the FORTRAN–
SUBSET used in
this text.

1. All numbers (except statement numbers or exponents) contain the decimal point.
2. The programming form must be properly filled out:
   a. Only statement numbers in Cols. 1–5.
   b. C for Comments in Col. 1.
   c. Programs must be written in Cols. 7–72.
   d. May use empty lines if desired.
   e. May use blanks if desired.
   f. May continue on next line of form by using any nonzero character in Col. 6.
3. Names of variables:
   a. Must use six or fewer characters.
   b. Do not start with I, J, K, L, M, N.
   c. Cannot start with a digit.
4. Sample statements:

   a. READ (5,5000) A, B, C
   b. WRITE (6,6000) X, Y, Z
   †c. $A = X*Y - X/Y - X**2 + Y**3.0 + X**Y$
   d. GØ TØ 10
   e. IF (A.LT.B) GØ TØ 175
   f. IF (X) 15, 30, 7

5. FORMAT statements:
   a. 5000 FØRMAT (8F10.2) for input.
   b. 6000 FØRMAT (8F15.5) for output.
6. Terminate the program by:

   7000 STØP
        END

7. Data sheet:
   a. All numbers contain a decimal point.
   b. Numbers are in Cols. 1–10, 11–20, etc.
   c. All columns 1–80 may be used.
8. FORTRAN decks must be put together in the following sequence:
   a. Job control cards.
   b. Program proper.
   c. Job control cards.
   d. Data.
   e. Job control cards.

† The exponential (power) operator is designated by **

SIMPLE ILLUSTRATIVE PROGRAMS

Invoice calculation

Figure B–11a shows the translation of the flowchart for invoice calculation (see Figure E–1 in Appendix two) into FORTRAN. **Figure B–11b** shows the printout.

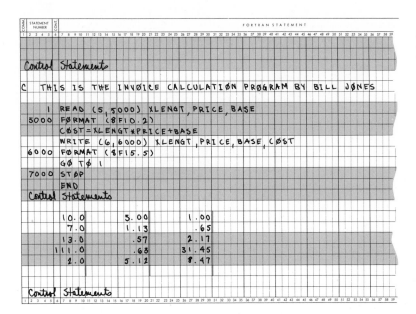

FIGURE B–11a
Invoice
calculation: How
to multiply.

The first statement in the program is a *comment*. Observe the letter C in Column 1. The computer recognizes the letter C in Column 1 and does no work on this statement (does not execute it). The purpose of writing comments in your program is to *document* your work. In other words, comments are to help you to write the program, to review it later, and to debug it—that is, to find errors in it.

Observe in the assignment statement that the multiplication is designated by an asterisk (*).

FIGURE B–11b
Computer printout
for invoice
calculation.

/DATA			
10.00000	3.00000	1.00000	31.00000
7.00000	1.13000	0.65000	8.55999
13.00000	0.57000	2.17000	9.58000
111.00000	0.63000	31.45000	101.37999
2.00000	5.12000	8.47000	18.70999

XLENGT is used rather than LENGTH or XLENGTH because of two of the rules in Figure B–10.

1. The first letter of the name of the variable in our FORTRAN–SUBSET must *not* be I, J, K, L, M, N (the I–N convention).
2. The name of a variable cannot contain more than six letters.

It is common practice among programmers to add an X at the beginning of a variable to avoid violating the I–N convention.

Sales analysis

Translation of the flowchart for the sales analysis problem, (Figure E–2) is shown in Figure B–12a, and the printout in Figure B–12b. Observe that division is designated by a slash (/). Why did

FIGURE B–12a
Sales analysis.

```
Control Statements
C    SALES ANALYSIS PROBLEM
   5 READ (5,5000) S1,S2,S3,S4,S5
     WDAY = S1+S2+S3+S4+S5
     READ (5,5000) S6,S7
     WEND = S6 + S7
     TOTAL = WDAY + WEND
     AVER = TOTAL / 7.0
     WRITE (6,6000) TOTAL,AVER
     WRITE (6,6000) WDAY,S1,S2,S3,S4,S5
     WRITE (6,6000) WEND,S6,S7
     GO TO 5
5000 FORMAT (8F10.2)
6000 FORMAT (8F15.5)
7000 STOP
     END
Control Statements
     15.61      341.16      972.89      251.13      493.63
    765.47      607.83
     49.16      317.09       99.16      190.27      161.91
    531.91      347.09
     72.42      710.00      800.50      342.72      351.67
     81.03       98.69
Control Statements
```

6 = Printer
5 = card reader

FIGURE B–12b
Computer printout
for sales analysis.

```
/DATA
 3447.70923      492.52979
 2074.40942       15.61000     341.14990     972.88985     251.12999     493.62988
 1373.29980      765.46997     607.82983
 1691.53906      241.64844
  812.53931       44.15999     317.03979      99.15999     190.26999     161.90999
  878.95976      531.90991     347.08984
 2457.02979      351.00415
 2277.30981       72.42000     710.00000     800.50000     342.71997     351.66992
  179.71999       81.03000      98.68999
```

we write 7.0 instead of 7? Remember that in our FORTRAN-SUBSET every constant (number) must be written with the decimal point.

Observe that our first READ statement has the statement number 5. The last statement in the program is: GØ TØ 5. Instead of the label 5 we could have used any number with not more than five digits, except 5000 or 6000. These labels are used for the FORMAT statements. (All statement numbers must be different.)

We have two READ statements corresponding to the two input boxes in the flowchart. Both READ statements reference the same FORMAT statement. We have three WRITE statements referencing the same FORMAT statement. To avoid confusion, we placed the FORMAT statement at the end of the program, but before the END statement. Some programmers prefer to start the program with FORMAT statements. You may place FORMAT statements anywhere in the program, but not after the END statement.

The shipping bill calculation

The FORTRAN translation of the flowchart for shipping bill calculation (Figure E–3) is shown in Figure B–13a, the printout in Figure B–13b. We happen to have chosen 15 as the statement number to READ the weights of the commodities. So the last statement in the program is: GØ TØ 15.

FIGURE B–13a
Shipping bill
calculation: How
to remember.

```
/DATA
      0.50000
     12.52000         23.09999        5.50000       7.10000      52.00000
      1.00000          1.00000        0.0           1.00000       1.00000
      4.00000         96.71997
      5.00000         12.00000        7.00000       2.00000       0.0
     26.00000        405.49951
      2.50000          3.00000       15.25000      20.00000      18.75000
     59.50000       1331.22485
```

FIGURE B–13b
Computer printout
for shipping bill
calculation.

BRANCHING PROBLEMS: DECISION MAKING AND LOGICAL OPERATIONS

Commission calculation: The logical IF statement

The program corresponding to the flowchart for commission calculation (Figure 2.10, Chapter 2) is shown in Figure B–14a, the printout in Figure B–14b. The third line in the program is a new kind of a statement:

IF (AMNT.GT.150.00) GØ TØ 30

FIGURE B–14a
Commission
calculation: How
to branch.

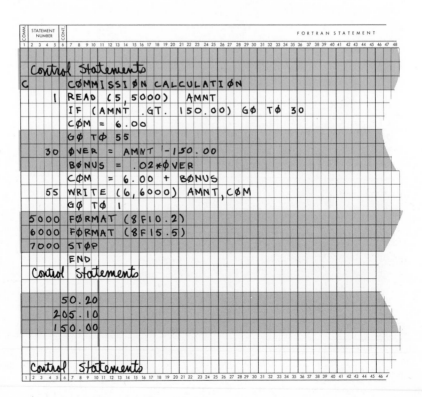

```
/DATA
       50.20000          6.00000
      205.09999          7.10200
      150.00000          6.00000
```

This is a logical **IF** statement,[3] to be read:

if amnt is greater than 150.00 go to 30.

If the amount is greater than $150, the program jumps to the statement labeled 30. The commission, including the bonus, is computed, and the correct answers are printed.

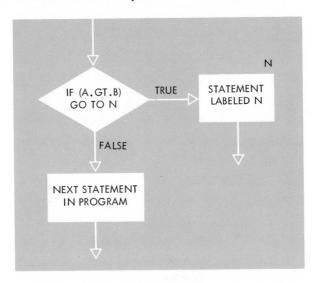

FIGURE B–15
Flowchart for
logical IF
statement. When
the IF statement
is not satisfied
the program drops
through.

What happens if the amount is less than (or equal to) $150? We say that the IF statement is not satisfied, that is, the logical statement **AMNT.GT.150.00** is false. So control is transferred not to statement 30 but to the statement immediately following the IF statement. *The program drops through;* that is, the IF statement is ignored by the computer (Figure B–15). So the commission is set to $6, control is transferred to the **WRITE** statement, and the correct answers are printed.

Figure B–16a shows the various logical IF statements of FORTRAN. Logical statements can also be combined, as shown in Figure B–16b.

---

[3] If your FORTRAN does not have logical IF statements you should proceed directly to the arithmetic IF section below.

FORTRAN	Meaning
IF (A.LT.B)	if A is less than B
IF (A.LE.B)	if A is less than or equal to B
IF (A.EQ.B)	if A is equal to B
IF (A.NE.B)	if A is not equal to B
IF (A.GT.B)	if A is greater than B
IF (A.GE.B)	if A is greater than or equal to B

FORTRAN	Meaning
IF ((A.LE.B).AND.(B.LE.C))	If A is less than or equal to B and B is less than or equal to C
IF ((A.LT.B).OR.(A.GT.C))	If A is less than B or A is greater than C
IF (.NOT. (A.LE.B))	If A is *not* less than or equal to B, that is A is greater than B

IF statements can be combined with assignment statements. For example, the commission calculation can be written as:

IF (AMNT.LE.150.00) COM = 6.00
IF (AMNT.GT.150.00) COM = 6.00 + .02 * (AMNT−150.00)

Multiple branching: The classification problem

A flowchart for multiple branching in the classification problem is given in Figure E–8 (Appendix two), which suggests a way to classify people by weight. The translation into FORTRAN-SUBSET is given for this problem in Figures B–17a and B–17b, and a computer printout is shown in Figure B–17c.

Commission calculation: The arithmetic IF statement

Some FORTRAN systems do not have logical IF statements, but all FORTRAN systems have arithmetic IF statements. As an illustration consider the statement

IF (X) 20,27,15

Then,

If X is less than 0, control is transferred to statement 20.
If X is equal to 0, control is transferred to statement 27.
If X is greater than 0, control is transferred to statement 15.

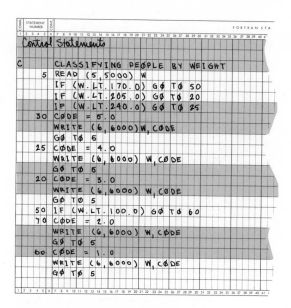

FIGURE B–17a
Program for
classifying people
by weight.

```
Control Statements
C     CLASSIFYING PEOPLE BY WEIGHT
   5  READ (5,5000) W
      IF (W.LT.170.0) GO TO 50
      IF (W.LT.205.0) GO TO 20
      IF (W.LT.240.0) GO TO 25
  30  CODE = 5.0
      WRITE (6,6000) W, CODE
      GO TO 5
  25  CODE = 4.0
      WRITE (6,6000) W, CODE
      GO TO 5
  20  CODE = 3.0
      WRITE (6,6000) W, CODE
      GO TO 5
  50  IF (W.LT.100.0) GO TO 60
  70  CODE = 2.0
      WRITE (6,6000) W, CODE
      GO TO 5
  60  CODE = 1.0
      WRITE (6,6000) W, CODE
      GO TO 5
```

FIGURE B–17b
Program for
classifying people
by weight.

```
5000  FORMAT (8F10.2)
6000  FORMAT (8F15.5)
7000  STOP
      END
Control Statements

      251.0
      173.0
      148.0
      230.0

Control Statements
```

FIGURE B–17c
Computer printout
for classifying
people by weight.

```
/DATA
      251.00000        5.00000
      173.00000        3.00000
      148.00000        2.00000
      230.00000        4.00000
       95.00000        1.00000
```

The arithmetic IF statement results in a three-way transfer of control, as shown in Figure B–18.

Figure B–19 shows the commission calculation program with the arithmetic IF. If the quantity in parentheses after the IF is less than 0, control is transferred to statement 10. If the quantity is exactly

FIGURE B–18
Flowchart for
arithmetic IF
statement.

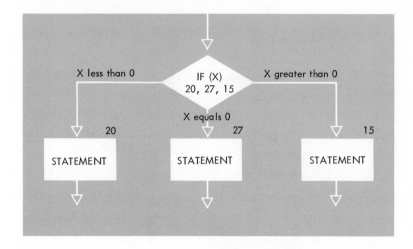

0, control is again transferred to statement 10. But, if the quantity is greater than 0, control is transferred to statement 30.

So, the IF statement in Figure B–19 will make the computer go to statement 10 if the amount is less than or equal to $150. But if the amount is over $150, the computer will go to statement 30.

You can verify with the aid of the flowchart that this is exactly what is required in the commission calculation.

Observe that if the amount is exactly $150 you could make the computer transfer control to statement 30, and still you would get the same correct answer to the problem. In most problems, you

FIGURE B–19
Commission
calculation
program with
arithmetic IF.

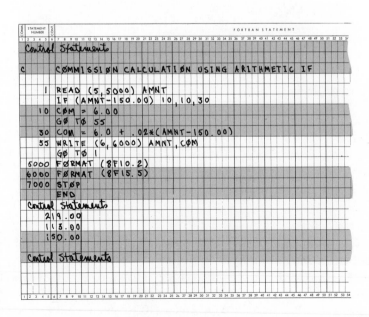

have such an option when the value in the parentheses is exactly 0, and in fact most of the time you use the arithmetic IF statement as a two-way transfer of control.

It is a risky practice to rely on an arithmetic IF statement as a three-way transfer of control. Computers often work only in approximate numbers, and therefore you may think that the value in the parentheses is exactly 0, but in fact in computer storage the value may be only approximately 0. Therefore, your transfer of control may be wrong if you rely on the equal branch of the arithmetic IF statement.

CONTROLLING LOOPS WITH THE DO STATEMENT

Turn to Figure E–26 (Appendix two) and study the problem described there of computing how many baby and adult rabbits there will be in 24 months. You should have no difficulty translating the flowchart into FORTRAN–SUBSET, but controlling loops with the aid of a DO statement can make the programming job a lot easier.

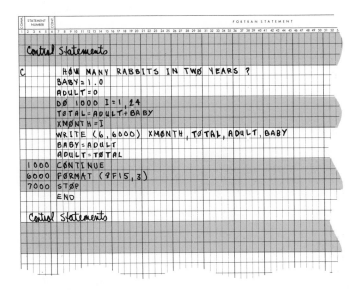

FIGURE B–20
Program to determine how rabbits multiply.

The first two assignment statements in Figure B–20 *initialize* BABY and ADULT. Then we have the DO statement to control the loop to be executed. Observe that:
1.   We open the DO statement by writing:

DØ 1000 I = number1, number2

2. We write the statements in the loop but omit *incrementing* I and *testing* whether I reached the upper limit.
3. We close the DO statement by writing:

1000 CØNTINUE

The opening statement specifies that the *counter* I is to run from number-1 to number-2. In this case the counter runs from 1 to 24, corresponding to the 24 months. The label 1000 indicates the last statement in the DO loop.

Examine how we translated the statements in Boxes 10, 15, and 20 in the flowchart of Figure E–26. The statement in Box 10 is directly translated, but why the XMØNTH = I statement? Our counter is I, corresponding to the month. So why don't we print I directly?

Here is a strange feature of FORTRAN. The counter in the DO loop *must* have a name starting with I, J, K, L, M, or N (standing for an integer variable). But in our FORTRAN–SUBSET we have no way to print such variables. So we must compute XMONTH by writing:

XMØNTH = I

In full FORTRAN you can print an integer variable, so you would print I directly.

The rest of the program presents no difficulties. You can verify in the printout (Figure B–21) that the program indeed works.

FIGURE B–21
Computer printout
showing how
rabbits multiply.

1.000	1.000	0.000	1.000
2.000	1.000	1.000	0.000
3.000	2.000	1.000	1.000
4.000	3.000	2.000	1.000
5.000	5.000	3.000	2.000
6.000	8.000	5.000	3.000
7.000	13.000	8.000	5.000
8.000	21.000	13.000	8.000
9.000	34.000	21.000	13.000
10.000	55.000	34.000	21.000
11.000	89.000	55.000	34.000
12.000	144.000	89.000	55.000
13.000	233.000	144.000	89.000
14.000	377.000	233.000	144.000
15.000	610.000	377.000	233.000
16.000	987.000	610.000	377.000
17.000	1597.000	987.000	610.000
18.000	2584.000	1597.000	987.000
19.000	4181.000	2584.000	1597.000
20.000	6765.000	4181.000	2584.000
21.000	10946.000	6765.000	4181.000
22.000	17711.000	10946.000	6765.000
23.000	28657.000	17711.000	10946.000
24.000	46368.000	28657.000	17711.000

If you wish to count not by 1 but, for example, by 2, you would open your DO statement by writing:

$$D\emptyset \ 1000 \ I = 1, 24, 2$$

WHAT COMPLETE FORTRAN CAN DO FOR YOU

There are a number of limitations in our FORTRAN–SUBSET which can be removed with full FORTRAN.

First, our flexibility with regard to printouts is strongly limited. In full FORTRAN you can prepare neat printouts with appropriate headings. You can space your answers to meet your needs. Numbers can be printed as whole numbers or decimals, and you can place the decimal point where you need it. Names and words, not only numbers, can be printed, and Englishlike messages can be provided.

Full FORTRAN allows you to work with whole (integer) numbers and also with floating-point numbers. Also, additional accuracy can be provided by using double precision numbers. Writing programs for calculations and working with rows, columns, and entire tables of numbers can be accomplished much more efficiently by using DO and DIMENSION statements.

When complicated programs are written, they can be divided into FUNCTION and SUBROUTINE subprograms. Each subprogram can be written separately and then combined into the final program. It is also possible to use the same subprograms over and over again, and many subprograms are provided by vendors. By maintaining a library of subprograms, much programming time can be saved.

In our FORTRAN–SUBSET we used a single input file (card reader) and a single output file (line printer). Full FORTRAN allows the use of many input and output files, including magnetic tapes and disks, and provides good data manipulation capability.

You must recognize that the FORTRAN–SUBSET covered in this chapter gives the most elementary aspects of FORTRAN and provides a basis for further study. Full FORTRAN is a powerful language for solving complicated problems efficiently.

DISCUSSION QUESTIONS AND ASSIGNMENTS

All assignments refer to the FORTRAN–SUBSET developed in the chapter.

1. State in what column you punch the following elements: (a) a statement number, (b) the symbol for a comment, (c) program statements, (d) the symbol to indicate a continuation card.

2. Describe job control cards to be used in your computer installation. Where do you place them in the FORTRAN deck? Where do you place the data cards?

3. State which of the following are not acceptable constants: (a) 25.73, (b) 73, (c) 15,123,710, (d) 1234.567, (e) +62.00, (f) .5, (g) $5.00.

4. State which of the following are not acceptable names for variables: (a) XXX, (b) NUMBER, (c) 5A3, (d) STOP, (e) K, (f) A00A00, (g) A1B2C3D, (h) PART-1, (i) PLUS, (j) MINUS, (k) XCUBE, (l) YSQUARE, (m) X1.4, (n) $5.00, (o) PART1a.

5. State which of the following assignment statements are unacceptable:

   a. $A = 2*a + 5$
   b. $C = C.X - 3.0$
   c. $D = A/B + 3.0$
   d. $E = A*/B$
   e. $X + Y = A - B$
   f. $BX6 = B + X + 6.0$
   g. $X = 6A - 3B$
   h. $A = \dfrac{X}{3.0}$

6. Do you have to label each statement?

7. A program has 100 statements. The 10th statement is:

$$123 \quad GØ\ TØ\ 501$$

The 35th statement is:

$$501 \quad GØ\ TØ\ 123$$

What would happen if the computer executes this program?

8. A program reads A, B, C and prints X, Y, Z. Below are given the statements between input and output:

$$X = A$$
$$Y = Z$$
$$Z = C$$
$$B = Y$$

What will happen if the computer executes this program? What happens if you have:

$$X = A$$
$$Z = C$$
$$Y = Z$$
$$Y = B$$

9. Do you need the decimal point in the data sheet?

10. Describe how FORMAT statements are used (Figure B–9). Give additional illustrations.

11. Can you use the same FORMAT statements for several input and output statements?

12. Explain how to print literals.

13. Describe how to prepare FORTRAN programs.
14. Correct the following statements:
 a. IF (X = Y) GØ TØ 175
 b. IF A.GT.10 GØ TØ 15.0
 c. IF (A − B.LT.7.2) GØ TØ 23
 d. IF ((A+B)X = 5.0) GØ TØ 17
 e. IF (7.0.GT.5.0) GØ TØ 1,000
 f. IF (A.LE.5.0) GØ TØ 52.
 g. N = 51
       IF (X.LE.7.2) GØ TØ N
15. Correct the following statements:
 a. IF (5) 58, 41, 35
 b. IF ((X+Y)Z) 10, 17, 3
 c. IF (A**2) 15, 20, 20
 d. IF (X−1) 82.0, 53.0, 82.0
 e. IF (X) 800, 900, 1,000
 f. N = 100
       IF (A.GE.17.5) N, N, 153
16. Discuss the advantages of full FORTRAN as compared with our FORTRAN–SUBSET.
17. Write FORTRAN–SUBSET programs for the data processing applications and problem solving assignments for Appendix two, Chapter E. Use headers and literals to make your printouts easily understandable.

ANSWERS TO SELECTED QUESTIONS

 1. (*a*) 1–5, (*b*) 1, (*c*) 7–72, (*d*) 6
 3. (*b*) no decimal point, (*c*) comma and no decimal point, (*g*) dollar sign
 4. (*b*) starts with N, (*c*) starts with a number, (*e*) first character is K, (*g*) 7 characters, (*h*) cannot have a hyphen, (*j*) starts with an M, (*l*) more than 6 characters, (*m*) cannot have decimal point, (*n*) cannot have dollar or decimal point, (*o*) cannot have a lower case letter
 5. (*a*) cannot have 2 or 5, must have 2.0 and 5.0, no lower case is permitted, (*b*) cannot have a period, (*d*) cannot have */, (*e*) cannot have + on lefthand side, (*g*) cannot have variables like 6A or 3B, (*h*) cannot have solidus (−) (fraction sign)
 6. No
 7. If either of the statements is reached, the computer gets into an infinite loop. Most computer installations have time limits imposed on programs, so when your time runs out you get kicked off the computer.
 8. In the first case Z appears on the right-hand side undefined. Thus Y will be garbage, and so will B. In the second case X becomes A, Y becomes B, and Z becomes C. But many FORTRAN compilers will set an undefined variable to 0. Then the first program gives the same X, Y, Z as the second, provided B is zero.

9. In our FORTRAN–SUBSET: Yes!

11. Yes

14. *a.* IF (X.EQ.Y) GØ TØ 175

But unless X and Y have 0s after the decimal point (like 17.0, 5.0) this is a risky statement. Due to internal conversion errors, you may never know whether the internal representations of X and Y are equal.

b. IF (A.GT.10.0) GØ TØ 15

c. IF ((A−B).LT.7.2) GØ TØ 23

d. IF ((A+B)∗X.EQ.5.0) GØ TØ 17

e. GO TO 1000

f. IF (A.LE.5.0) GØ TØ 52

g. IF (X.LE.7.2) GØ TØ 51

15. *a.* GØ TØ 35

b. IF ((X+Y)∗Z) 10, 17, 3

c. GØ TØ 20

d. IF (X−1.0) 82, 53, 82

e. IF (X) 800, 900, 1000

f. IF (A.GE.17.5) 100, 100, 153

Introduction to COBOL
programming

This chapter covers COBOL (*CO*mmon *B*usiness *O*riented *Lan*guage), the most widely used business computer language,[1] with emphasis on its fundamental aspects. To help you get on the computer quickly and obtain meaningful answers, we introduce a special COBOL–SUBSET language,[2] in which all our programs are written. Some of the features of full COBOL will be discussed at the end of the chapter.

GENERAL DESCRIPTION OF A COBOL PROGRAM

Every COBOL program is made up of four parts:

1. Identification division.
2. Environment division.
3. Data division.
4. Procedure division.

To run a COBOL program on your computer, you also need (job) control statements (Figure C–1). These control statements automate the scheduling and handling of programs on the computer system. They are not discussed in this text because they vary from installation to installation. Find out from your computer center what statements to use.

---

[1] The history and use of COBOL are discussed in Chapter 9.
[2] Our COBOL–SUBSET is also a subset of WATBOL (see Chapter 9).

FIGURE C–1
How to put a
complete COBOL
program together.

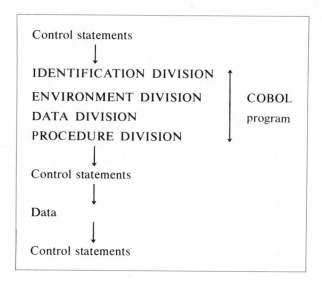

Control statements

↓

IDENTIFICATION DIVISION

ENVIRONMENT DIVISION   COBOL

DATA DIVISION   program

PROCEDURE DIVISION

↓

Control statements

↓

Data

↓

Control statements

Before your program can be executed you also must insert your
data between the last two sets of control statements.

Figures C–2, C–3, and C–4 show the COBOL program for the
account-balancing problem. Figure C–5 shows the data, Figure C–6
the computer listing of the program, and Figure C–7 the computer
output giving answers.

Before we discuss this COBOL program in detail, we will review
the general appearance of the program.

FIGURE C–2
Identification
division, environ-
ment division, and
file section of
data division of
COBOL–SUBSET
programs.

```
SEQUENCE                 COBOL STATEMENT                                      IDENTIFICATION
(Page)(Serial)
001010  IDENTIFICATION DIVISION.
   020  PROGRAM-ID. 'VAZSONY'.
   030  ENVIRONMENT DIVISION.
   040  INPUT-OUTPUT SECTION.
   050  FILE-CONTROL.
   060      SELECT DECK     ASSIGN TO 'SYS004' UNIT-RECORD 2540R UNIT.
   070      SELECT DOCUMENT ASSIGN TO 'SYS005' UNIT-RECORD 1403 UNIT.
   080  DATA DIVISION.
   090  FILE SECTION.
   100  FD DECK DATA RECORD CARD LABEL RECORD OMITTED
   110                          RECORDING MODE F.
   120  01 CARD PICTURE X(80).
   130  FD DOCUMENT DATA RECORD RESULT LABEL RECORD OMITTED
   140                          RECORDING MODE F.
   150  01 RESULT PICTURE X(120).
```

FIGURE C–3
Working-storage section of data division of account-balancing program.

```
002010  WORKING-STORAGE SECTION.
   020  01  INPUT1.
   030      02  OLD         PICTURE 9(8)V99.
   040      02  DEP         PICTURE 9(8)V99.
   050      02  CHECK       PICTURE 9(8)V99.
   060      02  FILLER      PICTURE X(50).
   070  01  OUTPUT3.
   080      02  OLDX        PICTURE Z(12).99.
   090      02  DEPX        PICTURE Z(12).99.
   100      02  CHECKX      PICTURE Z(12).99.
   110      02  BALX        PICTURE Z(12).99.
   120      02  FILLER      PICTURE X(60) VALUE SPACES.
   130  01  AUXILIARY.
   140      02  BAL         PICTURE 9(8)V99.
   150      02  TEMPORARY   PICTURE 9(8)V99.
   160      02  FILLER      PICTURE X(60).
```

FIGURE C–4
Procedure division of account-balancing program.

```
003010  PROCEDURE DIVISION.
   020      OPEN INPUT DECK OUTPUT DOCUMENT.
   030  PARAGRAPH1. READ DECK AT END GO TO FINISH.
   040      EXAMINE CARD REPLACING ALL SPACES BY ZEROS.
   050      MOVE CARD TO INPUT1.
   060      ADD OLD, DEP GIVING TEMPORARY.
   070      SUBTRACT CHECK FROM TEMPORARY GIVING BAL.
   080      MOVE OLD TO OLDX. MOVE DEP TO DEPX.
   090      MOVE CHECK TO CHECKX. MOVE BAL TO BALX.
   100      WRITE RESULT FROM OUTPUT3 AFTER ADVANCING 1.
   110      GO TO PARAGRAPH1.
   120  FINISH. CLOSE DECK DOCUMENT. STOP RUN.
```

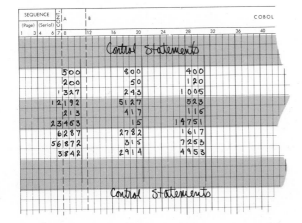

FIGURE C–5
Data for account-balancing problem.

```
                Control Statements

        500        800        400
        200         50        120
        327        243       1005
      12192        527        523
        213        417        116
      23453         15      14751
       6287       2782       1617
      56872         15       7253
       3842       2914       4953

                Control Statements
```

```
LINE NO. SEQ. NO.          SOURCE STATEMENT

    1    C0101C IDENTIFICATION DIVISION.
    2     020  PROGRAM-ID. 'VAZSONY'.
    3     030  ENVIRONMENT DIVISION.
    4     040  INPUT-OUTPUT SECTION.
    5     050  FILE-CONTROL.
    6     060      SELECT DECK     ASSIGN TO 'SYS004' UNIT-RECORD 2540R UNIT.
    7     070      SELECT DOCUMENT ASSIGN TO 'SYS005' UNIT-RECORD 14C3  UNIT.
    8     080  DATA DIVISION.
    9     090  FILE SECTION.
   10     100  FD  DECK DATA RECORD CARD LABEL RECORD OMITTED
   11     110                             RECORDING MODE F.
   12     120  01  CARD PICTURE X(80).
   13     130  FD  DOCUMENT DATA RECORD RESULT LABEL RECORD OMITTED
   14     140                             RECORDING MODE F.
   15     150  01  RESULT PICTURE X(120).
   16    C0201C WORKING-STORAGE SECTION.
   17     020  01  INPUT1.
   18     030      02  OLD       PICTURE 9(8)V99.
   19     040      02  DEP       PICTURE 9(8)V99.
   20     050      02  CHECK     PICTURE 9(8)V99.
   21     060      02  FILLER    PICTURE X(50).
   22     070  01  OUTPUT3.
   23     080      02  OLDX      PICTURE Z(12).99.
   24     090      02  DEPX      PICTURE Z(12).99.
   25     100      02  CHECKX    PICTURE Z(12).99.
   26     110      02  BALX      PICTURE Z(12).99.
   27     120      02  FILLER    PICTURE X(60) VALUE SPACES.
   28     130  01  AUXILIARY.
   29     14C      02  BAL       PICTURE 9(8)V99.
   30     150      02  TEMPORARY PICTURE 9(8)V99.
   31     160      02  FILLER    PICTURE X(60).
   32    C3001C PROCEDURE DIVISION.
   33     020      OPEN INPUT DECK OUTPUT DOCUMENT.
   34     03C  PARAGRAPH1. READ DECK AT END GO TO FINISH.
   35     040      EXAMINE CARD REPLACING ALL SPACES BY ZERCS.
   36     050      MOVE CARD TO INPUT1.
   37     06C      ADD OLD, DEP GIVING TEMPORARY.
   38     070      SUBTRACT CHECK FROM TEMPORARY GIVING BAL.
   39     08C      MOVE OLD TO OLDX. MOVE DEP TO DEPX.
   40     09C      MOVE CHECK TC CHECKX. MOVE BAL TC BALX.
   41     100      WRITE RESULT FROM OUTPUT3 AFTER ADVANCING 1.
   42     110      GO TO PARAGRAPH1.
   43     12C  FINISH. CLOSE DECK DOCUMENT. STOP RUN.
```

FIGURE C–6
Computer listing
of account-
balancing program.

```
// EXEC

        5.00          8.00          4.00          9.00
        2.00           .50          1.20          1.30
       13.27          2.43         10.05          5.65
      121.92         51.72          5.23        168.41
        2.13          4.17          1.15          5.15
      234.53           .15        147.51         87.17
       62.87         27.82         16.17         74.52
      568.72          3.15         72.53        499.34
       38.42         29.14         49.53         18.03
```

FIGURE C–7
Computer output
giving answers to
account-balancing
problem.

COBOL coding form

All programming work is done on COBOL coding forms. Observe that:

1. Each character (letter, number, etc.) of the program is written in a separate "cell" of the coding form (Figure C–8).

0, 1, 2, 3, 4, 5, 6, 7, 8, 9
A, B, C, D, E, F, G, H, I, J, K, L, M, N, O, P, Q, R, S, T, U, V, W, X, Y, Z

+ Plus sign
− Minus sign
* Asterisk
/ Slash
= Equal sign
$ Dollar sign
, Comma (optional)
. Period or decimal point
; Semicolon (optional)
' Quotation mark
(Left parenthesis
) Right parenthesis
> "Greater than" symbol
< "Less than" symbol

FIGURE C–8
Characters used in COBOL programs. When a blank (space) must be inserted in the coding sheet we designate the blank by the letter b.

2. Each line of the coding form must be keypunched, character by character, into a card (Figure C–9). Thus the 80 columns of the coding form correspond to the 80 columns of the punched card, and the program corresponds to a deck of cards.
3. There are no lowercase characters. The letter O (Oh) is often written as ∅ to differentiate from 0 (zero).
4. Columns 1–3 are reserved for a three-digit *page number*. Page 1 is numbered 001, page 2, 002, and so on.
5. Columns 4–6 are reserved for *line numbers*. The first line number is 010, the second 020, and so on. Thus 001120 means page 1, line 120.
6. Column 8 is the beginning of margin A; column 12 of margin B.
7. Programs start at margin A and must not go beyond column 72.

The identification division

The identification division, the first of the four divisions of COBOL (Figure C–2, Lines 010 and 020), consists of only a few

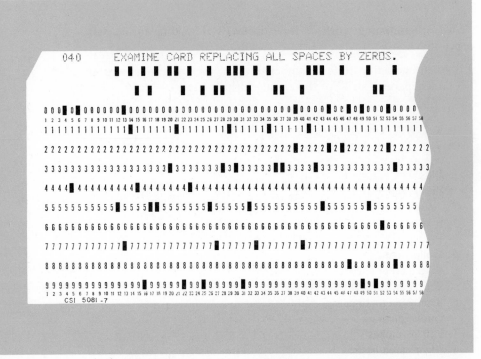

FIGURE C–9 A
COBOL punched
card.

lines to identify the program, the author, the data written, and so on. In our COBOL–SUBSET, the IDENTIFICATION DIVISION will always be written precisely as shown in Figure C-2.

The environment division

The environment division, the second of the four divisions of COBOL (Figure C-2, Lines 030 to 070), specifies the computer hardware to be used, storage size, console switches, and so on. *Before you write your program consult your computer center regarding the specifications to be used.*

In our COBOL–SUBSET the ENVIRONMENT DIVISION will always be written in precisely the same manner. Observe that the *input file* (input deck) to the system will be called DECK; the *output file* (output report or printout), will be called DOCUMENT.

The data division

The data division, the third of the four divisions of COBOL, contains the description of the files, records, and data items to be processed (Figure C-2, Lines 080 to 150 and Figure C-3, Lines

010 to 160). In our COBOL–SUBSET we will always have in the data division two sections: the FILE SECTION and WORKING-STORAGE SECTION.

In the FILE SECTION, the first file description—FD—(Figure C–2, Lines 090 to 110) states that the (input) file called DECK is made up of records, each to be called CARD. The LABEL REC-ORD (the special record at the beginning or end of the file) is OMITTED. Out of the several ways of RECORDING data (fixed word length, variable, unspecified), MODE F (fixed) is specified. The record CARD contains 80 characters as specified by PICTURE X(80). Later we will explain in detail the meaning of the PICTURE clause.

The second file description—FD—(Figure C–2, Lines 130 to 150) states that the (output) file (output report or printout) called DOCUMENT is made up of records (printout lines) to be called RESULT. The LABEL RECORD is again OMITTED and the RECORDING MODE is again F. The record RESULT contains 120 characters, as specified by PICTURE X(120).

In our COBOL–SUBSET the file section of the DATA DIVI-SION will always be written precisely as in Figure C–2.

In the WORKING–STORAGE SECTION (Figure C–3) we specify the names and types of variables and records we wish to use. Also we specify how the variables are organized into records.

The procedure division

In the procedure division we specify the steps the computer must carry out to solve our problem. All the assignment statements of our flowchart must be listed here in COBOL language.

WRITING A COBOL–SUBSET PROGRAM

In writing a COBOL–SUBSET program, we copy the IDENTI-FICATION DIVISION, the ENVIRONMENT DIVISION, and the FILE SECTION of the DATA DIVISION from Figure C–2. We write only the WORKING–STORAGE SECTION and the PROCEDURE DIVISION, so we will discuss only how to write these parts of the program.

Before we can go into detailed explanation of the program, however, we must describe a few specific features of the COBOL language.

The verbs MOVE, ADD, SUBTRACT, MULTIPLY, and DIVIDE

COBOL uses Englishlike statements to do computations (Figure C–10).

Example 1	Example 2
A ← B	A ← 0
MOVE B TO A	MOVE 0 TO A

Example 3	Example 4
B ← A + B	C ← A + B + C
ADD A TO B	ADD A AND B TO C
	ADD A, B TO C

Example 5	Example 6
COUNTER ← COUNTER + 1	C ← A + B
ADD 1 TO COUNTER	ADD A AND B GIVING C

Example 7	Example 8
D ← A + B + C	A ← A − B
ADD A, B, C GIVING D	SUBTRACT B FROM A

Example 9	Example 10
C ← A − B	D ← A − B − C
SUBTRACT B FROM A GIVING C	SUBTRACT B AND C FROM A
	GIVING D

Example 11	Example 12
B ← A * B	C ← A * B
MULTIPLY A BY B	MULTIPLY A BY B GIVING C

Example 13	Example 14
A ← A / B	C ← A / B
DIVIDE B INTO A	DIVIDE B INTO A GIVING C

Example 15	Example 16
D ← A + B − C	E ← A + B − C − D
ADD A, B GIVING X	ADD A, B GIVING X
SUBTRACT C FROM X GIVING D	ADD C, D GIVING Y
	SUBTRACT Y FROM X GIVING E

Example 17	Example 18
F ← A * B + C / D + E	F ← A * B * C + D − E
MULTIPLY A BY B GIVING X	MULTIPLY A BY B GIVING X1
DIVIDE D INTO C GIVING Y	MULTIPLY X1 BY C GIVING X2
ADD X, Y, E GIVING F	ADD X2, D GIVING X3
	SUBTRACT E FROM X3 GIVING F

FIGURE C–10
Sample COBOL
assignment
statements.

Watch for statements which do *not* have the word GIVING. For example, if A is 1 and B is 2, then after the assignment statement in Example 3 is carried out, B will be 3. Also if A is 1, B is 2, and C is 3, then after the assignment statement in Example 4 is carried out, C will be 6. Observe that you must not have TO and GIVING in the same statement.

Observe in Examples 15 to 18 that some assignment statements from the flowcharts require the introduction of auxiliary variables and the use of several COBOL statements.

Watch for certain illegal statements of COBOL. You cannot write: (1) ADD A TO 5 because you are not allowed to add to a number (literal), (2) SUBTRACT B FROM 3 because you are not allowed to subtract from a number (literal), (3) MULTIPLY 15 BY X because you are not allowed to multiply a number (literal), (4) DIVIDE A INTO 7, because you are not allowed to divide a number (literal).

The COMPUTE verb

Simple assignment statements can be easily written with the verbs ADD, SUBTRACT, MULTIPLY, and DIVIDE. For more complicated assignment statements, it is more convenient to use the COMPUTE verb. You can translate any of the assignment statements from the flowcharts by replacing the left arrow ($\leftarrow$) with the equal sign ($=$) and starting the statement with the verb COMPUTE. Figure C–11 shows some valid COBOL assignment statements.

FIGURE C–11 Sample COBOL assignment statements using the verb COMPUTE.

```
COMPUTE A = B
COMPUTE A = 0
COMPUTE B = A + B
COMPUTE C = A + B + C
COMPUTE COUNTER = COUNTER + 1
COMPUTE D = A + B − C
COMPUTE E = A + B − C − D
COMPUTE F = A * B + C / D + E
COMPUTE F = A * B * C + D − E
COMPUTE C = P1 * W1 + P2 * W2 + P3 * W3 + P4 * W4 + P5 * W5 + RATE * W
```

In writing these assignment statements, we insert a space (blank) ahead and after each of the signs: $=, +, -, *, /$.

HOW TO TRANSLATE A FLOWCHART INTO COBOL

The left side of Figure C–12 again shows the flowchart for the account-balancing problem. The right side shows the four steps in our method of translating flowcharts into COBOL.

Step 1   Translate each input statement directly. The names of the variables do not appear, and only the box number is affixed to the word INPUT, and so you

MOVE CARD TO INPUT1.

FIGURE C–12
How to translate
a flowchart into
COBOL.

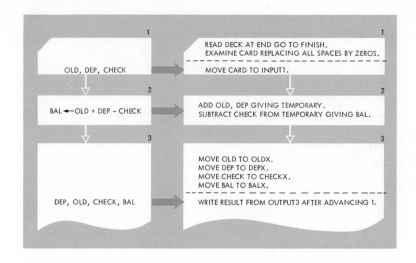

> **Step 2**   The assignment statements from the flowchart are translated into COBOL. Observe in Figure C–12 the auxiliary variable TEMPORARY. In flowchart language the first COBOL statement would be written as:

$$\text{TEMPORARY} \leftarrow \text{OLD} + \text{DEPOSIT}$$

The second statement as:

$$\text{BAL} \leftarrow \text{TEMPORARY} - \text{CHECK}$$

Instead of the two separate COBOL statements we could have simply written:

$$\text{COMPUTE BAL} = \text{OLD} + \text{DEP} - \text{CHECK.}$$

Observe that now we do not need the auxiliary variable TEMPORARY.

> **Step 3**   In COBOL before we produce our answers we must edit all the variables. We will do editing by introducing a new set of *display* variables, corresponding to the output variables in the flowchart. In our COBOL–SUBSET we will designate the display variables by adding an X to the name of each variable. Thus, instead of printing OLD, DEP, CHECK, BAL, we MOVE these variables to OLDX, DEPX, CHECKX, and BALX and then print these display variables. We hasten to add that this convention for our COBOL–SUBSET was instituted to make it easier to write COBOL programs. This convention has nothing to do with COBOL, and you could call these display variables DOG, CAT, RAT, and BAT.

> **Step 4**   Each output box from the flowchart is translated into

COBOL. The names of the variables do not appear. Only the box
number is affixed to the word OUTPUT. This is the reason we havê
OUTPUT3. The AFTER ADVANCING 1 advances the print
paper by one line and starts the printout at the first position. COBOL
does not automatically advance the paper after the verb WRITE.

THE ACCOUNT-BALANCING PROBLEM

The working-storage section

In the working-storage section of the program all the variables—
data names—of the problem must be specified.
First we write on Line 010 (Figure C–3):

WORKING–STORAGE SECTION.

Observe the period at the end of the statement. Every COBOL
statement must end in a period. Then we proceed to specify the
records needed in the problem.
On Line 020 we introduce the input record:

INPUT1.

In COBOL records are always on *level* 01. Observe in lines 020,
070 and 130 that the number 01 is written starting in margin A. The
names of records start at margin B. Observe that level 01 records
are made up of level 02 variables, and that level 02 is written starting at margin B. Input record INPUT1 has three data items: OLD,
DEP, CHECK, and a FILLER. What the PICTURE clauses mean
is explained below.

Numeric variables

The variables OLD, DEP, CHECK, and BAL are used for
computation; they are *numeric* variables. Figure C–13 shows how
numeric variables are specified in COBOL. In our case studies we
use mostly:

PICTURE 9(8)V99.

This PICTURE clause specifies that:

1. There are up to eight digits ahead of the decimal point.
2. There are two digits after the decimal point.
3. The field width is 10 (8 + 2).

Observe in the data sheet (Figure C–5) that all data is indeed
written with field width of 10. You must *not* include the decimal
point. The fact that there are two 9s after the V in the PICTURE

FIGURE C–13
PICTURE clauses
to specify numeric
variables.

	PICTURE	Field width	Examples and explanations
1	99999	5	12345 82932 00125 Five numeric digits
2	9(5)	5	Same as item 1
3	9999V99	6	1234.56 8293.21 0012.56 Four numeric digits ahead of the decimal point, two after the decimal point
4	9(4)V99	6	Same as item 3
5	9(8)V99*	10	12345678.90 00123456.78 Eight numeric digits ahead of the decimal point, two after the decimal point

* Will be used in most case studies.
Notes: The decimal point is not counted in the field width.
The V signifies the implied decimal point.
No minus sign (−) allowed.

clause implies that that there will be two digits after the decimal point. Thus:

5.00 is written as 500.
157 is written as 15700.
13.1 is written as 1310.

So far we have three variables in our INPUT1 record, with a total field width of 30 (3 times 10). But if you check Figure C–2, line 120, you observe that our input record, CARD, has a width of 80 characters specified by

CARD PICTURE X(80).

Here the letter X specifies that any character (numeric, alphabetic or special) may be used in the input record. So, following good programming practice in the input record, INPUT1, we add a FILLER with

PICTURE X(50).

Now INPUT1 has a total width of 80.

Display variables

Now we specify the output record (Figure C–3, Line 070):

OUTPUT3.

We have here four display variables: OLDX, DEPX, CHECKX, BALX, and a FILLER.

	PICTURE	*Field width*	*Examples and explanations*
1	*ZZZZZ*	5	12345 b1234 bb120 bbbbb Up to five numeric digits
2	*Z(5)*	5	Same as item 1
3	*ZZZ.999*	7	123.456 b12.345 bb1.201 bbb.000 Up to three digits ahead of the decimal point, decimal point, three digits after the decimal point
4	*Z(3).999*	7	Same as item 3
5*	*Z(12).99*	15	123456789012.34 bbbbbbbbbbbb.00 Up to twelve digits ahead of the decimal point, decimal point, two digits after the decimal point

* Will be used in most case studies.
Notes: Decimal point is counted in field width.
  All leading zeros ahead of decimal point suppressed.
  0s after decimal point printed.
  No minus sign (−) allowed.

FIGURE C–14
PICTURE clauses
to specify display
variables.

Figure C–14 shows the PICTURE clauses to be used with display variables. In our case studies we will use mostly

PICTURE Z(12).99.

meaning that:

1. Fields with the width of 15 will be used in the printout (12 + decimal point + 2).
2. The decimal point will be printed (taking one position out of the 15).
3. Two digits will be printed after the decimal point.
4. There may be up to 12 digits ahead of the decimal point.
5. Leading zeros will be suppressed (Z is the initial for *zero* suppression).

So far we have four variables in our OUTPUT3 record, with a total field width of 60. Checking in Figure C–2, line 150, observe that our output record RESULT has a field width of 120 characters specified by

RESULT PICTURE X(120).

So we add a FILLER specified by

PICTURE X(60) VALUE SPACES.

The last clause will clear the FILLER (with blanks or SPACES). If we fail to add the clause, the computer may print the garbage occupying the FILLER.

If you check the flowchart in Figure C–12 you observe that we still have two computational variables to specify: BAL and TEMPORARY. All variables must be listed and so on line 130 (Figure C–3) we establish an AUXILIARY record with these variables and a FILLER to create a total field width of 80 characters.

Negative numbers

The business world rarely uses negative numbers. In all our work so far we have tacitly assumed that none of the numbers are negative. If you must include negative numbers in your computations you need different PICTURE clauses.

The PICTURE clause for numeric variables to include negative numbers must start with an S. So instead of 99999 or 9(8)V99, we write: S99999 or S9(8)V99. To show the minus sign (−) in printout, for display variables we must replace Z by −. So instead of ZZZZ or Z(12).99, we write: −−−− or −(12).99.

When we write a negative number on the data sheet we do not write the minus (−) sign in front of the number, but *overpunch* it in the position of the last (far right) digit of the number. For example, −25.22 would be punched as:

2522

The procedure division

In the procedure division we first write on line 010 at margin A (Figure C–4):

PROCEDURE DIVISION.

Observe that the statement is terminated by a period. Every COBOL statement must be terminated by a period, followed by a space.

In line 020 you OPEN (margin B) the two files DECK and DOCUMENT. (These were defined in lines 100 and 130 in Figure C–2.) These two lines of the PROCEDURE DIVISION will be the same in every COBOL program you write.

In line 030 you start the input statement. Observe that COBOL programs are divided into paragraphs; so we start in line 030 our

PARAGRAPH1 of the program. Paragraphs must start at margin A. (Do not forget the space after the period.) Now we READ our INPUT file DECK. We also specify that after the last record is read, control is to be transferred to the last paragraph of the program, FINISH.

In line 040 we EXAMINE the record CARD (defined in Figure C–2, line 100) which we just READ. COBOL reads spaces (blanks) not as 0s but as spaces. So we must tell the compiler: EXAMINE CARD REPLACING ALL SPACES BY ZEROS.[3] (If you write the 0s yourself in your input card, this statement is unnecessary.) In line 050 we MOVE our CARD to INPUT1 so we can start our assignment statements.

Lines 030 to 050 will be similar in all programs.

Lines 060 and 070 are the assignment statements to do the calculations.

Lines 080 and 090 edit all numeric variables by using the MOVE verb.

In line 100 we WRITE one record called RESULT (defined in Figure C–2, line 130) FROM OUTPUT3, that is, our output record. Printing is done AFTER ADVANCING 1., which advances the paper in the printer by one line.

Line 110 transfers control back to PARAGRAPH1 to read another card.

Line 120 is the last paragraph in our program: FINISH. Here the two files, DECK and DOCUMENT, are closed. The RUN is stopped. This last paragraph will be similar in all programs.

Reserved words of COBOL

Choosing names for your variables ordinarily presents no problem. You cannot use more than 30 letters or numbers, and at least one of the characters must be a letter. However, you must avoid the use of the *reserved* words of COBOL. A typical list is shown in Figure C–15. Consult your computing center for the precise list used in your implementation.

> ### Do not write any COBOL programs
> ### before you know your reserved words

In addition, in our COBOL–SUBSET you must not use the words DECK, DOCUMENT, CARD, or RESULT, because we used them in Figure C–2.

---

[3] WATBOL does not conform to standard COBOL in this respect and so does not require this statement.

ABOUT	ENDING-FILE-LABEL	MODE	RESERVE
ACCEPT	ENDING-TAPE-LABEL	MODULES	REVERSED
ADD	END-OF-FILE	MOVE	REWIND
ADDRESS	END-OF-TAPE	MULTIPLE	RIGHT
ADVANCING	ENTER	MULTIPLIED	ROUNDED
AFTER	ENVIRONMENT	MULTIPLY	RUN
ALL	EQUAL		
ALPHABETIC	ERROR	NEGATIVE	SAME
ALPHANUMERIC	EVERY	NEXT	SECTION
ALTER	EXAMINE	NO	SELECT
ALTERNATE	EXCEEDS	NO-MEMORY-DUMP	SENTENCE
AN	EXIT	NOT	SENTINEL
AND	EXPONENTIATED		SEQUENCED
APPLY		NOTE	SIGN
ARE	FD	NUMERIC	SIGNED
AREA	FILE		SIZE
AT	FILE-CONTROL	OBJECT-COMPUTER	SOURCE-COMPUTER
	FILLER	OBJECT-PROGRAM	SPACE
BEFORE	FIRST	OCCURS	SPECIAL-NAMES
BEGINNING	FLOAT	OF	STANDARD
BEGINNING-FILE-LABEL	FOR	OFF	STATUS
BEGINNING-TAPE-LABEL	FORMAT	OMITTED	STOP
BITS	FROM	ON	SUBTRACT
BLANK		OPEN	SUPERVISOR
BLOCK	GIVING	OPTIONAL	SUPPRESS
BY	GO	OR	SYNCHRONIZED
	GREATER	OTHERWISE	
CHARACTER		OUTPUT	
CHECK	HASHED		TALLY
CLASS	HIGH VALUE	PERFORM	TALLYING
CLOCK-UNITS		PICTURE	TAPE
CLOSE	IF	PLACE	TEST-PATTERN
COBOL	IN	PLUS	THAN
COMPUTATIONAL	INCLUDE	POINT	THEN
COMPUTE	INPUT	POSITION	THROUGH or THRU
CONFIGURATION	INPUT-OUTPUT	POSITIVE	TIMES
CONSTANT	INTO	PREPARED	TO
CONTAINS	I-O-CONTROL	PRIORITY	
CONTROL	IS	PROCEDURE	UNEQUAL
COPY		PROCEED	UNTIL
CORRESPONDING	JUSTIFIED	PROTECT	UPON
		PURGE-DATE	UPPER-BOUND
DATA	LABEL		USAGE
DATE-WRITTEN	LEADING	QUOTE	USE
DECLARATIVES	LEAVING		
DEFINE	LEFT	RANGE	VALUE
DEPENDING	LESS	READ	VARYING
DIGIT	LIBRARY	RECORD	
DISPLAY	LINE	RECORD-COUNT	WHEN
DIVIDE	LOCATION	RECORDING	WITH
DIVIDED	LOCK	REDEFINES	WORK
DIVISION	LOWER-BOUND	REEL	
DOLLAR	LOW-VALUE	REEL-NUMBER	
		RENAMES	WORKING-STORAGE
ELSE	MEMORY	RENAMING	WRITE
END	MEMORY-DUMP	REPLACING	
ENDING	MINUS	RERUN	ZERO (ZEROS, ZEROES)

FIGURE C–15
Typical COBOL
reserved words.

One certain way to avoid using reserved words is to add a number at the end. For example, INPUT is a reserved word, but INPUT1, INPUT25 are not reserved. OUTPUT is a reserved word, but OUTPUT0, OUTPUT1, OUTPUT100 are not.

The DISPLAY verb

The DISPLAY verb is very convenient when only a limited amount of data is to be produced. For example, in the account-balancing problem, you can produce your answers by writing:

DISPLAY OLDX, DEPX, CHECKX, BALX.

or more simply:

DISPLAY OUTPUT3.

In order to advance the paper in the printer you need to know how to print *nothing* or an *empty* line. Since blanks are characters you need only learn how to print *literals*. If you write:

DISPLAY 'ANDREW VAZSONYI'.

the computer will print the author's name. In other words, the computer will print literally the characters in the quote marks. If you write:

DISPLAY.

the computer will print nothing on the line and will advance the paper by one line.

Figure C–16 presents a new version of the PROCEDURE DIVISION of the account-balancing problem.

Observe that in line 030 we print *headers* of width 15 for the

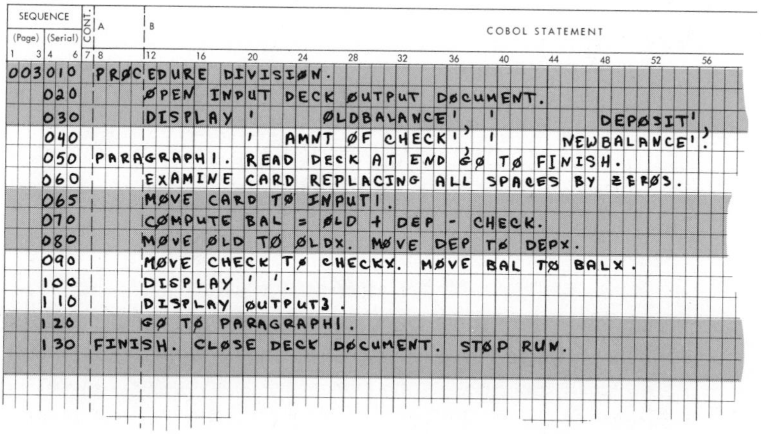

```
SEQUENCE
(Page) (Serial)                    COBOL STATEMENT
003010   PROCEDURE DIVISION.
   020       OPEN INPUT DECK OUTPUT DOCUMENT.
   030       DISPLAY '     OLDBALANCE' '        DEPOSIT'
   040                 '  AMNT OF CHECK'         'NEWBALANCE'.
   050   PARAGRAPHI. READ DECK AT END GO TO FINISH.
   060       EXAMINE CARD REPLACING ALL SPACES BY ZEROS.
   065       MOVE CARD TO INPUTI.
   070       COMPUTE BAL = OLD + DEP - CHECK.
   080       MOVE OLD TO OLDX. MOVE DEP TO DEPX.
   090       MOVE CHECK TO CHECKX. MOVE BAL TO BALX.
   100       DISPLAY ' '.
   110       DISPLAY OUTPUT3.
   120       GO TO PARAGRAPHI.
   130   FINISH. CLOSE DECK DOCUMENT. STOP RUN.
```

FIGURE C–16
Alternate PROCEDURE DIVISION for account-balancing problem.

output columns; in line 070 we COMPUTE BAL. In line 100 we advance the paper, and in line 110 we print the answers.

If you use the DISPLAY verb in a program, you must not use the WRITE verb because in some implementations the sequence of the printout will be garbled.

SUMMARY RULES OF COBOL-SUBSET

For convenience, the most important rules you need to know to write programs in our COBOL-SUBSET are summarized below:

1. Working-storage section
    All records are at level 01.
    All variables are at level 02.
2. Numeric PICTURE clause

    PICTURE 9(8)V99.

    or

    PICTURE S9(8)V99.

    if the variables may become negative.
3. Display PICTURE clause

    PICTURE   Z(12).99.

    or

    PICTURE   −(12).99.

    if the variables may become negative.
4. Fillers
    Fillers use X code for PICTURE clause. Input records must total 80 characters, output record must total 120 characters and include the clause VALUE SPACES.
5. Procedure division
    a. *Variables.* Variables cannot use more than 30 characters and may use letters and numbers, but at least one character must be a letter. Variable names must not be the reserved words of COBOL of your installation or the special words in COBOL-SUBSET: DECK, CARD, DOCUMENT, and RESULT.
    b. *Spaces.* There must be a space before and after each sign: =, +, −, *, /, and a space after each period. In mathematical formulas, there must be a space before the opening parenthesis and after the closing parenthesis. There must *not* be a space after the opening parenthesis or before the closing parenthesis.

    c. *Statements.* There must be a period after each statement. Statements must be in columns 12–72. Paragraphs start at column 8. Statements may run over from one line of coding sheet to others, or several statements may be on the same line.

    d. *Data sheet.* Use mostly the field width of 10 for PICTURE 9(8)V99, and do not include the decimal point. It is implied that the decimal point is two places to the left. The last digit is placed in columns 10, 20, and so on.

HOW TO PREPARE A COBOL PROGRAM

Step 1 Working-storage section. Choose data names and lay out the input, output, and auxiliary records and variables. Watch for reserved words. Use numeric PICTURE clauses for input and computations. Use display PICTURE clauses for output.

Step 2 Procedure division. Take care of opening preliminaries. Read your input. Translate your flowchart into COBOL assignment statements. MOVE variables to output. Take care of printing and final statements in the program.

Step 3 Prepare the data sheet. Use no decimal points in the data.

Step 4 Assemble the program into:

1. Copy of Figure C–2.
2. Working-storage section.
3. Procedure division.
4. Data sheet.

Step 5 Add control statements 0.

Step 6 Keypunch your deck.

SOME ILLUSTRATIVE COBOL PROGRAMS

The invoice calculation

In preparing a COBOL program for the invoice calculation, we first inspect the flowchart (Figure E–1, Appendix two, Chapter E). Observe that we need the numeric variables LENGTH, PRICE, COST, BASE, and the display variables LENGTHX, PRICEX, COSTX, BASEX. Figures C–17 and C–18 show the WORKING-STORAGE SECTION.

Note the FILLERS we have used in the output record. Our purpose is to spread the data in the printout to improve readability and appearance. We also introduce two auxiliary records called

FIGURE C–17
WORKING–
STORAGE
SECTION for
invoice calculation.

```
002010 WORKING-STORAGE SECTION.
   020 01  INPUT1.
   030 02    LENGTH     PICTURE 9(8)V99.
   040 02    PRICE      PICTURE 9(8)V99.
   050 02    BASE       PICTURE 9(8)V99.
   060 02    FILLER     PICTURE X(50).
   070 01  OUTPUT3.
   080 02    FILLER     PICTURE X(10) VALUE SPACES.
   090 02    LENGTHX    PICTURE Z(12).99.
   100 02    FILLER     PICTURE X(5)  VALUE SPACES.
   110 02    PRICEX     PICTURE Z(12).99.
   120 02    FILLER     PICTURE X(5)  VALUE SPACES.
   130 02    BASEX      PICTURE Z(12).99.
   140 02    FILLER     PICTURE X(5)  VALUE SPACES.
   150 02    COSTX      PICTURE Z(12).99.
   160 02    FILLER     PICTURE X(35) VALUE SPACES.
   170 01  AUXILIARY.
   180 02    COST       PICTURE 9(8)V99.
   190 02    FILLER     PICTURE X(70).
```

HEADLINE and NOTHING.[4] We will use these records to print headlines to mark the columns in the output.

Figure C–19 shows the PROCEDURE DIVISION. Line 040 advances the paper in the printer by three lines. If instead of 3 we write 0, the printer will advance the paper to the next page.

Observe the use of the verb COMPUTE in Line 080. This saves us the trouble of introducing auxiliary variables.

Figure C–20 shows the data sheet.

FIGURE C–18
WORKING–
STORAGE
SECTION for
invoice calculation
(continued).

```
003010 01  HEADLINE.
   020 02    FILLER  PICTURE X(20) VALUE 'LENGTH OF MATERIAL'.
   030 02    FILLER  PICTURE X(20) VALUE 'PRICE OF MATERIAL'.
   040 02    FILLER  PICTURE X(20) VALUE 'BASE PRICE'.
   050 02    FILLER  PICTURE X(20) VALUE 'COST TO BE CHARGED'.
   060 02    FILLER  PICTURE X(40) VALUE SPACES.
   070 01  NOTHING.
   080 02    FILLER  PICTURE X(120) VALUE SPACES.
```

Sales analysis

The flowchart for the sales analysis problem is shown in Figure E–2.

To help lay out the WORKING–STORAGE SECTION, Figure C–21 shows the input/output layout as it will appear in the cards

---

[4] There are many alternatives to print empty lines which we do not discuss in this text.

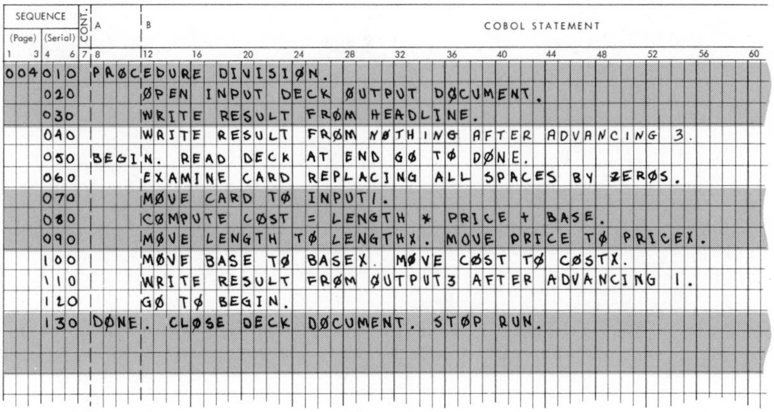

FIGURE C-19
PROCEDURE
DIVISION for
invoice calculation.

SEQUENCE				COBOL STATEMENT
(Page)	(Serial)			

```
004010    PROCEDURE DIVISION.
   020        OPEN INPUT DECK OUTPUT DOCUMENT.
   030        WRITE RESULT FROM HEADLINE.
   040        WRITE RESULT FROM NOTHING AFTER ADVANCING 3.
   050    BEGIN. READ DECK AT END GO TO DONE.
   060        EXAMINE CARD REPLACING ALL SPACES BY ZEROS.
   070        MOVE CARD TO INPUT.
   080        COMPUTE COST = LENGTH * PRICE + BASE.
   090        MOVE LENGTH TO LENGTHX. MOVE PRICE TO PRICEX.
   100        MOVE BASE TO BASEX. MOVE COST TO COSTX.
   110        WRITE RESULT FROM OUTPUT3 AFTER ADVANCING 1.
   120        GO TO BEGIN.
   130    DONE. CLOSE DECK DOCUMENT. STOP RUN.
```

and in the printout. Each input is provided with two cards. Observe that the first card has five, the second two data items.

In the output we will have a line with two data items, then a blank line, then a line with six data items, followed by a line with three data items. We will have two blank lines between each set of outputs.

The WORKING-STORAGE SECTION is shown in the two parts of Figure C-22. Corresponding to the flowchart, we introduce two input records—INPUT1 and INPUT3, and three output records—OUTPUT5, OUTPUT6, and OUTPUT7. We also need an AUXILIARY record for WDAY, WEND, TOTAL, and AVER.

The PROCEDURE DIVISION is shown in Figure C-23. Observe that in the first paragraph we read the first CARD, and then we MOVE it to INPUT1 and do our calculations. In the second paragraph, we do the same thing for the second CARD and then MOVE it to INPUT3.

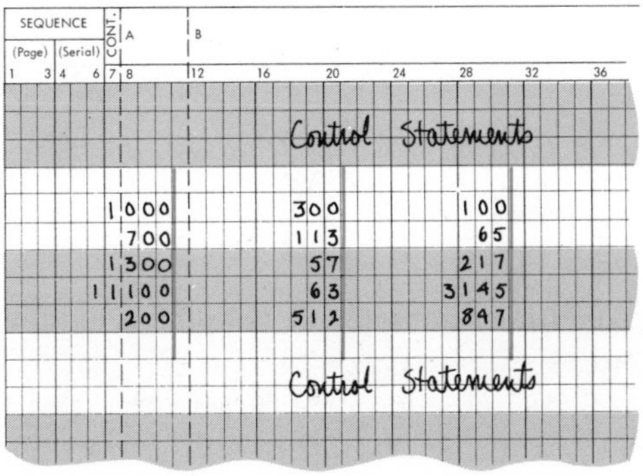

FIGURE C-20
Data for invoice
calculation.

SEQUENCE				
(Page)	(Serial)			

```
                   Control Statements

        1000        300        100
         700        113         65
        1300         57        217
       11100         63       3145
         200         512        897

                   Control Statements
```

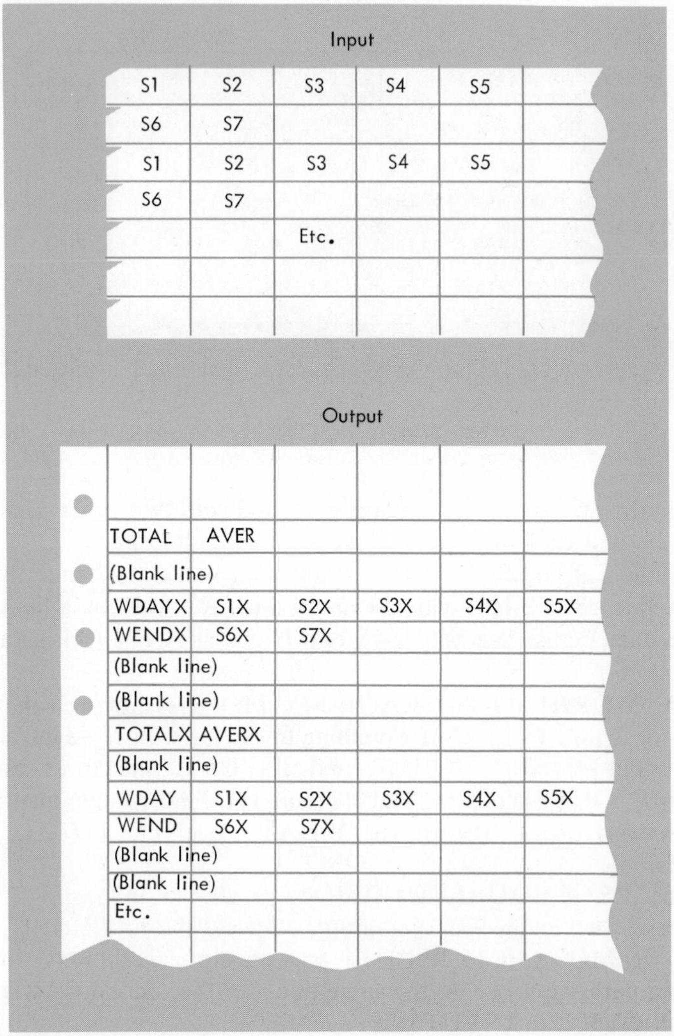

FIGURE C–21
Input/output
layout for sales
analysis.

Input

S1	S2	S3	S4	S5	
S6	S7				
S1	S2	S3	S4	S5	
S6	S7				
		Etc.			

Output

TOTAL	AVER				
(Blank line)					
WDAYX	S1X	S2X	S3X	S4X	S5X
WENDX	S6X	S7X			
(Blank line)					
(Blank line)					
TOTALX	AVERX				
(Blank line)					
WDAY	S1X	S2X	S3X	S4X	S5X
WEND	S6X	S7X			
(Blank line)					
(Blank line)					
Etc.					

Paragraph 3 with the MOVE and WRITE statements is self-explanatory.

Figure C–24 shows the data input sheet.

Counting, keeping a running total, and computing the average

The flowchart for counting and keeping a cumulative total is shown in Figure E–6. To make the problem more practical, we will add an extra computation in the flowchart. After all the records are read, we will print the average value of the amounts.

```
SEQUENCE      CONT. A    B                                    COBOL STATEMENT
(Page)(Serial)
1   3 4   6   7     8    12   16   20   24   28   32   36   40   44   48   52   56
002 010             WØRKING-STØRAGE SECTIØN.
    020             01   INPUT1.
    030                  02   S1              PICTURE 9(8)V99.
    040                  02   S2              PICTURE 9(8)V99.
    050                  02   S3              PICTURE 9(8)V99.
    060                  02   S4              PICTURE 9(8)V99.
    070                  02   S5              PICTURE 9(8)V99.
    080                  02   FILLER          PICTURE X(30).
    090             01   INPUT3.
    100                  02   S6              PICTURE 9(8)V99.
    110                  02   S7              PICTURE 9(8)V99.
    120                  02   FILLER          PICTURE X(60).
    130             01   ØUTPUT5.
    140                  02   TØTALX          PICTURE Z(12).99.
    150                  02   AVERX           PICTURE Z(12).99.
    160                  02   FILLER          PICTURE X(90) VALUE SPACES.
```

FIGURE C–22a WORKING–STORAGE SECTION for sales analysis problem.

```
SEQUENCE      CONT. A    B                                    COBOL STATEMENT
(Page)(Serial)
1   3 4   6   7     8    12   16   20   24   28   32   36   40   44   48   52   56
003 010             01   ØUTPUT6.
    020                  02   WDAYX           PICTURE Z(12).99.
    030                  02   S1X             PICTURE Z(12).99.
    040                  02   S2X             PICTURE Z(12).99.
    050                  02   S3X             PICTURE Z(12).99.
    060                  02   S4X             PICTURE Z(12).99.
    070                  02   S5X             PICTURE Z(12).99.
    080                  02   FILLER          PICTURE X(30) VALUE SPACES.
    090             01   ØUTPUT7.
    100                  02   WENDX           PICTURE Z(12).99.
    110                  02   S6X             PICTURE Z(12).99.
    120                  02   S7X             PICTURE Z(12).99.
    130                  02   FILLER          PICTURE X(75) VALUE SPACES.
    140             01   AUXILIARY.
    150                  02   WDAY            PICTURE 9(8)V99.
    160                  02   WEND            PICTURE 9(8)V99.
    170                  02   TØTAL           PICTURE 9(8)V99.
    180                  02   AVER            PICTURE 9(8)V99.
    190                  02   FILLER          PICTURE X(40).
```

FIGURE C–22b WORKING–STORAGE SECTION for sales analysis problem (continued).

Figure C–25 shows the WORKING–STORAGE SECTION. Observe in the AUXILIARY record the variables COUNT and SUM; in the flowchart (Figure E–6), these variables are initialized to 0. We could accomplish this in COBOL by moving ZERO to the variables SUM and COUNT. However, we can do the same thing by adding to the PICTURE clause:

VALUE ZERO.

The PROCEDURE DIVISION is shown in Figure C–26. Observe that after the last CARD is read, control is transferred to

FIGURE C-23
PROCEDURE
DIVISION for sales
analysis problem.

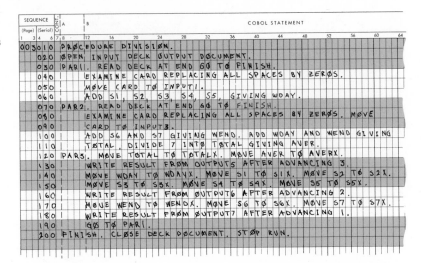

```
003010  PROCEDURE DIVISION.
   020      OPEN INPUT DECK OUTPUT DOCUMENT.
   030  PAR1. READ DECK AT END GO TO FINISH.
   040      EXAMINE CARD REPLACING ALL SPACES BY ZEROS.
   050      MOVE CARD TO INPUT1.
   060      ADD S1, S2, S3, S4, S5, GIVING WDAY.
   070  PAR2. READ DECK AT END GO TO FINISH.
   080      EXAMINE CARD REPLACING ALL SPACES BY ZEROS. MOVE
   090      CARD TO INPUT3.
   100      ADD S6 AND S7 GIVING WEND. ADD WDAY AND WEND GIVING
   110      TOTAL. DIVIDE 7 INTO TOTAL GIVING AVER.
   120  PAR3. MOVE TOTAL TO TOTALX. MOVE AVER TO AVERX.
   130      WRITE RESULT FROM OUTPUT5 AFTER ADVANCING 3.
   140      MOVE WDAY TO WDAYX. MOVE S1 TO S1X. MOVE S2 TO S2X.
   150      MOVE S3 TO S3X. MOVE S4 TO S4X. MOVE S5 TO S5X.
   160      WRITE RESULT FROM OUTPUT6 AFTER ADVANCING 2.
   170      MOVE WEND TO WENDX. MOVE S6 TO S6X. MOVE S7 TO S7X.
   180      WRITE RESULT FROM OUTPUT7 AFTER ADVANCING 1.
   190      GO TO PAR1.
   200  FINISH. CLOSE DECK DOCUMENT. STOP RUN.
```

FIGURE C-24
Data for sales
analysis problem.

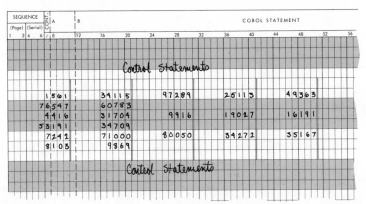

```
                    Control Statements

     1561      34115     97289     25113     49363
  76547        60783
   4416        31704      9916     19027     16191
  53191        34709
   7242        71000     80050     34272     35167
   8103         9869

                    Control Statements
```

FIGURE C-25
WORKING-
STORAGE
SECTION for
counting and
keeping a running
total.

```
002010  WORKING-STORAGE SECTION.
   020  01  INPUT21.
   030      02  A              PICTURE 9(8)V99.
   040      02  FILLER         PICTURE X(70).
   050  01  OUTPUT43.
   060      02  COUNTX         PICTURE Z(15).
   070      02  AX             PICTURE Z(12).99.
   080      02  SUMX           PICTURE Z(12).99.
   090      02  FILLER         PICTURE X(75) VALUE SPACES.
   100  01  AUXILIARY.
   110      02  COUNT          PICTURE 9(10) VALUE ZERO.
   120      02  SUM            PICTURE 9(8)V99 VALUE ZERO.
   130      02  AVERAGE        PICTURE 9(8)V99.
   140      02  FILLER         PICTURE X(50).
   150  01  FINAL-OUTPUT
   160      02  FILLER         PICTURE X(15) VALUE SPACES.
   170      02  FILLER         PICTURE X(10) VALUE 'AVERAGE = '.
   180      02  AVERAGEY       PICTURE Z(10).
   190      02  FILLER         PICTURE X(85) VALUE SPACES.
```

```
SEQUENCE                        COBOL STATEMENT
(Page) (Serial)
1   3 4   6 7 8   12    16    20    24    28    32    36    40    44    48    52    56    60    64
003010  PROCEDURE DIVISION.
   020     OPEN INPUT DECK OUTPUT DOCUMENT.
   030  PAR1. READ DECK AT END GO TO WRAPUP.
   040     EXAMINE CARD REPLACING ALL SPACES BY ZEROS.
   050     MOVE CARD TO INPUT21.
   060     ADD 1 TO COUNT.
   070     ADD A TO SUM.
   080     MOVE A TO AX. MOVE COUNT TO COUNTX. MOVE SUM TO SUMX.
   090     WRITE RESULT FROM OUTPUT43 AFTER ADVANCING 1.
   100     GO TO PAR1.
   110  WRAPUP. DIVIDE COUNT INTO SUM GIVING AVERAGE.
   120     MOVE AVERAGE TO AVERAGEX.
   130     WRITE RESULT FROM FINAL-OUTPUT AFTER ADVANCING 3.
   140  DONE. CLOSE DECK DOCUMENT. STOP RUN.
```

FIGURE C–26
PROCEDURE
DIVISION for
counting and
keeping a running
total.

line 110 to paragraph WRAPUP. Here we compute the AVERAGE and move it to AVERAGEX.

Finally, in lines 130 and 140 we write our answers and complete the program. Figure C–27 shows the data.

BRANCHING PROBLEMS: DECISION MAKING AND LOGICAL OPERATIONS

Commission calculation

The flowchart for this problem is shown in Figure 2.10, Chapter 2. The COBOL program and data are shown in Figures C–28, C–29, and C–30. Note in Figure C–29, lines 060 and 070, how branching is accomplished in COBOL.

The flowchart calls for a transfer of control to Box 10 if the amount is less than (or equal to) $150.00; and to Box 30 if the amount is over $150.00. The corresponding COBOL statement in lines 060 and 070 says the same thing, but in a slightly different manner.

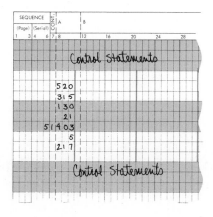

FIGURE C–27
Data for counting
and keeping a
running total.

FIGURE C–28
WORKING–
STORAGE
SECTION for
commission
calculation.

```
SEQUENCE      A   B                                    COBOL STATEMENT
(Page)(Serial) CONT.
002010  WORKING-STORAGE SECTION.
   020  01  INPUT.
   030      02  AMOUNT        PICTURE 9(8)V99.
   040      02  FILLER        PICTURE X(70).
   050  01  OUTPUT55.
   060      02  AMOUNTX       PICTURE Z(12).99.
   070      02  COMMISSIONX   PICTURE Z(12).99.
   080      02  FILLER        PICTURE X(90) VALUE SPACES.
   090  01  AUXILIARY.
   100      02  OVER          PICTURE 9(8)V99.
   110      02  BONUS         PICTURE 9(8)V99.
   120      02  COMMISSION    PICTURE 9(8)V99.
   130      02  FILLER        PICTURE X(50).
```

FIGURE C–29
PROCEDURE
DIVISION for
commission
calculation.

```
SEQUENCE      A   B                                    COBOL STATEMENT
(Page)(Serial) CONT.
003010  PROCEDURE DIVISION.
   020      OPEN INPUT DECK OUTPUT DOCUMENT.
   030  PAR1.  READ DECK AT END GO TO FINISH.
   040      EXAMINE CARD REPLACING ALL SPACES BY ZEROS.
   050      MOVE CARD TO INPUT.
   060  PAR5.  IF AMOUNT IS NOT GREATER THAN 150.00
   070          GO TO PAR10 ELSE GO TO PAR30.
   080  PAR10. MOVE 6.00 TO COMMISSION.
   090          GO TO PAR55.
   100  PAR30. SUBTRACT 150.00 FROM AMOUNT GIVING OVER.
   110      MULTIPLY 0.02 BY OVER GIVING BONUS.
   120      ADD 6.00 TO BONUS GIVING COMMISSION.
   130  PAR55. MOVE AMOUNT TO AMOUNTX.
   140      MOVE COMMISSION TO COMMISSIONX.
   150      WRITE RESULT FROM OUTPUT55 AFTER ADVANCING 1.
   160          GO TO PAR1.
   170  FINISH. CLOSE DECK DOCUMENT. STOP RUN.
```

FIGURE C–30
Data for
commission
calculation.

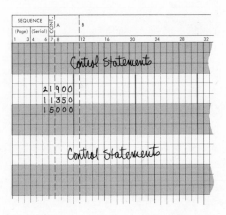

```
SEQUENCE      A   B
(Page)(Serial) CONT.
        Control Statements

            21900
            11350
            15000


        Control Statements
```

The rest of the COBOL program is self-explanatory.

COBOL has a variety of IF statements. The most important ones are:

IF A IS GREATER THAN B
IF A IS NOT GREATER THAN B
IF A IS LESS THAN B
IF A IS NOT LESS THAN B
IF A IS EQUAL TO B
IF A IS NOT EQUAL TO B

You can write, for example:

IF AMOUNT IS NOT GREATER THAN 150.00 MOVE 6.00 TO
COMMISSION ELSE COMPUTE COMMISSION = 6 + .02∗
(AMOUNT − 150).

You can also combine IF statements:

IF SEX = 1 AND SALARY IS GREATER THAN 150.00 GO TO
PAR10 ELSE GO TO PAR5.

IF COLOR = 1 OR COLOR = 2 MOVE A TO B ELSE
MOVE A TO C.

Nonnumeric comparisons

Suppose NAME-1 stands for Carson and NAME-2 for Hitch. then the statement:

NAME-1 IS LESS THAN NAME-2.

is true because Carson precedes Hitch in the alphabet. Such comparisons are necessary in data processing jobs like sorting and collating records.

Suppose CODE stands for the color of some material, and in the input data the colors RED, GREEN, BLACK, and WHITE are listed. You can make a test by writing

IF CODE = 'BLACK' GO TO PARAGRAPH1 ELSE GO TO
PARAGRAPH2.

Such comparisons are necessary programming jobs which involve classifying records.

Multiple branching: A classification problem

The flowchart for multiple branching, illustrating how to classify people by weight, is in Figure E–8, Appendix two. The COBOL

FIGURE C–31
WORKING-
STORAGE
SECTION for
classifying people
by weight.

```
SEQUENCE  CONT  A    B                          COBOL STATEMENT
(Page)(Serial)
002010  WORKING-STORAGE SECTION.
  020   01  INPUT.
  030     02  W              PICTURE 9(9)V9.
  040     02  FILLER         PICTURE X(70).
  050   01  OUTPUT.
  060     02  WX             PICTURE Z(13).9.
  070     02  CODEX          PICTURE Z(5).
  080     02  FILLER         PICTURE X(100) VALUE SPACES.
```

FIGURE C–32
PROCEDURE
DIVISION for
classifying people
by weight.

```
SEQUENCE  CONT  A    B                          COBOL STATEMENT
(Page)(Serial)
003010  PROCEDURE DIVISION.
  020     OPEN INPUT DECK OUTPUT DOCUMENT.
  030  PAR1.  READ DECK AT END GO TO FINISH.
  040     EXAMINE CARD REPLACING ALL SPACES BY ZEROS.
  050     MOVE CARD TO INPUT.
  060  P10.  IF W IS LESS THAN 100 GO TO P35 ELSE GO TO P15.
  070  P15.  IF W IS LESS THAN 170 GO TO P40 ELSE GO TO P20.
  080  P20.  IF W IS LESS THAN 205 GO TO P45 ELSE GO TO P25.
  090  P25.  IF W IS LESS THAN 240 GO TO P50 ELSE GO TO P30.
  100  P35.  MOVE 1 TO CODEX.  GO TO P60.
  110  P40.  MOVE 2 TO CODEX.  GO TO P60.
  120  P45.  MOVE 3 TO CODEX.  GO TO P60.
  130  P50.  MOVE 4 TO CODEX.  GO TO P60.
  140  P30.  MOVE 5 TO CODEX.  GO TO P60.
  150  P60.  MOVE W TO WX.
  160     WRITE RESULT FROM OUTPUT AFTER ADVANCING 1.
  170     GO TO PAR1.
  180  FINISH.  CLOSE DECK DOCUMENT.  STOP RUN.
```

program and data are shown in **Figures** C–31, C–32, and C–33.

We have simplified writing the COBOL program by providing a single output record with the variables WX and CODEX and transferring control with the aid of four IF statements.

FURTHER COBOL FEATURES

Mixed alphabetic and numeric input

So far in all our input records we have used only numeric data. The example below illustrates how to work with a record which has mixed alphabetic and numeric (alphanumeric) data.

Figures C–34, C–35, and C–36 show the commission program rewritten so that in the input record we have the name of the salesman followed by the amount of sale. There is only one technique we need to illustrate when writing the program. Namely, first we read in the record with a PICTURE clause having an X form, and then we MOVE the numeric data to a computational PICTURE with a 9 form.

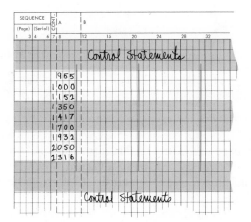

FIGURE C–33
Data for
classifying people
by weight.

```
SEQUENCE  C A B                          COBOL STATEMENT
(Page)(Serial)O
1  3 4  6 7 8   12   16   20   24   28   32   36   40   44   48   52   56   60   64
0 0 2 0 1 0  WORKING-STORAGE SECTION.
    0 2 0  0 1  INPUT1.
    0 3 0      0 2  ALPHABETIC-DATA      PICTURE X(30).
    0 4 0      0 2  NUMERIC-DATA         PICTURE X(10).
    0 5 0      0 2  FILLER               PICTURE X(40).
    0 6 0  0 1  OUTPUT55.
    0 7 0      0 2  SALESMANX            PICTURE X(30).
    0 8 0      0 2  AMOUNTX              PICTURE Z(12).99.
    0 9 0      0 2  COMMISSIONX          PICTURE Z(12).99.
    1 0 0      0 2  FILLER               PICTURE X(60) VALUE SPACES.
    1 1 0  0 1  AUXILIARY.
    1 2 0      0 2  AMOUNT               PICTURE 9(8)V99.
    1 3 0      0 2  OVER                 PICTURE 9(8)V99.
    1 4 0      0 2  BONUS                PICTURE 9(8)V99.
    1 5 0      0 2  COMMISSION           PICTURE 9(8)V99.
    1 6 0      0 2  FILLER               PICTURE X(40).
```

FIGURE C–34
WORKING–
STORAGE
SECTION for
mixed alphabetic
and numeric input.

```
SEQUENCE  C A B                          COBOL STATEMENT
(Page)(Serial)O
1  3 4  6 7 8   12   16   20   24   28   32   36   40   44   48   52   56   60   64
0 0 3 0 1 0  PROCEDURE DIVISION.
    0 2 0      OPEN INPUT DECK OUTPUT DOCUMENT.
    0 3 0  PAR1.  READ DECK AT END GO TO FINISH.
    0 4 0      MOVE CARD TO INPUT1.
    0 5 0      EXAMINE NUMERIC-DATA REPLACING ALL SPACES BY ZEROS.
    0 6 0      MOVE NUMERIC-DATA TO AUXILIARY.
             Continue Program
```

FIGURE C–35
PROCEDURE
DIVISION for
mixed alphabetic
and numeric input.

In the WORKING-STORAGE SECTION (Figure C–34), our
INPUT1 is split into two records—ALPHABETIC-DATA and
NUMERIC-DATA. The other two 01 level records—OUTPUT55
and AUXILIARY—are self-explanatory.

Look at the first five lines of the COBOL program in Figure
C–35. There is nothing new in the first three lines, but line 050 is:

EXAMINE NUMERIC–DATA REPLACING ALL SPACES BY
ZEROS.

We must do this in order to fill in the blanks with zeros. Then line
060 is:

MOVE NUMERIC–DATA TO AUXILIARY.

Observe that we do not specify that the record be moved directly
to AMOUNT. The reason is that COBOL does not allow you to
move an X record to a 9 record directly. You must move the record
either to an 01 level record, or to a record which is split into sub-
records. (You must move the record into a *group* record which is
not followed directly by a picture clause.)[5]

The rest of the program is not included in Figure C–35, as our
original program in Figure C–29 already contains all the essential
information.

COBOL allows many other ways to deal with mixed alphabetic
and numeric records.

FIGURE C–36
Data for mixed
alphabetic and
numeric input.

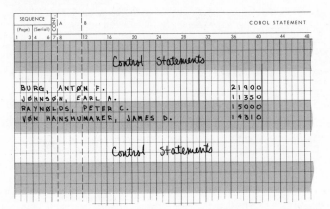

Mnemonic notation

So far we have tried to abbreviate the names of our variables
for the sake of simplicity. COBOL allows the use of more meaningful names which remind us of what variable we are referring to. For
example, we can use:

OLDBALANCE

or we are allowed (as you may have observed in Figures C–34 and
C–35) to hyphenate words:

---

[5] WATBOL does not have this restriction of standard COBOL and therefore
dealing with mixed alphabetic and numeric input is simple and does not require the
discussion presented here.

OLD-BALANCE
AMOUNT-OF-CHECK
NEW-BALANCE

Instead of using PARAGRAPH1 we could say:

PARAGRAPH-1.
START.
FIRST-PAR.
BEGIN-HERE.

or we could write:

GO TO LAST-INSTRUCTION.
GO TO WRAPUP.
GO TO BONUS-CALCULATION.
GO TO FEMALE-CASE.

You must *not* have a space between words representing a variable. For example OLD BALANCE is illegal. Also, you must *not* leave a space before or after a hyphen.

Avoiding auxiliary records

Most of our programs have had some variables which were parts neither of input nor of output records. COBOL allows introducing such variables without an auxiliary record by the use of 77-level variables. For example, in Figure C–3 we could have written:

WORKING-STORAGE SECTION.
77   BAL   PICTURE 9(8)V99.
77   TEMPORARY   PICTURE 9(8)V99.

The use of 77-level variables must be directly after the WORKING-STORAGE SECTION statement and must precede all other variables.

Printing literals, headers, and blank lines

We are not covering a new subject here; only summarizing. In discussing the invoice calculation we showed how literals and headers can be printed. We used the VALUE clause with PICTURE statements in the WORKING–STORAGE SECTION (Lines 010 to 080 in Figure C–18) and the corresponding WRITE statements in the PROCEDURE DIVISION (Figure C–19). We also showed how to skip a line in the printout (Line 040 in Figure C–19) and how to start a new page by using AFTER ADVANCING 0.

The PERFORM verb

In Figure C–23, look at the READ statements in Lines 030 – 040 and 070–080. It is a nuisance to repeat the same lines twice. But suppose we need to read ten cards. Do we have to repeat the two statements ten times? No. The PERFORM verb can save time. We write in the program (preferably just before the FINISH statement):

READING. READ DECK AT END GO TO FINISH. EXAMINE
CARD REPLACING ALL SPACES BY ZEROS.

(Here READING is a paragraph name; so the R must be in column A, that is, in column 8 on the coding sheet.) Now when we want to READ a card, we simply write in the program:

PERFORM READING.

(Of course we can use any other paragraph name instead of READ-ING.)

The PERFORM verb can do many other programming jobs. For example, see the flowchart in Figure E–26,[6] which shows how to compute the number of rabbits there will be in two years. We can translate this into COBOL without difficulty, but the PERFORM verb makes the job easier. First we translate Box 5, then write a paragraph for Boxes 10, 15, and 20. (Omit Box 25.) We call this paragraph RABBITS. Now if we write:

PERFORM RABBITS 24 TIMES.

the loop will be executed 24 times.

An alternate way to write the program is to omit setting MONTH to 1 in Box 5. Then when we write our new paragraph, RABBITS–ALTERNATE, we omit the last statement, that is, the incrementation of MONTH, the second statement in Box 20. We just write:

PERFORM RABBITS-ALTERNATE VARYING MONTH FROM 1
BY 1 UNTIL MONTH 24.

Then MONTH will be automatically incremented and the loop executed 24 times.

If we wish to vary a counter from 10 to 20 in increments of not 1 but, for example, 2, we would write the clause:

FROM 10 BY 2 UNTIL COUNTER 20.

There are some other useful options in connection with the PERFORM verb, but they will not be discussed here, as they are required only for more advanced work.

---

[6] The rest of this section assumes that you already covered Figure E–26 in Appendix two.

WHAT COMPLETE COBOL CAN DO FOR YOU

There are a number of limitations in our COBOL–SUBSET which can be remedied when you use Full COBOL.

You can make the computer produce edited printouts to meet a wide variety of user requirements. Appropriate headings, spacing of data, the layout of pages can all be easily arranged. Both alphabetic and numeric data can be printed in a manner to satisfy business requirements (Figure C–37).

1	$131.40 $ .08	Dollar sign
2	$128.51 $1.10 $.05	Floating dollar sign
3	25.17 DB 1.52 CR	Debit Credit
4	5,252.17 3,115,701.50	Comma to mark thousands, millions, etc.
5	$**1,252.71 $*72,512.18 $******.05	Leading asterisks to protect checks
6	$3.125.91 DB $712.00 CR $.81 CR	Floating dollar and debit, credit

FIGURE C–37
Sample COBOL printouts to illustrate editing of data.

Additional language techniques allow writing of more complex data processing programs in a simpler manner. COBOL is particularly suitable for working with many files and managing large amounts of data. In our COBOL–SUBSET we used only level 01 and 02 records. In full COBOL you can use groupings of data on many levels and can process groups of data as easily as we have processed elementary data items.

In all our examples we read a deck of cards and printed output reports. COBOL allows you to read or write on other input/output media, such as magnetic tapes or disks.

You must recognize that the COBOL–SUBSET of this chapter covers only the most elementary aspects of COBOL. It provides you with a basis for further study. Full COBOL is a powerful language for efficiently solving complicated data processing problems.

DISCUSSION QUESTIONS AND ASSIGNMENTS

1. What are the divisions of a COBOL program? For what are the divisions used? In what sequence must they appear in the program?

2. What are the "fixed segments" of COBOL–SUBSET programs you need only to copy from the book? State what the following words designate in the COBOL–SUBSET: DECK, DOCUMENT, RECORD, RESULT.

3. Describe the job control cards to be used in your computer installation. Where do you place these cards in the COBOL deck?

4. Describe the use of the COBOL coding form. In which column do you write the numbers, paragraph names, statements, level numbers? In which column are margins A and B?

5. Is the use of the period optional at the end of a statement?

6. Can you have only one statement in a paragraph? More than five?

7. Can you have two statements on the same line of the coding form? Do you have to start each statement on a new line?

8. Must each paragraph have a name?

9. Which of the following constants are not acceptable:
   a. 1234.56
   b. − 8.25
   c. 5,000.00
   d. 95.15 −
   e. 1000000
   f. + 25.73
   g. 542.
   h. = 142.51

10. What is the difference between the following constants:
    a. 512.00
    b. 512.000
    c. 512

11. How do you keypunch − 142.51?

12. If your flowchart has three input boxes and four output boxes, how many READ and WRITE statements will you have?

13. Which of the following are illegal paragraph names: PAR3, PAR-3, PARAGRAPH-17, FINISH-LAST, LAST-STATEMENT?

14. Below are given examples of assignment statements. Determine the value of the variables after the statements are executed. Mark the illegal statements:

   a. ADD   A   B   GIVING   C
   Before   2   5   3
   After   ?   ?   ?

   b. ADD   X TO Y
   Before   5   7
   After   ?   ?

   c. ADD   P TO Q GIVING X
   Before   2   3   5
   After   ?   ?   ?

d. ADD   A, B, C GIVING D
Before 4   3   2   1
After   ?   ?   ?   ?

e. ADD   A AND B TO C GIVING D
Before 4   3   2   1
After   ?   ?   ?   ?

f. ADD   A, B, C TO D
Before 1   2   3   4
After   ?   ?   ?   ?

g. ADD   2 TO COUNTER
Before   10
After   ?

h. SUBTRACT P FROM Q
Before   10   15
After   ?   ?

i. SUBTRACT X FROM Y GIVING A
Before   5   10   1
After   ?   ?   ?

j. MULTIPLY P BY A
Before   5   10
After   ?   ?

k. MULTIPLY A BY C GIVING B
Before   2   3   3
After   ?   ?   ?

l. DIVIDE A INTO B
Before 2   6
After   ?   ?

m. DIVIDE A INTO B GIVING C
Before 2   6   1
After   ?   ?   ?

15. When do you use TO and when do you use GIVING?

16. Each of the following statements is illegal. Explain why.
a. ADD COUNTER TO 1.
b. SUBTRACT X FROM 0.
c. MULTIPLY 5 BY A.
d. DIVIDE X INTO 2.
e. MULTIPLY A TIMES B GIVING C.
f. DIVIDE X BY Y.
g. ADD TWO TO COUNTER.

17. Assume values of your own choice for the variables on the right-hand side of the statements in Figure C–11 and evaluate the left-hand side values.

18. What is the WORKING–STORAGE SECTION?

19. When do you use numeric variables? When do you use display variables? Illustrate appropriate PICTURE clauses. When do you count the decimal point in the field width?

20. Give examples of PICTURE clauses for different field widths and number of digits after the decimal point. Illustrate numeric, display, and negative variables.

21. Illustrate the use of the verb DISPLAY. Can you mix it with WRITE statements?

22. Describe the use of FILLERS.

23. Describe limitations in the names of variables.

24. When must you have spaces in a COBOL program? When must you not have them?

25. Describe the filling out of data sheets.

26. Describe preparation of a COBOL program.

27. List the various IF statements. Do you need a period before the ELSE?

28. What is meant by nonnumeric comparison?

29. How do you handle mixed alphabetic and numeric input?

30. Rewrite a program of your choice, using mnemonic notation.

31. Explain the use of 77-level entries in the WORKING–STORAGE SECTION. Where do you place these entries?

32. Can you list two different variables under the same name in the WORKING–STORAGE SECTION?

33. Discuss the advantages of full COBOL as compared to our COBOL–SUBSET.

34. Write COBOL programs for the data processing applications and problem solving assignments for Appendix two, Chapter E. Use headers and literal messages to make your printouts easily understandable.

ANSWERS TO SELECTED QUESTIONS

5. No! It is mandatory.

6. Yes. Yes.

7. Yes. No.

8. No.

9.   *b.*   No space allowed between − sign and digits.
      c.   No comma allowed.
      d.   − sign must be ahead.
      g.   Cannot end in a decimal point.

10. None.

11. 14251 and overpunch the − on the last 1: 1425+ (Do not punch the decimal point!)

12. Three and four.

13. None.

14.   *a.*   A = 2, B = 5, C = 8
      b.   X = 5, Y = 12

    c. Illegal. Cannot have both TO and GIVING.

    d. A = 4, B = 3, C = 2, D = 9

    e. Illegal.

    f. A = 1, B = 2, C = 3, D = 10

    g. COUNTER = 12

    h. P = 10, Q = 5

    i. X = 5, Y = 10, A = 5

    j. P = 5, A = 50

    k. A = 2, C = 3, B = 6

    l. A = 2, B = 3

    m. A = 2, B = 6, C = 3

15. If you use TO the value of a variable will be lost and cannot be used later. For example, if you write ADD A TO B the old value of B is lost. If you write ADD A, B GIVING C, both A and B remain unchanged.

16. *a.* Cannot add to a number (it must be a variable).

    b. Cannot subtract from a number (literal).

    c. Cannot multiply a number (literal)

    d. Cannot divide a number (literal)

    e. Should be: **MULTIPLY A BY B GIVING C.**

    f. Should be: **DIVIDE Y INTO X.**

    g. Should be: **ADD 2 TO COUNTER.**

19. For input and computations. For printout. Only in display variables.

21. No!

27. You must not have a period before ELSE.

31. Right at the beginning of the WORKING–STORAGE SECTION.

32. No.

Introduction to BASIC
programming

In this chapter we cover the elements of BASIC (*B*eginners' *A*ll-purpose *S*ymbolic *I*nstruction *C*ode), the most widely used computer language in the time-sharing mode.[1] BASIC has been specially designed as an easy-to-learn language, but it has not been standardized. Therefore your system may deviate slightly from the one covered here. Our approach is to translate flowcharts into BASIC programs, and we begin by writing a program for the commission calculation.

However, it is not enough to learn how to translate the flowcharts into BASIC programs because you will be working at a terminal, and you must interact with the computer system to write, execute, and modify your programs. The language required to perform these functions is called the *command* language, and the best way to learn this is by working at a terminal and composing a program. So our approach in learning the command language is to present a man-machine programming dialog at a terminal. You must first modify the dialog to match the command language of your own computer system and then repeat this terminal session with your system.

THE COMMISSION CALCULATION IN BASIC

When you type a program on your terminal in BASIC you must number each statement. In the example in Figure D–1, the first

---

[1] The history and use of BASIC are discussed in Chapter 9.

```
15 READ A
20 IF A <=150 THEN 50
30 LET C=6.00+.02*(A-150)
40 GØ TØ 60
50 LET C=6.00
60 PRINT A,C
70 GØ TØ 15
80 DATA 85.32, 200.10, 500.00, 15.50, 1000, 210.50, 352.20
90 END
```

statement has the line number 15. It is a **READ** statement, which will read the first value of the amount. Observe that in our program all variables are designated by a single letter. In BASIC we can go one step further and add a single digit to the names of variables. Thus we can write:

$$B5, \quad F2, \quad X0$$

As a result of this restriction on the names of variables we cannot use mnemonic notation in BASIC.

A possible input statement:

$$17 \quad READ \quad L2, \quad B, \quad D5$$

illustrates in a more general manner how to read data in BASIC. The data itself is listed at the end of the program. In line 80 of (Figure D–1) our example the word DATA and the values of the data items are typed in.

Observe that the lines are numbered in an increasing order, but the numbers do not have to be consecutive. Line 20 illustrates *conditional branching*. If the value of A is less than 150 then control will be transferred to line 50; otherwise, the program drops through to line 30.

Line 30 illustrates how assignment statements are written in BASIC. Observe the word LET before the assignment statement.[2]

Line 40 is an *unconditional transfer* instruction. Line 50 is a simple assignment statement where the value of C is set to 6.00. (We could have written simply 6 instead of 6.00.) Line 60 illustrates how output is provided. Line 70 is an unconditional transfer to line 15 to read another data item.

Every BASIC program must terminate in END.

MORE ABOUT BASIC

How do we print alphanumeric messages or literals? If we add in Figure D–1 the initial lines:

---

[2] Some systems do not require the word LET.

```
10   PRINT "AMØUNT", "CØMMISSIØN"
11   PRINT
12   PRINT
```

the printer will print the *headers* for the columns, leave two empty lines, and print the answers. We can print anything we wish; all we have to do is put the message into quote marks.

As an alternate, we could replace line 60 in Figure D–1 by

```
60   PRINT "IF THE AMØUNT = $", A,
61   PRINT " THEN THE CØMMISSIØN = $", C,"."
```

and the computer would print

IF THE AMØUNT = $ 85.32 THEN THE CØMMISSIØN = $ 6.00.
IF THE AMØUNT = $ 200.10 THEN THE CØMMISSIØN = $ 7.002.

and so forth.

FIGURE D–2
Summary of rules
for BASIC.

---

1   Each line must be numbered in increasing order.
2.   Names of variables:

Single letter: X, A, C
Single letter followed by single number: X5, A0

3.   Sample statements:

```
READ W5, X0
PRINT A, B, X + Y, X/Y
PRINT "FØR SALE ØF," A, "PRØFIT IS," X
LET A = X*Y − X/Y − X↑3 + Y↑X
GØ TØ 201
IF A < B THEN 103          Conditional branch
INPUT C5, X
```

4.   Data should be placed before the END:

```
1000   DATA   85.32, 200.10, 500.00
1001   END
```

↑ to the power of

** Fortran

Figure D–2 summarizes the rules of BASIC. Note that in the PRINT statement expressions like X + Y and X/Y are allowed because in BASIC you can combine computations and printing. For example, you could replace

```
50   X = A + B − C/D + E
60   PRINT A, B, X
```

by

```
60   PRINT A, B, A + B − C/D + E
```

Observe in the 4th statement in Figure D–2 that exponential operator is designated by ↑. Thus, instead of A*A you write A↑2 (instead of B*B*B*B, B↑4) and so forth. (The exponent may also be a fraction.)

There is one further statement in Figure D–2, the INPUT statement, which we need to discuss.

INTERACTIVE COMPUTER PROGRAMS

Look at the account-balancing program in the upper part of Figure D–3 and at the printout in the lower part. The INPUT statement (line 10) creates a question mark in the printout. Then we

FIGURE D–3
Interactive version of the account-balancing problem. What you type is in frames; the rest shows the computer response.

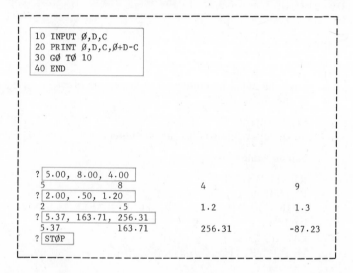

type in the values of the old balance, deposit, and check, and the computer types back the answers.

This type of program is very convenient for a user who is not interested in getting involved in programming. All he has to do is type in the data after the question mark, and the computer provides the answer.

As a further illustration consider the interactive program for the commission calculation in Figure D–4. Statements 10 to 45 create the questions shown in the lower part of Figure D–3. Statement 60 provides the answer if the amount is less than or equal to $150 and statement 80 when it is over $150.

Thus the computer generates the questions in the lower part of Figure D–4, the user types in the amount, and the computer automatically provides the answer.

```
10 PRINT
20 PRINT
30 PRINT " WHAT IS THE AMØUNT ØF EARNING" ,
40 INPUT A
45 PRINT
50 IF A > 150 THEN 80
60 PRINT " ØN $" A "THE CØMMISSIØN IS $ 6.00 . "
70 GØ TØ 10
80 LET C=6.00 + .02*(A-150)
90 PRINT " ØN $" A "THE CØMMISSIØN IS $" C "."
100 GØ TØ 10
110 END
```

WHAT IS THE AMØUNT ØF EARNING? 85.32

ØN $ 85.32   THE CØMMISSIØN IS $ 6.00

WHAT IS THE AMØUNT ØF EARNING? 200.10

ØN $ 200.1   THE CØMMISSIØN IS $ 7.002

WHAT IS THE AMOUNT ØF EARNING? 500

ØN $ 500   THE CØMMISSIØN IS $ 13.

WHAT IS THE AMØUNT ØF EARNING? STØP

FIGURE D-4
Interactive version of the commission calculation problem. All the user has to do is to answer the computer-posed question; the computer will automatically calculate the commission.

CONTROLLING LOOPS WITH FOR AND NEXT

Turn to Appendix two, Chapter E and look at Figure E–26. Study the problem described there on computing numbers of adult and baby rabbits. You should have no problem translating this flowchart into BASIC. Using the special BASIC features to control loops can make your programming job a lot easier.

The program at the left in Figure D–5 illustrates the approach. Lines 10 and 20 *initialize* B (for BABY) and A (for ADULT). Line 30 has the FOR statement to control the loop to be executed. Observe:

1. We open the loop by writing:

    FØR M = number-1 TØ number-2

2. We write the statements in the loop, but omit incrementating M and testing whether M reached the upper limit.
3. We close the loop by writing:

    NEXT M

FIGURE D-5
Program and
printout to
determine how
rabbits multiply.

```
                                    1   1     0     1
                                    2   1     1     0
                                    3   2     1     1
                                    4   3     2     1
                                    5   5     3     2
                                    6   8     5     3
                                    7  13     8     5
10  LET B=1                         8  21    13     8
20  LET A=0                         9  34    21    13
30  FOR M=1 TO 24                  10  55    34    21
40  LET T=A+B                      11  89    55    34
50  PRINT  M,T,A,B                 12 144    89    55
60  LET B=A                        13 233   144    89
70  LET A=T                        14 377   233   144
80  NEXT M                         15 610   377   233
90  END                            16 987   610   377
                                   17 1597   987   610
                                   18 2584  1597   987
                                   19 4181  2584  1597
                                   20 6765  4181  2584
                                   21 10946  6765  4181
                                   22 17711 10946  6765
                                   23 28657 17711 10946
                                   24 46368 28657 17711
```

It is the opening statement that specifies that the counter M is to run from number-1 to number-2 (in our case 1 to 24). Of course, instead of M we can use any other variable for the counter.

WHAT FULL BASIC CAN DO FOR YOU

There are a number of limitations of the BASIC system presented here which can be removed if you learn more about BASIC and its extensions.

BASIC includes a DIM statement which allows you to work with rows, columns, and entire tables of numbers. Also with the aid of subroutine and function capability you can write programs separately and then combine them conveniently into the main program. Special provisions to work with matrix algebra are also included.

Flexibility with regard to printouts is limited in some versions of BASIC, though features to improve printout layouts are available in other versions.

MAN-MACHINE PROGRAMMING DIALOG

The command language for a time-sharing system enables you to communicate directly with the computer system. The instructions are immediately transmitted to the computer system and are executed. Thus you can get the attention of the computer system. You can compose a program, modify it, and change it. You can perform all the manipulations required to make your program valid and cause the computer to execute your program.

The computer language required to manipulate BASIC programs varies slightly from one computer system to another. We will discuss the command system used for the Hewlett-Packard 2000F. If you use another computer system, you should obtain a user's manual and modify the discussions presented here.

The discussion considers only the most essential features of the command language which enable you to compose and execute a great variety of programs for many problems. Mastery of these features will make it easier to learn further commands for more sophisticated applications. Commands can be written in their *extended* form, meaning that the entire word for the command is typed, or in the *short* form, meaning that only three characters from the extended form are used. We cover the following eleven commands:

Extended form	Short form
HELLØ	HEL
NAME	NAM
RUN	RUN
LIST	LIS
SAVE	SAV
SCRATCH	SCR
RENUMBER	REN
CATALØG	CAT
GET	GET
KILL	KIL
BYE	BYE

We use the following notation:

Symbol	Meaning
r	Carriage return
X^c	Type X with the control key pressed
←	Upper case Ø
Ø	Character O (Oh)
0	Digit 0

Before you begin to compose a program you must learn how to *get on* the system, how to *get off*, how to *escape*, and how to *edit* your statements.

How to get on

Type in HEL-account number, password r.

How to get off

Type in BYE r.

How to escape

1. To escape from operating in the input mode:
   The computer is said to be in the *input mode* when it is waiting for you to type in some input. The computer types ? and then stops for your action. To *escape* from the input mode, type in c^{c}r. The computer responds with DØNE and then *hangs*.
2. To escape from operating in the output mode:
   The computer is said to be in the *output mode* when it is typing out something. To escape from the output mode, press the BREAK/INTERRUPT key. The computer responds with STØP and then hangs.

Note: If everything fails you could escape by turning off the terminal. However, in this case you will lose your currently active program.

How to edit

1. By deleting characters from the current line being typed in:
   Pressing the upper case key Ø provides a left arrow (←) or underscore bar (__) which deletes the immediately preceding character. For example, the word NAME1 can be typed as:

   NAMEA←1
   NAAME1←←←← ME1
   NAMM←E2←1

2. By deleting an entire line:
   Type in the corresponding line number followed by the carriage return key. For example, if line 60 is to be deleted, type in 60r

3. By replacing a line:
   Type in the corresponding line number followed by the new

contents of that line. For example, if line 11 is to be replaced with END, type in **11 END** r

4. By inserting a new line between two lines:

Type in any number between the numbers of surrounding lines, followed by the contents of the new line. For example, if **PRINT A** is to be inserted between lines 10 and 20, type in **13 PRINT A** r

Note: Any number between 10 and 20 could have been used instead of 13.

A TERMINAL SESSION ✳

This section presents a series of exhibits describing a terminal session in which three different versions of the account-balancing problem (Chapter 2, Figure 2.6) are composed. You are to repeat the steps described in the exhibits on your system. The typing you have to do is shown in the exhibits in color within frames, and all details outside the frames are typed by the computer system. Many of the steps in the exhibits are self-explanatory; we comment only on those steps that require explanation.

Exhibits

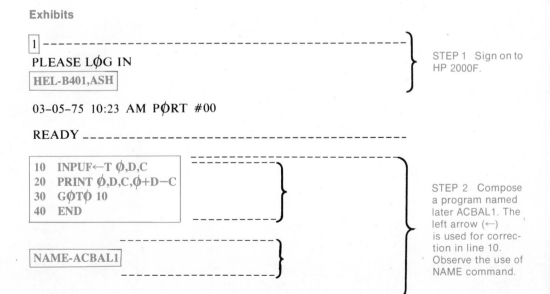

1 ─── ⎫
PLEASE LØG IN   ⎬ STEP 1   Sign on to HP 2000F.
| HEL-B401,ASH |

03–05–75   10:23 AM PØRT #00

READY ───

| 10   INPUF←T Ø,D,C |
| 20   PRINT Ø,D,C,Ø+D−C |
| 30   GØTØ 10 |
| 40   END |

STEP 2   Compose a program named later ACBAL1. The left arrow (←) is used for correction in line 10. Observe the use of NAME command.

| NAME-ACBAL1 |

RUN

ACBAL1

? | 5.00,8.00,4,0←←.00 |

5   8   4   9

? | 2.00, .50, 1.20 |

2   .5   1.2   1.3

? | EXiT |

DONE

STEP 3   Run ACBAL1. The left arrow is used for correction of input. Also observe the use of C^c, depicted by □. (This character has been used for the same purpose in many other steps also.)

LIST

ACBAL1

```
10    INPUT Ø,D,C
20    PRINT Ø,D,C,Ø+D−C
30    GØTØ 10
40    END
```

STEP 4   List ACBAL1.

Stop, Tonight

STEP 5   Save ACBAL1 in your library. Saving a program from your *current work space* for your *library* does not destroy the current work space.

SAVE

RUN

ACBAL1

? | 100, 50.0, 75.49 |

100   50   75.49   74.51

? | 100, 0, 150 |

100   0   150   −50

? | |

DØNE

STEP 6   Run ACBAL1.

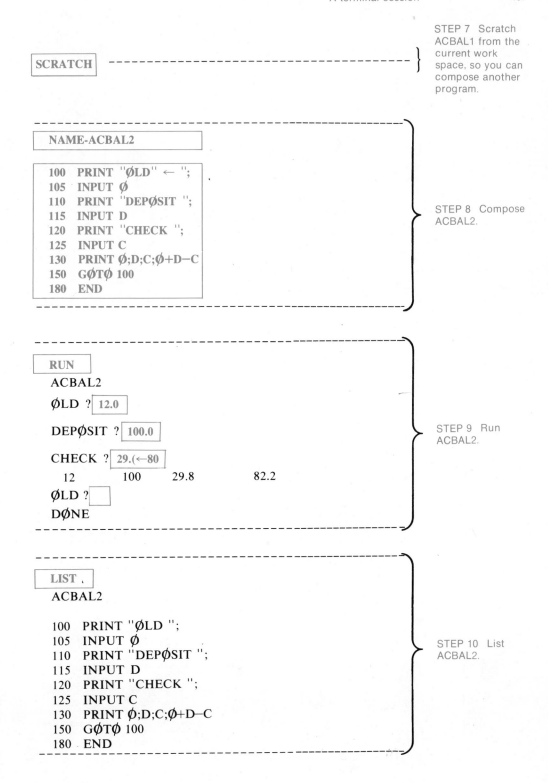

STEP 7 Scratch ACBAL1 from the current work space, so you can compose another program.

SCRATCH

NAME-ACBAL2

```
100   PRINT "ØLD" ← ";
105   INPUT Ø
110   PRINT "DEPØSIT ";
115   INPUT D
120   PRINT "CHECK ";
125   INPUT C
130   PRINT Ø;D;C;Ø+D−C
150   GØTØ 100
180   END
```

STEP 8 Compose ACBAL2.

RUN
ACBAL2

ØLD ? 12.0

DEPØSIT ? 100.0

CHECK ? 29.(←80
   12   100   29.8   82.2
ØLD ?
DØNE

STEP 9 Run ACBAL2.

LIST .
ACBAL2

```
100   PRINT "ØLD ";
105   INPUT Ø
110   PRINT "DEPØSIT ";
115   INPUT D
120   PRINT "CHECK ";
125   INPUT C
130   PRINT Ø;D;C;Ø+D−C
150   GØTØ 100
180   END
```

STEP 10 List ACBAL2.

STEP 11
Renumber the
statements of
ACBAL2. Compare
listings in steps 10
and 12.

REN –––––––––––––––––––––––––––––––––––––––

LIST ––
ACBAL2

```
10   PRINT "ØLD ";
20   INPUT Ø
30   PRINT "DEPØSIT ";
40   INPUT D
50   PRINT "CHECK ";
60   INPUT C
70   PRINT Ø;D;C;Ø+D−C
80   GØTØ 10
90   END
```

STEP 12 List the
renumbered
ACBAL2.

SAVE –––––––––––––––––––––––––––––––––––––

STEP 13 Save
ACBAL2 in your
library.

STEP 14 Check
contents of your
library and find
that you have
two programs in
your library.

CAT –––––––––––––––––––––––––––––––––––––––
```
NAME   LENGTH   NAME   LENGTH
ACBAL1       20   ACBAL2       48
```

SCRATCH ––––––––––––––––––––––––––––––––––

STEP 15 Scratch
ACBAL2 from your
work space.

GET-ACBAL1 ––––––––––––––––––––––––––––––––

STEP 16 Retrieve
ACBAL1 from your
library.

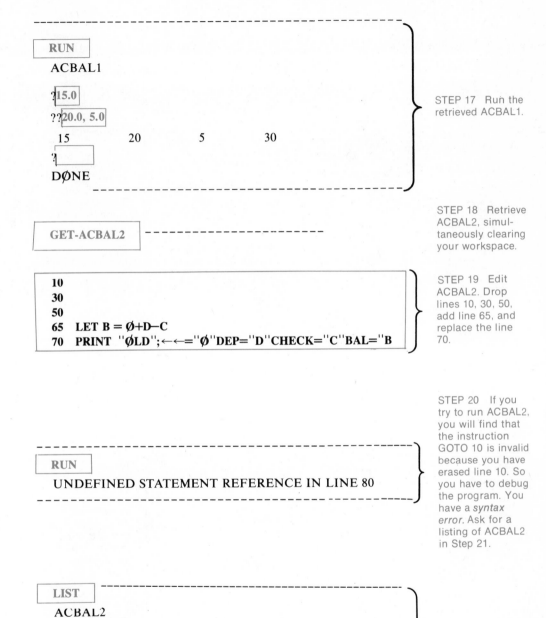

RUN

ACBAL1

?15.0

??20.0, 5.0

  15   20   5   30

?

DØNE

STEP 17   Run the retrieved ACBAL1.

STEP 18   Retrieve ACBAL2, simultaneously clearing your workspace.

GET-ACBAL2

```
10
30
50
65    LET B = Ø+D−C
70    PRINT "ØLD";←←="Ø"DEP="D"CHECK="C"BAL="B
```

STEP 19   Edit ACBAL2. Drop lines 10, 30, 50, add line 65, and replace the line 70.

STEP 20   If you try to run ACBAL2, you will find that the instruction GOTO 10 is invalid because you have erased line 10. So you have to debug the program. You have a *syntax error*. Ask for a listing of ACBAL2 in Step 21.

RUN

UNDEFINED STATEMENT REFERENCE IN LINE 80

LIST

ACBAL2

```
20    INPUT Ø
40    INPUT D
60    INPUT C
65    LET B=Ø+D−C
70    PRINT "ØLD="Ø"DEP="D"CHECK="C"BAL="B
80    GØTØ 10
90    END
```

STEP 21   List ACBAL2.

STEP 22   You try to *rename* the edited ACBAL2 as ACBAL3, but RENAME is an invalid command. Since only the first three characters of a command are used for its identification, the computer thinks you are trying to *REN*UMBER the currently active program. The computer objects to your use of a name instead of a number after REN by saying "BAD PARAMETER." No action is taken by the computer.

RENAME-ACBAL3

BAD PARAMETER

STEP 23   You try to save the edited ACBAL2 in your library, but, there already is another program with the same name. Though the contents of two programs with same name ACBAL2 are different (check steps 12 and 21), still the computer is objecting to your instruction. This is because it recognizes only names and not contents of programs.

SAVE

DUPLICATE ENTRY

NAME-ACBAL3
SAVE

STEP 24 Name edited ACBAL2, the currently active program, as ACBAL3 and then save it.

GET-ACBAL2
LIST

ACBAL2

```
10   PRINT "ØLD ";
20   INPUT Ø
30   PRINT "DEPØSIT ";
40   INPUT D
50   PRINT "CHECK ";
60   INPUT C
70   PRINT Ø;D;C;Ø+D−C
80   GØTØ10
90   END
```

STEP 25 Retrieve ACBAL2 and list.

STEP 26 Retrieve ACBAL3 and try to correct the syntax error detected in the program ACBAL3 at step 20. Note that correction can only be done to the currently active program and not to the program in your library. Replace statement 80.

GET-ACBAL3

80 GØTØ 20

```
RUN
ACBAL3
? 10.0,40.0
EXTRA INPUT-WARNING ONLY
? 40.0
? 60.0
ØLD= 10   DEP= 40   CHECK=60   BAL=−10
?
DØNE
```

STEP 27 Run corrected ACBAL3. You inadvertently provide an extra input. Program was asking for the value of Ø, i.e., only one number.

```
KILL-ACBAL3
SAVE
```

STEP 28 *Kill* the incorrect, old version of ACBAL3 and *save* the correct version (corrected at step 26).

```
CAT
```

NAME	LENGTH	NAME	LENGTH	NAME	LENGTH
ACBAL1	20	ACBAL2	48	ACBAL3	42

STEP 29 Check your library.

```
SCRATCH
```

STEP 30 Scratch current work space.

```
GET-ACBAL3
LIST
ACBAL3

20   INPUT Ø
40   INPUT D
60   INPUT C
65   LET B=Ø+D−C
70   PRINT "ØLD="Ø"DEP="D"CHECK="C"BAL="B
80   GØTØ 20
90   END
```

STEP 31 Retrieve ACBAL3 and list it.

STEP 32   Edit
ACBAL3. Errone-
ously you type
INPUF instead
of INPUT. The
computer returns
with ERROR in
next line. Type
":" followed by
r to find out the
nature of the
error. Later, type
line 20 once again.

```
20 INPUF Ø,D,C
```

ERRØR: MISSING ASSIGNMENT ØPERATØR

```
10   PRINT "ØLD ";
20   INPUT Ø
30   PRINT "DEP ";
40   INPUT D
50   PRINT "CHK ";
```

```
RUN
```

ACBAL3

ØLD ? `100`

DEP ? `200`

CHK ? `300`

ØLD= 100   DEP= 200   CHECK= 300   BAL= 0

? `10`

DEP ? `       `

DØNE

STEP 33   Run the
edited ACBAL3.

STEP 34   Correct
a *semantic* error
in ACBAL3. The
program did not
print OLD? while
asking for input.
Replace line 80.

```
80   GØTØ 10
```

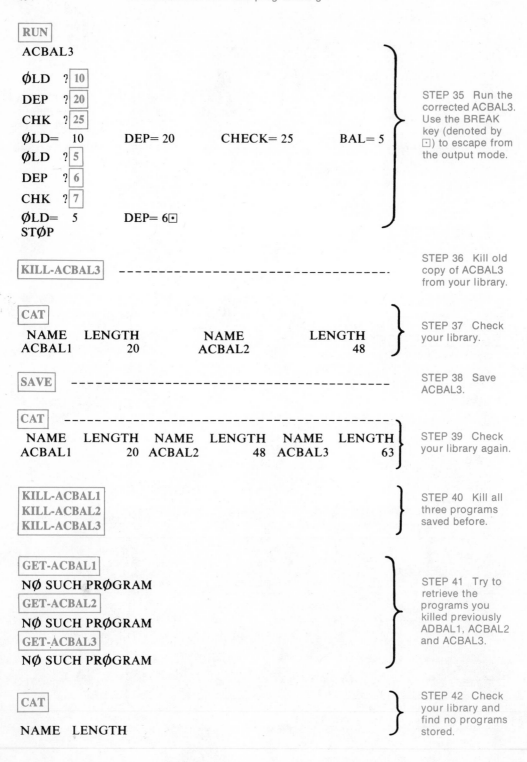

```
RUN
ACBAL3

ØLD   ? 10
DEP   ? 20
CHK   ? 25
ØLD=   10        DEP= 20        CHECK= 25        BAL= 5
ØLD   ? 5
DEP   ? 6
CHK   ? 7
ØLD=   5         DEP= 6⊡
STØP
```

STEP 35 Run the corrected ACBAL3. Use the BREAK key (denoted by ⊡) to escape from the output mode.

```
KILL-ACBAL3  ------------------------------------------
```

STEP 36 Kill old copy of ACBAL3 from your library.

```
CAT

NAME    LENGTH              NAME              LENGTH
ACBAL1        20            ACBAL2                  48
```

STEP 37 Check your library.

```
SAVE  ------------------------------------------------
```

STEP 38 Save ACBAL3.

```
CAT  ------------------------------------------------
NAME   LENGTH   NAME   LENGTH   NAME   LENGTH
ACBAL1      20  ACBAL2      48  ACBAL3      63
```

STEP 39 Check your library again.

```
KILL-ACBAL1
KILL-ACBAL2
KILL-ACBAL3
```

STEP 40 Kill all three programs saved before.

```
GET-ACBAL1
NØ SUCH PRØGRAM
GET-ACBAL2
NØ SUCH PRØGRAM
GET-ACBAL3
NØ SUCH PRØGRAM
```

STEP 41 Try to retrieve the programs you killed previously ADBAL1, ACBAL2 and ACBAL3.

```
CAT

NAME   LENGTH
```

STEP 42 Check your library and find no programs stored.

BYE
‾‾‾⎤
0   ⎬ STEP 43   Log off.
                                                   ⎦

31 MINUTES ØF TERMINAL TIME

DISCUSSION QUESTIONS AND ASSIGNMENTS

1. Which of the following assignment statements are unacceptable?

   a. LET A = 2*A + 3*5.0
   b. LET A5 = −2*A2 + 15.00
   c. LET X1 = A/B + C5 + 5C − XY
   d. LET Z3 = P.Q − 3.21
   e. LET U = X*/X
   f. LET X + Y = A − B
   g. LET U5 = (A + B)*(C + D)
   h. LET E = $\dfrac{A}{B}$
   i. LET A12 = X + Y
   j. LET A = X3/Y2

2. Must you number each line?

3. The computer is in the midst of a program. At the moment the current values of variables are:

$$
\begin{array}{ll}
A1 & 2.5 \\
B & -6.6 \\
F3 & 0 \\
K1 & -5.2 \\
Q & -1 \\
T & 99.2 \\
Z7 & 99.2
\end{array}
$$

   For each of the following statements, determine whether or not the computer will branch to statement 150:

   a. IF Z7 <   T   THEN 150
   b. IF A1 >   F3 THEN 150
   c. IF A1 <   F3 THEN 150
   d. IF Q >   .5 THEN 150
   e. IF Z7 < = T   THEN 150
   f. IF B <   K1 THEN 150
   g. IF A1 >   100 THEN 150

4. Find errors if any in the following statements:

   a. PRINT A, B, 5.2, A/B
   b. PRINT "IS IT "VAZSØNYI" OR "VASZØNYI"?"
   c. PRINT "A=", A, "B=", B
   d. PRINT "IF X=Y Then D=", X−Y
   e. READ A, B, X + Y

5. A program has 100 lines. The 10th line is:

$$10 \quad G\emptyset T\emptyset \quad 81$$

The 81st line is:

$$81 \quad G\emptyset T\emptyset \quad 10$$

What would happen when the computer executes this program?

6. Write BASIC programs for the data processing applications and problem solving assignments for Appendix two, Chapter E. Use headers and literal messages to make your printouts easily understandable.

ANSWERS TO SELECTED QUESTIONS

1. Cannot have:
   c. variable names like 5C or XY
   d. period between P and Q
   e. */
   f. X + Y on left-hand side
   h. solidus (/) (fraction sign)
   i. A12 as variable name

2. Yes.

3. a. No.
   b. Yes.
   c. No.
   d. No.
   e. Yes.
   f. Yes.
   g. No.

4. Cannot have:
   b. quotes within quotes
   e. READ X + Y

5. If either of the statements is reached the computer gets into an infinite loop. Most computer installations have time limits imposed on programs, so when your time runs out, you get kicked off the computer.

appendix two

Data processing applications and flowcharting supplement

All data processing applications can be divided into a number of simple elementary applications. In this supplement we present a series of highly simplified data processing applications with two purposes in mind:

1. To present applications that you can study without a knowledge of programming and from which more complicated data processing systems can be assembled.
2. To provide a set of flowcharts which you can translate into computer programs.

Before you can translate the flowcharts into computer programs you must realize that the flowcharts are suitable for any computer language, but the name of the variables may not meet the special requirements of the language you are studying. Therefore, your first task is to replace the names of the variables with acceptable names for the language you are using, when this is necessary. A good approach is to prepare a table in which you list the names of the variables in the flowchart on the left and the new names you are introducing on the right.

You should also examine the sample data presented in the flowcharts. The particular language you use may require editing of the data.

AN INVOICE CALCULATION

Warren Kelly is in the process of composing a program to support a data processing system for producing invoices for the national distributor of Textiles Incorporated. Part of Kelly's program determines the price of materials to be shipped. In the flowchart for this problem we concentrate only on this simple component of the program to be prepared.

The rule for computing the price of a material to be shipped is simple: (1) the LENGTH of the material is multiplied by the unit COST, and (2) a fixed BASE cost is added to cover a general charge for shipping and other expenses. The assignment statement expressing the rule is:

$$COST \leftarrow LENGTH * PRICE + BASE$$

Note that the sign of multiplication is the asterisk (∗). The flowchart and sample data for the problem are shown in Figure E–1.

Box 1 reads the LENGTH of the material sold, the PRICE, and the BASE to be added. For example, in the first sample input we have the numbers 10, 3.00 and 1.00, meaning that 10 yards of goods

FIGURE E–1
Invoice calculation
flowchart.

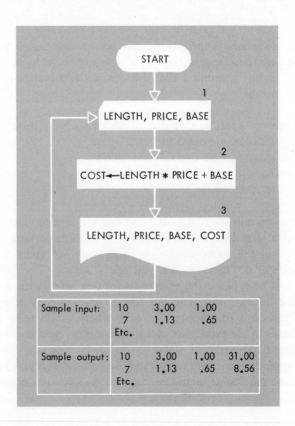

are sold, the unit price is $3.00, and the base to be added is $1.00. The price to the customer will be:

$$10 * 3 + 1 = 31$$

In Box 2 is the assignment statement already discussed. Box 3 provides for the output.

If you compare this flowchart with the flowchart for the account-balancing problem (Figure 2.6, Chapter 2), you note that the former omits the decision box for the last card read. We introduce this simplification in all our flowcharts. When you translate your flowcharts into programs you may be required to use special programming features to deal with this problem.

SALES ANALYSIS: HOW TO SUMMARIZE

Stan Hudson, a merchant, keeps daily records of certain types of goods sold. He wants to make a sales analysis by summarization and comparison. Specifically, he wants to

1. Compare sales on weekdays and on weekends.
2. Compute the sum of (summarize) the weekday sales.
3. Compute the sum of (summarize) the weekend sales.
4. Compute the sum of (summarize) all the sales.
5. Compute the average daily sales.

Figure E–2 shows the flowchart for solving this problem.

First, examine a sample input to the program. Observe that the first input card has the five sales figures for weekly sales; the second input card has the Saturday and Sunday sales; the next two cards have similar figures for the next week. And so on.

Box 1 reads the weekday sales: S1, S2, S3, S4, S5.

Box 2 computes WDAY, the sum of the weekday sales.

Box 3 reads the second card with S6 and S7, the Saturday and Sunday sales.

Box 4 shows three different assignment statements. We could put them into separate boxes, but for the sake of simplicity we allow a sequence of assignment statements to be put into a single box.

The first assignment statement computes the weekend sales, WEND, or the sum of Sunday and Saturday sales. The second assignment statement computes TOTAL, the sum of all the sales. And the third assignment statement computes AVER, the average daily sale.

Observe that division is designated by a slash (/). This is common practice in most computer languages. All assignment statements can be broken down into the four arithmetic operations: addition, subtraction, multiplication, and division.

Box 5 is an output statement to print TOTAL, the sum of all the sales, and AVER, the average sale.

Box 6 is again an output statement to print WDAY, the sum of

FIGURE E–2
Flowchart for sales
analysis showing
how to summarize.

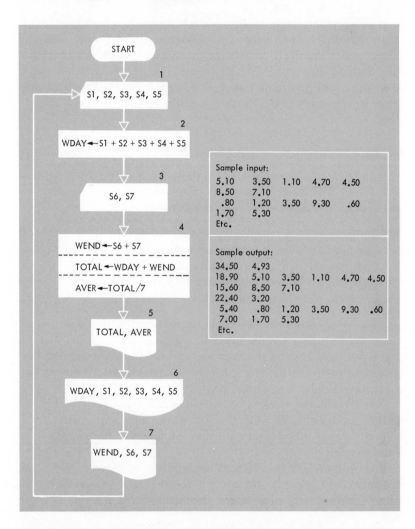

the weekday sales, and S1, S2, S3, S4, and S5, a repeat of the input of the five weekday sales.

Box 7 is an output statement to print WEND, the sum of the weekend sales, and S6 and S7, the Saturday and Sunday sales.

Is there any reason for the particular sequence of the boxes in the flowchart? Why read the five weekday sales first and then compute the sum of the weekday sales and only then read the weekend sales and then do the other computations? There is no compelling reason to do so. We could have designed the flowchart to read first the five weekday sales, then the two weekend sales, and then do all the computations. Observe that the same data processing problem can be worked equally well many ways. But certain things you must keep in mind.

The flowchart cannot do computations until the required data is available. Thus data must be obtained from input cards, or the data must be the result of some previous computations. The flowchart cannot print data until the data is available. Thus the data must be either read from input cards or computed prior to printing.

In arithmetic operations, there is one thing you must always watch for: it is impossible to divide by 0! If inadvertently you command the computer to do so, execution of the data processing job will fail.

COMPUTATION OF A SHIPPING BILL

Ronald Edwards is a wholesale distributor dealing with such commodities as coffee, sugar, and pepper. For simplicity, assume that Edwards deals with only five commodities. Commodity prices change daily, so each morning Edwards sets the prices of the commodities and prepares the invoices for the various orders to be filled. He needs to compute the total cost of the commodities to be billed in each invoice.

The total cost is computed in five steps which provide various figures:

1.   Unit price times weight in pounds shipped gives individual commodity cost.
2.   Sum of individual costs gives net cost.
3.   Sum of weights in pounds shipped gives total weight.
4.   Total weight times shipping rate per weight in pounds gives shipping charge.
5.   The total cost to be charged to the customer is obtained by adding net cost and shipping charge.

For example, on a particular day the shipping rate per pound was 50 cents and the prices of the commodities were $12.52, $23.10, $5.50, $7.10, and $52.00 (Figure E–3). Milton Hughes purchases 1 pound of the first, second, fourth, and fifth commodities, and nothing of the third commodity. The total cost to be charged to Hughes will be:

$$\$12.52 + \$23.10 + 0 + \$7.10 + \$52.00 + \$2.00 = \$96.72$$

FIGURE E-3
Shipping bill
calculation
flowchart.

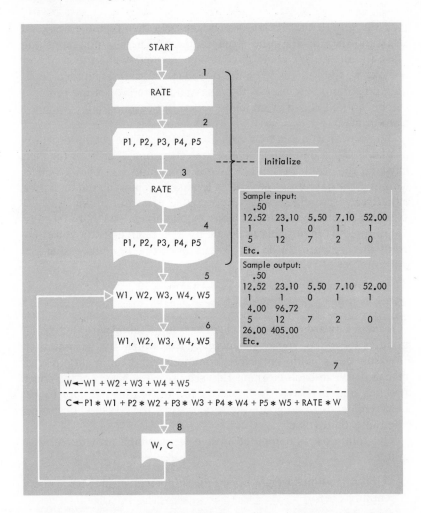

Consider the sample input in Figure E–3. In the first card there is a single number, the shipping rate per pound. The second card gives the price of the five commodities, which will hold for all the shipments to be made. Then follows a deck of cards. For each customer there is a single card listing the pounds of commodities to be shipped.

In the flowchart, Box 1 reads the shipping RATE, and in Box 2, P1, P2, P3, P4, and P5, the prices of the five commodities are read. Boxes 3 and 4 provide a printout for the shipping rate and the prices. Box 5 reads the five values of pounds of commodities sold. Box 6 provides a printout of the weights.

Box 7 carries out the computations with the aid of two assignment statements. The first assignment statement computes W, the total weight of the shipment. The second assignment multiplies the weight of each commodity by the unit price, adds the individual costs, and finally adds the shipping charge (shipping rate times total weight).

Box 8 calls for the total weight of the commodity and the total cost to be printed.

Then a return is made to Box 5 and from the next card the weights of the next five commodities are read. Observe that control must not go back to Box 1. The shipping rate and the prices of the commodities are provided once for all the computations, and these values must remain unchanged. It is customary to say that Boxes 1, 2, 3, and 4 *initialize* the process, while Boxes 5, 6, 7, and 8 form the data processing loop. Initialization is done only once; the loop itself is executed as many times as there are customers.

KEEPING YOUR OWN CHECKBOOK

In Chapter 2 you learned how to balance an account in the bank. Now we show how to automate the process of keeping your own checkbook.

Figure E–4 shows the flowchart and sample inputs and outputs to the problem. Look at the outputs first.

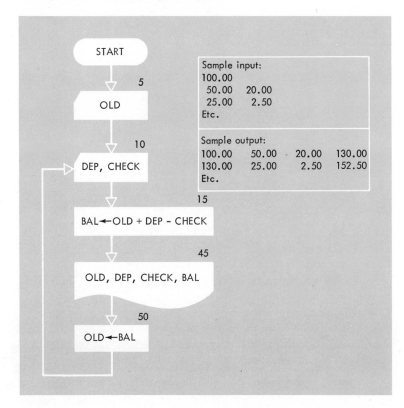

FIGURE E–4
Flowchart for keeping your own checkbook.

If you start with an initial deposit of $100, then deposit $50 and write a check for $20, your balance is $130. The next line in the output shows the balance forwarded of $130. The new deposit is $25, the new check is $2.50, and the new balance is $152.50. And so on. If you compare this output with the output of the account-balancing problem (Figure 2.6, Chapter 2) you observe that now the ending balance in each line is the same as the starting balance on the new line, namely the balance forwarded.

FIGURE E–5
Flowchart showing
alternate solution
to the problem
of keeping your
own checkbook.

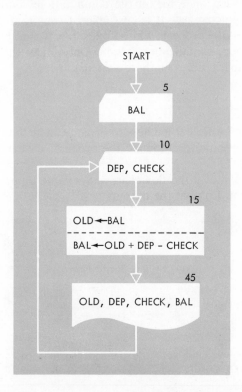

Now look at the sample input in Figure E–4. Observe that in the first input card there is a single number with the starting deposit of $100. Then each card has a pair of data for a single deposit and a check.

Now that we understand the problem, we must introduce names for the variables. We might as well use the same names as in our account-balancing problem. We even have the assignment statement to get the balance from the old balance, the deposit, and the check. So we start by writing this assignment statement into a box on the flowchart. We number this Box 15, as we do not know yet what boxes will precede and follow this assignment statement in the flowchart.

We know that we want to print OLD, DEP, CHECK, and BAL, so we write the output box in the flowchart. We number it 45. We can also write the input box and number it 10.

We could have used entirely different numbers for the boxes, because the numbering system is only for our convenience, but we like to have the flowchart boxes in a somewhat ordered fashion. Therefore we use these numbers, allowing for the possibility of inserting a box somewhere in the flowchart.

We now have the three boxes: 10, 15, and 45. Now we must take care of the forwarded balance, that is, we must make the first number in each line of the output the same as the last number in the previous line. So we write the assignment statement in Box 50.

Are we through? Not yet! When the processing of the cards starts, a single card with the first balance must be read. So now we write the input statement in Box 5. Then we close the loop with the arrows, and we have the flowchart.

Is the flowchart in Figure E–4 the only solution to the problem? Obviously not! Data processing problems usually have many solutions. In Figure E–5 we show an alternative solution.

COUNTING AND KEEPING A RUNNING TOTAL

Robert Casey keeps a daily record of his expenses and wants to keep a running total or cumulative total of his expenses. Figure E–6 shows the flowchart and a sample input and output for the problem. Observe that each input card has a single number: the daily expense. In the output, the first column is a sequence number: 1, 2, 3, etc. The second column is a printout of the daily expenses listed on the input cards. This third column is the cumulative sum or the total of the daily expenses so far read from the input cards.

Examine in the sample output the cumulative totals shown in the third column. On the first day both expenses and cumulative expenses are $5.20. The second day's expense is $3.15, and so the cumulative expense is $8.35, obtained by adding the expense of $3.15 to the previous expense of $5.20. The expense on the third day is $1.30, so the cumulative expense is $9.65, obtained by adding the $1.30 to the $8.35.

Now we introduce names for the three variables. We call the sequence number COUNT, the amount of the expense A, and the cumulative sum SUM. We start the flowchart by writing the output statement as shown and number the box arbitrarily 43.

Next we write the input statement, Box 21, which reads A from

FIGURE E–6
Flowchart for
counting and
keeping a running
(cumulative) total.

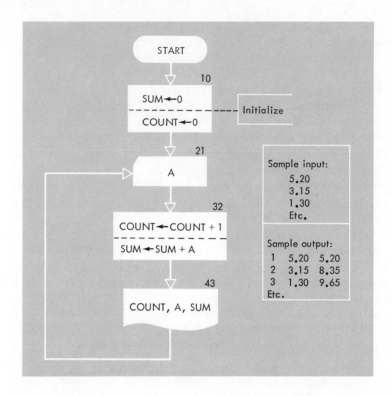

the card. Then in the first assignment statement in Box 32 1 is added
to COUNT, that is, COUNT is *incremented* by 1 each time control
goes around the loop. The second assignment statement adds A
to SUM.

What about Box 10? The assignment statements in Box 32 make
no sense when the process starts, because on the right side COUNT
and SUM have no values yet. They should be zeros. This *initialization* to zero is accomplished in Box 10. One of the common traps

FIGURE E–7
Code assignment
for classifying
people by weight.

Weight (in pounds)		
At least	*But less than*	*Code to be assigned*
—	100	1
100	170	2
170	205	3
205	240	4
240	—	5

programmers fall into is forgetting to initialize variables to zero when required.

MULTIPLE BRANCHING: HOW TO CLASSIFY

As part of a dietary study of the U.S. Department of Health, Education and Welfare, people are classified by weight. Figure E–7 shows how the codes are assigned. Figure E–8 shows the flowchart. Figure E–9 shows an alternate flowchart.

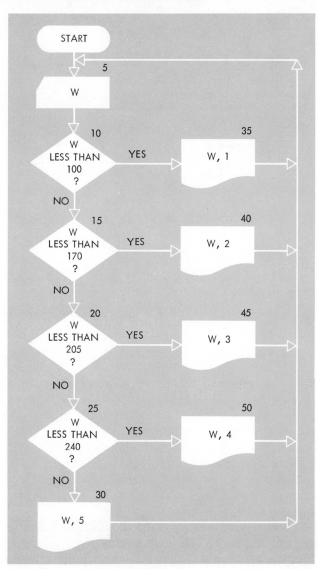

FIGURE E–8
Flowchart for classifying people by weight.

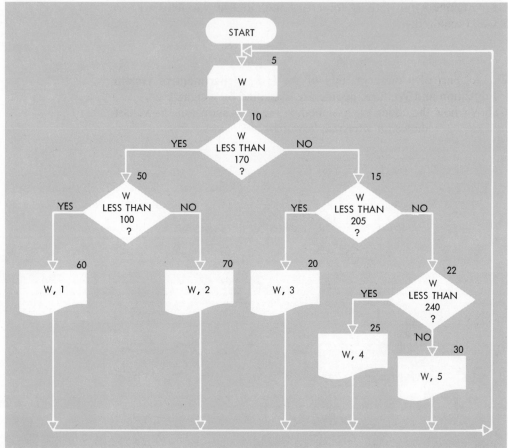

FIGURE E–9
Alternate
flowchart for
classifying people
by weight.

TOTALING DATA AND EDITING

Often in data processing tables of numbers are given, and the problem is to total, edit, and classify the data in various ways. For example, data on sales are often to be summarized by product lines, sales territories, salespeople, or customer type. It also often happens that the manner in which the data is provided is not suitable for output, and the user requires editing of the data. A typical example is when tables of numbers are to be edited so that rows become columns, and columns rows. A typical, simplified example is given below.

Richard Johnson is a national distributor of typewriters, dictating machines, and calculators. He gets weekly reports on the sale of these three commodities in his two sales territories, the East and the West. In the first two rows of the sample input in Figure E–10a,

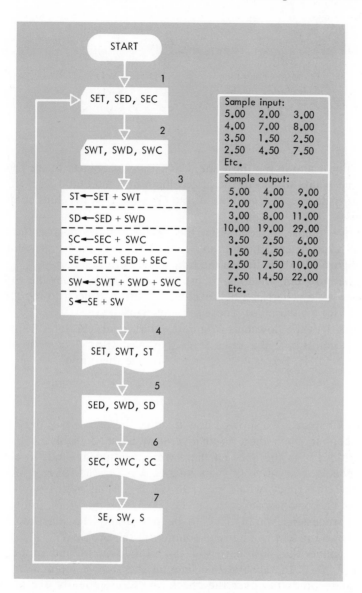

FIGURE E-10a
Flowchart for
totaling and
editing data.

the first row refers to the sales territory of the East, and the second to the West. The first column of figures refers to typewriters, the second to dictating machines, and the third to calculating machines. Sales figures are in thousands. For example, in the first week the sale of dictating machines in the East amounted to $2 thousand and the sale of typewriters in the West amounted to $4 thousand.

The sample output illustrates what Johnson needs. In the first line he wants the sale of typewriters; in the second line, dictating

	East	West	Total
Typewriters	SET	SWT	ST
Dictating machines	SED	SWD	SD
Calculating machines	SEC	SWC	SC
Total	SE	SW	S

machines; and in the third line, calculating machines. In the fourth line he wants totals. In the first column he wants total sales in the East; in the second column, in the West; and in the third column, totals.

For example, in the first line the third figure, $9.00, gives the sale of all typewriters (in thousands). In the fourth line, first column, the figure $10.00 indicates the total sales in the East.

The problem, then, is to produce the output from the input. Before a flowchart can be developed, there is a need to introduce names for the variables. These are shown in Figure E–10b.

Box 1 of the flowchart (Figure E–10a), reads the sales from the East, and Box 2 the sales from the West. Box 3 computes the various totals. Boxes 4, 5, 6, and 7 provide the output.

ACCOUNT BALANCING WITH OVERDRAW

In Chapter 2 we showed how to solve the problem of balancing an account when there is an overdraw under a highly simplified condition; if in the account there were insufficient funds to cover the check, a negative (minus) balance was printed. In real life, of course, the check would be returned, a special notice would be issued and/or other action would be taken, and, therefore, additional data processing would have to be performed. To illustrate this point, we present an alternate solution to the problem.

Examine the flowchart and the sample input and output in Figure E–11. In the first two lines of the sample input there are adequate funds to cover the check and, consequently, the output is like the output shown in Chapter 2. But examine now the third line of the input.

For account no. 0221 there is an old balance of $15.00, a deposit of $3.00, and a check for $21.50. Insufficient funds! The output provides a printout of the account number, the old balance, and the deposit. But the fourth check column shows 0. The fifth balance column shows $18.00 because as the sixth column indicates, the check of $21.50 was returned. The seventh column, for reference shows $3.50, which indicates the amount by which account no. 0221 is deficient.

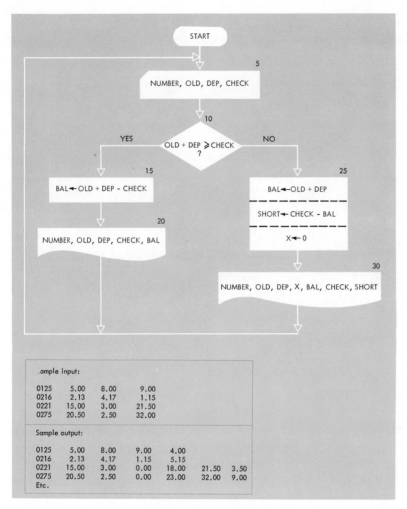

FIGURE E–11
Flowchart for
account balancing
with overdraw.

In the flowchart Box 5 reads the account number, the old balance, the deposit, and the check. Box 10 indicates a test as to whether there are sufficient funds. If so, control goes to Boxes 15 and 20, as in the example in Chapter 2. But if funds are insufficient, it goes to Box 25, where the new balance and the shortage are computed and X is set to zero. Then Box 30 provides the printout.

RETRIEVING AND LISTING RECORDS

One of the common data processing jobs is scanning and retrieving records. For example, there may be a need to retrieve sales records, personnel records, equipment and tools, inventories of

FIGURE E-12
Flowchart for
listing male
employees making
over $4 per hour.
SEX is 1 for
males, 2 for
females.

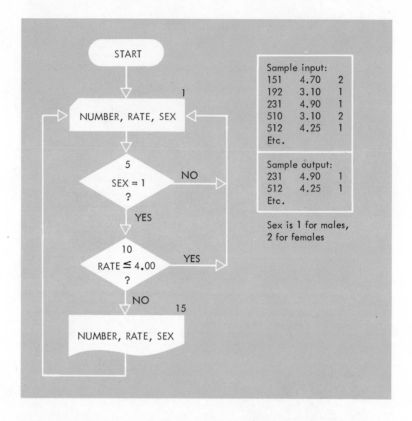

goods, and so on. Figure E-12 shows a simple example of scanning a personnel file and listing certain employees.

Specifically, the problem is to list male employees making over $4 per hour. To simplify matters, assume that there are only three items in each record—the employee number, the rate of pay, and sex. The code for males is 1, and for females 2.

Box 1 reads the data. Box 5 tests the sex, and Box 10 tests the pay rate. Finally, Box 15 provides the answers.

SEQUENCE CHECKING

In all data processing jobs, a great variety of checks and controls must be made on accuracy. It can often happen that the computer is fed wrong data, errors are made, cards are lost, and so on. Figure E-13 shows one of the common data processing controls of testing that records in a file are not out of sequence.

The flowchart tests the employee number in a personnel file, record by record, and if any of the numbers are out of sequence, processing is stopped.

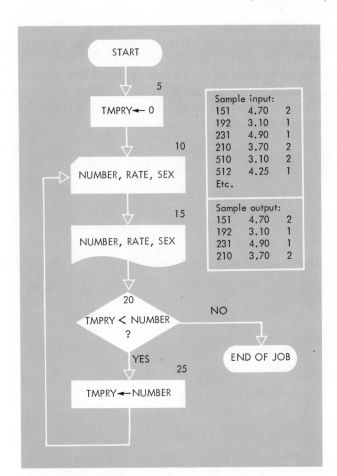

Box 5 initializes a temporary variable, TMPRY to 0. Box 10 reads a record, and Box 15 prints it. In Box 20 a test is made on employee number. If it is larger than TMPRY the record is in proper sequence, and in Box 25 the value of TMPRY is reset to the employee number. However, if the record is out of sequence, the test in Box 20 fails, and processing is terminated.

SIMPLIFIED TAX COMPUTATION

When we discussed the commission calculation problem in Chapter 2, the commission had to be computed in a different manner when the sales were under or over $150. There are many data processing jobs where amounts must be computed in different ways depending on the particular "bracket" in which the input variable happens to be. For example, there may be a graduated commission paid to salesmen, and if the amount goes over $250, they get a 4 percent bonus instead of 2 percent. Interest rates on small loans depend on the amount of the loan, and discount calculations must be performed depending on the amount of sale. There are many data processing problems involving either a maximum or a minimum amount, independent of the value of a variable. A typical problem of this nature is the federal tax computation.

FIGURE E–14
Flowchart for
simplified federal
tax computation.

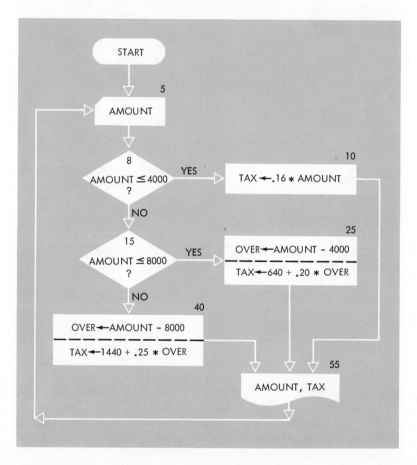

In Figure E–14 a simplified version of such a tax computation is shown. Box 5 reads the amount, and Box 8 makes a test. If the amount is less than or equal to $4,000, the tax is 16 percent of the amount, as shown in Box 10. But if the amount is over $4,000 but less than or equal to $8,000, the tax rate becomes higher. In Box 15 the test is made, and in Box 25 the tax is computed by the formulas shown. If the amount is over $8,000 the tax is computed by the formulas shown in Box 40.

Finally, Box 55 provides a printout of the amount and the tax given.

SORTING THREE NUMBERS

One of the common data processing jobs is to sort the records in a file into alphabetic or numeric order. Programs to do sorting are usually provided by the manufacturer, and it is not necessary to know the details of how sorting is done. However, it will be useful to know how a very simple sorting task, namely, sorting three numbers into ascending order, can be accomplished.

In the logic of the flowchart shown in Figure E-15, Box 5 reads A, B, and C, the three numbers to be sorted. Box 10 provides a printout of A, B, and C. Box 15 compares A with B. If A is less than (or equal to) B the process continues in Box 25. Otherwise, it goes to Box 20, where A and B are swapped. Specifically, first A is assigned to X. (This is necessary, as the value of A must be retained.) In the second assignment statement in Box 20, B is assigned to A. Now A equals B, and X equals A. So, in the third assignment statement, X is assigned to B. Now A and B are swapped, and A will be smaller than B.

Box 25 compares A and C. If A is less than (or equal to) C the process goes to Box 35; otherwise to Box 30, where A and C are swapped. Finally, Box 35 compares B and C and, if necessary, Box 40 swaps them.

WEEKLY SALES ANALYSIS

The input to the problem of weekly sales analysis is a column of figures representing sales for weeks. The problem is to provide a daily count, a printout of the input, and the subtotal on every seventh line. The flowchart is shown in Figure E-16.

In the logic of the flowchart, Box 5 sets TOTAL and COUNT to 0. Box 10 reads SALES, and Box 12 computes TOTAL and COUNT. Then Box 14 makes a test of whether COUNT has reached 7. If not, the flowchart just prints COUNT and SALES. If yes, it prints COUNT, SALES, and the TOTAL, and goes back to Box 5 to start the process again for next week's data.

COMPUTING AVERAGE GRADES FOR SCHOOL CLASSES

There is often a need for statistical analysis; for example, the average of a set of numbers must be computed. Figure E-17 shows how to compute the average grade for various school classes.

Inspect the sample input. The first number is the course number.

FIGURE E–15
Flowchart for
sorting three
numbers into
ascending order.

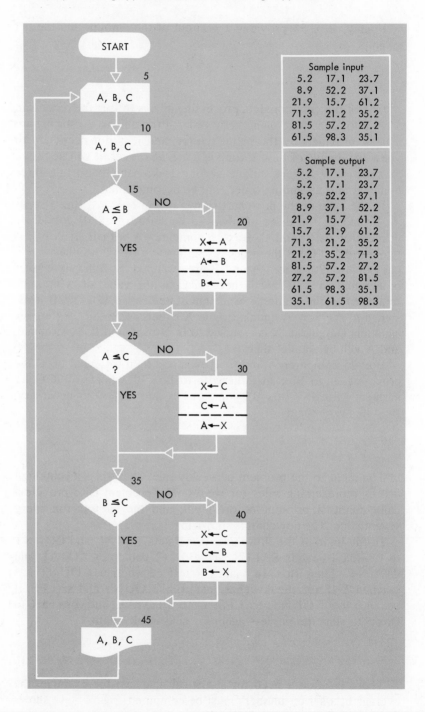

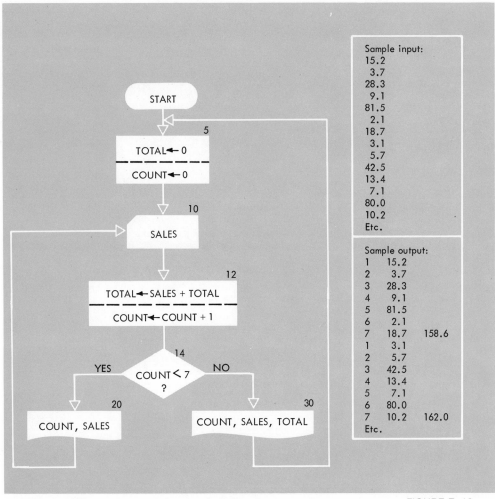

Sample input:
15.2
3.7
28.3
9.1
81.5
2.1
18.7
3.1
5.7
42.5
13.4
7.1
80.0
10.2
Etc.

Sample output:

1	15.2	
2	3.7	
3	28.3	
4	9.1	
5	81.5	
6	2.1	
7	18.7	158.6
1	3.1	
2	5.7	
3	42.5	
4	13.4	
5	7.1	
6	80.0	
7	10.2	162.0

Etc.

FIGURE E–16
Flowchart for
weekly sales
analysis.

There are only three students in the class, and their grades are given in numeric form as 3, 1, and 2. What does the next −1 stand for?

Somehow we must tell the computer that the grades for all the students in Course 123 have been listed. So, we add a last data item, a *flag,* with the value −1. We know that grades cannot be represented by the number −1, so we can write our flowchart such that the computer will recognize that the last grade has been read in.

The sample output provides the number of the class, the number of students, and the average grade.

In the logic of the flowchart, Box 5 initializes the variables

FIGURE E–17
Flowchart for
determining
average grades
with trailer card.
The value of
GRADE is –1 in
the trailer card.

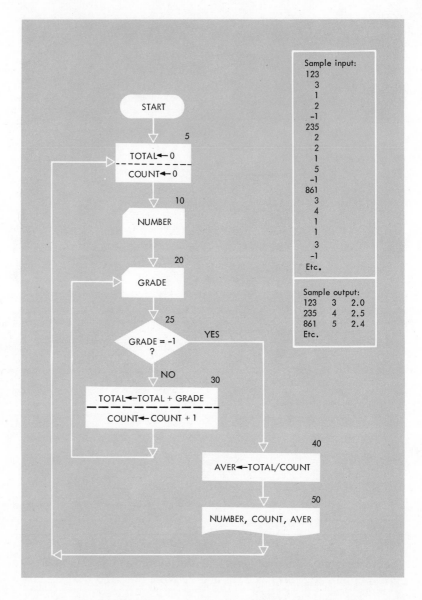

Sample input:
123
3
1
2
–1
235
2
2
1
5
–1
861
3
4
1
1
3
–1
Etc.

Sample output:
123   3   2.0
235   4   2.5
861   5   2.4
Etc.

TOTAL and COUNT to 0. Box 10 reads the class number, and Box 20 reads the GRADE.

Box 25 makes a test: If GRADE is –1, the last grade has been read. Box 40 computes the average, and Box 50 provides the print-out. However, if the test in Box 25 fails, control is transferred to Box 30 where TOTAL and COUNT are computed. Then control returns to Box 20 to read another value of GRADE.

Why did we use −1 as the flag? We could have used any other number that cannot be a grade. For example, we could have used 999 or 100 because they can never occur as grades.

This technique of adding a special flag to mark the end of the data group is common practice in data processing. Sometimes data processing people refer to such a data item as a trailer, a terminal item, or a sentinel.

COMPUTING SUBTOTALS

Figure E–18 shows the flowchart and the sample data for computing subtotals. The input is a column of numbers with flags of −1.00 indicating the end of each group of numbers. The output is a printout of the input, and each time a trailing flag is reached the subtotal is printed. For example, the first three numbers are 5.25, 4.50, and 7.50; so in the output in the third line there is the sub-

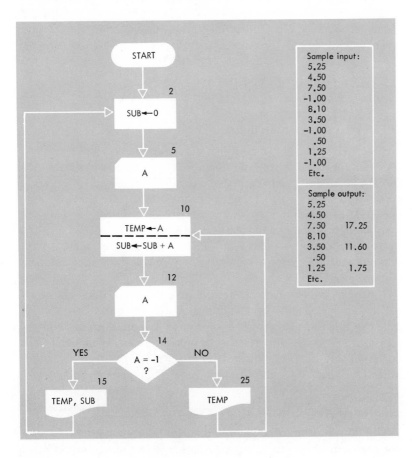

FIGURE E–18
Flowchart for computing subtotals with trailer card. The value of A is −1 in the trailer card.

total 17.25. Then there are the inputs 8.10 and 3.50, so in the fifth line of the output there is the subtotal 11.60, etc.

According to the flowchart logic, Box 2 sets SUB, the subtotal to 0. Box 5 reads a card. We do not know yet whether we wish to print this number, as the next card may have a −1 on it, in which case we wish to print both the number and the subtotal. So Box 10 assigns A to TEMP, a temporary variable. Also SUB, the value of the subtotal is updated. Then Box 12 reads another card. Observe that TEMP has the value from the previous card and A has the value from the last card. Now Box 14 makes a test. If A is −1, the flowchart must print TEMP and SUB (Box 15) and go back to Box 2. But if the statement in Box 14 is false, it must print only TEMP (Box 25) and go back to Box 10.

AVERAGE SALARY RATE OF MALE AND FEMALE EMPLOYEES

The flowchart in Figure E-19 is designed for counting the number of male and female employees and also computing their average salary rates. We use the flag 3 for SEX in the last card to mark the end of all data. We not only must count the number of male and female employees but add the salary rates of the males and females, so we can get the average. Box 5 sets to 0 the following variables:

1. SM, the sum of the male rates.
2. SF, the sum of the female rates.
3. CM, the count of the males.
4. CF, the count of the females.

Box 10 reads the card with the record of the employee. The statement in Box 12 gives the signal that the last card has been read and the averages (AM for males, AF for females) are to be computed. If there is no signal, control drops through and a test is made in Box 15 as to whether the employee is male or female, and in each case the appropriate count and sum are updated.

In Box 60 the count of the males and their average rate are printed, and in Box 65 the count of the females and their average rate are printed.

If, due to an error, a card contains a code that does not equal either 2 or 3, the flowchart will classify the record in Box 15 as a male. So this flowchart is not foolproof. To avoid this possibility, a decision box to test for SEX = 1 could be added. If this test fails, the flowchart should indicate an error message or some other action.

SALARY ANALYSIS BY GROUP AND DIVISION

The flowchart and the sample data for salary analysis by group and division are given in Figures E-20a, b, c, and d. Observe in

the sample input the four columns of numbers. The first one lists
the division number, the second the group number, the third the
employee number, and the fourth, the salary of the employee. The
problem is to provide a printout of the input, as well as to total
the salaries by groups and divisions. Observe, for example, that in
Division 012 and Group 002 there are two employees. The salaries

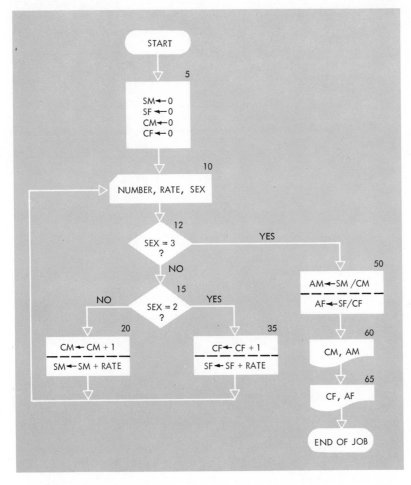

FIGURE E-19
Flowchart for
computing
average salary
rate of males and
females. SEX is 1
for males, 2 for
females; SEX is 3
in trailer card.

are: $150 and $121, so in the output in Line 2 we have the group
sum salary of $271. The sixth line of the printout provides the group
sum of $668 for Group 004 in Division 012 and also the divisional
sum of $939 for Division 012.

Before we describe the flowchart, inspect the names of the variables shown in Figure E-20d.

FIGURE E–20a
Flowchart for
salary analysis
by group and
division.

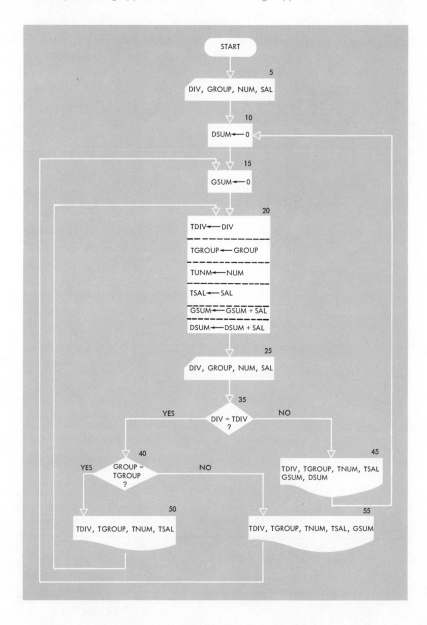

Figure E–20a shows the logic of the flowchart. Box 5 reads the record. Boxes 10 and 15 set DSUM and GSUM to 0.

Box 20 first prepares a temporary copy of the input record. This is necessary, because only after reading the next card can it be determined what to print. Then GSUM and DSUM are computed.

	Sample input		
DIV	*GROUP*	*NUM*	*SAL*
012	002	512	150
012	002	121	121
012	004	007	140
012	004	050	135
012	004	132	212
012	004	041	181
024	024	062	179
024	030	205	200
024	030	251	132
024	031	132	142
030	005	501	190
999	0	0	0

FIGURE E–20b
Sample input data for salary analysis by group and division.

		Sample output			
DIV	*GROUP*	*NUM*	*SAL*	*GSUM*	*DSUM*
012	002	512	150		
012	002	121	121	271	
012	004	007	140		
012	004	050	135		
012	004	132	212		
012	004	041	181	668	939
024	024	062	179	179	
024	030	205	200		
024	030	251	132	332	
024	031	132	142	142	653
030	005	501	190	190	190
999	0	0	0		

FIGURE E–20c
Sample output data for salary analysis by group and division.

DIV	Division number
GROUP	Group number
NUM	Employee number
SAL	Salary
DSUM	Sum of divisional salaries
GSUM	Sum of group salaries
TDIV	Temporary DIV
TGROUP	Temporary GROUP
TNUM	Temporary NUM
TSAL	Temporary SAL

FIGURE E–20d
Names of variables for salary analysis by group and division.

Box 25 reads the next record, and Box 35 makes a test. If the division number has not changed, the test is satisfied and the flowchart is still dealing with employees of the same division. So control goes to Box 40 where the group number is tested. If the group number has not changed either, the flowchart is still in the same group in the same division, and so control goes to Box 50, provides a printout and then to Box 20 to prepare a copy of the record just read in.

On the other hand, if the test in Box 40 fails, this means that the flowchart has completed a group within a division, and so control goes to Box 55, where a printout of the input and a group sum of the salaries is provided. Then control goes to Box 15, where the group sum is reset to 0.

If the test in Box 35 fails, this means that a division is completed; so Box 45 provides a printout of the input, a group sum, and a divisional sum of the salaries. Then control is transferred to Box 10 to reset the divisional sum to 0.

SHIPPING BILL CALCULATION BY TABLE LOOK-UP

The shipping bill calculation was illustrated above in Figure E–3. This time, however, we assume that each customer orders only a single commodity. We will code the five commodities by the numerals 1, 2, 3, 4, and 5. As you can see in the sample input in Figure E–21, the input now is the code of the commodity and the weight ordered.

For example, the first line in the sample input implies that commodity 2 was sold in the quantity of 4 pounds. If you check the sample input in Figure E–3 you find that the price of the second commodity was $23.10 per pound. Therefore, 4 pounds of the commodity will cost $92.40. We also need to add the shipping cost of 50 cents per pound, or $2. Thus in the first line of the sample output the cost to be charged to the customer is $94.40.

To solve this data processing problem we need to find the price of each commodity corresponding to the code. Data processing people refer to a problem of this type as a table look-up problem. For each code or entry to the table one must find the value in the table, in our case the price of the commodity. Our flowchart in Figure E–21 shows how to solve such a problem.

The first four flowchart boxes are the same as those in Figure E–3 and are not reproduced here. Box 10 reads the code of the material and the weight. Then in five successive tests it is determined which code is used in the input and which price is to be used. Box 40 computes the cost to be charged to the customer, and Box 50 provides the printout.

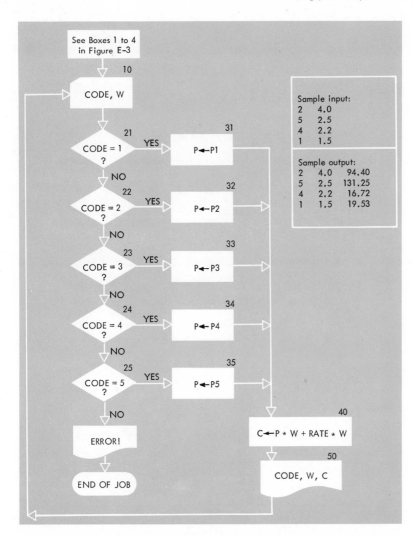

SOLVING PERCENT PROBLEMS

The flowchart in Figure E–22 illustrates how a single flowchart can solve a group of related problems. In a percent calculation we may have three different problems:

1. Given the amount and percent, find the percentage.
2. Given the amount and percentage, find the percent.
3. Given the percent and percentage, find the amount.

Figure E-22 shows the sample input and output. In the first line of the input there is a given amount of $200 and a given percent of

FIGURE E–22
Flowchart for
solving percent
problems.

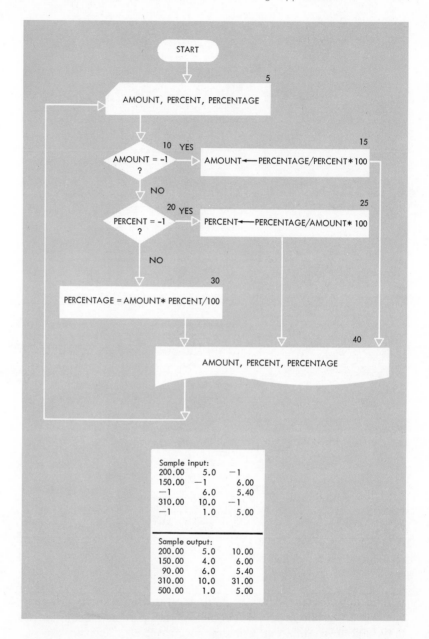

5.0. The problem is to find the percentage. We indicate this by including the flag of −1 as a third data item.

In line 2 there is an amount of $150 given, and a percentage of $6. The unknown is the percent, and this is indicated by a flag of −1 as a second data item.

In the third line of the input the percent of 6.0 and the percentage of $5.40 are given. The unknown is the amount, as indicated by the flag of -1 as the first data item.

In the flowchart, Box 5 reads AMOUNT, PERCENT, and PERCENTAGE. Observe that one of these variables will be the flag of -1. So Boxes 10 and 20 test for the flag of -1, and Boxes 15, 25, and 30, compute the corresponding unknown in the problem. Box 40 prints the answer.

DETERMINING WHO IS THE HEAVIEST PERSON

In many data processing jobs it is necessary to find the highest or lowest paid person, the best selling product, or the largest or smallest of a set of numbers. Figure E–23 shows how to find the heaviest person on the payroll.

Observe in the sample input that the first number is the payroll number of the person, and the second number is the weight. The last data card has a flag with a 0 and 999, as we do not expect to have an employee weighing that much.

In the flowchart Box 5 sets a temporary weight, TWEIGHT, to 0. Box 10 reads the payroll number and the person's weight. Box 15 signals when all the numbers have been read, and Box 30 provides the answers.

In the logic of the flowchart, Box 20 compares the weight of the person with TWEIGHT. At the first go-around this test yields of course NO, and so Box 25 sets TWEIGHT to the weight of the person, and TNUMBER to the payroll number of the person. Then control goes to Box 10 where another record is read. Observe that the test in Box 20 yields NO when the record of a person whose weight is larger than any weight so far encountered is read. Consequently, as the processing goes on, the payroll number and the weight of the heaviest person will always be updated. Finally, when the signal is given by Box 15, the payroll number and weight of the heaviest person are printed.

COMPUTING A MOVING AVERAGE

In many financial problems (like analysis of the prices of stocks), it is necessary to compute a moving average. In Figure E–24 a moving average of three numbers of a set of input numbers is computed.

Observe the sample input and output. In the output in the third line we compute the average of the three numbers 2, 3, and 1. (We add the numbers and divide by 3.) In the fourth line we show the

FIGURE E–23
Flowchart for
finding the
heaviest person.

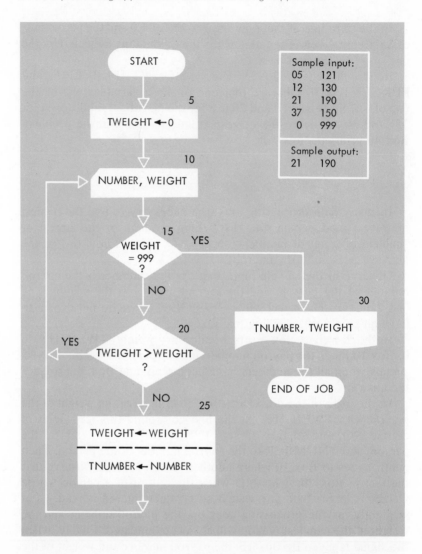

average of the three numbers 3, 1, and 5. In the fifth line we provide
the average of the three numbers, 1, 5, and 6, etc.

According to the logic of the flowchart, Box 5 reads FIRST, the
first input number. Box 10 prints the number. Box 15 reads SEC-
OND and prints it in Box 20. Then Box 25 reads THIRD.

Box 30 computes the average of the three numbers. Box 35
prints the number and the moving average.

Now comes the essence of the moving average calculation. Box
40 sets FIRST to SECOND and SECOND to THIRD. So now the
process has FIRST and SECOND and Box 25 reads THIRD. Then
again in Box 30 the average is computed, and so on.

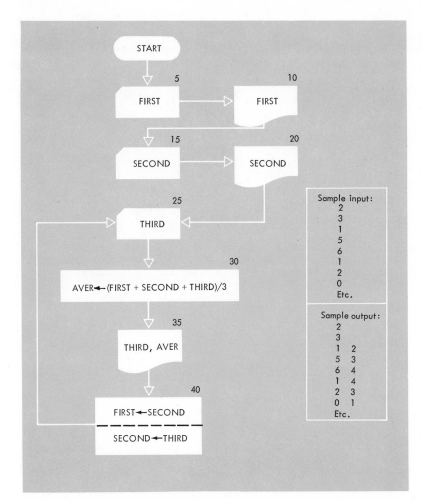

FIGURE E–24
Flowchart for
computing a
moving average.

MULTIPLYING RABBITS

This is a tale of a colony of female rabbits (Figure E–25). It all begins with a baby female rabbit, which, after the *first* month's time, matures into an adult rabbit. So at the beginning of the *second* month we have one adult rabbit and no baby rabbits. In the course of the second month the rabbit bears a baby rabbit. So at the beginning of the *third* month we have one adult rabbit and one baby rabbit, a total of two rabbits.

Now the one adult rabbit bears another baby rabbit, and the former baby rabbit matures into an adult. So at the beginning of the *fourth* month there are two adult rabbits and one baby rabbit, a total of three rabbits.

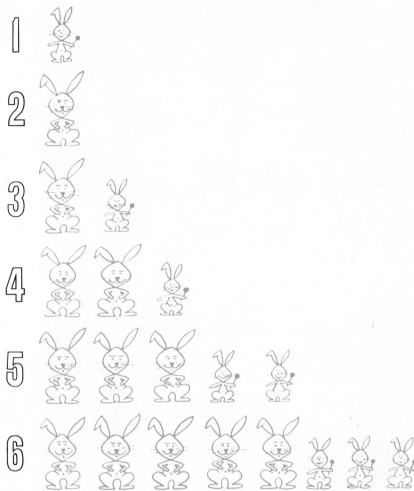

FIGURE E–25
The rabbits of
Leonardo
Fibonacci da Pisa.

Reprinted with permission from Andrew Vazsonyi, Problem Solving by Digital Computers with Pl/1
Programming, © *1970, Prentice-Hall, Inc., Englewood Cliffs, New Jersey.*

Now each of the two adult rabbits bears one baby rabbit, and the former baby rabbit matures into an adult. So at the beginning of the *fifth* month there are three adult rabbits and two baby rabbits, a total of five rabbits.

Each of the three adult rabbits bears one baby rabbit, and the two former baby rabbits mature into adults. So at the beginning of the *sixth* month there are five adult rabbits and three baby rabbits, a total of eight rabbits.

How many rabbits will there be in total in 24 months, or two years?

The flowchart is given in Figure E–26. Inspect first the output. The first column shows the month, the second the total number of rabbits, the third the adult rabbits, and the fourth the baby rabbits. Observe the way the numbers "slide" down. For example, in the seventh month there are 13 rabbits in total; in the eighth month, 13 adult rabbits, and in the ninth month, 13 baby rabbits. We need to put this relationship between the numbers into our flowchart.

Box 5 initializes MONTH to 1, BABY to 1, and ADULT to 0.

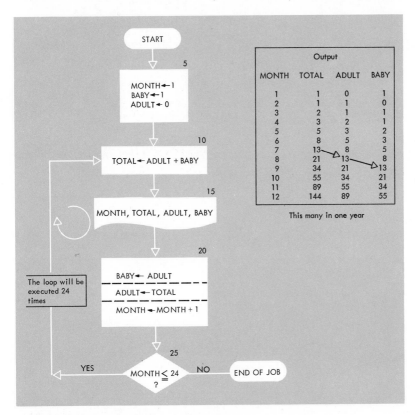

FIGURE E–26 Flowchart for computing how many rabbits in two years.

Box 10 computes TOTAL and MONTH. Box 15 produces the printout. Observe that at the first go-around the numbers 1, 1, 0, and 1 will be printed.

In Box 20 the two statements express the "sliding" of the numbers. First we put into an assignment statement the fact that each adult is going to have a baby; then that the total number of rabbits become adults. Box 25 calls for a test, so the computation will end after the 24th month or second year.

You may be interested to know that the number of rabbits, that is, the sequence of numbers, 1, 1, 2, 3, 5, 8, etc., form the series of Fibonacci numbers. These numbers, which have fascinated mathematicians for hundreds of years, are of great importance in mathematics.

INTEREST CALCULATION

Suppose you deposit a certain amount of money in the bank and collect 4 percent yearly interest. How would you develop a ten-year schedule of the amounts accumulated in the bank?

FIGURE E–27
Flowchart for ten-year interest table at 4 percent interest.

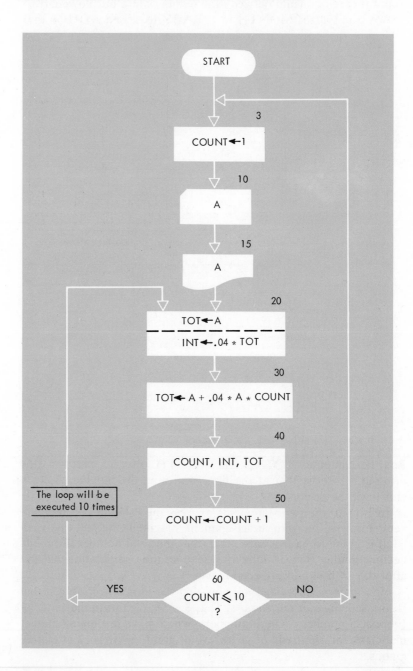

This problem is solved in the flowchart in Figure E–27. Box 3 sets COUNT to 1. Then Box 10 reads the amount initially deposited, and Box 15 provides for a printout.

Box 20 sets TOT, the total amount in the bank to A and computes INT, the interest. Box 30 computes TOT, the total amount. Box 40 prints COUNT, INT, and TOT. Box 50 increments COUNT by 1. Box 60 makes a test as to whether the computations have been

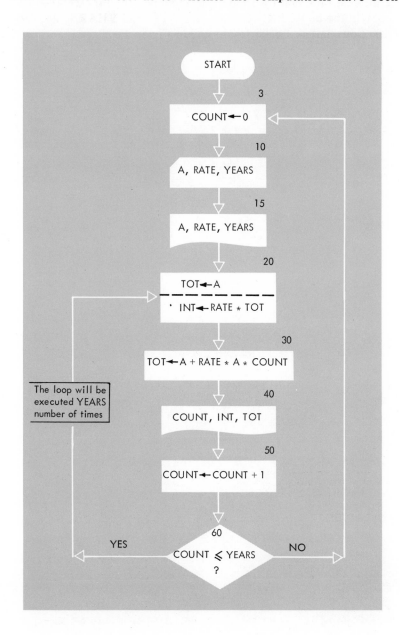

FIGURE E–28
Flowchart for computing simple interest tables.

carried out for the required ten years. If COUNT is less than or equal to ten another line for the printout must be computed, so control goes back to Box 20. Otherwise, control goes to Box 3 and starts a new interest table.

In **Figure E-28** we show a flowchart to solve the problem under more general conditions. We designate by A the amount, by RATE the interest rate, and by YEARS the number of years we keep the money in the bank. Box 10 reads A, RATE, and YEARS. The rest of the flowchart is similar to the one in Figure E-27.

FIGURE E-29
Flowchart for computing compounded interest tables.

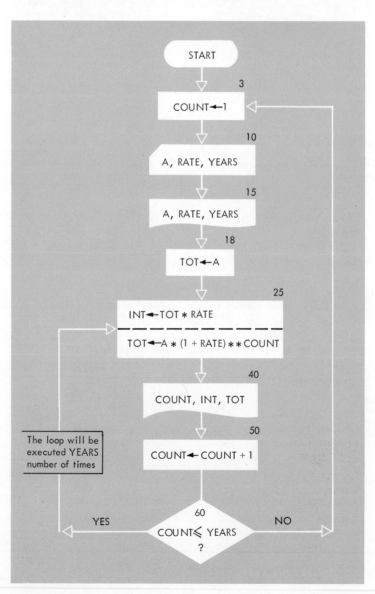

In Figure E–29 we solve the same problem, but now assume that interest is compounded yearly. The computations are carried out in Box 25. The first assignment statement computes the interest, which will vary from year to year. The second assignment statement computes the total amount accumulated in the bank. Observe that the exponential operator is designated by the double asterisk ($**$). (Proof of this interest formula is omitted.)

ASSIGNMENTS

1. Write FORTRAN, BASIC, and COBOL programs for each case study in this chapter. Make your printouts meaningful by printing headers and other user-oriented messages.

PROBLEM-SOLVING ASSIGNMENTS

You are to prepare a flowchart first, then translate the flowchart into a program. In many of the problems a sample set of inputs and outputs is provided to make certain you understand the problem. Make your printouts more meaningful by printing headers and other user-oriented messages.

1. Change the invoice problem (Figure E–1) by allowing one or two materials for each customer. If there is only one material, set LENGTH2 to zero. Replace the BASE price by DISC, the discount allowed to customers.

2. Change the sales analysis flowchart (Figure E–2) in the following manner:
   a. First read all input, then do all processing; finally prepare the outputs.
   b. Compute and print only the TOTAL, the AVER, the weekday average, WDAYAV, and the weekend average, WENDAV.

3. In the shipping bill calculation (Figure E–3) customers are given a discount stated as a percent of the net price:

$$\text{DISC} \leftarrow \text{PERCENT} * \text{NETPRICE}.$$

4. Change the problem of keeping your own checkbook (Figure E–4) by allowing two deposits, DEP1 and DEP2, and two checks, CHECK1 and CHECK2. Prepare flowchart and output for three sets of data.

5. Change the account-balancing problem (Figure 2.6) by counting the transactions (as in Figure E–6) and keeping a running total of deposits (SMDEP) and checks (SMCHECK). The output will have two lines for each transaction:
   a. OLD, DEP, CHECK, BAL
   b. COUNT, SMDEP, SMCHECK

6. You are selling carpeting, the PRICE of which is $35 per yard. If you sell over 50 yards you give a 10 percent discount on the yardage

over 50 yards. Input is LENGTH and PRICE; output is LENGTH and COST to buyer.

7. Modify the previous problem by introducing a minimum COST to buyer of $175. Develop flowchart, execute it, and provide output.

8. Instead of classifying people by weight (Figure E–8), classify them by age, using the figures below:

	Age in years		
Classification	At least	But less than	Code to be assigned
Infant	—	2	1
Child	2	10	2
Adolescent	10	18	3
Young	18	30	4
Not so young	30	50	5
Middle aged	50	80	6
Old	80	—	7

9. Modify the commission calculation the following way: There is a base commission of 5 percent on sales. If the amount is over $100 the salesman gets an additional 3 percent bonus on the amount over $100. If the amount is over $200 he gets a second bonus of 2 percent on the amount over $200.

Sample input	
50.00	
100.00	
150.00	
200.00	
250.00	
300.00	

Sample output	
50.00	2.50
100.00	5.00
150.00	9.00
200.00	13.00
250.00	18.00
300.00	23.00

10. Modify Problem 9 the following way: The commission is never less than $4 and never more than $24.

11. Rework some of the problems in the text by printing messages like the following:

a. If the deposit in the account-balancing problem is over $1,000 print: "LARGE DEPOSIT"; if the check is over $500: "LARGE CHECK"; if the balance is over $10,000: "YOU ARE RICH"

b. If the bonus in Problem 9 is over $25.00 print: "GOOD WORK"

12. Write a program for a generalized commission computation. The first inputs are three numbers: the BASE commission, the LIMIT over which there is a bonus, and the bonus to be computed as PERCENT of the amount over the LIMIT. Then follows a series of inputs for the AMOUNTS representing sales:

Sample input		
6.00	150	2
50.20		
205.10		
150.00		
Sample output		
6.00	150.00	2.00
50.20	6.00	
205.10	7.10	
150.00	6.00	

13. The input to a program is two numbers: H, the height of a man in inches, and W, the weight in pounds. IF

a. $W > 4.2 * H - 132$ print "OVERWEIGHT"

b. $W < 3.8 * H = 118$ print "UNDERWEIGHT"

c. else print "OK"

14. The formulas in Problem 13 apply only if the person is not shorter than 5 feet or not taller than 6 feet and 6 inches. Modify the program in Problem 13 by printing only

a. IF $H < 60$: "TOO SHORT"

b. IF $H > 78$: "TOO TALL"

15. The input is X and Y, the two sides of a rectangular metal sheet, both measured in inches. The price of the metal is $15.25 per square foot. The output is a printout of X and Y and the cost to the buyer.

16. Modify Problem 6 on carpeting the following way: If you sell over 150 yards, there is an additional 5 percent discount on the yardage over 150 yards.

17. An employee works H hours a week and is paid at a rate of R dollars per hour. The inputs to the program are H and R. Earnings are computed the following way:

a. Regular time; if he works less than 40 hours earnings are:

$$E = H * R$$

b. If he works 40 or more hours but less than 48 hours, he gets 50 percent higher pay for the excess hours:

$$E = 40 * R + 1.5 * R * (H - 40)$$

    c. If he works over 48 hours, he gets double time:

$$E = 40 * R + 1.5 * R * (H - 40) + 2 * R * (H - 48)$$

The output is H, R and earnings E.

18. In a certain hardware store each nut is 8 cents and each bolt is 12 cents. If your bill is over $5 you get a 10 percent discount on the amount over $5. Inputs are: number of nuts N and number of bolts B. Output is N, B, and amount A to be paid.

Sample inputs		
15	10	
30	40	
Sample outputs		
15	10	2.40
30	40	6.98

19. A certain material can be bought from two suppliers. Number 1 charges $30 per ton but charges an additional flat charge of $500 for each order. Number 2 charges $50 per ton and only an additional flat charge of $200 per each order. You order from the supplier, who charges less. Inputs are the number of tons you order. Outputs are the number 1 or 2 depending which supplier you order from and the cost to you.

Sample inputs		
10.0		
15.0		
20.0		
Sample outputs		
10.0	2	700.00
15.0	1	950.00
20.0	1	1100.00

20. In a certain country a letter can be mailed if no side is less than 6 inches and no side is longer than 12 inches. The input to the program is the two sides S1 and S2, and the printout is the input and "YES" or "No."

Sample inputs	
4.1	11.2
10.6	7.2
8.2	11.8
11.6	3.1
15.1	7.2
6.8	12.5

Sample outputs		
4.1	11.2	NO
10.6	7.2	YES
8.2	11.8	YES
11.6	3.1	NO
15.1	7.2	NO
6.8	12.5	NO

21. The dimensions of a shoebox are 6, 8, and 14 inches. The lengths of the dimensions of a brick are the inputs, but the inputs are not necessarily in increasing order. The outputs are the printout of the inputs and "Yes" or "No," depending on whether the brick will fit into the box.

22. A real estate office charges a percent commission on the selling price of property. The input to the program is the PERCENT and net RECEIPTS to the seller. The output is a printout, the commission and selling price of the real estate.

Sample input	
10.0	45000.00
6.0	37600.00
8.0	55200.00

Sample output			
10.0	45000.00	5000.00	50000.00
6.0	37600.00	2400.00	40000.00
8.0	55200.00	4800.00	60000.00

Use the formula:

$$\text{NET RECEIPTS} = \frac{\text{SELLING PRICE}}{(1 - \text{PERCENT}/100)}$$

23. The table below shows monthly sales for years 1973, 1974, and 1975 for a certain product. This 12 by 3 table of numbers is the input. The output is a printout of the input, the monthly and yearly totals, and the grand total.

Month	1973	1974	1975	Total
January	331.66	227.21	371.97	_____
February	175.49	249.93	196.21	_____
March	581.72	427.31	632.47	_____
April	433.43	568.57	357.14	_____
May	75.24	108.09	210.79	_____
June	857.25	824.01	613.64	_____
July	496.21	584.31	767.07	_____
August	145.72	231.96	319.46	_____
September	96.21	216.72	157.44	_____
October	867.08	713.64	521.49	_____
November	598.80	542.96	391.50	_____
December	86.43	73.46	297.87	_____
Total	_____	_____	_____	_____
			Grand total	_____

24. Modify problem 23 by printing in the fourth column the average of monthly sales and in the 13th row the average sales for each year. Also print the average of all (36) monthly sales.

25. Modify Problem 23 by printing in the fourth column the highest sale in each month.

26. Modify Problem 23 by printing in the 13th row the lowest sale in each year and in the bottom the all-time low.

27. Print a table for the first 100 whole numbers. Print them in five columns and 20 rows.

28. Modify Problem 27 by printing the first 100 odd numbers.

29. Modify Problems 27 and 28 by printing also the average of the numbers.

30. Prepare a table of compound interests for a deposit of $1. Use five columns with interests of 4, 5, 6, 7, and 8 percent and 20 rows for the 20 years.

31. Modify the problem in Figure E–8 in the following way: there are exactly 20 people to be classified. Count the number of people in each class.

32. Modify Problem 31 to the effect that you also print the average weight for each class.

33. Modify the problem in Figure E–12 in the following way: there are exactly 20 employees. Count male employees making over $4.00 per hour. What is the average and the highest wage rate for males?

34. Work the problem in Figure E–19 without a trailer card but by knowing that there are exactly 20 employees.

Selected bibliography
and periodicals

FORTRAN programming

Anderson, Decima *Computer Programming: FORTRAN IV*. New York: Appleton-Century-Crofts, 1966.

Couger, J. Daniel, and Shannon, L. E. *FORTRAN IV: A P.I. Approach Including Structured Programming*. 3d. ed. Homewood, Ill.: Richard D. Irwin, 1976.

Cress, Paul; Dirksen, Paul; and Graham, J. Wesley *FORTRAN IV with WATFOR and WATFIV*. Englewood Cliffs, N.J.: Prentice-Hall, 1970.

Farina, Mario V. *FORTRAN IV Self-Taught*. Englewood Cliffs, N.J.: Prentice-Hall, 1966.

McCameron, Fritz *FORTRAN IV*. Rev. ed. Homewood, Ill.: Richard D. Irwin, 1974.

McCracken, Daniel D. *A Guide to FORTRAN IV Programming*. New York: John Wiley & Sons, 2nd ed. 1972.

COBOL programming

McCameron, Fritz *COBOL Logic and Programming*. 3d. ed. Homewood, Ill.: Richard D. Irwin, 1974.

McCracken, Daniel D., and Garbassi, Umberto *A Guide to COBOL Programming*. 2d ed. New York: John Wiley & Sons, 1970.

Murach, Mike *Standard COBOL*. Chicago: Science Research Associates, 1971.

Spitzbarth, L. M. *Basic COBOL Programming*. Reading, Mass.: Addison-Wesley Publishing Co., 1970.

Sprowls, R. C. *Computing with COBOL.* San Francisco, Cal., Canfield Press, 1974.

PL/I programming

Bates, Frank, and Douglas, Mary L. *Programming Language/One.* Englewood Cliffs, N.J.: Prentice-Hall, 2d ed. 1970.

Conway, Richard, and Gries, David *An Introduction to Programming: A Structured Approach Using PL/I and PL/C.* Cambridge, Mass.: Winthrop Publishers, 1973.

Lecht, Charles Philip *The Programmer's PL/I.* New York: McGraw-Hill Book Co., 1968.

Scott, R. C., and Sondek, N. E. *PL/I for Programmers.* Reading, Mass.: Addison-Wesley Publishing Co., 1970.

Sprowls, R. Clay *Introduction to PL/I Programming.* New York: Harper & Row, 1969.

Vazsonyi, Andrew *Problem Solving by Digital Computers with PL/I Programming.* Englewood Cliffs, N.J.: Prentice-Hall, 1970.

Weinberg, G. M. *PL/I Programming Primer: A manual of style.* New York: McGraw-Hill Book Co., 1970.

BASIC programming

Farina, M. V. *Programming in BASIC.* Englewood Cliffs, N.J.: Prentice-Hall, 1968.

Gately, W. Y., and Bitter, G. G. *BASIC for Beginners.* New York: McGraw-Hill Book Co., 1970.

Sharpe, William F. and Jacob N. *BASIC.* Rev. ed. New York: Free Press, 1971.

RPG programming

Brightman, R. W., and Clark, J. R. *RPG I and RPG II Programming.* New York: Macmillan Co., 1970.

Seeds, Harice L. *Programming RPG RPG II.* New York: John Wiley & Sons, 1971.

Programming in other languages

Gilman, Leonard, and Rose, Allen J. *APL/360: An Interactive Approach.* New York: John Wiley & Sons, 2d ed. 1974.

Sammet, Jean E. *Programming Languages: History and Fundamentals.* Englewood Cliffs, N.J.: Prentice-Hall, 1969.

Staff of Computer Usage Company. *Programming the IBM System/360.* New York: John Wiley & Sons, 1966.

Computer systems

Bartee, Thomas C. *Digital Computer Fundamentals*. 3rd ed. New York: McGraw-Hill Book Co., 1972.

Gordon, Geoffrey *System Simulation*. Englewood Cliffs, N.J.: Prentice-Hall, 1969.

Gruenberger, Fred (ed.) *Critical Factors in Data Management*. Englewood Cliffs, N.J.: Prentice-Hall, 1969.

Kanter, Jerome *Management Guide to Computer System Selection and Use*. Englewood Cliffs, N.J.: Prentice-Hall, 1970.

Martin, James *Computer Data-Base Organization.* Englewood Cliffs, N.J.: Prentice-Hall 1975.

Orlicky, Joseph *The Successful Computer System: A Management Guide*. New York: McGraw-Hill Book Co., 1969.

Information systems

Benjamin, Robert I. *Control of the Information System Development Cycle*. New York: Wiley Interscience Div. of John Wiley & Sons, 1971.

Couger, J. D., and Knapp, R. W. *System Analysis Techniques*. New York: John Wiley & Sons, 1974.

Couger, J. D., and McFadden, F. R. *Introduction to Computer Based Information Systems*. New York: John Wiley & Sons, 1975.

Davis, Gordon B. *Introduction to Management Information Systems: Conceptual Foundations, Structure, and Development*. New York: McGraw-Hill Book Co., 1974.

Greenwood, William T. *Decision Theory and Information Systems*. Cincinnati: South-Western Publishing Co., 1969.

Head, Robert V. *A Guide to Packaged Systems*. New York: Wiley-Interscience Div. of John Wiley & Sons, 1971.

Kelly, Joseph F. *Computerized Management Information Systems*. New York: Macmillan Co., 1970.

Lyon, John K. *An Introduction to Data Base Design*. New York: Wiley Interscience, Div. of John Wiley & Sons, 1971.

Martin, James *Computer Data-Base Organization*. Englewood Cliffs, N.J.: Prentice-Hall, 1975.

McFarlan, F. W., Nolan, R. D. (eds.) *The Information Systems Handbook*. Homewood, Ill.: Dow Jones-Irwin, 1975.

McFarlan, F. W.; Nolan, R. L.; and Norton, D. P. *Information Systems Administration*. New York: Holt, Rinehart & Winston, 1973.

Murdick, Robert G., and Ross, Joel E. *Information Systems for Modern Management.* Englewood Cliffs, N.J.: Prentice-Hall, 1971.

Prince, Thomas R. *Information Systems for Management Planning and Control.* 3d. ed. Homewood, Ill.: Richard D. Irwin, 1975.

Rappaport, Alfred (ed.) *Information for Decision Making.* Englewood Cliffs, N.J.: Prentice-Hall, 1970.

Shaw, John C., and Atkins, William *Managing Computer Systems Projects.* New York: McGraw-Hill Book Co., 1970.

Williams, Thomas H., and Griffin, Charles H. *Management Information: A Quantative Accent.* Homewood, Ill.: Richard D. Irwin, 1967.

Computers and social implications

Bemer, R. W. (ed.) *Computers and Crisis: How Computers are Shaping Our Future,* Petrocelli, 1971.

Myers, Charles A. *Computers in Knowledge-Based Fields.* Cambridge, Mass.: M.I.T. Press, 1970.

Rothman, Stanley, and Mosmann, Charles *Computers and Society.* Chicago, Ill.: Science Research Associates, 1972.

Sackman, Harold *Mass Information Utilities and Social Existence.* New York, Mason Charter, 1971.

Periodicals

Business Automation Business Press International, Inc., 288 Park Avenue, West, Elmhurst, Ill. 60126. Monthly, 85-page journal on various EDP subjects. Free to qualified individuals.

Communications of the ACM Association for Computing Machinery (ACM), 1130 Avenue of the Americas, New York, N.Y. 10036. Journal covering technical articles and subjects of general interest.

Computer Decisions Hayden Publishing Company, Inc., 50 Essex Street, Rochelle Park, N.J. 07662. Magazine covering current and prospective developments in the data processing field. Free to qualified individuals.

Computing Newsletter for Schools of Business J. Daniel Couger (ed.). School of Business Administration, University of Colorado, Colorado Springs, Colorado.

Computing Reviews Association for Computing Machinery, 211 E. 43d Street, New York, N.Y. 10017. Journal presenting evaluation of books, articles, and films on various aspects of computing.

Computing Surveys Association for Computing Machinery (see above for address). Journal covering survey and tutorial technical articles.

Datamation F. D. Thomas Publications, Inc., 35 Mason St., Greenwich, Conn. 06830. Magazine covering current and prospective developments in the data processing field. Free to qualified individuals.

Index*

* Page numbers in color refer to words defined in Key Words and Phrases sections.

547

This book has been set in 10 point and 9 point Times Roman, leaded 2 points. Chapter numbers are 48 point Helvetica bold and chapter titles are 18 point Helvetica. The size of the type page is 32 by 47$\frac{1}{2}$ picas.